I0643193

The Age of Wild Ghosts

The Age of Wild Ghosts

Memory, Violence, and Place
in Southwest China

Erik Mueggler

UNIVERSITY OF CALIFORNIA PRESS

Berkeley / Los Angeles / London

University of California Press
Berkeley and Los Angeles, California

University of California Press, Ltd.
London, England

© 2001 by The Regents of the University of California

Library of Congress Cataloging-in-Publication Data

Mueggler, Erik, 1962–
    The age of wild ghosts : memory, violence, and place in Southwest
    China / Erik Mueggler.
        p.   cm.
    Includes bibliographical references and index.
    ISBN 0-520-22623-2 (alk. paper) — ISBN 0-520-22631-3 (pbk. :
    alk. paper)
    1. Ethnology—China—Yunnan Sheng. 2. Yunnan Sheng (China)—
    Social conditions. I. Title.

DS793.Y8 M83 2001
305.8′00951′35—dc21   00-055164

Printed in the United States of America

10 09 08 07 06 05 04 03 02 01
10 9 8 7 6 5 4 3 2 1

The paper used in this publication meets the minimum requirements of
ANSI/NISO Z39.48–1992 (R 1997) (*Permanence of Paper*). ♾

For the people of Zhizuo
and in memory of Karl, Max, and Keith

his ears are millstones	nó pɔ lɔ̀ ka le
his eyeballs stars	me sæ̀ kǽ mo le
his arms iron pillars	lè vɔ̀ hɔ̀ vɔ̀ le
his fingers iron bars	lè ni hɔ̀ ka le
when you meet him	kʼo nì tʼà mo jæ
that king of death	mó mi yà lɔ̀ wú
don't you hesitate	ni kʼo nì tʼà ngò sæ̀
don't be afraid	kʼo nì tʼà jo sæ̀

Contents

Illustrations

Figures

Tables

Acknowledgments

I have accumulated debts of many kinds while researching and writing this book, and none of them can be reciprocated with words alone. My first debt is to people in Zhizuo, who fed me, drank with me, tutored me endlessly, and tolerated my eccentricities, bad manners, and foolish questions. I have written this work in a spirit of gratitude to them, though I fear it is a poor return for their kindness and generosity.

Without the kind help of Professor He Yaohua of the Yunnan Academy of Social Sciences and Professor Liu Yaohan of the Chuxiong Yi Culture Research Institute, as well as that of many efficient administrators in Kunming, Chuxiong, Yongren, and Zhonghe, I could never have done the field research for this book.

I am indebted to several institutions that provided funding for research and writing. The Woodrow Wilson Foundation's Andrew W. Mellon grants for language study funded no less than three summers of intensive language study, in 1987, 1990, and 1991. A grant from the Johns Hopkins University Program in Atlantic History, Culture, and Society funded my first field research in Yunnan in 1989; the Wenner Gren Association for Anthropological Research and the National Academy of Sciences Committee for Scholarly Communications with China funded much more extended field research in 1991–1993. A Woodrow Wilson Foundation Andrew W. Mellon Dissertation Writing Award and a National Endowment for the Humanities Dissertation Writing Fellowship funded the writing of the dissertation out of which this book eventually grew. Much of the book itself was written while I held a faculty fellowship from the University of Michigan Institute for the Humanities. Earlier versions of two chapters have appeared as articles: chapter 4 (Mueggler 1998c, reprinted by permission of the Royal Anthropological Institute of Great Britain and Ireland; Mueggler 2000) and chapter 8 (Mueggler 1999, reprinted by permission of Cambridge University Press).

Emily Martin, William Rowe, and Gillian Feeley-Harnik shaped the first, halting drafts of these chapters with vigilance and compassion. Stevan Harrell, Ashraf Ghani, Michel-Rolf Trouillot, Monica Schock-Spana, Felicity Northcott, and Elizabeth Ferry were also incisive critical readers. I am grateful to David Bradley for his early advice on transcribing Yi languages; Bruce Mannheim and Webb Keane provided brief but indispensable suggestions for formatting transcriptions of poetic language. P. Steven Sangren, Ralph Litzinger, Kenneth Pomerantz, and Norma Diamond read the entire manuscript. I am deeply indebted to them for their comments. This book owes much to my colleagues at the University of Michigan for the support and guidance that have sustained my intellectual growth over the past four years. I owe a special debt to Katherine Verdery for her unwavering friendship, encouragement, and example. Pen and ink drawings by Sean McCabe grace these pages; I thank Sean for being a brother when my other brother, to whom this book is dedicated, could no longer be. Finally, writing, and life itself, would be impossible without the friendship, tolerance, and love of my partner in all things, Min Kim.

A Note on Orthography
and Transcription

Romanizations of Chinese in this book do not distinguish between standard Chinese and its Yunnan variant; both are romanized as though they were standard Chinese, using the pinyin system. Where necessary, I have distinguished words as Chinese by prefacing them with the abbreviation "Ch." the first time they appear.

Most transcriptions in the book are not of Chinese but of a Tibeto-Burman language that its speakers call Lòlongo. Linguists in China classify Lòlongo as one of the Lipo subdialects (Ch. *tuyu*) of the Central dialect (Ch. *fangyan*) of Yi, a Loloish Tibeto-Burman language (Yang H. 1990, 117). Some linguists have noted that the subdialects grouped under the Central dialect of Yi are closer to Lisu than they are to other dialects classified as Yi (Bradley 1978). Unlike speakers of many Yi dialects, Central dialect speakers have never developed writing systems, and linguists have developed no standard orthography. To represent Tibeto-Burman languages in general, Chinese linguists have adopted a version of the International Phonetic Alphabet (as in Chen, Bian, and Li 1984); I have modified this system to minimize the use of exotic symbols. The system of transcription that has resulted, while not a perfect phonetic representation, is sufficient to make the necessary phonemic distinctions.

Consonants are transcribed as single letters or as sequences of letters that are already familiar conventions in English-language writing (see Table 1). There is also an initial glottal stop, represented only by the absence of an initial graph before a vowel. The voiceless affricate *j* and aspirated affricate *ch* are palatal before the front vowels *i, e, ɛ,* and *æ* and

Table 1 *Consonants*

	Labial	Dentilabial	Dental	Retroflex	Palatal	Velar
Voiceless stop	p		t			k
Aspirated stop	p'		t'			k'
Voiced stop	b		d			g
Voiceless affricate			ts	j	j	
Aspirated affricate			ts'	ch	ch	
Voiceless fricative		f	s	sh	c	h
Voiced fricative		v	z			
Nasal	m		n			ng
Lateral			l			
Voiced flap				r		
Continuants	w				y	

retroflex before other vowels. A great deal of variation is found in the velar voiced stop *g*, which frequently becomes fricative.

There are eleven basic vowels; I represent a few with International Phonetic Alphabet symbols not used in English-language writing (see Table 2). The vowel I represent as *r* occurs only after affricates and fricatives (such as *ts*, and *j*). Ramsey's description of similar vowels in Nasu pertains: "In either case the tip of the tongue remains at, or very near, the position where the affricate is articulated. Thus, as voicing begins, the vowel is heard after dental affricates as the buzzing sound *z*, and after retroflexes as a sound very much like a Midwestern American *r*. These two different sounds are very nearly the same as those heard in the [standard Chinese] words *sì* 'four' and *shì* 'persimmon'" (1987, 255). Many vowels may be laryngalized—pronounced with a tight larynx, in a "creaky" voice; I have marked laryngalization by underlining the vowel (*a*).

Chen, Bian, and Li (1984, 211–212) distinguish five tones in the Central dialect: high, level ([55]); mid-high, level ([44]); mid, level ([33]); low, falling ([21]); and low, rising ([13])—the last of which appears only in loan

Table 2 *Vowels*

i	ɯ	u	r
e	ə	o	
ɛ	a	ɔ	
æ			

Table 3 *Tones*

high, level	á
mid-high, level	a
mid, level	a
low, falling	à
low, rising	à

words from Chinese. The system of transcription used here is simpler, dividing the tones into high, middle, and low, without distinguishing between the mid-high, level tone and the mid, level tone, nor between the low, falling tone and the relatively rare low, rising tone. I use accent marks to mark tones, as shown in Table 3.

The Central dialect of Yi shares with Lisu an extreme phonological poverty at the end of the syllable (Ramsey 1987, 261). In Lòlongo, consonants are used only as initials except in loan words from Chinese. The construction of words is simple: most are one syllable long, consisting at the most of an initial consonant followed by a vowel (sometimes laryngalized) and a tone. There is a great deal of microregional variation within Lòlongo, and I have made no efforts to standardize across the variants I recorded, except in the case of place names and single words I use repeatedly (such as *ts'ici*).

In transcribing ritual speech, I have indicated units of lines and stanzas. Lines are commonly five or seven syllables long (sometimes longer), with a pause at the end of each line; stanzas, separated by additional space, are sets of interrelated lines. I have made free use of indentations to draw attention to interrelations between lines and among stanzas.

CHAPTER ONE

Introduction

Sometimes I think it all began the day I met Li Yun.[1] I was taking tea in a graceful riverbank mansion, once the home of a local despot, now the seat of a township government in Yunnan Province. Li Yun staggered through the door, bent under a load of firewood. He was an elderly man in horn-rimmed glasses, very thin and very drunk. He spotted me, dumped his firewood in a corner, and bellowed, "American comrade! Chairman Mao sent this one from America to help the minority people carry out socialist reconstruction! You wear glasses and carry a pen! I too am a member of the Communist Party assigned by Chairman Mao to the task of building the new China!" I could only open my mouth and stare until a township official gently drew Li Yun into another room.

Later that afternoon, I watched the old man set off up the canyon road, stumbling and singing in the rain. The road—a footpath, really—led to a scattering of mountain villages, the township's largest and poorest brigade,[2] inhabited mainly by "minority people," officially of the "Yi nationality." For several months, I had been seeking permission to live in this brigade, known as Zhizuo in Chinese and as Júzò ("little valley") in the local Tibeto-Burman language.[3] A few days later, I followed the same path twenty kilometers up a canyon to a narrow valley, the center of Zhizuo, where I eventually found a place to live in an elementary school.

Living in Zhizuo, I learned to fear Li Yun's approach. Sometimes I had warning. I would hear him coming, bellowing fragments of slogans, and I would slip out the school's back door. Or I would spot him from afar, descending from his village on the sun-drenched eastern slope, and I would guess that he was headed across the valley to the large village where I lived, eventually to find his way to my room. Sometimes he ambushed me. He would materialize out of the crowd at a wedding or funeral, take my hand in a lockwrench grip, and bellow outdated Maoist slogans into my face. For these harangues, he never used either the flowing Tibeto-Burman tongue employed here in daily life or the harsher Yunnan dialect of Chinese used to communicate with outsiders. Instead, he enunciated his slogans with precision, in formal standard Chinese, the language of officialdom: "Without the Communist Party there would be no new China! Ten thousand years to Chairman Mao!" I would wince, smile patiently, and wait for some kind soul to divert his attention. Li Yun was not threatening; he was just unbearably friendly. His mission, which he pursued with energy for more than a year, was to take me home for dinner; his method was brute force. He was very strong, and once he got hold of my hand and started along the path toward his house, I could only stumble along behind until he relaxed enough for me to twist out of his grasp, voice a quick apology, and dash away.

I was desperate to ignore Li Yun. He represented a side of life here that I hated. When officials from higher levels of government visited, I watched his antics through their eyes. Filthy, alcoholic, crazy as a loon, he seemed to shamefully confirm their complaints about the local "minority population": they drank too much; they were unsanitary and superstitious; they were enamored of their own poverty; they had no education and no culture. When he accosted me in public, I watched myself through his eyes. Clearly powerful, with connections, spectacles, and a pocket pen, I was a person with whom to ingratiate oneself, if only with a dinner of rice and chicken soup—and how could I not share most officials' perceptions of himself and his neighbors as dirty, alcoholic, and degenerate? I tried to put Li Yun out of my mind as I went about my business of conducting interviews, listening to stories, recording statistics, attending rituals, and transcribing poetry.

But he was always there, at the edges of my perception, comic, furious, and emaciated, stumbling along the valley paths, shouting anachronistic political slogans to the melodies of courting songs, singing laments properly reserved for mortuary rituals. "He is mad [*t'a,* implying possession]," my friends in Zhizuo said, tolerating his interruptions with the cheerful public demeanor I soon came to expect of them. Yet what kind of madness, among the many forms they could diagnose, not even the experts on spirit possession I had begun to consult could say. All I learned was that everyone around him associated Li Yun's affliction in some way with his long tenure as an official—among the most eminent this brigade had produced. Beginning in the mid-1950s, he had served as the head of a neighboring township. He had been hospitalized for mental illness in 1966, as the Cultural Revolution began. He was formally reinstated to his position a few years later; he retired early in 1976, returning home to Zhizuo. His wife was dead, but he had one daughter, who worked in the country town and sent him money. I learned virtually nothing more: I could not talk to Li Yun, and others deflected my questions about him.

Still, I found I could not stop thinking about Li Yun's mad incantations, those startling eruptions of anachronistic speech that heralded his presence at so many public gatherings. Were they merely symptoms of a personal derangement? Or did they issue instead from a collective past that also haunted others? Why did they take the form of political slogans? What was the singular power of those formulas in an alien tongue that they could haunt or possess one, and how could they still be echoing through this valley so many years after their meaning and authority had faded away? Above all, I was troubled by the enormous pain that seemed to darken Li Yun's bellowing voice. What wounds did it reopen for those who heard it; what histories did it conceal? And how might such wounds and histories relate to the entity that Li Yun's slogans named and renamed with such obsessive energy: the socialist state?

I was to learn that Li Yun's affliction was not exceptional. Many people in this community referred to the present age, beginning with the catastrophic famine that followed the Great Leap Forward in 1958–1960 and continuing through the 1990s, as the "age of wild ghosts." This phrase captured the sense that life in this era was inflected by eruptions into the present of unreconciled fragments of the past, often personified as the ghosts of people (or spirits) who had met bad ends and who frequently possessed or killed their descendants. Most such eruptions were quieter than Li Yun's roaring. Yet many gathered force and persistence as they were elaborated in stories, their origins divined, their qualities explicated, their symptoms treated. Some eventually accumulated the coherence of strategies—to subvert state projects, to enunciate calls for justice, or to open up avenues for healing.

This book traces the struggles of the people of Li Yun's community to find their place at the end of a century of violence and at the margins of a nation-state. These were efforts to shape a habitable place—in bodies, houses, and the national landscape—in a time when ordering space was a principal mode of state power. They were attempts to reshape past and present time in a place where ordering time was the central project and exclusive prerogative of the state. In a specific and limited sense, then, this is an ethnography of the state. It approaches the state *first* not as a system of institutions, a network of power relations, or a history of policies and programs, but as an aspect of the "social imaginary," in the sense that Cornelius Castoriadis gave this term. Every social community, Castoriadis reflected, must answer a few fundamental questions:

> Who are we as a collectivity? What are we for one another? Where and in what are we? What do we want; what do we desire; what are we lacking? Society must define its "identity," its articulation, the world, its relations to the world and to the objects it contains, its needs and its desires. Without the "answer" to these "questions," without these "definitions," there can be no human world, no society, no culture—for everything would be an undifferentiated chaos. The role of imaginary significations is to provide an answer to these questions, an answer that, obviously, neither "reality," nor "rationality" can provide. . . . Society constitutes itself by producing a *de facto* answer to these questions in its life, in its activity. It is in the *doing* of each collectivity that the answer to these questions appears as an embodied meaning; this social doing allows itself to be understood only as a reply to the questions that it implicitly poses itself. (1987, 147)

States pose and answer such constituting questions in reference to the imagined communities they govern. In practice, states are loosely coordinated systems of institutions, policies, symbols, and processes. Their capacity to affect events, produce meanings, or work themselves into the bodies of their subjects depends on how they are imagined collectively as unitary entities. As Ann Anagnost (1997) argues, the socialist state in China, especially during the Mao era, was particularly striking in this regard. It was a weak and disorganized institution; its power depended on its capacity to impose its own visions of itself on the social world. It was a "magnanimous sorcerer," to borrow Fernando Coronil's words, which "sieze[d] its subjects by inducing a condition or state of being receptive to its illusions—a magical state" (1997, 5).

This book investigates concrete practices and poetics as resources for engaging, diverting, or replacing the tangible "illusions" of this magical state, and thus for submitting to or deflecting its grasp. Among these practices

are ritualized methods for doing useful things: treating physical and psychic afflictions; promoting the fertility of crops, animals, and people; rid-
ding bodies, houses, and the proximate landscape of undesirable nonhuman entities. These methods involve two formalized "languages." One is a
language of materials: everyday objects such as twigs, grasses, string, clothing, and bowls, used to sculpt representations of ghosts or spirits. The
other is a verbal poetic language: ritual chants used to communicate with
nonhuman entities, their vocabulary drawn largely from daily practice.
These languages are resources for thinking about the practiced diligence of
everyday life—the acquired capacities for taking care of oneself, one's family, and one's community—and for evading the domination of others,
human or nonhuman, living or dead. At the same time, as is typical of ritualized languages in China, they produce manifold, mutable images of the
state. The state they imagine is not external to the fundamental concerns of
daily life, nor does it penetrate this intimate sphere only from the outside.
It is a constitutive force at the heart of the social world. To envision it is to
pose and answer questions about the social world, about relations to this
world and the objects it contains, about social needs and social desires.

A story I was told in the context of a mortuary ritual reflects on the
state in this sense, as framing the conditions for social existence. I heard
several versions of this story—this one from a man in his fifties at the funeral of one of his affines. It is about the careful operations of mourning,
in which material objects such as bamboo sieves and paper screens are
ritually manipulated to regulate transactions between the living and the
dead, allowing the living to escape being dominated by their grief. In
this story, it is the state, in the form of market officials, that sets the rules
for grief's transactions and oversees the discriminations that mourning
creates between the living and their objects of loss:

> Long ago, the living [ts'ɔ] could see the dead [nè], and the dead could see
> the living. Living and dead both attended the market: on that side of the
> street the dead sold their things; on this side the living sold theirs; and
> the dead took the same form as the living. At that time they used copper
> money, not paper. The dead used paper to stamp out coins that looked
> just like the copper coins of the living, and with this money they bought
> things from the living. But the living were not to be trifled with. They put
> the coins in a pan of water: the real coins made of copper sank, and the
> paper coins made by the dead floated. They returned the false money to
> the dead, and gradually the dead could no longer buy from the living;
> they could buy only from other dead. If your father died, you could go to
> the market the next day and see him. But it was not permitted for living

and dead to speak to each other. The dead were punished if they spoke to the living—their officials taxed and fined them—and the living were afraid to speak to the dead. So living and dead could only look at each other. Then, as now, the dead sometimes harmed [*k'ə*, literally "bit"] the living, but the living could beat the dead in return, so the dead had no power over them. Disgusted with this situation, the dead petitioned for a bamboo sieve to be set up between them and the living. The living could see the dead only vaguely, but the dead [being closer to the sieve's holes] could see the living clearly. The living did not like this, for the sieve was too thick to beat the dead through. The living were stupid: some say they asked for a paper screen to be placed on their side of the street; they could beat the dead through the paper, but they could not see them at all.

The state is held at a distance in this tale. It is glimpsed only once, through its representatives, officials who tax and fine the dead. Yet the entire scene takes place under its watchful gaze. Its authority glimmers in the authentic copper coins that sink in water, cutting off market transactions across the street; its permission erects the sieves and screens that curtail the "bite" of loss. The imagined state is seen to enable and structure mourning, yet it is also found to be an agent of loss: the story is told in the context of a mortuary rite that sends back to the underworld realm "police" who, on orders of higher officials, arrest and chain the souls of the living to lead them away to death.

The ritual techniques examined here imagine such a state: a constitutive presence at the center of the social world with an intimate relation to loss. In these rites, the state is found to be a strange image, abstract and uncanny, divided from this world as shade is from sunlight, as insubstantial as it is omnipresent. It is sensed as an absent subject, from which issue acts and commands governed by alien principals, like omens that bridge the gulf between this world and the underworld to bring muffled messages from the dead. The nationscape is a body, ordered spatially and morally like a digestive tract, the nearby mountains at its head and the governing cities at its excretory end. The imagined state has a proper place, at the bottom of the digestive tract. Its strange powers come from beyond even there, in the absolute otherness of the sky and sea, from whence descend the calamities of mass starvation, suicide, or violent death. To imagine the state in this way is to find it to be at once remote and intimate, at once alien and familiar. The body of the nation can be mapped onto individual bodies, the digestive flow of its rivers onto corporeal digestive tracts. Ritual techniques for healing find the body and the national landscape to coexist as a single, extended, "collective unity of habitations" (Stein 1957a, 1957b; Boltz 1983). To heal physical or psychic pain is to reorder this unity. It is to release the knots or reversals in the body's flows; it is to locate a habitable place in a morally ordered national landscape and to guide violence and loss back toward their origins at the rivers' ends.

Enunciated in the ritual languages of healing, such images of state and nation shaped the stories people in this community told about how wounds treated with ritual had been inflicted. This book retells many such stories. To make them intelligible, I have recast them in the standard chronological framework through which we are accustomed to viewing the great transformations of rural Chinese society in the twentieth century's last half: Liberation, land reform, collectivization, the Great Leap Forward, the Cultural Revolution, the revival of household cultivation, market reforms, birth planning campaigns. This framework is the effect of an official perspective on time that structures both scholarship in the West and histories produced within Chinese state agencies. From this perspective, the state appears in its conventional guise: institutions, processes, policies, projects. I use this framework as a device for translation. My objective is to show how stories of past events were used to assemble an oppositional practice of time, a practice that deliberately undermined the temporality of official history. To be intelligible as historical practice, however, these stories must be translated through a more familiar vocabulary. The outlines of an alternative temporal strategy emerge from the dissonances of translation, its incapacity to fully render narrated memories as simple instances of a known history, subject to a familiar temporality. I employ this procedure because it seems to me that the alternative is to cast what is strange in these narratives outside history altogether—as effects of the tellers' personal vagaries or as simple instances of the "popular beliefs" (or, as the official voices of the Chinese state still render them, "superstitions") of a marginal people.

The stories I retell here persistently raise questions about what it means to live as a community in the aftermath of violence—in particular, the violence of hunger in the Great Leap famine and of revenge in the Cultural Revolution. They converge on a dream of community—a bad dream, embodied in the life, death, and ghostly revenance of a single local institution. This institution was called the *ts'ici* by local people and a Ch. *huotou* by outside officials and scholars. Oral accounts of the *ts'ici* of the 1930s and 1940s described it as an arrangement by which a title and a well-defined set of political and ritual responsibilities rotated yearly among the area's most affluent households. The *ts'ici* system distributed the burdens and risks of hosting influential and demanding outsiders among these wealthiest community members. Each year, the household that accepted the title of *ts'ici* became a kind of guest house, where visiting officials and soldiers were lodged well, fed abundantly, entertained politely, and sent quickly on their way. The host household provided a stage on which the region's local despot judged disputes among community members; it fed and lodged prisoners arrested by agents of the local state; and it carried letters, repaired footpaths, and buried dead outsiders. It also sponsored a yearly cycle of public rituals for a family of collective ancestors. Many of its expenses were paid with the harvest of a collectively held and communally farmed ancestral estate, a fertile swath of rice land.

People in Zhizuo remembered the *ts'ici* as creating a houselike community, descended from a single apical ancestor and bound together in a circle of affinal relations. Their stories of the socialist period lingered over the slow disintegration, traumatic killing, and ghostly rebirth of the *ts'ici*. In the 1950s, local agents of the new state quickly took over most of the *ts'ici*'s political functions. The circle of affluent residents who had elected the host households was decimated, some executed as counter-revolutionaries, many attacked as landlords and rich peasants. Still, people in Zhizuo found ways to keep the *ts'ici* alive throughout the 1950s, as land and labor were collectivized. In 1965, shortly before the advent of the Cultural Revolution, this embattled emblem of community was ritually killed at a theatrical mass meeting. This killing transformed the family of collective ancestors into a cabal of wild ghosts, which haunted the community for the next thirty years. During the Cultural Revolution, these ghosts killed off those held responsible for the *ts'ici*'s destruction and the devastation of the Great Leap famine; during the period of national reconciliation and market reforms, they continued their depredations in other forms.

Taken together, such stories about the *ts'ici* constitute a narrative of a tortured relationship between a wounded community and an imagined state. In this narrative, the state gradually transforms itself from a personified external Other into an abstract internal Other. The *ts'ici* system remembered from the 1940s kept the violent and tattered Republican state outside and at a distance by inviting its agents within, moving them on their way, and managing the social and moral threats their incursions entailed. In the 1950s, the socialist state efficiently penetrated this community, installing itself within, as the center of production and social reproduction. By the time of the Great Leap famine, this center had revealed itself as hollow, a spectral presence whose essence was felt in endless demands for grain and praise. During the Cultural Revolution, this ghostly state was seen to possess the bodies of ambitious activists and fearful officials (such as Li Yun), who used their mouths to voice its slogans and demands. Later, after collective land had been divided among households, the state was found to be obsessively concerned with human reproduction—it was seen to penetrate to the most intimate core of body and community: fertile and infertile wombs. As they show the state attaining an ever more invasive presence at the core of lived social and corporeal worlds, these stories describe it as ever more abstract, ever more difficult to grasp in concrete, human terms. This rift between the state's presence at the intimate core of the social and corporeal worlds and the growing difficulties of imagining it concretely inflected many aspects of social life in the early 1990s, the period of my fieldwork.

Several of the coming chapters show this narrative emerging with many diversions, contradictions, and ironies from nostalgic stories about a dream of lost community, bitter stories about hunger and injustice, comic stories about ghostly possession and toppling buildings, serious stories about killings and suicides, anxious stories about surgeons' scalpels and dying wombs. The question that dominates these chapters is, why this narrative? What did these stories, structured in this particular fashion, do? My answer, arrived at only gradually, is that they produced an oppositional practice of time and an alternative mode of history. This was a critical history, a calculated mistranslation of the constitutive questions about the social world that the state was heard to pose and answer. It was a history of an alternative kind of *doing* (to echo Castoriadis again), a subversive embodiment of alternative questions and answers about the ways a human community articulates with its lived world. I read these stories as efforts to find ways to live together in a community rent by past violence, as attempts to trace the responsibility for violence to its morally ambiguous origins, as struggles to enunciate calls for justice and to articulate longings for reconciliation. In this sense, I read them as means for creating collective ethical responses to past violence and its inevitable returns to the present and the future.

This is also an ethnography of place. It is a record of my own efforts to understand how people *inhabit* particular places—how habitable places are made in language and in the material world and how they become foundations for social being. To this end, I have structured this book as a journey through places I found people to inhabit intensely. This journey begins (in chapter 2) with an afflicted body, the dwelling place for an improbable entity: the soul of an animal destined to be reborn repeatedly as a stillborn fetus. I suggest that this body is not simply contained within its inhabited world like an egg in a basket; rather, it is involved with the world in a mutual interleaving of place and flesh. This theme is revised and complicated several times as the journey continues. The next stage (chapter 3) is a tour through the close domestic places of houses. I investigate houses not as simple containers for lives but as material foundations for social relations that could not exist in the same way without them. Then (in chapters 4 and 5) houses open up into a valley and its surroundings. I suggest that people fashion their closely inhabited landscape on the model of a house; it is the place-foundation for a houselike community, always in disintegration and always being reconstituted through the work of memory. From the known landscape, the journey ventures onto paths that link the closely inhabited world with the imagined nation and cosmos (chapters 6, 7, 8, and 9). The directions of these paths and the flow of traffic along them situate a lived community in this more expansive imagined space. These are paths of danger and healing; they are the routes along which the worst calamities enter the lived world—yet they are walked also by people in search of relief or reconciliation.

This journey inverts a common trope of ethnography, the trope of the "setting." Much ethnographic writing finds place to be a container for social being or a surface on which social life is played out. Ethnographies in this mode often begin with a "setting" chapter, which dispenses with the question of where the subjects of the inquiry are located in place and time. In contrast, this question animates this entire book. Neither place nor time is given in nature or by power; both are made. People are subject to the economic and political geographies that shape landscapes, but they are actively subject; they refashion these geographies locally and find their own routes through them. So too with the dominant architectures of time. My ambition is to keep the questions of where and when alive throughout this work.

Like most ethnographic ambitions, however, this one can be realized only in small part. Again, this is a work of translation: everything it communicates must move first through familiar vocabularies; it repeatedly imposes conventional spatial and temporal contextualizations in order to let unconventional understandings of place and time emerge in an intelligible way. I would like to stop there, allowing orientations in time and space to unfold gradually in the journey from body through house, valley, and imagined nation, but I know this would make some of what follows less readable, especially to those less familiar with China. So a few pages of "setting" follow. Much of what they state will be expanded and complicated in further chapters.

Zhizuo comprises some twenty-four villages and hamlets built on the slopes of a small mountain valley and its tributaries. These valleys lie in the Baicaolin Mountains, part of a vast chain of mountain ranges that forms the frontier between two of the economic and physiographic macroregions into which G. William Skinner (1977, 1985) divides China—and which scholars of China across many disciplines have found to be indispensable aids to analysis. These are the Yungui macroregion, covering most of Yunnan and Guizhou Provinces, and the Upper Yangtze macroregion, coinciding largely with Sichuan Province. Skinner notes that each of these regional systems has a core-periphery structure with further, internal cores and peripheries. In general, key resources such as arable land, population, and capital investment are concentrated in the lowland riverine core areas. Agriculture is more intensive there, transport more efficient, economic transactions more dense, towns and cities closer together; all these goods thin out toward the mountainous peripheries (Skinner 1997). Zhizuo is triply peripheral in this regional-systems methodology. It lies in a peripheral region of the nationally peripheral Yungui macroregion, an area now known as Chuxiong Yi Autonomous Prefecture. It is perched on this prefecture's northern edge, in mountains that divide two of its economically least significant counties, Dayao and Yongren. During the twentieth century, Zhizuo was swapped several times between these counties; today it lies mostly in Yongren.[4]

The occupants of these mountains have long been marked as different from their lowland neighbors by their language, customs, clothing, and "character." In the nineteenth and early twentieth centuries, their Chinese-speaking neighbors knew them as Luoluo. The Dayao County gazetteer of 1825 called them White Luoluo to distinguish them from the Black Luoluo living in the Liangshan Mountains to the north. Unlike the latter, the gazetteer noted, they were little trouble to administer. They did not often engage in banditry, and they did not raid lowland villages for slaves; they were poor, timid, and peaceable: "The White Luoluo are tame and foolish of character. The men wrap their heads, go barefoot, and throw a black goatskin over their shoulders; the women plait their hair. Occasionally men and women come into town to sell hempen cloth, hempen thread, honey, and pitch pine" (DXZ 1825, 7,1b). In 1922, the gazetteer of Yanfeng County, established eleven years earlier to administer the salt mines where many men from these mountains worked as porters, made similar observations about these people, calling them Yi and describing a few of their "customs": "The Yi men dress in goatskins and hempen cloth; the women are distinguished by cloth capes on their backs and also by goatskins. They live in grass-roofed houses or houses roofed with wooden shingles. Men and women are free to choose marriage partners. When they fall ill, they don't use medicine; they do a sorcerer's dance and chant, and that is enough" (YXZ 1922, 3,61b).

Apart from such brief characterizations, the local histories and gazetteers of the late Qing and Republican years took little notice of these people. Still, administrators did remark on one aspect of their lives: many of their villages appeared to form cooperative associations, founded on land held in common. In 1912, negotiators attempting to resolve a dispute over the boundary between Dayao and Yanfeng Counties took note of one such group of Luoluo villages in the border area, in a place called Liushutang: "These five small villages and the seven small villages on the road to the temple make up a *huotou* territory. This is a community organization. Up and down the road they hold real estate in common, and when they encounter disaster, they distribute its burdens" (YXZ 1922, 1,16a). The existence of this "community organization" supported an argument that these villages should not be split up but should instead belong as a unit to one of the two disputing counties. In these mountains, administrators noted, many groups of villages were united in similar *huotou* territories, with land held in common and rules that rotated ritual and political responsibilities among villages and households.

More detailed descriptions of these mountain residents did not appear until the 1950s, when the new socialist government conducted a series of social history projects among the nation's "minority" peoples.[5] About two hundred investigators, trained in the Soviet model of ethnography, descended upon China's mountainous and border areas to study the culture and society of non-Han peoples. At least two separate teams assembled reports on the history, folklore, and economic circumstances of people living in the Baicaolin Mountains. Like the compilers of gazetteers and local histories before them, these ethnographers noticed many cooperative associations with elected heads and common funds of grain and land used for collective rituals (YSB 1986, 109, 111). They too remarked that locals treated death, illness, and affliction with "sorcerer's chants" directed to a bewildering variety of nonhuman entities. One team collected some such chants from Zhizuo and its environs, compiled them with songs and chants from nearby regions, and translated them into Chinese; the text that resulted remains the most comprehensive written record of this area's extraordinary oral literature (YSMWCD 1959).

These efforts were part of a nationwide project to systematically assign official "nationality" designations to all the non-Han groups in China. In this task, ethnographers were initially guided by Joseph Stalin's four criteria for defining a unique nationality: common language, common territory, common economic base, and common psychological character (Fei 1980). Among the varied and scattered peoples of the southwest, however, most of these criteria proved impractical, and investigators of the peoples formerly called Luoluo largely abandoned their use. Chinese scholars had dreamed for two decades of discovering a common historical relationship among these peoples; the ethnologists of the 1950s continued this work by tracing genetic relationships among linguistic vocabularies and cultural traits to assemble most into a single "nationality" (Harrell 1995). They gave this group the name "Yi"—pronounced the same as the term "Yi" that had once been applied generally to non-Han peoples in the southwest, but written with a less derogatory character. This is now among the largest and least well understood of the "minority nationalities" on China's official list of fifty-five, with a current population of more than six million.

Linguists in the 1950s distinguished six mutually unintelligible dialects spoken by Yi peoples. The speakers of the Northern dialect proved most problematic for the socialist state, and only they have been objects of substantial social or historical research. Notorious for enslaving their neighbors, many clans of Northern dialect speakers resisted incursions of the People's Liberation Army into stronghold territories in Sichuan's Liangshan Mountains until 1956, when they were pacified and their slaves liberated.[6] Speakers of the other five dialects have been written about very little in Chinese and almost not at all in Western languages.[7] Despite great historical and cultural differences among Yi groups, even the best descriptions of minority languages and cultures in English still take Northern dialect speakers as representative of Yi. Most describe this "nationality" in blanket terms as descendants of the famous "independent Luoluo" and as organized into exogamous clans and strictly divided into endogamous and hierarchical castes, including noble "Black Yi," commoner "White Yi," and slaves (see, for example, Ramsey 1987). At best, this applies only to the minority of Yi who speak the Northern dialect and reside mainly in Sichuan's Liangshan Prefecture and Yunnan's Ninglang County. Baicaolin Mountain residents, like most of the varied peoples called Yi who are scattered throughout Yunnan, Guizhou, and Guangxi Provinces, have been under state rule for centuries and have never had exogamous clans, caste hierarchies, or slaves.

Most residents of the Baicaolin range speak what is now known as the Central dialect of Yi. Some linguists have noted that this dialect is much closer to the language of another "nationality," Lisu, than to any other Yi dialect (Bradley 1978). Chinese ethnographers have divided Central dialect speakers into Lipo and Luoluopo (omitting the offensive "dog" radical from the first two characters), according to dialect differences and reported self-appellations (Yang H. 1990, 117). The non-Han residents of the Baicaolin are classed as Lipo, a group that numbers about ninety-four thousand people. While many in Zhizuo were pleased to claim kinship with other Central dialect speakers in the surrounding mountains, they rejected as ridiculous the notion that they could share a "nationality" with Northern dialect speakers, who once preyed on their villages as bandits and still ate like barbarians, tearing chunks of meat from the bone without chopsticks. Most applied the term "Yi" to themselves only when traveling or speaking Chinese to outsiders. They found the designation "Lipo" more accurate: many traced their ancestry to people they called Líp'ò (in their own language) from a few valleys to the south. Nevertheless, most were agreed, the proper appellation for non-Han in the Zhizuo *ts'ici* (or *huotou*) was not Líp'ò but Lòlop'ò or, more formally, Lòlop'ò Lòlomo, "Lòlo men and women." And the language spoken in this region should be called Lòlongo, "Lòlo language." These terms, Zhizuo residents insisted, were unrelated to the contemptuous Chinese appellation "Luoluo." They derived instead from *lò*, an ancient word for "ox" or "tiger," still used in ritual language. Of course, all these claims were inflected by the discourse on "nationalities"; during the period of my fieldwork, some in Zhizuo were pushing the idea that Lòlop'ò should be considered its own nationality, the nation's smallest, exclusive to the occupants of the Zhizuo *ts'ici*. About 5 percent of Zhizuo residents considered themselves not Lòlop'ò but Han (or Cep'ò). Many formerly Han families had become Lòlop'ò after moving to Zhizuo; these remaining Han spoke Lòlongo as their first language, intermarried with their Lòlop'ò neighbors, and found themselves hard pressed to preserve their Han identity.

These mountains, with their high elevations, narrow valleys, and deeply peripheral situation, have always been a difficult place to make a living. The 1950s ethnographers found most families getting by on a mixture of farming, goat herding, and household-based hempen cloth production. Zhizuo's central valley lay on a trade route from the nearby salt wells of Baijing[8] to the lowlands. During the Republican era, many men worked as porters or muleteers along this route, but these opportunities melted away in the 1950s as the salt business was brought under firmer state control. Land in these mountains was divided between precious irrigated paddy land on the valley floors for rice and winter wheat; unirrigated terraces for maize, wheat, and barley on hillsides near the villages; and swidden land for oats, buckwheat, potatoes, and hemp higher in the mountains. Land of all classes was scarce. Before the land reform movement, a few landlord households produced enough grain on their own land to feed their numbers for the entire year. Afterward, however, virtually no household could feed itself entirely on its own land (of about 2.1 mu[9] per capita); all supplemented their grain income with hempen cloth production.[10] These mountains had long been renowned in Yunnan for the quality and quantity of their hempen cloth; during the first three decades of socialism, more hempen cloth flowed from here than from any other part of the province. Women raised hemp on swidden acreage high in the mountains; soaked and washed it in the cold streams; pounded, boiled, spun, and wove it in their courtyards; and sold it to state-run supply and marketing cooperatives to make grain bags.

From 1952 to 1978, the state subsidized hemp prices relative to prices for grain and cotton. High hemp prices brought unprecedented prosperity to these mountains for nearly three decades, in a period when real incomes for most peasants in China were stagnating and declining. But this good fortune ended with market reforms. In 1978, the state raised prices for grain; in 1980, it instituted a floating price for hemp procurement. China had begun to produce synthetic fibers in the 1970s, and one of their earliest uses was to replace hemp in bags for grain and fertilizer.

Hemp prices plunged more than 12 percent in one year, and they never recovered. By the early 1980s, households in the Baicaolin Mountains could not sell hempen cloth for any price.

Hempen cloth production, like cotton production in the Yangze Delta, had encouraged population growth and made grain land even more scarce. In the 1980s and 1990s, Zhizuo residents farmed about .93 *mu* per capita of unirrigated land and .36 *mu* per capita of irrigated land.[11] Most households could grow enough grain on this land to suffice for about half the year; nearly all relied heavily on state relief grain. Some households raised herds of black-haired goats; some had a few walnut trees; many harvested timber illegally from higher in the mountains; a handful opened tiny shops or developed businesses as tinkers; the most fortunate produced educated sons and daughters who found work in lowland towns or cities and sent money home. Everyone ate two meals a day, usually of steamed grain with a soup of boiled greens on the side. Most households killed one small pig a year, salted its meat, and used it sparingly in cooking for the entire year. On special occasions, people killed a chicken, burned off its feathers, and boiled it in a soup. At weddings and funerals, goats were slaughtered and eaten in quantity. During the rainy season, however, when the fall harvest was but a dim memory and relief grain was running out, many people routinely went hungry.

The rapid economic expansion that transformed many parts of China in the 1980s and 1990s bestowed few benefits on this deep periphery. By the mid-1990s, Zhizuo still had no village industries and no legal sideline occupations that turned a profit. One youth had a tape deck on which he recorded courting songs; three or four families had battery-powered radios. Some houses sported electric lines—the remains of past, failed attempts to electrify villages by installing small generators in mountain streams—but not a single house had electricity. Although pipelines had been installed from mountainside springs to tanks in the centers of the largest villages, many of the pipes were broken, and residents walked the steep, root-strewn paths to draw water from the streams. Zhizuo residents had expended immense effort during the Great Leap Forward to build a road to span the twenty-five steep kilometers from the township center, but it was rough and dangerous, and the only vehicles to bounce up it were the jeeps of county officials on their semiannual visits. For most people, life was growing gradually harder, as prices rose and entitlements for free medical care and education disintegrated.

After following Li Yun to Zhizuo, I settled on the valley's populous "sunny side" in an elementary school that served the entire brigade. I lived there for thirteen months. It had taken me repeated visits to Yunnan over four years and many months of negotiation to be allowed to do extended fieldwork in a single location, and throughout my stay I was always uncertain how long I would be allowed to continue. For the first six months, in adherence to regulations governing foreign field researchers in China, I was accompanied by one of two "companions" (Ch. *peitong*) who had been assigned to facilitate my research and report back to my sponsoring institutions, the Yunnan Academy of Social Sciences and the Chuxiong Yi Culture Research Institute, on its progress and results. After six months, I was quietly allowed to continue research on my own.[12] I occupied a small, earth-floored room, separated from a roomful of sixth-grade boys by a wall of planks and newspapers and overlooking a courtyard that filled several times a day with cheerful schoolchildren. I could not have found a more auspicious place to live. My first friends were children, who laughed at my stumbling Lòlongo, offered me gifts of sunflower seeds, and competed to take me home for dinner. Their trust was the foundation for all the conversations with their parents and other kin around which this book is built.

I often sat outside the school gate in the evening with a friend or two, watching the sunlight melt off the mud-brick houses on the opposite slope. The fields below gleamed jewel-bright, while dark figures trudged up the paths toward home. One of the ritual poems I had begun to learn (quoted in chapter 2) described this view: "Look over at that slope, only cliffs and caves; look at this slope, only thorns and brambles; not land enough to turn a plow, not land enough to place a sieve, rocks below the feet, cliffs at every corner." It was a bitter place to live, all its inhabitants agreed. Yet many also seemed to believe that no other place was anything like it: in no other place were words and things so close to each other, shadowing each other, completing each other. The warp and woof of lived experience here—upstream and downstream, this slope and that slope, sunny side and shady side—were the cloth on which the poetic languages of healing, courtship, mourning, and pain needled their intricate embroidery. This tree up here, that rock down there, this courtyard, that wall—each breathed a history of words, formal and informal, fluent and chaotic, secret and available, accordant and contested. One could sit up here like this and listen to the fields and slopes below speak one's histories and those of others, with their comings and goings, deaths and wounds, bitter rifts and healing accords. I know this because it is from such a perch that many of the stories in this book began, as someone pointed out a house, a gully, a grave, or a deforested slope and began to talk about it. It was a difficult place to live: high, poor, cold, far from the luxuries of cities and markets, and in troubled relation to the nation below. It was even an accursed place, as chapters 6 and 8 will show. But it was a place that, in being lived so intimately and known so well, offered its inhabitants abundant resources for engaging with the afflictions, uncertainties, and consolations of memory.

"Why study a minority when we still know so little about the Han?" an eminent economic historian of China once asked me. "It's all very interesting, but is it China?" commented an ascendant anthropologist of China after a presentation on ritual in Zhizuo. Historians and anthropologists have long imagined China to form a cultural whole. The classic anthropology of China, which has taught us most of what we know about "Chinese culture," made this a founding principle. To study any village, no matter how peripheral—and most were in the far peripheries of Taiwan and Hong Kong's New Territories—was to investigate a culture common to the Chinese people. For anthropologists, this common cultural core was first captured in the conceptual triune of Chinese lineage, Chinese household, and Chinese family, brilliantly described by Maurice Freedman (1958, 1966). Feminist anthropologists have long since dismantled Freedman's triune, but the idea of a common cultural core has continued to infuse much anthropology of China, sometimes as a foil against which to bring out local differences, sometimes as a resource to fill in gaps in analysis. The idea of a Han nation (Ch. *minzu*) as the carrier of this common culture was invented by Sun Yatsen and other nation builders during the Republic; later, anthropologists in search of "Chinese culture" accepted this idea almost without questioning it.

Many still assume that an ethnography of any locale is relevant or interesting only insofar as it sheds light on this cultural whole. Studies of people now identified as "minority nationalities," it is assumed, can make little contribution to this enterprise. These peoples are either culturally distinct and thus not "Chinese," or they are in the process of being "sinicized" and thus neither reliable representatives of Chinese culture nor very interesting on their own. In this context, the ethnography of "minority" peoples in China has taken two predominant forms. In the West, most of such work is about ethnicity. It delineates cultural and linguistic differences among ethnic groups, elucidates the processes by which ethnic difference is created in dialogue with the Chinese state, and shows how Han have attained a unified ethnic identity by marking off "minorities" as exotic others.[13] The other form of ethnography investigates a "minority" as a cultural isolate, making no claims to contribute to knowledge about "Chinese culture." In China, this is an industry: "ethnic studies" (Ch. *minzuxue*) departments of universities and research institutes now churn out descriptions of every officially defined nationality, emphasizing the attributes that distinguish them from Han.[14]

Recent scholarship has begun to show that the cultural features we identify as "Chinese" have multiple historical origins, including contributions from different ethnicities within and outside China (see Rawski 1996 for a review). This scholarship dismantles the notion of "Chinese culture" as a unity belonging to a Han people engaged in a long historical process of converting to this culture each of the various non-Han peoples within their realm. It allows us to think instead of an open and flexible field of cultural practices, fashioned in the interactions of many different peoples. This field is not centered on any single deep-seated common cultural core; it is historically and regionally diverse, and it ranges across ethnic and national boundaries. In this view, present-day "minority nationalities" are neither outside a cohesive entity called "Chinese culture" nor in any simple process of being assimilated by it. Instead, these peoples seed a diverse cultural field with fresh influences; they selectively appropriate its elements, reworking or embellishing them; they imagine coherent versions of it against which to pose self-consciously, inventing themselves as different.

I take the subjects of my inquiry to be participants in such a field. Lòlop'ò in Zhizuo see themselves as no less "Chinese" than any of their neighbors, yet they also believe themselves to occupy a unique and troubled place within the Chinese nation. Their experience as participants in late twentieth-century China has been dominated by the same massive political and economic transformations that have shaped the lives of people throughout the countryside, yet they have drawn on distinctive cultural resources to respond to these transformations in uncommon ways. Readers familiar with scholarship on Chinese culture will recognize much about them, yet they will also find much of what they recognize to be distorted or amplified in ways that make it seem strange. Note that all of this might also be said of any of the rural people in the People's Republic about whom anthropologists have recently written as, in some way, representative.[15] In this sense, Zhizuo might be seen as just one more locale in the vast and diverse landscape of rural China, neither typical nor unique, neither marginal nor central. As an ethnography of such a place, this book is not limited to exploring "ethnicity" or to investigating practices assumed to be interesting because they are distinct. Still, to write of a people presumed to be different is to feel some special restraints. The most obvious is that "Chinese culture" cannot be invoked to explain local practices or fill in ethnographic lapses. I have found this restraint to be productive. It has forced me to give closer attention to the specificities of daily practice, and it has granted me the freedom to let my questions emerge from the local ethnographic terrain. But it has also constrained me to search for other means to show how this local terrain articulates itself with the whole that "China" is imagined to be. The questions about transactions between daily practices and the imagined state and nation that animate this inquiry have emerged from this mix of freedom and constraint.

The first half of this book explores closely inhabited places and dreams of domestic community. Chapter 2 tells of Li Qunhua's troubled dreams during a birth planning campaign, of how she found these dreams to be caused by the soul of a domestic animal lodged in her womb, and of the ritual that drove this thing out of her body and house. This story introduces one of the book's central themes: how people inhabit their most intimate surroundings in the face of loss or violence. Chapter 3 broadens the investigation of domestic space. It uses houses and their representations in material and poetic languages to describe the flow of social relations through intimately inhabited places. The next two chapters use stories of Zhizuo's *ts'ici* system of the 1930s and 1940s to show how people modeled dreams of a larger domestic community on houses. Chapter 4 retells some of these stories, while chapter 5 looks at the ritual forms that accompanied them to examine ideas about memory and representation. The book's second half explores the infirmity, death, and rebirth of this dream of community. Chapter 6 relates stories of the first decade after Liberation, beginning with the new state's deliberate conquest of intensely inhabited places in the early 1950s and culminating in the Great Leap famine of 1958–1960. This unforgettable catastrophe commenced the "age of wild ghosts," forever transforming the character of community in this place. Chapter 7 investigates the rites of exorcism with which people traced the double origins of pain and loss to the famine dead and the imagined state. Chapter 8 picks up the narrative of the *ts'ici* system once more, showing how people used stories of its traumatic death and reappearance as a cabal of vengeful ghosts to explore themes of community and justice. The concluding chapter returns to the theme of birth planning. It tells the story of a campaign in which more than eighty women in Zhizuo were forcibly sterilized and the active resistance this campaign engendered. This story gathers and sharpens the questions of place, memory, violence, and community that have inspired this study.

CHAPTER TWO

An Intimate Immensity

In songs of grief performed upon the deaths of their parents,[1] Lòlopʼò women invoke images of mothers bearing (*bùu*) infants on their backs and carrying (*te̠*) them in their arms. These songs recall the debts children owe their dead mothers, measured in the flesh of their arms and backs, worn away in the labor of bearing and carrying.

2.1

mother bore this orphaned daughter	su mo né chi̠ bùu væ̀ do̠
bore this orphaned son	zò chi̠ bùu væ̀ do̠
bore this daughter for three years	né bùu sa kʼò lɔ
she played with tiles at the courtyard's head	kæ wú ngæ̀ kʼà tsə
played with bowls at the courtyard's tail	kæ mæ si̠ kʼà tsə
made dolls of *le̠* leaves	le̠ pʼè æ næ pe̠ je wò
made little oxen of *le̠* branches	le̠ kə lò zò pe̠ je wò
loved to eat from her little bowl	tsò mi si̠ zò nó ngɔ̀ ga
loved to drink from her little cup	dɔ mi ló zò nó ngɔ̀ ga
mother bore her for three years	su mo né bùu sa kʼò lɔ
carried her for three years	né te̠ sa kʼò lɔ
wore her back raw with bearing	pʼa ká bùu chi̠ ka
wore her arms thin with carrying	le̠ kò te̠ chi̠ ka

Li Qunhua, a mother of four, recorded the song from which this fragment is taken, sitting with my tape recorder beside the singer at her mother's funeral. When she helped me translate this long lament, she explicated this passage with particular care, pointing out its eloquent parallelisms and delighting in the image of a child in the courtyard fashioning dolls from the leaves and branches of a *le* tree. With quick gestures of her fingers, she demonstrated how to twist and tie *le* leaves to make a doll. On another occasion, she showed me how to tie an embroidered head cloth to bear a child on one's back.

How do people inhabit worlds fissured by violence and loss? This question is elusive in its every aspect. How are we to represent another's pain, and with what methods might we seek its meanings? How do violence and loss rend the dense intercalations of body and the world involved in intimately inhabited places? What manner of living in the world do people envision, and on what resources do they draw, as they struggle to heal these wounds? Though this passage does not appear on its face to address violent or accidental death, it clearly expresses the desolation of loss: it is an orphaned daughter's public announcement of her grief for her dead mother. It speaks to the heavily gendered transactions between body and language that, as Veena Das (1997, 68) has noted, the work of mourning employs in many societies to re-create the world in the face of loss. In Lòlop'ò poetry of grief, such transactions involve interactions among memory, place, and the pain and fatigue of labor, especially the gendered labor of bearing and nourishing children. This fragment hints that the world is to be inhabited on these terms, in the thickness of these connections. Might such hints about "ordinary" forms of loss and pain become a foundation for understanding struggles to inhabit worlds shorn by memories of more violent loss?

The memories this passage evoked were more likely of carrying and raising one's own children than of being carried as an infant. Li Qunhua had raised four children. The youngest was a quietly inquisitive girl of twelve, another daughter and a son were in middle school, and an eldest son occupied a bureaucratic position in the county town. By the standards of the neighborhood, it was a brilliantly successful family. Li Qunhua had paid for her children's education by buying cloth, thread, and machine-embroidered strips in the cities of Chuxiong and Kunming, hauling them home by bus and foot, and carrying them on her back around the mountains to sell to highland women. She expected to continue to bear her children's weight, as she put it, for several years, until all graduated from middle school. I guessed that this passage gave Li Qunhua so much pleasure because its words attached to acts and materials that elicited memories of her children in infancy. She completed the words' meanings by demonstrating such acts to me, who lacked any such memories.

Infants seemed much on Li Qunhua's mind at the time. Her husband told me that she had been dreaming about bearing and carrying babies. Every night she saw herself with an infant in her arms or strapped to her back. At night, the dreams disturbed her sleep; during the day, she felt lethargic and depressed. These dreams alarmed her husband. If she had been pregnant, he told me, they might well have been omens that she would lose the child. But he didn't think she was, and, given a recent tightening of birth control policies, she would never have another child to lose.

Like many in Zhizuo, Li Qunhua and her husband had been deeply frightened by a recent mass sterilization campaign. The local government had adopted revised family planning regulations stipulating that every woman under the age of forty who already had two or more children must be sterilized. Li Qunhua's nephew, who had just been appointed Party secretary for Zhizuo, had publicly vowed to carry out the policy thoroughly and quickly in his brigade. Every day, a list was posted on the wall of the brigade government building naming women who were to walk to the township clinic to undergo tubal ligation. Those who resisted, the Party secretary announced, would be fined, and their livestock confiscated; in addition, they would be arrested and led in handcuffs to the clinic, where the operation would be performed without anesthetic.

Culturally specific understandings of the manner in which the body and its energies are embedded in the world (explored in chapter 9) led most Lòlop'ò women to believe that tubal ligation would injure their capacities for life and labor, in addition to reproduction, by halting the flow of sexual energy through their bodies. They would no longer enjoy sex; the "explosive strength" that allowed them to lift and carry heavy loads would wane; their kidneys would gradually swell with stagnant sexual energy; and they would spend the rest of their lives ill and weak. Still, more than eighty women were frightened into undergoing tubal ligation before collective outrage forced a halt to the campaign. Li Qunhua barely escaped sterilization. Her husband paid a relative in the brigade government to alter his household registration, changing her age from thirty-nine to forty-nine and thus exempting her from the sterilization requirement.

All of this had a presence in the couple's worried response to Li Qunhua's dreams. Her husband pointed out that the dreams could be read conventionally as omens of injured reproductive capacity, indicating the future loss of a child. Li Qunhua had already given up the opportunity to bear further infants, but the threat of sterilization endangered her capacity to haul the loads that paid for her children's education. This threat was a naked reminder that the relations of nurture and debt between herself and her children were not an isolated circuit. Present in these relations from their conception and permeating them to their core was the power of the state to create and regulate political subjects. In the 1980s and 1990s, the struggle to regulate women's reproductive capacity was a crucial arena for the generation of state power: even the most intimate of familial relationships and daily activities were shaped by the sustained scrutiny of agents acting on the state's behalf. And to bear and raise children in this context was inevitably to participate in imagining the nation as a subjectivized body, a massive and problematic population managed and disciplined by the state (Anagnost 1997; Handwerker 1995). For Zhizuo residents, the reminder that state power ran through the circuits of debt and labor between parents and children was at this moment focused in the image of a surgeon's knife cutting into bodies, perhaps without anesthetic, severing the conduits of life energy. Violence and disabling pain, projected through the distant but nevertheless everpresent image of nation and state, flickered implicitly in the background of the couple's troubled preoccupation with Li Qunhua's dreams.

Laments like the one quoted in fragment 2.1 gave pain a home in a narrative of worn flesh and debt—of a mother bearing and nourishing her children within the intimately inhabited places of house and courtyard. The elaborately beautiful language of ritual laments formalized this narrative, helping transform the "strangeness of the world revealed by death . . . into a world in which one can dwell again in full awareness of a life lived in loss" (Das 1997, 68–69). Li Qunhua found a place for the threatened violence implicit in her dreams in a distorted reflection of this healing narrative, in which a malevolent force inserted itself like a scalpel into the circuits of labor and debt that bind parents and children, reducing them to quick, repetitious cycles of injury and death. In this chapter, I examine this counternarrative as performed in a ritual with which Li Qunhua and her family responded to her dreams of infants. Here, the question of how to inhabit a world shorn by violence turns on the dense intertwining of body, language, and lived place. To heal the world one inhabits most intimately is to bring back the body in language to the lived spaces that surround it—to bring to language a mutual enfolding of flesh and place.

Investigating the techniques Li Qunhua and her family used to address her disquieting dreams will not provide direct answers to questions about pain, violence, and healing. But it will provide an opportunity to probe some of the ramifications of these questions, which animate this study. How are the relations that fill people out as social beings involved in the material places of houses and landscapes or in the imagined spaces of nation and cosmos? How did the people in this peripheral place make distinctive use of their relations to such places as they sought ways to address the many kinds of pain and loss they, like people throughout China, experienced in the last half of the twentieth century? This performance also introduces part of a mimetic sequence that was crucial to Zhizuo residents' sense of the interfolding of body and place and to their efforts to respond to loss and pain in many contexts. This sequence involved several square-framed enclosures and openings, each of which stood in imperfectly for the others: wombs, granaries, door frames, courtyards, carved wooden boxes, and the enfolding ridges of a mountain valley. These were among the most deeply significant of material habitations to Zhizuo residents, and we will find them to be central to their struggles to find ways to dwell together in their injured worlds.

This healing ritual addressed a relation through which persons and the world shape each other in a process we might call "sedimentation." Maurice Merleau-Ponty (1962, 130) used this term to name a process by which the categories of thought and language permeate the perceptual world, organizing it, structuring it, and enriching it with deposits of meaning and possibility. Li Qunhua and her family sought to heal the deep unease brought about by her dreams through a performance that addressed the affects, memories, and disciplinary imperatives sedimented into the intimately inhabited places of their house. This healing performance raised the possibility of encountering these places as though their meanings had yet to be fixed and of finding in this encounter a smoother integration of body and place and an easier mode of inhabiting the world close at hand. This performance is a good place to begin because it involves places close to the daily experience of Zhizuo residents and at the heart of their ideas about how social persons reproduce each other—a bed in an upstream room and a threshold, porch, and courtyard. Examining these places as resources for healing will lay a foundation for investigating other, more expansive, places: houses, the facing slopes of an inhabited valley, a houselike territory of several valleys, the rivers that bind and differentiate a nation's center and its peripheries.

Divining

Li Qunhua's husband, Li Zhiwu, began to attach himself to me not two weeks after my arrival in Zhizuo. He was insatiably curious about my research, which he imagined to be a comprehensive study of the many ritual techniques (*nèpi*) used in Zhizuo. After I convinced my institutional sponsor to allow me to hire research assistants locally, I paid Li Zhiwu a small fee to accompany me in the time he had free from farming.

On one trip to a village about eight hours' walk away, Li Zhiwu, Li Qunhua, and I stopped at the house of a diviner, an elderly woman who lived alone, not far from our route. Li Qunhua had prepared a bag of husked rice as a gift; diviners often read the answers to questions posed to them in the patterns formed by rice grains shaken in a wooden scoop or bowl. The couple had prepared a list of topics to discuss with the diviner: how their children would fare in life, what they might do to make peace between Li Qunhua's two quarreling brothers, when they might expect the elderly kinswoman who lived with them to die. Li Qunhua also mentioned her disturbing dreams. One needn't read the patterns in a rice scoop to interpret those dreams, the diviner told her. She had been inhabited by a *mæ*, the soul of a domestic animal that invades pregnant women's bodies and makes them miscarry or causes their infants to die before growing teeth. Had their dog recently died? It had—Li Qunhua's brother had stolen it and killed it to augment a banquet for a visiting official. The soul of the dead dog was clearly attacking her. She should ask a ritual specialist to perform a *mæho* for her, to appease the dog's soul and drive it away.

Li Zhiwu had taught me that the first rule of dream interpretation is that any dream scene may be an omen that its opposite might soon occur: a dream of one's own wedding is a warning of one's coming funeral, a dream of sudden wealth an omen of impending financial disaster. The diviner interpreted Li Qunhua's dreams of bearing infants according to this rule, as a sign that her reproductive capacity was being injured by a *mæ*. I heard of these entities frequently during my stay in Zhizuo. Diviners and ritual specialists said that a diagnosis of *mæ* possession could be made under two conditions. The first was when a woman repeatedly miscarried or when her children died one after another before reaching the age of four months. The second was when an infant developed sores in its armpits, on its buttocks or mouth, or around its anus, penis, or vagina. Especially if such sores contained broken skin, they could indicate that the baby had little time to live.

Mæ were the souls of the higher-order domestic animals that shared courtyards with human beings: dogs, cats, rabbits, horses, donkeys, and mules. In funeral lore, such animals were said to carry the souls of human beings who had been reborn as animals to atone for their sins. The other, inferior, inhabitants of the courtyard—cattle, chickens, pigs, and goats—did not possess souls, or at least not souls that could become *mæ*. The soul of a dead cat, dog, or horse could take refuge in a woman's womb and be miscarried, stillborn, or born as a sickly infant that quickly expired. An infant with a *mæ* for a soul could not develop into a healthy human being, for *mæ* were fated to be reborn as animals. It was said that sometimes a fetus or infant was marked as a *mæ* by a deformity, such as hooflike hands or a dog's head.

Once a *mæ* inhabited a woman's body, it was likely to return repeatedly, causing further miscarriages or deaths. In Zhizuo, to ensure that a dead fetus or infant did not return to its mother's womb, the parents often buried it under rocks in the path, where the feet of passersby would punish it for its sins of previous lives and disperse its soul along the roads. In nearby Nijiu, dead fetuses or infants were sometimes cut into pieces and discarded on a path, again so travelers' feet would scatter the soul. In the town of Yongren, also nearby, people had once placed dead infants high in the crooks of trees, where ravens and vultures would perform the same task. When dead infants were not disposed of in one of these ways, they were given unmarked graves far from the tombs of their families. In Li Qunhua's village, the site for burying infant corpses was on the north side of the hill on which the houses sat, where the flow of wind and water from south to north would tend to carry the souls away from the habitations. But ritual specialists claimed that none of these techniques were likely to be effective unless accompanied by a *mæho,* the ritual Li Qunhua was advised to perform.

Li Qunhua and Li Zhiwu began immediately to plan a *mæho.* They appeared to think that Li Qunhua's dreams were related to dreams that were plaguing her husband at the same time. He dreamed of walking along a mountain road far from home and discovering suddenly that his bag was gone, the bag that held all his family's possessions. "It is as if on the road to China," he said to me, "you suddenly lost everything you were carrying, everything you owned, and there you were, one person alone on the road." He would awake with a start, and for the entire day he would be out of sorts, with a headache and sore feet. This dream might well be a sign of coming wealth, I argued, but he disagreed. Dreams aren't always omens of their opposites, he said. They might just as easily be echoes of similar events in the living world. Husband and wife began to speak of the two sets of dreams in the same breath. Li Qunhua also had a sense that she had lost something, and she too, it now turned out, had symptoms of fatigue, headaches, and sore feet. Perhaps a *mæho* would address the sense of loss that husband and wife both seemed to be experiencing both in their bodies and through their dreams.

I found all of this puzzling. Why would Li Qunhua want to drive away the soul of an animal usurping the place of an infant in her womb if it was clear to her that her capacity to reproduce had already been trumped by the state's birth planning policies? Attempts by others in Zhizuo to bear a third or fourth child had recently been met with heavy fines and confiscations of livestock. In addition, although Li Qunhua had not reached menopause, she gave no indication of wanting another child. Still, in the context of the recent sterilization campaign, it was not possible to separate thoughts of bearing or not bearing children from the difficult and ambiguous topic of state power. Might it be that the *mæ* stood for the official threat to take final control of Li Qunhua's reproductive potential? Sterilization, she believed, would have sapped her capacity to perform the heavy labor of bearing and carrying that was necessary to continue supporting her children, since it would short-circuit the flow of sexual energy through her body, just as *mæ* shorted out reproductive cycles. Still, by the time her dreams became an issue, Li Qunhua and her husband had already evaded this threat. It seemed clear that in planning a *mæho* the couple were not responding to any explicitly defined effect of state power in their relations to their children. They were dealing with more elusive symptoms: unnameable anxiety, confusing physical pains, a vague shared sense of loss. The task of diviners was to gather together such dispersed influences at the root of a client's suffering and fix them with a name so that they might be dealt with in word and in gesture. In naming the *mæ,* the diviner associated this indeterminate anxiety and loss with the image of a surgeon's scalpel cutting into the sources of life and life energy, an image Li Qunhua and her husband both mentioned repeatedly in conversation. Might a *mæho* address this reminder of the dispersed but inescapable influence of state power in shaping the circuits of nurture, debt, and gratitude between parents and children?

Speaking

I did not sleep at Li Zhiwu and Li Qunhua's house, but for months I had taken many of my meals there. Also eating there were the couple's youngest daughter, who was twelve years old, and an elderly kinswoman they had taken into their household after her own descendants had passed away. Li Qunhua addressed me as "your elder brother" (*ni àtá*), giving me generational and birth-order rank in relation to her daughter. Li Zhiwu had explained that *mæho* was "a household matter," which should be performed at night in a sealed house, with only household members and one ritual specialist present. Nevertheless, since I ate at their fire most days, he said, he saw no harm in inviting me to attend. Li Qunhua invited her father's sister, Luo Lizhu, to direct the ritual. Luo Lizhu was a ritual specialist who had mastered a large repertoire of chants and techniques for communicating and exchanging with ghosts and spirits (*nè*). Most such specialists in Zhizuo were men, but Li Qunhua and many of her friends preferred Luo Lizhu over male ritualists, especially for intimate, small-scale ceremonies such as *mæho*. Luo Lizhu had learned her techniques from her father as a young girl, and she was renowned for her impish sense of humor and the exquisite poetry of her chants. Moreover, like most women, she didn't drink. She was thus a less expensive guest than most male ritualists, and she could be trusted not to make the errors of language and gesture that tended to plague their performances after they had downed a few glasses.

Two hours after dark, Luo Lizhu arrived at Li Qunhua's house, where the couple waited with their youngest daughter, their elderly relative, and me. She carried in her back basket most of the materials she would need: an old sieve, some thorny brush, a few branches and vines, some cloth, and some hemp string. Li Zhiwu had visited his wife's brother's house that day and found the worn pestle, or "beak," of a treadle grain pounder in the trash heap. This was a cylindrical chunk of pine, which was inserted into the long lever of the treadle to pound grain in a stone mortar. He had also borrowed two musical instruments. After letting the ritualist into the courtyard, Li Zhiwu scooped some ashes from the fire and scattered them on the ground just outside the gate. Ashes were often used to seal houses for private occasions. They warned human visitors to stay away, and they were said to show footprints of nonhuman entities entering or leaving. Sealing with ash made a house a self-contained receptacle, within which relations were isolated from external influences in order to effect internal transformations.

Li Qunhua sat gingerly on the edge of the bed she shared with her husband until the ritualist laughed at her, pulled a goatskin cape to the bed's head, and pushed her against it. "Lie down," she said. "Pretend you're a new mother." After making sure Li Qunhua would lie still, the ritualist stepped out to the porch and drew materials from her back basket to build a sculptural representation of the *mæ*. Such representation were called *nègu*, literally "ghost bodies"; I refer to them as "effigies." They were central to all rituals in Zhizuo except for those funeral rites in which the corpse itself was available to represent the deceased. An effigy was intended to gather a ghost, spirit, or ancestor from the surrounding landscape and give it substance, a fixed location, ears to hear the ritualist's words, eyes to see the offerings being presented, and a mouth to eat them with. At the same time, the effigy served as part of the offering, explicitly given to the nonhuman entity along with meat, grain, wine, tea, and words.

To construct this effigy, the ritualist tied the ends of three willow sticks to the old sieve and bound them together above it to form a three-cornered arch. She bundled their leafy tips into a piece of white cloth and tied the neck of the bundle with a piece of the malodorous dog vine, used often in healing rituals to bind and contain malevolent entities. With a brush and a bottle of ink, she painted a face—two eyes, a mouth, and two ears—on the cloth. "The *mæ* is the white tiger and the dog that eats the moon," she later explained. "The white tiger contains the dog, the horse, and the cat—or the rabbit, because rabbits and cats are basically the same thing. They are the *mæ*'s ancestors." The cloth bundle hovering over the sieve, she said, was the moon and the white tiger, while the sieve was the "world of people" (*ts'ɔmi*, the opposite of *nèmi*, the "world of ghosts"). Pregnant women and new mothers "within the month" should never go outside during an eclipse of the moon, since the dog that eats the moon is the *mæ* that eats a fetus or new infant. A horse or donkey left outside during an eclipse is also likely to miscarry. "Han sometimes put a pan of water in the middle of the courtyard at night," she said. "They capture the moon's reflection in the water and then throw it away. That's the same thing as *mæho*."

Behind this grinning effigy, the ritualist leaned three groups of objects against the wall. Each contained a forked pine branch, a miniature flag of chopsticks and paper, and a group of five sticks. She marked the sticks with her knife to represent the *mæ*'s face, its ears, a dog's claws, a tiger's claws, and a limit of three years, three generations, or three hundred years, before which the *ma* was not to return. Each group of objects was for one of the three domestic animals contained in the white tiger: the dog, the horse, and the cat or rabbit. On the sieve, she placed a bowl of husks with a piece of sugar candy and a bone. This was the "rank and fragrant offering" given at the funeral of a domestic animal.

Upon finishing this effigy, the ritualist made another. She took the worn beak of the grain pounder inside and, by the light of the fire, carefully drew the face of an infant on its blunt end, complete with fat cheeks and a toothless smile. She drew a long strip of cloth from her basket and tied one end to this wooden infant, placed it under the bed on which Li Qunhua was lying, and trailed the cloth strip from under the bed, across the room, and over the threshold to the porch. She was ready to begin. Li Zhiwu handed me one of the two bamboo pipes he had borrowed—sorrowful, buzzing instruments that use a thin tongue of bamboo as a reed. "Blow when I blow," he said. The ritualist poured out three bowls of alcohol, set them in front of the effigy on the porch, and slit the throats of two small chickens. As she bled the chickens into an empty bowl, she began to chant.

The first few lines of Luo Lizhu's chant were a formula used with variations in nearly every healing ritual—and which no ritual specialist I talked to could consistently translate into ordinary language. Ritualists said that this formula was intended to "get the attention" of ghosts and spirits (*nè*). It framed the subsequent words and gestures, setting them off from the ordinary flow of daily life and marking them as communication with a nonhuman entity.[2] After intoning this opening in a low voice, Luo Lizhu began to describe the pain the spirit had inflicted on its victim. This too was a formula used in most healing rituals, but one that any experienced listener could understand. Luo Lizhu's words followed the pain's trajectory through ever more specific spaces, from the sky and earth, to the family harmed, to the body on the bed, and finally to the center of that body, its bone marrow, and the pupils of its eyes.

2.2

ghosts of ridges attack	sa k'á lɔ ne kɔ́ lɔ
ghosts of gullies attack	sa bùɪ lɔ ne kɔ́ lɔ
descend from the sky	mùɪ ti gu lɔ
arise from the earth . . .	mi ti ta lɔ . . .
pain floods her head	su rɔ̀ chì wú chì kɔ t'è
her torso and her feet	chì gɔ chì chì t'è

of an entire family harmed	bo du rɔ̀ chì vɛ
the harm centers on her bed	jo du rɔ̀ chì hæ
of thirty of their men	sa tsr rɔ̀ p'ò zò
thirty of their women	sa tsr rɔ̀ mo zò
of all in this house	chì he chì go le
You beat *her* head with clubs	wú tæ̀ mæ jæ lɔ
shoot *her* breast with crossbows	gɔ tæ̀ ché pa lɔ
she can't sleep a wink	bɯ́ nà chì me wò nó
can't sit a moment	ti nà chì sɔ wò nó
can't stretch her legs	chì ká n chà
can't lift her hands	lè ká n du
her food won't digest	tso tsò yi n chi
her drink won't stay down	ji do se n go
her bones have no marrow	wɯ̀ ká pɯ̀ n jɔ
pain pierces her pupils	me̱ ká no̱ lé ne
invades even her pupils	me̱ ká ja̱ lɔ bɔ
pain pierces her bone marrow	wɯ̀ ká no̱ lé ne
invades even her marrow	wɯ̀ ká ja̱ lɔ bɔ

The pain has a source, Luo Lizhu continued, and the source has been discovered in divination. It has come out in the pulse of the left wrist and the lines of the left hand; it has been seen in the cock's beak and the goat's shoulder blade; it has appeared in the patient's finger joint and a length of cloth stretched along her forearm, in a Ch. *dou* of grain, a Ch. *sheng* of rice, a chunk of salt, a bowl of wine, a pot of wine, a stick of incense. The ghost has been seen squatting on the table's corner and crouching on a pack saddle. It has come out in offerings of silver and gifts of gold. After reciting this list, Luo Lizhu used language specific to the *mæho* chant to name the *mæ* as the source of pain. As she chanted lines mentioning the white tiger, she switched to Chinese. She later explained that, like some other foul spirits associated with dogs and cats, the white tiger is Han, and one must use its own language to say its name.

2.3

white-haired stud *mæ*	mæ p'ò mæ wú p'u
yellow-fanged bitch *mæ*	mæ mo mæ jæ cæ̱
scruffy-thighed bitch *mæ*	mæ mo mæ dɔ pè
mæ of nine mares	mò mo ko̱ mæ
mæ of seven cats	mǽ mi shr̀ mæ
mæ of seven dogs	á nò shr̀ mæ

sky dog white tiger	tian gou bai hu
sky dragon white tiger	tian long bai hu
great white tiger	da tou bai hu
small white tiger	xiao tou bai hu
white-haired stud *mæ*	mæ p'ɔ̀ mæ wú p'u
yellow-fanged bitch *mæ*	mæ mo mæ jæ cæ
biting, clawing, entangling, maddening	k'ɔ lɔ chí lɔ ví lɔ là lɔ
it is you!	ni na nga lú bɔ

Having identified the pain's cause, Luo Lizhu described the offerings, with exuberant exaggeration. Magpies, pheasants, fish, shrimp, wild geese and wild ducks, jays, crows, ducks and green pigeons, frogs and bullfrogs, bees, bumblebees, ants, grasshoppers, long-tailed dragonflies, a flapping hen, a struggling cock, three hundred pine branches as long as a forearm, twelve sticks marked with faces, twelve cut with a limit of time, twelve marked with ears, twelve cut with dogs' claws and tigers' claws, a *dou* of unhusked rice, three hundred white bowls of tea, and three hundred more of the best alcohol bought from the hands of Han merchants—all this she claimed to offer to the *mæ*. She went on:

2.4

the sky's seven corners	mừ wú shr̀ ngɔ̀
the earth's four sides	mé mi lí p'æ
take my offerings back to the sky	ngo ho ne mừ k'ò te
return to the sky for us	mừ k'ò te gɔ̀ ga
take my offerings back to the earth	ngo ho ne mi k'ò yi
return to the earth for us	mi k'ò yi gɔ̀ ga
I now begin to drive off the *mæ*	æ mæ ngo mæ kà tu lɔ ne

With this announcement, she picked up a bundle of thorned branches, strode into the room, climbed on top of the bed, and began to sweep with her thorned wand at the dark corner where the roof beam met the wall. As she named each part of the room in order from head to tail, she swept it with the thorns, not sparing the bed, where Li Qunhua still lay, and swept finally through the dark courtyard to the front gate.

2.5

I drive you from the roof peak	he bɔ wú t'è̠ kà
descend from the roof peak	he bɔ wú t'è̠ je
descend to the beam's corners	jà mo ngɔ̀ là je
I drive you from the beam's corners	jà mo ngɔ̀ là kà
I drive you from the walls	k'à chi wú t'è̠ kà
descend from the walls	k'à chi wú t'è̠ je

descend to the golden bamboo mat	mo cæ ngɔ̀ lɔ je
I drive you from the golden bamboo mat	mo cæ ngɔ̀ lɔ ka̱
descend to the fireplace	ko̱ tɔ mùɪ t'è̱ je
I drive you from the fireplace	ko̱ tɔ mùɪ t'è̱ ka̱
I sweep you with pine branches	ngo t'à p'ò kɔ lɔ ja
thrust thorns in your eyes	cá pu mé lɔ t'ɔ
truly in your eyes!	mé lɔ t'ɔ tu ngo
snare your neck with dog vines	á nò chì ji li lí lɔ p'æ
truly around your neck!	lí lɔ p'æ tu ngo
I drive you, *mæ,* over the threshold	mæ ka̱ á dù tí t'è̱
the yard's head, the yard's tail, I drive you	kæ wú kæ mæ ka̱
that corner, that side, I drive you	k'o ngɔ̀ k'o p'æ ka̱
this end, this side, don't stay there!	chɔ vɔ̀ chɔ p'æ ni t'à jɔ
that end, that side, don't stand there!	k'o vɔ̀ k'o p'æ ni t'à hɔ̱

She kicked the gate open, stepped outside, and waved her thorns as she sent the *mæ* down over the ridges and gullies, to the river that flowed through the valley below.

2.6

come out through the gate	á dù ti̱ t'è̱ do̱ lɔ do̱
out along eleven gullies	ts'ɪ̌ tí kà̱ chì do̱
out through twelve streams	ts'ɪ̌ nì kà̱ lí do̱
descend to the ridges	wò wú kɔ̀ chè je̱
I drive you from the ridges	wò wú kɔ̀ chè ka̱
descend to the long roads	jo cí mè t'è̱ je̱
I drive you from the roads	jo cí mè t'è̱ ka̱
I drive you, *mæ*	ngo mæ ka̱
drive you to the river	lɔ ka t'è̱ yi ka̱
wild fruit	cà hɔ nà
grows in its stones, it is said	ló p'ò ló go chì mi jo
sandy beaches line its banks, it is said	hɔ̀ ji bɛ lɛ chì mi jo
your companions live there	pe dù k'o ka jɔ
your friends live there	ni chɔ̀ dù k'o ka jɔ
your ancestors live there	ni cì dù k'o ka jɔ
your origins are there	p'í dù k'o ka jɔ
return to those sandy beaches, that place	ni hɔ̀ ji bɛ lɛ chì mi kò
three pairs of dogs die there	á nò sa tsɛ shr
three pairs of boars and wildcats die	ve po̱ vɔ̀ ngɔ́ sa tsɛ shr
three pairs of wild dogs die	pu̱ yì pu̱ vè sa tsɛ shr
three pairs of rabbits and weasels die	t'à lo hɔ lò sa tsɛ shr
three pairs of mares die	mò mo sa tsɛ shr
three pairs of cats die	mæ mi sa tsɛ shr

your *mæ* friends live there	mæ chɔ̀ kʼo ka jɔ
mæ companions live there	mæ pe kʼo ka jɔ
go to where your *mæ* friends live	ni mæ chɔ̀ jɔ dù yi
go to where *mæ* companions live	mæ pe jɔ dù yi

Squatting again in front of the moon-faced effigy, Luo Lizhu went through the rest of the chant. Her next task was to convince the *mæ* that the places it had recently inhabited were no match for the sandy riverbank, strewn with dead animals.

2.7

she lives in this land of Júzò [Zhizuo]	su rɔ̀ mi jɔ Júzò
these two centers of Chezò and Chemo	Chezò Chemo nì ká ne
look over at that slope	kʼo bò hɔ le ne
only cliffs and caves	vé sà jɔ̱ ne jɔ
look at this slope	hé bò hɔ le ne
only thorns and brambles	chù sa kɔ́ ne jɔ
no land to turn a plow	lò chè chì và mi n jɔ
not land enough to place a sieve	wò je chì và mi n jɔ
rocks below the feet	chì tʼà ló ngɔ̀ mi
cliffs at every corner	ngɔ̀ kʼò vé jɔ mi

On the rocky fields and paths of Zhizuo, Luo Lizhu continued, the patient, by not counting the days of the month, ran afoul of the *mæ*. She plowed on the fourteenth, traveled on the fifteenth, washed hemp on the day of the snake, carried water on the day of the tiger, husked grain on the day of the rabbit, cut wood on the day of the monkey, mended clothing on the day of the chicken. But now, like a fox she will count the days and like a rabbit count the nights. No longer will she wash hemp on the day of the snake, carry water on the day of the tiger, and so on. When you, *mæ*, walk on the center of the path, she will retreat to the path's edge; when you walk on the path's edge, she will retreat to the center.

Just as undesirable a residence for a *mæ* as Li Qunhua's valley and village, the ritualist pointed out, were her house and body. This, Li Zhiwu told me later, was his favorite part of the chant. "That old woman can really talk," he said. "People say that ghosts and spirits have their own tastes. Even the worst love cleanliness; they don't like goat or horse meat, and they hate Sichuan pepper worse than anything."

2.8

look at the roof tiles	he pʼì hɔ ne le
the tiles emit no smoke	he pʼì kʼɔ̀ n sɔ̱

look at the fire stones	ko lo hɔ lé ne
the stones bear no soot	ko lo bò n ne
look at our fire pit	ngæ ho pì hɔ lé ne
the pit has no wood	ho pì sɨ n hɔ
look at the head of our bed	ngæ gɔ̀ wú hɔ lé ne
the bed's head stinks	gɔ̀ wú ɔ nè jɔ
look at the bed's tail	gɔ̀ mæ hɔ lé ne
the bed's tail has vomit	gɔ̀ mæ ts'ɔ nè jɔ
look at her head	rɔ̀ wú hɔ lé ne
her hair reeks of sweat	rɔ̀ wú mè jì ne
look at her feet	rɔ̀ chì hɔ lé ne
her feet stink of rot	rɔ̀ chì chr tsè ne
she eats goat meat	chì ji chì hò tsò
drinks horse soup	mò ji mò yi dɔ
lies on goatskins	chì ji k'a lɔ́ mo
stuffs her pillow with pepper	zɔ̀ lé wú kæ̀ mo
burns pepper branches for firewood	zɔ̀ p'è sɨ ká pe
boils pepper leaves for soup	zɔ̀ p'è và jé pe
she truly lives like this	k'o nì pe tu ngɔ
an evil place to live, you *ma*	ni mæ jɔ kæ n tsæ
you white-haired stud *ma*	ni mæ p'ò mæ wú p'u
yellow-fanged bitch *ma*	mæ mo mæ jæ cæ

Calling again on the *ma* to return to the sky and the earth, Luo Lizhu finished the chant. The pain in the patient's head now disappears, she intoned, the pain in her torso flows away, the swelling of her feet diminishes. Let this one sacrifice suffice for an entire family; let one family's sacrifice suffice for a hundred.

The ritualist set her thorns down, and Li Zhiwu poked me in the ribs. "Now blow," he directed, and he started to wail on his bamboo pipe. ("The pipe—Ooooh! Ooooh! Ooooh!—is the baby crying," he explained later.) Luo Lizhu pulled slowly on the end of the long cloth strip that led from under the bed, across the threshold, and to the side of the effigy on the porch. As the head of the grain pounder with its infant's face emerged from under the bed and bumped across the floor, Li Qunhua squirmed on the bed and shrieked, "My child! My child!" Her husband and I blew the baby's cries, and the ritualist reeled in the wooden baby, wrapped the cloth streamer around its body, and dumped it in the sieve under the moon-faced "white tiger."

Li Qunhua sat up, wiped her face on her sleeve, and set to work boiling the chickens. The ritualist offered the cooked chickens to the *ma* once more, and Li Zhiwu chopped one of them up. We ate a subdued meal of rice, broth, and chicken; the usually lively Li Qunhua ate little and didn't say a word. The ritualist then bundled the two effigies together, placed them in the sieve, put the second chicken on top, and led Li Zhiwu and me out the door, leaving mother and daughter to wash up. We walked to the edge of a gully. After slipping the second boiled chicken into her bag, Luo Lizhu dumped the sieve with its swaddled infant and leering round head in the ravine, and the three of us went home separately to bed, our paths lit by the nearly full moon.

Dwelling

People had often spoken to me of *mæ* as a problem of the too-intimate coexistence of animals and humans. Residents of Zhizuo were separated from their domestic animals as they ate and slept only by the threshold that divided a room's interior from porch and courtyard. This threshold was the site of continual incursions: cats slept curled by the fire within; dogs coursed anxiously back and forth through the doorway in search of food; and, though horses stayed in the barn, their grain passed through attics or granaries in the house's dwelling places on its way to their mouths. When they buried the corpse of a cat, dog, or horse, Zhizuo residents marked this intimacy by dribbling a bit of saliva from their mouths into a "rank and fragrant" mixture of husks, sugar, and bones offered to the dead animal. This proximity was the sign of a distance between Zhizuo residents and people in the surrounding lowland communities. Han officials complained that sharing a courtyard with domestic animals was unsanitary; other visitors remarked on it as a clear symptom of the moral and economic backwardness of these minority people.

Zhizuo residents were aware of these perceptions. They admitted that *mæ* were particularly dangerous in Zhizuo because of the copresence of humans and animals in houses there—as though recognizing the links between a very high incidence of infant mortality and the poverty indexed in their small and crowded houses. Yet they also argued that separating barns from houses was inefficient and inconvenient, and even those who could afford to build new houses rarely built walls between human courtyards and animal dwellings. I found it difficult to imagine how the mere spatial proximity of humans and animals might open human bodies to the souls of other beings. It was as though the intimacy of humans and animals in Lòlop'ò houses was something altogether different from simple coexistence in space as I imagined it to be.

Indeed, this ritual seems to exhibit a sense of a "meaningful core of existence" (to borrow a phrase from Merleau-Ponty) not confined to a bodily interior. The *mæho* seems to have treated Li Qunhua's room, house, and courtyard as places where different kinds of spatial relations apply than those we commonly accept as natural when we imagine the articulation of social persons and the material world. In casting back among the words and gestures of this rite for hints about what it means to dwell in a house in Zhizuo and how dwelling and healing are related, I draw on a pair of distinctions that roughly correlate. The first is a distinction Luo Lizhu made between two kinds of *mæ;* the second is a distinction anthropologists once commonly made between two principles of "magical" action.

In the days that followed this performance, I enlisted Luo Lizhu's help to record, transcribe, and translate her *mæho* chant. During these sessions, Luo Lizhu took care to make certain I understood what she regarded as the essential facts about *mæ*. Others had clearly not explained some aspects of these spirits to me, she observed, probably because they lacked expertise. There are two types of *mæ*, she said, dry and wet. The ritual she performed for Li Qunhua was intended to drive off both, but it was nevertheless important to distinguish them. Although the wet *mæ* acts only in concert with the dry *mæ* and afflicts only women's wombs, the dry *mæ* sometimes acts alone. The symptoms of a dry *mæ* attack are terrible: it afflicts only one side of the body, leaving it in great pain. The patient's eyes stare up at the sky, and she can lie only on one side because the other hurts so badly. Whereas a wet *mæ* occupies a woman's womb, a dry *mæ* might afflict anyone. It often assaults people who have been exposed to a lunar eclipse: it is as though one half of the body is eaten when the dog eats half the moon. The dry *mæ* is the white tiger and the dog that eats the moon, Luo Lizhu continued, and it resides in the sky. Its effigy is the moon-faced head suspended above the sieve, representing the world of people, and the groups of sticks placed behind it in the courtyard. The wet *mæ* is the one that flows downstream. Its effigy is the beak of the treadle pounder, which one pulls out from under the bed and through the doorway. It is the one you drive out of the house, down the ravines, and to the sandy river banks. When she announced, "I now begin to drive off the *mæ*," it was the wet *mæ* against which she brandished her thorned wand.

Luo Lizhu's contrast of dry *mæ* and wet *mæ* is similar to a distinction between two principles anthropologists once identified as foundational "laws" of magical action. Drawing on James Frazer's classic work *The Golden Bough* (1890), Marcel Mauss and Henri Hubert named these principles *contiguity* and *mimetic sympathy*. A third principle, *opposition* or *antipathy*, Mauss and Hubert saw as a variation on mimetic sympathy (1972, 64–74). Under the principle of contiguity, beings and things are in sympathy by virtue of their close proximity in space. Influences, ideas, and sentiments flow from one being to those that adjoin it in a spatial ensemble. When one part of the ensemble is removed, the flow of influence from it through its formerly contiguous objects or beings does not necessarily cease, and the part may act as a substitute for the whole. Mauss and Hubert noted that the flow of influence is never indiscriminate: magical action precisely limits it to particular properties abstracted and detached from the whole. In mimetic sympathy, iconic images act on their referents in two ways: "like produces like . . . ; and like acts upon like, and in particular, cures like" (1972, 68). The flow of influence depends on similarity, though not necessarily on its precision or accuracy. Mimetic sympathy produces antipathy as well: "When like is found to cure like, what we have in fact is the opposite. The sterilizing knife produces fertility, water produces the absence of dropsy, etc. . . . A complete formula would be: like drives out like in order to produce the opposite" (1972, 71). The contrasting modes of action Luo Lizhu described for dry and wet *mæ* and the different techniques she mustered to counter them correspond roughly to mimetic sympathy/antipathy (dry *mæ*) and contiguity (wet *mæ*). As she addressed and manipulated these entities, Luo Lizhu engaged a play of mimesis and contiguity that she found to inhere in the world and to shape the character of spatial relations among body, house, and universe. Dry and wet *mæ*, mimesis and contiguity correspond to distinct but complementary modes of dwelling in proximate space.

Mimesis

Mimetic sympathy and antipathy have thickened the weave of this narrative from the outset. A diviner found in Li Qunhua's dreams an inverted reflection of her waking existence, of infertility rather than fertility, of bearing a dog's soul rather than an infant's. A soul (*yɛho*) is a reflection or double of a living body—sometimes a mirror reflection, as when Zhizuo residents comb the hair of a corpse straight up from its scalp to invert the hairstyle of the living. This is true also for animal souls, which Lòlop'ò dispatch by the dozens in mortuary rituals to inhabit the dead person's underworld house and provide it with meat. In most cases of *mæ* possession, a dog's soul would also double for a miscarried fetus or a dead infant; in Li Qunhua's case, divination doubled a dream infant in a dog's corpse, finding the corpse's reflection in Li Qunhua's body by virtue of its resemblance to an infant's absent soul. Luo Lizhu assembled sticks, sieve, and cloth to make an image of this redoubled absence in the effigy of the dry *mæ*. She doubled the dead dog's soul again in the spherical tiger's face suspended above the sieve—an icon for the "world of people." She tripled it in the three groups of sticks, which reflected the dry *mæ*'s specific characteristics: three pine branches to indicate its humanlike qualities, three flags to show that it was both Han and an official, three groups of five sticks carved with a face, ears, claws, and a limit.

These assemblages gathered a further series of resemblances among body, house, and universe. The moon hangs over the courtyard as the moon-faced tiger's head hangs over the sieve; the dog of the sky eats the moon and devours half a body; the dog of the courtyard and threshold passes into a woman's womb and devours her fetus. These resemblances do not depend on a homologous logic in which a body or a house is structured according to dispositions or orientations assumed also to structure the universe (as in Bourdieu 1990). The house is not a microcosm of the universe; the body does not represent at one level a logic embodied in a house or universe at a different level. Instead, body, house, and universe all double, enfold, and invade one another. The moon is captured in a pan of water placed in the courtyard and thrown out the door; the universe, composed of sieve, cloth, and branches, is set down on the porch, offered up to the tiger in the sky, and then tossed into the gully; the dog that eats the sky's moon also eats the moon enclosed in the womb; a woman's body enfolds the animal life of the courtyard.

Gaston Bachelard articulated a similar sense of living in the world as inhabiting a series of mutually enfolded and enfolding places in his explorations of poetic images of "felicitous space" (1964, xxxi). Bachelard argued for a "topoanalysis"—a "systematic psychological study of the sites of our intimate lives" (1964, 8). The "topography of our intimate being" is to be found in the surroundings we inhabit most closely, particularly our houses. The meanings of these localities are released in their images in memory, reverie, dreams, or poetry: for Bachelard, a poetic image of a child playing in a courtyard or a dream of bearing an infant through a house's rooms would be a significant site for topoanalysis (1964, 230). Such images of closely inhabited surroundings are a "first world," a "first universe" that grounds our further experience of more extensive space: "What human beings know first—and never forget—are the intimate values of inside space. Dwelling in these material images is not delimited by the simple opposition of inside and outside that Euclidean geometry leads us to expect" (Bachelard 1964, 7, 4, 212).

Through the apertures of a dwelling—a doorway, the opening of a courtyard to the sky—the intimacies of lived space and the immensities of the imagined universe come into communication. In this interchange, "limitless night ceases to be empty space," and an "osmosis between intimate and undetermined space" obtains (Bachelard 1964, 230). A house's boundaries—its thresholds or ash-sealed doorways—are enabling limits rather than confining ones; they are means by which the difference between inside and outside, even if painful, is felt in dwelling. They allow inner and outer space to enfold each other. To inhabit domestic space, especially the mimetic spaces of memory and poetic image, is to find the vastness of the outer world already present within; one first comes to know and inhabit the world through intimate relations with and in dwellings. As Edward Casey, reading Bachelard, puts it, "I feel at one with the universe not because I am extended out into it, or can merely project myself there, but because I experience its full extent *from within* my discrete place in the house. Felt from the very being of within, the most redoubtable being of without comes easily within one's compass. Limits fade and concentration occurs as I connect the tiny and the enormous in a single stroke" (1997, 294).[3]

Divination found the "most redoubtable being of without," bearing danger and pain, already within Li Qunhua's most intimate compass. Luo Lizhu acknowledged this osmosis of intimate and immense as she doubled the exterior universe in a miniature world of sieve, bamboo, and grinning moon assembled in the courtyard. In gathering into this icon resemblances among womb, courtyard, and universe, she called on the resources of intimate space to establish authority over the "limitless night," where the distant and mysterious authority of officialdom was reflected in the flag-bearing, Mandarin-speaking "sky dog white tiger." Bachelard wrote that poetic images of intimate spaces "give us back areas of being, houses in which the human being's certainty of being is concentrated, and we have the impression that, by living in such images as these, in images that are as stabilizing as these are, we could start a new life, a life that would be our own, that would belong to us in our very depths" (1964, 33). Such stabilizing certainties are a clue to the magic of mimetic sympathy. If, as Mauss and Hubert put it, "like acts on like, and in particular, cures like," it is perhaps by giving one back, through mutual reflections of intimate and indeterminate space, areas of being that have been lost to oneself. If the *mæho* referred to such a lost area of being, it was at once the closest and the most distant: the enigmatic flourishing (or failure to flourish) of another's soul within one's own body and the official attitudes, pronouncements, and actions on that most interior of processes, reflected in the soul-devouring dry *mæ* in the night sky. To concentrate both sides of that indeterminate space within the intimate compass of the courtyard was to delimit and determine it with the apertures and boundaries of the lived dwelling.

Contiguity

Fragments 2.3 and 2.4 of Luo Lizhu's *mæho* chant were exemplary of the mimetic doublings of dwelling and universe involved in confronting the dry *mæ*. Fragment 2.3 named and described the dry *mæ*, referring to it (in Lòlongo) as the soul of the dogs, cats, and horses of the courtyard but addressing it with its official names (in Chinese, its "own language") as the dog, dragon, and white tiger of the sky. Fragment 2.4 extended this reflection of courtyard and sky as it paired "the earth's four sides" with "the sky's seven corners." In contrast to these relatively static passages, the other five sections quoted moved the *mæ* through body, house, and universe as they described its attack and drove it away. According to Luo Lizhu, these passages referred to the wet *mæ*. They described a mode of dwelling in intimate space of a different order than that explored so far, a mode we might approach through Mauss and Hubert's principle of contiguity.

Bachelard held that the capacity of poetic language to confer psychic benefit flowed from its raveling of lived experience and imagination. In poetic language, "we are offered a veritable cure of rhythmo-analysis through the poem which interweaves real and unreal and gives dynamism to language by means of the dual activity of signification and poetry" (1964, xxxi). Luo Lizhu's poem "interweaves real and unreal" by alternating between the most concrete deictic significations and the most insubstantial poetic abstractions as it outlines the pain's advance through the patient's world and body (in fragment 2.1) and derives it away (in fragments 2.5 through 2.8). "Descend to the beam's corners, I drive you from the beam's corners; I drive you from the walls, descend from the walls": each pair of verses indicates, on the one hand, the visible and tactile material of body and house and, on the other, the sources, textures, and trajectories of another's pain. This oscillation binds pain tightly to the shared material of lived experience, revealing a world where neither pain nor illness is confined within the body's skin. Pain's trajectory begins in the sky and earth with the wild ghosts of ridges and gullies, descends on an entire family, and then centers on a single bed, saturating the patient from head to foot and diving to the pupils of her eyes and the marrows of her bones.

As the pain penetrates the patient's body, it suffuses the world that surrounds her. The cause of the pain appears to the diviner in the patient's pulse, in the lines of her hands, and in patterns formed by grains of rice or buckwheat, a length of hempen cloth, a cock's beak or goat's shoulder blade, grains of salt, a bowl of wine. Exceptionally skilled diviners, who, like crows, can see the world of people with one eye and the world of ghosts with the other, sometimes spy the source of pain as it springs grinning out of a table's corner or squats drooling on a roof beam. The symptoms of an illness erupt in the spaces surrounding the body just as they appear in the body itself. To be inhabited by a malevolent entity is to have one's entire proximate world flooded with its being. Pain is no longer an inner experience that isolates one and destroys communication; it becomes part of the world one inhabits with others by virtue of the body's close contact with the places around it. The principle of contiguity described by Mauss and Hubert depends in each of their examples on such an interfolding in language of "real and unreal." The magic of contiguity closely interweaves intersubjectively experienced material realities with the imagined pain of others.

The intertwining of lived experience and imagination that Bachelard found in poetic language is echoed in the "founding" relation that grounded the thought of his younger contemporary, Merleau-Ponty, about the way subjects *inhabit* the world. For Merleau-Ponty, lived and embodied perception of the world and its material and social realities founds and gives rise to expression in language. The perceived world bodies forth in words (Das 1997, 70). As M. C. Dillon puts it in his reading of Merleau-Ponty, "I am drawn toward signification by something that needs to be said and which imposes on me the task of finding words for it in order to learn, myself, what it is that I want to say" (1988, 199). Expressive (or imaginative) structures generated in perception are sedimented back into the sensible world—as language, as memory, as culture—and become further material for perception. Perception is in this way an active and open relation with the world, bringing the sentient subject and the sensible object into their ongoing existence. The perceiving body and the world it inhabits are folded one into the other; the body is at once sentient and sensible; it sees and it sees itself seeing, touches and touches itself touching; it is part of the world one senses as well as the sensing instrument. It is thus contiguous with the world in the most fundamental sense: it is *surrounded* by that world "not on a plane of which it would be an inlay, it is really surrounded, circumvented." Body and world are related in an "embrace." Between them "is not a frontier but a contact surface" (Merleau-Ponty 1968, 271).

The "driving" (*kà*) sections of Luo Lizhu's chant (fragments 2.5 through 2.8) brought language to bear directly on the contact surface between body and world. Sweeping the beams, walls, mats, and threshold of the house as she chanted, Luo Lizhu intended to sweep away the pain, personified in the *mæ*, that inhabited the folds of body and house. She moved it along a route guided by gravity, as though it were a stream of water flowing from the roof's peak to the beams below it, down the walls, along the bed from head to foot, into the fire pit, out the door, through the courtyard, into the gutters dug beneath the outside walls, down through the ravines to the river. She left the patient's body on the bed out of the flow of words like the gap between bed and floor or the space between fire pit and threshold, as though it were not inlaid in this inhabited world but "circumvented" so completely by it that it need not be featured at all. As she called on the *mæ* to look back at the miserable place it was leaving behind—the rocky valley, the cold and smokeless house, the vomit-stained bed—she reinserted the patient's stinking head and rotten feet into the chant as two among many dwelling places the *mæ* would have to stomach were it to return. Her words made Li Qunhua's pain visible in the "intermundane space" (Merleau-Ponty 1968, 269) shared with those who inhabited her house, overcoming its isolating effects by making it manifest in language and the material world. Here, the magic of contiguity makes a resource of the reciprocal involvement of body and world. It makes explicit what is implicit there: that pain and affect are never simply or completely enclosed within an individual body, that one person's pain is always partially accessible to others (for good or ill) through their mutual engagement in a shared world.

Belonging

We have followed Luo Lizhu's suggestion that dry *mæ*
and wet *mæ* be distinguished, by considering each to be an instance of
one of the two great principles of magic delineated by Mauss and Hubert. The mimetic techniques applied to the dry *mæ* show body, house,
and sky to reciprocally reflect, invade, and envelop one another. The
techniques of contiguity applied to the wet *mæ* show that body and
proximate space share a broad and interfolded contact surface, as pain
personified in the *mæ* carves a single conduit through the beams, mats,
limbs, and torso of body and house. Yet as Mauss and Hubert pointed
out, the principles of mimesis and contiguity are not so easily separated.
Sympathy usually involves contact, and contiguity always involves some
form of mimesis. Magical actions are often "so complicated that it is
only with great difficulty that they can be ordered into one or other of
our two categories" (Mauss and Hubert 1972, 72). Such complexity
characterizes the culminating act of Li Qunhua's *mæho*, in which mimesis and contiguity—body, house, and sky as mutually enveloping like-
nesses, and body and world as a single surface of contact—were folded
together in the birth or miscarriage the family dramatized for the *mæ*'s
benefit.

After sweeping the wet *mæ* through the house and out the door, the
ritualist pulled on the streamer of cloth leading from under the bed to
the porch, while Li Qunhua shrieked and her husband and I played the
infant's wails on bamboo reed pipes. She pulled the wooden effigy of
the fetus through the house along the route over which she had just
driven the wet *mæ*. At the same time, she delivered it repeatedly from
enveloped aspects of the world into enveloping ones. The effigy
emerged from under the bed into the space in which infants had been
born ever since this house was built. Li Qunhua had given birth to her
four children squatting there beside her bed as her husband sat on the
bed behind her, supporting her by the armpits. Were the *mæho* ritual to
be performed for more typical reasons, the wooden fetus would pass
from beneath the patient on the bed into the space into which she
hoped to give birth to a healthy child. The patient's presence on the bed
figured the dark space beneath the bed as a womb, out of which the
wooden fetus emerged into the precise place where real infants enter
the world.

As Luo Lizhu pulled the fetus over the threshold, it was born a second time. Parents taught children never to sit on the wooden lintel of a threshold or to chop anything against it. "People say that if you chop something on a lintel and a woman in the house is pregnant, her child will be born with a cleft lip," one woman told me. Doorways between sleeping rooms and the courtyard were both mouths and vaginal openings—here, the vagina of a woman within the house and the mouth of a fetus in her womb. The doorway made the room a womb, enclosing other wombs within. The container for an unborn child was at once a woman's body, her bed, and her room, and actions at the openings to any of these places could affect the infant within.[4] In the courtyard, the wooden infant was wrapped in its cloth streamer as a baby is wrapped in clothes and set in the sieve beneath the moon-faced bundle of cloth and leaves that reigned over its miniature sieve-universe. With this action, Luo Lizhu gave the wooden infant over to the "sky dog white tiger" as a substitute for a real baby. Her final act in the ritual was to bundle up this entire miniature universe, carry it out of the courtyard on the route along which the illness flowed out of the patient's world, and dump it in the gully, where it would eventually disintegrate and be washed into the creek and down the river toward which she had sent the personification of Li Qunhua's distress.

The effigy emerged from the bed to the room's womb, to the courtyard, and to the representation of the universe, each of which was a likeness of the others; and it simultaneously flowed along a trajectory that made each of these spaces contiguous with the others. As Michael Taussig notes in his study of mimesis and alterity in sympathetic magic, the interpenetration of mimesis and contiguity makes it impossible to distinguish sign from thing, to separate representations (of a person's body, affect, or affliction) from actual substance (1993, 155–157). The play of similarity and contact in the *mæho* ritual made the inhabited spaces of Li Qunhua's house simultaneously sign and substance. Her house was a likeness of her body, standing in for it partially and imperfectly. But its materials and spaces also extended her body, forming a single ensemble with it. Li Qunhua's pain or loss *inhabited* her house not only because the house stood in for her body, and not only because she lived in and through her house, but also because of the intertwining of these modes. The *mæho* combined these modes in a drama that culminated with the mother's shrieks: "My child! My child!" It was as though Li Qunhua was at that moment encouraged to experience simultaneously these two modes of inhabiting spaces close at hand—to find her body, her room, the courtyard, and the sky shining into it as mutually enveloped and enveloping and to find her head and feet contiguous with the mat, walls, beams, and fire pit with which they were aligned. She was asked to experience her loss again in a moment when her intimate world appeared as a single field in which inside and outside replace each other and relief as well as pain flows from one contiguous space to another. This was a world similar to the one Merleau-Ponty evoked when he wrote of freedom: "Nothing determines me from the outside, not because nothing acts on me, but, on the contrary, because I am from the start outside myself and open to the world. We are *true* through and through, and have with us, by the mere fact of belonging to the world, and not being merely *in* the world . . . all that we need to transcend ourselves" (1962, 456; emphasis in original).

Conclusion

Divination and ritual rendered the origin of Li Qunhua's symptoms at once precise and indeterminate. In divination, a vague collection of psychic and corporeal afflictions—distressing dreams, lethargy, depression, and headaches—was gathered and brought to language. In the *mæho* ritual, the origin of these afflictions was named with precision: an animal's soul doubling as the soul of an infant, occupying the spaces in which the work of bearing and nourishing children took place and rendering that work barren. In the context of the recent mass sterilization campaign, this image could not but be associated with the sustained though erratic efforts of the state to intervene in this work, encapsulated of late for Zhizuo residents in the threat of a surgeon's knife cutting into the most intimate of dwelling places. Yet when the origin of this violence was named as a *mæ*, its connections to real actors, policies, and institutions were severed, and it was given over instead to the indeterminate realm of the "sky dog white tiger." This entity was unmistakably identified with Han officialdom in the language used to address it directly, the names assigned to it, and the trappings of flags and incense it carried. Nevertheless, these associations were of the most general kind, not pointing directly at the township officials who planned the campaign, nor at the brigade Party secretary who brought it to Zhizuo, nor at the clinic doctors who performed the sterilizations.

This combination of precision and imprecision in reference to the pain that violence brings was characteristic of the efforts of Zhizuo residents to bring ritual to bear as a resource for imagining the powers of officialdom and living with their effects. The tangible origins of violence were always uncertain, scattered, and incomplete. As we shall see in a later chapter, many in Zhizuo who did not escape the scalpel attempted to pin the blame for this sterilization campaign on the brigade's Party secretary. Yet, at the same time, they were aware that behind each of his acts lay officials they could not name, policies they did not fully understand, and institutions whose full scope they could not grasp. The effects of this violence were tangible and immediate, yet every attempt to fix a tangible cause receded from one mysterious actor, policy, or institution to another yet more distant one.

The language and gestures of the *mæho* ritual figured the powers of officialdom as a unified if indeterminate source of violence: this source was the Mandarin-speaking, flag-bearing dog that eats the moon and floods courtyard, house, and body with its pain-laden influence; it was an immense, imagined background against which the immediate daily work of bearing and nourishing people was carried out. At the same time, the *mæho* ritual acknowledged that the imagined state and the potential for pain it carried, though distant and mysterious, were always already present within the intimate compass of daily life. The state's imperatives, helping to determine not only when and how one might give birth but also what and how much one's family ate, and how and when they worked, were sedimented into the very material of a house—its beds, granaries, and attics (as chapter 3 describes). In Luo Lizhu's efforts to exorcise the source of Li Qunhua's pain from the beams, walls, and fire pits of her house, the ritual specialist gave voice to this intimate involvement of state power, however vaguely conceived, in daily existence.

To find this indeterminate outside already within was to find it in one's grasp. In the *mæho* ritual, to reveal the source of pain hiding within the matter of body, house, and universe was to claim authority over it— the robust authority that filled out the ritualist's words and gestures as she ordered the *mæ* out of the house and down the gullies and rivers. What were the grounds of this authority? Why did it hold out the promise of healing? At every turn of the *mæho* ritual, a play of mimesis and contiguity opened out the patient's existence to the closely inhabited spaces that surrounded and circumvented her. It drew into signification her state of being already outside herself and open to the world. It brought private pain, unspoken dreams, and unvoiced anxiety into the public world of language. It opened interior suffering out into the world of mutually shared household space, making Li Qunhua's distress "a household matter" (to quote Li Zhiwu again), shared by all those who occupied with her the ash-sealed receptacle of her house.

We cannot escape the implication that divination and ritual made others responsible for Li Qunhua's suffering. It acknowledged that each of those who shared Li Qunhua's dwelling was implicated in bringing the pressures and imperatives of official power to bear on the household work of birthing and nurturing people; each participated in bringing into the intimate compass of the household the distant and mysterious imagined unity of this power, reflected in the white tiger in the sky. A concrete reference for this responsibility might have been Li Qunhua's brother, who had released a *mæ* into Li Qunhua's courtyard by stealing the family dog and killing it to prepare a feast for a visiting official. Or it might have been Li Qunhua's nephew, the young Party secretary credited with bringing the sterilization campaign to Zhizuo. Li Qunhua's *mæho* did not rely on these tangible references. By finding the source of violence to be a mysterious entity linked to the indeterminate image of official power, and by finding that entity already implicated in the very matter of shared household space, this ritual distributed the responsibility among all those closely involved in Li Qunhua's world. We might begin to think of divination and healing ritual as methods for creating an ethics to deal with the violence of power, especially state power, in daily life. This ethics acknowledges the pain that violence brings as a shared burden (Das 1997, 88). But, even more crucially, it distributes the burden of responsibility for pain.

CHAPTER THREE

An Empty Frame

Participants in the *mæho* ritual encountered pain as present in a public world of household space, an "intermundane space" where "gazes cross and perceptions overlap" (Merleau-Ponty 1968, 269). But domestic spaces generate divisions and differences just as clearly as they generate mutual engagement or shared perceptions. In the "orphan's song" quoted at the beginning of the previous chapter, the singer contrasts her silent house, emptied by the loss of her mother, to a remembered dwelling. In that earlier, happy place, her family clustered around the fire pit, ordered meticulously by gender and generation through the distinction of near and far beds and the division of each bed into head, middle, and tail.

3.1

when mother was alive	su mo jɔ t'ù ga
we mixed nettles with buckwheat	ngǽ ló p'ɔ̀ kò mə na̠ pe le
mixed greens with rice	và je k'o mo je pe le
daughter-in-law and mother ate together	chì ka̠ mo ka̠ tsò
daughter and mother ate together	né ka̠ mo ka̠ tsò
son and father ate together	zò ka̠ p'ò ka̠ tsò
the grain was delicious	chɨ̀ tsò chɨ̀ chi ga
the wine made us drunk	ji ta ji chi ga
mother sat at the bed's head	mo jɔ gɔ̀ wú tḁ
father sat at the [other] bed's head	p'ò jɔ gɔ̀ wú tḁ
daughters sat in the bed's middle	né jɔ gɔ̀ jò tḁ
sons sat in the [other] bed's middle	zò jɔ gɔ̀ jò tḁ
grandchildren and great-grandchildren near	lí jɔ le jɔ ko̠ ta̠ ti
the door	

This song describes a shared place crosscut by differentials of gender and generation that fix a position for each inhabitant. As Li Qunhua helped me translate it, she pointed out each line's location in an ideal "upstream room"—the room where people cook and eat together in most Zhizuo households. Mother, daughter, and daughter-in-law would eat together on the outside bed, the woman's bed, against the room's outer wall. The men would eat on the opposite, inside bed. Older generations would sit on the inside, "upstream" heads of both beds, younger generations on their outside, "downstream" tails. In later sections of this song, the mourner describes how the gap left by her dead mother is filled, as the daughter-in-law moves up to take her place: "father's burden has passed to his orphaned son, mother's burden to her orphaned daughter." It is a vision of an ideal household, where social differences sedimented into a house's places become orderly flows along determined vectors: nurturance flows from the parents at the beds' upstream heads to the children and grandchildren at their downstream feet; generations flow the opposite way, as children gradually replace parents.

This chapter examines houses in Zhizuo as technologies for producing differential social relations (Bray 1997). With few exceptions, the ethnography of China has described families and households as combinations of persons already configured by attributes of gender and generation. Feminist anthropologists began to argue more than twenty years ago that social persons might better be understood as *effects* of the structured relations of family and kinship (Rubin 1975; Cowie 1978; Strathern 1988). Along these lines, Tani Barlow (1994b) has shown how kinship might be considered a "production line for subjectivities." Barlow demonstrates that women in late Imperial China were produced variously as daughters, mothers, or wives—rather than as generic "women"—through moral discourses about differential kin linkages.[1] Francesca Bray (1997) has adapted this approach to the concrete realm of daily life, writing of late Imperial houses as technologies for producing social relations. Chinese houses of that period, Bray states, might be thought of as looms on which individual lives were woven into typically Chinese social patterns: "through the long warp threads of the descent line, stretching back through decades or even centuries, were woven the horizontal weft threads of present marriages and alliances" (1997, 57).[2]

The mud-brick houses of mountainous northern Yunnan might also be understood as a technology in a "production line for subjectivities." Like houses everywhere in rural China, they were certainly an indispensable means of *material* production, second only to land. They performed innumerable transformative tasks that depended on differentials of light, heat, moisture, and air quality. Their orientation in relation to the sun, the situation of fire pits and cisterns, the directions of drainage, and the overhang of eaves created dry and sunny places where hemp could dry quickly, dry and dark places where grain would lose its moisture slowly, smoky places where meat would not rot, warm and wet places where straw and manure would decompose into compost, cool and wet places where vegetables would keep, cool and dry places where eggs could mature into chickens and kids into goats. The attributes of these places also attached to persons. Young women were associated in word and habit with cool, wet corners where vegetables were kept fresh; senior men were linked with dry, smoky attics where emblems of their inherited wealth, skills, and authority were preserved. Such attributes arose from productive technologies to structure the fields of relations out of which social persons were composed. As means of material production, houses also generated social relations.

These means were shaped by the larger social world and its most prominent and enigmatic, agent, the socialist state. The houses I encountered in Zhizuo were molded into their present form by the rural reform program that made households the basic level of agricultural production and resource management.[3] Households had long been crucial objects of bureaucratic control, but with rural reform they became intense foci for state imperatives to manage production and consumption, reform and "civilize" social relations, provide social services, collect tax revenue, alleviate poverty, and regulate population growth. The household registration system was the formal mechanism through which these projects operated. This system designated each person a member of a single household and assigned each member privileges and obligations in relation to the state. As Ellen Judd (1994, 169) points out, actual residence was more variable than official definitions, and family ties were wider, more ambiguous, and less accessible to state surveillance and control than were official households. Nevertheless, households, as officially defined, were the sites where the state reached deep into domestic life to participate in the production of social relations.

Houses accommodated many such transformations in material and social relations. But they were also resistant and enduring; the histories and dispositions sedimented into them inflected every social transformation. Here, I examine some of these accommodations and obduracies. Following Henri Lefebvre (1991), I conceive of domestic space broadly, as perceived in *spatial practices,* conceived in *representations of space,* and lived in *representational spaces.*

Social relations emerged from spatial practices. Differentials of shady side and sunny side, inside and outside, back and front guided the movements of persons through domestic spaces as they came of age, courted, married or remained single, built or inherited houses, bore children or remained barren. Representations of space actively shaped these practices. Ritualized language and gesture divided and ordered domestic space, generating axes of material and social difference. Poetic representations of houses used in rituals of passage correlated gendered and generational relations with the arrangements of rooms, beds, and fire pits and aligned transformations in social status with movements through space. Effigies for spirits, sculpted from branches, paper, vines, and household objects, inhabited every house, gathering and condensing signs of social relations in specific corners of rooms and courtyards.[4] And less formal representations—stories, complaints, recollections, rationalizations, and jokes—also saturated spatial practice.

The perceived space of practices and the conceived space of representations gave rise to lived representational space. This was the enveloped, enveloping, and contiguous space addressed in Li Qunhua's *mæho* ritual. It was the space in which sign and substance mutually inhered and where magic had its effects. Representational space, Lefebvre wrote, "is space as directly *lived* through its associated images and symbols, and hence the space of 'inhabitants' . . . It overlays physical space, making symbolic use of its objects"; it embodies "complex symbolisms, sometimes coded, sometimes not, liked to the clandestine or underground side of social life" (1991, 39, 33; emphasis in original). Bachelard's "topoanalysis" was an attempt to explore some of the fragmented and uncertain connections between poetic representations of space and lived representational spaces. The house image, wrote Bachelard, is "one of the greatest powers of integration for the thoughts, memories and dreams of mankind . . . in the life of man the house thrusts aside contingencies, its councils of continuity are unceasing. Without it, man would be a dispersed being. . . . Life begins well, it begins enclosed, protected, all warm in the bosom of the house" (1964, 6–7).

Practices and representations of domestic space in Zhizuo were sources of difference and hierarchy, but they also projected values similar to those Bachelard describes. Houses embraced the productive unions at the origins of life and encouraged stable and continuous flows of human relations. Their structured differentials tended to open up every position or relation to the view of another, generating possibilities for each person to occupy, partially and ephemerally, another's place. In this way, the doublings and couplings of domestic space absorbed differential relations into dreams of unity.

Sunny Side and Shady Side

From the gate of Li Qunhua's house in the village of Chemo, one could see most of Zhizuo's central valley. Clusters of warm mud-brick walls and tile roofs blanketed the slope before and behind the gate. Across a deep gully, Zhizuo's other large village, Chezò, meandered along another hillside. People in Zhizuo called this side of the valley the "sunny side" (*pido*). It faced east, and its houses were warmed early in the morning by the sun rising over the mountains opposite. This and a lively creek flowing between the two villages made the sunny side Zhizuo's most desirable neighborhood, supporting more than half the brigade's population (of almost exactly three thousand in 1990). Below and beyond, the mountain slopes were roughly terraced into maize and barley fields. Still further below, the valley bottom glowed in the summer with the translucent green of rice seedlings and in the winter with the duskier shades of wheat. A stream wound between the irrigated fields, flowing north toward the Jinsha River. Across the valley, on its "shady side" (*dəp'æ*), lived about three hundred people in four hamlets, the largest of which was called Méabò (literally "facing slope"). The mountain behind these hamlets shaded most of the houses and fields until after noon, and a single, small rivulet ran intermittently, making rice cultivation on this edge of the valley bottom perilous. With its steep, bare slopes and difficult access to water, that side was indeed "only cliffs and caves."

On both slopes, houses took their orientation from the steeply tilted land. Builders laid out a houses' one or (usually) two rectangular main buildings lengthwise along the slope's contour and approximately parallel to the stream below. Carpenters said that the ideal house would exactly parallel the stream in the valley bottom, with the slope falling off to the east. Building sites with these precise characteristics were rare, of course, and most dwellings were tilted off this ideal axis. Even so, on approximately east-facing slopes, the downhill side of a residential building was called the "sunny side" and the uphill side the "shady side"; on approximately west-facing slopes, it was the opposite. In this way, the sunny and shady sides of a house paralleled and inverted the shady and sunny slopes of the valley. This uphill/downhill axis, decided mainly by the natural slope of the building site, determined a perpendicular upstream/downstream axis, roughly parallel to the river below. One end of a house was called *lɔwú,* "upstream," or, more literally, "the river's head"; the other end was called *lɔmæ,* "downstream," or "the river's tail." One referred to houses neighboring one's own on the upstream side as *lɔwú* and to those on the downstream side as *lɔmæ,* and the same went for upstream and downstream villages. The village farthest upstream had come to be called simply Lɔwú, and the gorge below the valley carried the name Lɔmæ.

A couplet common in mourning songs and ritual chants mentions two kinds of houses:

3.2

| our happy shingled house | cí mo lè he he chì he |
| our great tiled house | næ̀ mo t'á he he chì he |

A "shingled house" (*címo*) was built of pine logs trimmed to eight flat surfaces and piled to form the walls, with a roof of loose pine shingles weighted with rocks. A few such buildings dotted Zhizuo's villages, but most were used to shelter animals rather than humans. Shingled houses were used mainly as seasonal habitations in high-mountain areas—bases from which to herd goats, farm potatoes, or cut timber. Most Zhizuo residents made their permanent habitation in a "tiled house" (*næ̀mo*), with a pine pillar-and-beam skeleton, mortared mud-brick walls, and a tile roof.

The perpendicular axes of uphill/downhill and upstream/downstream were built into a tiled house's very bones. A saying common in the lowlands held that a man contributed the bones of a child while a woman contributed its flesh. Lòlop'ò revised this to say that a house's wooden frame, shaped and erected by men, was its bones, while the mud bricks of its walls, molded and carried by women, were its flesh. Every bone in the post-and-beam skeleton had a proper orientation. Carpenters in this region used the Ch. *tailiang* framing system (described in Knapp 1986, 70–71), in which beams of progressively shorter length defined the roof's slope. In the most common configuration, five pillars supported three beams across the house's width. Seven purlins were laid across the beams to define the roof line, and rafters were placed across the purlins. Gray baked-clay roof tiles were laid directly on the rafters in an alternating convex and concave pattern.[5] On residential buildings (and some-

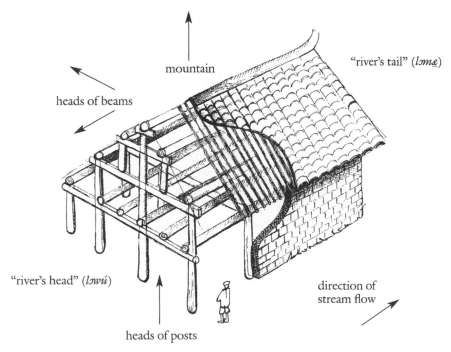

Figure 3.1 The orientation of posts and beams in a house on a slope's sunny side.

times barns), the front wall was built back along the second row of pillars, leaving a deep eave over a porch that ran the house's front length.

When cutting pillars, beams, purlins, and rafters, carpenters marked the end that had pointed upward in the tree as the timber's "head" (*wúdə*); the other end was its "tail" (*mɛdə*). Even when these marks were omitted or obliterated, skilled carpenters could divine from the grain which end of a timber had pointed upward in the tree. Builders oriented the head of every timber to point "up" in one of three directions: the heads of posts pointed toward the sky; the heads of beams, running perpendicular to the mountain's slope, pointed into the slope; and the heads of purlins, running parallel to the slope, pointed upstream. Even short, supporting beams and rafters were placed with their heads toward the sky, into the slope, or upstream (see Figure 3.1). Carpenters stressed that the proper orientation of every bone of this skeleton was crucial to a house's success. A pillar with its head in the ground or a beam pointing downstream or downhill evoked social evil in the form of the ghosts of people who had died badly (*chènè*).

The complex relation of these entities to the spatial orientations of bodies, houses, and the landscape is explored in chapter 7. Here it is enough to say that improperly oriented timbers were thought to harm the fundamental balance of life within a house, making livestock infertile, people quarrelsome, death frequent, and wealth elusive.

Like most houses in this area, Li Qunhua's had as its core two buildings facing each other across a central courtyard. On the courtyard's uphill side was a two-story residential "proper building" (Ch. *zhengfang*) with three rooms side by side. The rooms opened onto a stone porch running the length of the building, raised above the courtyard and sheltered by an overhanging eave. On the courtyard's opposite side was the "facing building" (Ch. *mianfang*), or barn, also two stories tall and three rooms wide. Carpenters cautioned that to make parallel buildings the same height would be to pit the inhabitants of one building against those of the other, forcing their life energies into a covert struggle for supremacy. At worst, this would result in death and infertility in the barn when those in the residential building were doing well and cause illness, infertility, and quarrelsomeness in the residential building when those in the barn—animals and adolescents—were thriving. Most houses were built on slopes, making this opposition easy to avoid; on level ground, carpenters built the barn a few feet shorter.

On the valley's sunny side, this dissimilarity in height created a differential of light and warmth. The low roof of the barn allowed the morning sun to strike full into the front of the residential building, heating its stone porch and filtering through the windows, doors, and open-work wooden walls to warm the house. In the afternoon, the residential building and the mountain behind it blocked the sun: the open side of the barn rarely saw sunlight. Cooking fires in the residential building and the rotting compost in the barn deepened this contrast between the light, dry, warm uphill building and the dark, wet, cold downhill one. On the shady side of the valley, the differential of light and warmth was reversed, and people inhabited the shade of their own residential buildings until late in the day. Residents of the sunny side spent part of every winter morning sitting on the porch, letting the sun warm their faces and chests and feeling it reflect off the warm walls behind them. Residents of the shady side sat in an open barn loft later in the day or found a sunny place outside the house to warm up.

Inhabiting any position on either the sunny or shady side of valley or house thus meant facing its visible, inverted alternative. To step over the threshold of a residential building on the valley's sunny side was to face the dark barn and shaded mountains opposite, but it was also to face full into the warming morning sun, with the activity of the coming day beckoning from fields and paths below. To step back into the residential building was to view the warm, sunny front of the house and the sunny mountain behind, but it was also to face the darkness of within and one's ancestral spirits sleeping on the wall opposite the doorway.

In his study of the "Kabyle house" (1990, 271–283), Pierre Bourdieu accumulates similar examples of spatial couplings and inversions, correlates them with social differentials of gender and generation, and derives a limited set of oppositions, or "generative schemes," that he posits to underlie and inform the practices of inhabitation. In Zhizuo, the pace of life little resembled the measured rhythms Bourdieu found to correlate comings and goings over the threshold with the cycles of the day and of growth and death in Kabyle. The irregular rhythms of domestic work and the need to seek warmth from sun or fire filled each day with continual shifts of place and perspective through a house's many differentials. Often, this experience resembled that of the *mæ* in Luo Lizhu's chant, preparing to depart over the threshold: "the yard's head, the yard's tail . . . that corner, that side . . . this end, this side, don't stay there! that end, that side, don't stand there!" The alternations and inversions involved in moving from this side to that side or from sun to shade disturbed corporeal habits and routines. The homology of sunny side and shady side with the front and back sides of the body as one turned toward the sun did not reduce these alternations to the contained *habitus* of a practical corporeal geometry, as Bourdieu argued for Kabyle. Instead, it repeatedly opened up bodily routines toward opposite, inverted, or simply different alternatives. To inhabit the residential building was to measure one's life energies against those of animals and adolescents in the barn; to inhabit the sunny side was to live in full view of those on the opposite slope, with their various inverted experiences. A house's intersecting differentials tended to open each position up to the view of another, and these intersecting gazes made houses open fields of social relations.

Upstream and Downstream: Brotherly Contention

The residential space of houses in Zhizuo was structured as three steps following the stream's flow, rather than as a central hall

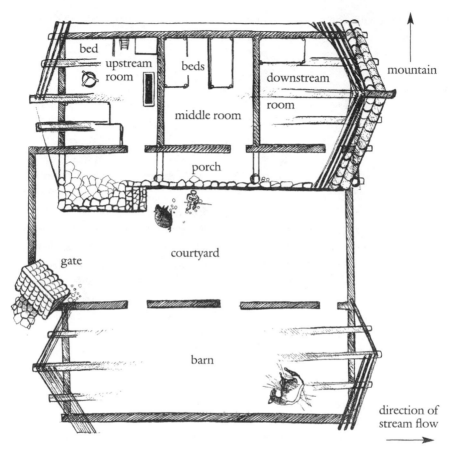

Figure 3.2 The arrangement of rooms in a house on a slope's sunny side.

with two wings as was common in much of rural China.[6] Li Qunhua and her husband slept at the upstream end of the residential building, in the "upstream room" (*lɔwú chìkà*). This was the center of a house's activity and, whenever space permitted, the residence of a household's senior couple. By its single bed was an open cooking fire around which meals were prepared and eaten and guests entertained. Beside this room was the "middle room" (*kɔ chìkà*), and beside that the "downstream room" (*lɔmæ chìkà*) (see Figure 3.2).

In Li Qunhua's house, the middle room held two beds on which her two sons, attending school and working in the county town, slept when they visited home. The couple entertained kin and friends from Zhizuo in their upstream room, but they brought officials and outsiders to the middle room. This practice honored the expectations of lowland out-siders that a middle room should be a house's innermost space, and it also distanced them from the true intimacies of the upstream room. The downstream room was the residence of a childless kinswoman whom Li Qunhua and Li Zhiwu had taken into their household in return for her inheritance. There, at a distance from the upstream room, she main-tained a degree of independence from the rest of the household, cooking many of her meals over her own fire.

The couple hoped their younger son would finish middle school, marry, and inhabit the middle room with his wife. After his parents' deaths, he would inherit their house and the contracted land and move into the upstream room. Li Zhiwu told me he felt fortunate that his elder son had a job and residence in the county town: because the brothers did not have to share residential space, their bickering was kept to a minimum. "People say that brothers' quarrels start in a previous life," he noted. "In the underworld, one says to the other, 'You obnoxious creature, I'm not finished with you. I'll follow you to the family you are born into, and we'll continue this argument there.'" A key source of brotherly con-tention was limited household space. Brothers expected to absorb equal parts of their parents' care and wealth, but the realities of birth order usually required that resources be spent earlier and disproportionately on elder brothers. Ideally, marriage meant that a son gained a separate room in the residential building, downstream of his parents. One son's marriage frequently forced his brothers to move to less desirable rooms. These brothers then had to choose between delaying their own mar-riages or setting up married residence in an undesirable part of the house—in the barn above the animals, or in a side building or lean-to.

Few joint households—in which two or more married brothers co-habited with their parents—existed for long in Zhizuo. Though all the grain, livestock, and vegetables produced by household members were kept in common, married couples saved income from activities other than farming and herding to build their own houses. (Before 1978, the most common source of this sideline income was hempen cloth produc-tion. After this no longer proved profitable, illegal timber harvesting took its place.) Older brothers expected to combine these savings with help from their parents to build a new house within a few years of their first child's birth. As in Li Qunhua's family, it was most often the youngest son who was expected to live with his parents in their old age and inherit their house upon their deaths. For families with more than two sons, this ideal was very difficult to achieve, and every step toward its fulfillment carried the potential for serious brotherly discord. Men with more than two or three married brothers were often forced to marry uxorilocally, moving in with their wives' families, because their parents had exhausted their resources building houses for the other brothers.[7]

Houses and Barns: Adolescent Sex

Li Qunhua's two daughters slept on the house's shady side, in the barn. On the valley's sunny side, the space of the courtyard separated stable and unstable generative relations. The sunny residential building housed an orderly progression of secure productive unities, with married sons succeeding their married parents. The shaded barn was the site of fertile relations among animals on the ground floor and volatile sexual relations among adolescents in the loft. Most girls in Zhizuo were given beds in their parents' barn lofts at the age of twelve or thirteen. Few, however, spent every night there.

In 1913, the French missionary Alfred Liétard observed of Lòlop'ò in nearby Yaoan County: "Upon arriving at a certain age (twelve to fourteen years), the boys sleep in groups, as do the girls, and frequently the sexes mix. Certain nights, the young men of one village make a tryst in the mountains with the girls of another. They sing, they dance, they make music, and this is how many marriages are decided" (1913, 152). In Zhizuo in the 1990s, unmarried girls still gathered in groups of two to seven or more to sleep in their girlfriends' rooms. Boys in their teens and early twenties also gathered at night to tour barn lofts in their own or neighboring villages. These bands walked from house to house singing, whistling, and playing flutes, gourd-pipes, and bamboo pipes. Girls and young women watched from small windows in the backs of barn lofts, sometimes inviting the boys inside, where, as older Lòlop'ò put it, they "warmed each other around the fire." This warmth began with laughter, courting music, handfuls of sunflower seeds, and sometimes a shared bottle. Eventually, it included sex. Most young men and women used these occasions to experiment with a variety of sexual partners before settling on a serious lover. If all went well, and if the parents on both sides approved, such attachments led to marriage.[7]

Parents of adolescent girls spoke of these activities with wry tolerance. Li Zhiwu complained of the bands of young men making nightly rounds from house to house: "They act like they are in a department store, choosing this, rejecting that, and moving on to something else." "You can't just order your daughter to stay home," another father said, "because the boys make so much noise, singing and shouting, sometimes until the sun comes up. And you have to get up and open the front gate for them all night. So you just let her go where she wants to go so that you can get some sleep." The same man grumbled, "If you cross over to the barn to tell them to shut up, you end up regretting it. Respect for the elderly breaks down in the dark. If an old grandmother tries to scold them, one of them might drag her around the courtyard by the hand and play rough jokes on her. She'll never know who it is, because she can't see his face. Your only option is to shut your eyes, cover your ears, and pretend to sleep."

Parents spoke as though adolescent sex was confined to the barn in order to keep its disruptive energy as far as possible from the rooms where adults and young children slept. Married sex, in contrast, was supposed to be stable and monogamous, taking place only in the couple's own room and only at night. Some parents worried that the mobile, rambunctious, and indiscriminate nature of adolescent sex made it physically dangerous. During my stay in Zhizuo, a young man fell ill a few days after his father surprised him in a daytime dalliance with his girlfriend. The herbalist who treated him told me that his sudden fright in being discovered had obstructed his sexual fluids (*và*) at the height of their flow, backing them up into his kidney area. The accumulation obstructed his penis; he could not urinate, and his abdomen swelled until he died. Milder forms of this condition are common among young men who don't care when or where they sleep with young women, the herbalist claimed, and a similar ailment can afflict a young woman who takes more than one sexual partner in a single night. The sexual fluids of her partners do combat in her womb, causing it to swell painfully—fatally if left untreated.

But parents worried most about the instability of adolescent sex because it threatened their marriage plans for their children. It was a foolish parent, I was told, who believed it was possible to dictate a child's choice of partner. Most marriages began in barn lofts, out of sight of all but the most vigilant parents. Responsible parents took note of any youth who lingered frequently in their barn, granting approval by inviting him in for a morning meal or two or withholding it by ignoring him. Marriages begun this way were formalized with a simple shift of residence. After obtaining the approval of both sets of parents and registering with the township government, a youth chose an auspicious day to bring the woman's family a pot of sticky rice with two pieces of fat on top and then return home with his bride. Formal wedding ceremonies were delayed until after the birth of a first child.

Managing one's children's marriage choices took sustained and energetic "thought work" (Ch. *sixiang gongzuo,* a term borrowed from political discourse). In the ideal scenario, parents said, the child would present his or her mother with a list of several possible partners. The parents would discuss the list and approve one or more names. Frequently, however, parents had other aspirations altogether. Those who had daughters but no sons demanded that one daughter find a partner who would agree to reside in their house, care for them in their old age, and arrange their funerals in return for a portion of their property. Like men in much of rural China, men in Zhizuo found such uxorilocal residence unpalatable, agreeing to it only when they had little chance of substantial inheritance from their own parents.[8] Uxorilocal marriages could be effected simply by formalizing a man's sporadic residence in his partner's household after the birth of a first child. A more prestigious option was to cement the marriage with a wedding in which the ritual roles of groom and bride were switched.

To illustrate the difficulties of managing their children's marriage choices, some parents brought up the practice of delayed-transfer marriage. Before the land reform movement, a few of Zhizuo's wealthiest families, determined not to leave the important matter of forging alliances with other families of influence to childish whims, betrothed their children before they reached adolescence. Such betrothals were extremely expensive, and only those wealthy enough to be later labeled "rich peasants" or "landlords" attempted them. After negotiating a suitable match, the boy's parents would consolidate the alliance with an expensive three-day wedding. The girl was not adopted into the boy's family and raised as a potential bride, as was sometimes the case in other regions, especially the southeast (Wolf and Huang 1980; Wolf 1995). Instead, both children lived with their own parents until they were seventeen or eighteen. Each year during rice-planting season, the two households reconfirmed their alliance by exchanging the betrothed children's labor.

Having been promised to another family rarely prevented the betrothed children from participating in courtship after they reached adolescence, however. For youths of both sexes, these nightly gatherings were the high point of their social lives, and few parents could prohibit their children from joining in. It is not surprising, then, that the majority of youths betrothed in childhood eventually resolved to marry someone else. If a girl failed to carry out a virilocal marriage (or if a boy balked at a uxorilocal one), the family who had paid for the wedding demanded compensation for wedding expenses. Compensation was undertaken only after the girl began to cohabit with her chosen partner, and it was usually paid by that partner's family, with the understanding that the couple would not receive a wedding ceremony. In some cases, when the new partner's family could not pay, the girl's own family paid the compensation. Parents who described these practices estimated that only one or two out of ten childhood betrothals resulted in marriage.

Burning Torches, Stinging Leaves

The separation of barn from residential building generated and enforced gender difference. Children were divided across the courtyard in early adolescence, girls given over to the barn's fertile instability, boys sheltered within the residential building's orderly progression of productive unities. Children inhabited these assigned places as points along an anticipated trajectory that would spin off the occupants of barn lofts to other households, while binding the occupants of the residential building's rooms ever more firmly into relations of filiation and descent. In this way, houses provided a means for moving people along specific social paths with determined futures. Social relations also emerged from domestic space through ritualized acts that sedimented expectations about the future into movements over thresholds or across courtyards—from acts as simple as a father building his daughter a bed in the barn to acts as complex as ritually uprooting a bride's soul from her parents' house and transporting it to that of her husband in a wedding ceremony. Most such rites employed the meticulous architecture of poetic language to lay out trajectories through domestic places. In many ways as substantial and resistant to manipulation as the walls of a house (Keane 1995), this architecture provided models for imagining the future paths of social relations.

Every mention of sons' relations to their parents in poetic language firmly coupled them to the relations of daughters to their parents.[9] For instance, this couplet appears in both wedding speeches and mourning songs:

3.3

| [you] raised sons like tree trunks | kə k'ὰ zò ho t'ù |
| raised daughters like stinging leaves | p'ὲ dɔ̀ né ho t'ù |

Sons are to daughters as the branching tree trunk of descent is to its leaves, which sting as they are raised, only to be shed. Vegetable metaphors also pair parents' relations to married-out daughters (here, fragrant cedars) and parents' relations to married sons (ground-squash roots):

3.4

fragrant cedars are here	mɔ̀ ngɔ́ pe jɔ lu
ground-squash roots are here	chi sæ jo jɔ lu
three stages of grandchildren	sa jɛ́ lɪ́ zò jɔ
three layers of great-grandchildren	sa tə le zò jɔ
two generations of nephews	nì tsɪ́ zò du jɔ
three generations of nieces	sa tsɪ́ né du jɔ

Fragrant kin, said the women who helped me translate this song, are those with whom relations are smooth and comfortable—you can sit with them on a bed for a long time without being offended by their odor. Daughters remain fragrant even as they become widely scattered, like cedars. Sons are like ground-squash roots—bound in a network of agnatic relations. The "three stages of grandchildren" and "three layers of great-grandchildren" refer to the imagined architecture of filial and affinal descendants, respectively. A "stage" (*jɛ́*) is a vertical increment, like a year's growth of a pine branch or a ring on a water buffalo's horns. A "layer" (*tə*) is a horizontal increment, like a plowed furrow in a field. The descendants of sons accumulate in vertical stages, the descendants of daughters in horizontal layers.

    As in these two examples, the poetic language of mourning songs and ritual chants is largely built of distichs, two-line verses bound together by semantic and formal similarities. Such poetic couplets encourage people to imagine each form of relationship as coupled with another. The relations of sons to the household of their birth form such a dyad with the relations of daughters to their parents' houses: a family spreads through both its roots and its fragrance, and any gathering of kin for a wedding or funeral is a failure unless roots and cedars, stages and layers, are present in force. In these examples, the distichs of poetic language employ a simple dyadic architecture. Often, however, poetic language makes use of more elaborate structures to embed differential relations in a complex texture of alternation and reversal. Here, for instance, in a wedding song, vegetable metaphors are coupled with references to domestic places in a pair of parallel distichs:

3.5

the radish rots from within	và tsr̀ và kɔ fu
this courtyard must marry off [a daughter]	fu mo he chì kæ
make torches of mountainside pines	bɛ bò shɔ́ bò pe
this courtyard must speak [for a son]	bɛ dù he chì kæ

The first distich is parallel to the second both semantically and formally. Alternating lines are also paired—the first and third lines couple son and daughter with rotting radish and pine sap; the second and fourth pair the marriage of a daughter with that of a son—and this semantic parallelism is given force by the repetition of "this courtyard" (*he chì kæ*). These alternations couple a pair of spatial differentials (inside/outside and fire/cistern) with the consequences of a son or daughter marrying or not marrying. An unmarried daughter is like a radish left too long in a field.[10] Before the introduction of leafy vegetables to Zhizuo in 1962, radishes—fresh, dried, or pickled—were the main vegetable accompaniment to grain at meals. They were grown on the rims of rice paddies, in the field but not within it, like a daughter sleeping on a house's margins. Left too long in the field, they rotted from the heart outward. An unmarried son is like a mountainside pine. A son might seem to wander much farther afield than a radishlike daughter: father-son relations were fraught with divisive expectations in a way that mother-daughter relations were not. Yet the image of a pine on a mountain slope is central to Lòlop'ò imagination of the relations of filiation and descent that eventually bind a son firmly to his parents.[11]

Marriage brings both radish and pine within. To avoid letting them rot, radishes must be uprooted and piled with other things that need to be kept cool and wet, under a water cistern near the door. Cut from a pine tree's heart, pitchy pine torches are placed at the room's opposite end, on a smooth stone by the fire, shedding their light over the room.[12] People pointed out that the placement of a water cistern and a fire pit was crucial to the harmony of a house's upstream room. Like a residential building with its stable sexual unities and a barn with its unstable sexual fluidities, a fire pit and a cistern were potentially in opposition. A cistern placed directly opposite the fire pit could overcome the fire (as water overcomes fire in the circle of the five elements), making it sullen and smoky. Cisterns were to be positioned near the door on the room's downstream wall, around the bed's corner from the fire. This differential parallels the relation between the position of a daughter-in-law, brought inside the upstream room of a residential building yet kept at its margins near the door, and that of a son, who lights up the household from his place near the fire.

The same song continues:

3.6

A son who can't speak for a daughter-in-law	zò jɔ chì m bɛ
stands like Wòlòbo̱ in the courtyard	ti kæ Wòlò lɔ há n dɔ̀
a daughter who doesn't marry out	né jɔ ro m fu
stands like the itchy girl on the cliff	p'o mo vɛ́ t'ɛ̀ chì ni hɔ lɔ há n dɔ̀

In Lòlop'ò mythology, Wòlòbo̱ are immensely strong, tigerlike creatures, whose gigantic footprints can be seen in flat rocks at the valley's tail.[13] Four of them support the earth at its corners in myths of creation, and one sometimes plays straight man to the trickster Jimìabamo, lifting houses or hauling stones at her command. But Wòlòbo̱ have no mates and no descendants. A son who refuses to marry stands alone in the courtyard, as immobile and solitary as a Wòlòbo̱. A daughter who does not marry ends up like the "itchy girl," whose imprint can still be seen on a cliff near the high-mountain village of Heinila. As the father of two marriageable daughters told this story, the itchy girl was a beautiful young woman, an only child who refused to marry. Desperate for a son-in-law to inherit their house and care for them in old age, her parents quarreled with her daily:

They could not agree which suitor she should marry. The good-looking ones slept all day, the hard-working ones had harelips. One day a honeybee flew through the house, humming, "Zang, zang, a bee will carry off your only daughter, zang, zang." After that, her parents watched her during the day; they locked her in a cupboard at night. One day they let her attend a mortuary ritual: she would be safe in the crowd. When the ritual was half over, a big deer ran by. The people looked up; they ran after it. It ran up into the hill of graves and disappeared. The people looked back; the girl was floating in the sky. She floated across the valley and over the ridge; her mother ran below. Her mother climbed the ridge; the girl was already above the next range. She floated all the way to a cliff near Heinila. Her mother found her there, standing halfway up the cliff. She could not climb up; she could not climb down. She was not dead, but she could not move. Her mother boiled dumplings and tied branches together into a long pole. She fed her by spearing dumplings on the end of the pole, but she could not bring her water. After eight days, the daughter said, "Mother, don't bring me dumplings tomorrow. My saliva has dried up, I can't eat any more." The mother came back the next day, and her daughter was dead. She was still standing on the cliff; she is still there.

Failure to achieve a productive union freezes both Wòlòbo̱ and itchy girl into solitary immobility. But while the Wòlòbo̱ remains in the courtyard, the itchy girl suffers the most severe of dislocations, transported from itchy (or lustful) confinement in her parents' house to distant immobility on a cliff. Whether lighting up the house from the fire pit or standing in the courtyard like Wòlòbo̱, a son remains always in a relatively stable position within a house's embrace; a daughter is always in motion between the center and the outermost perimeters. At adolescence, a daughter forms with her mother the tight core of household activity while sleeping at the house's unstable margin; at marriage, she moves into an inner room of another household but remains near the door. If she does not marry, her position becomes untenable: she can choose only between a dead, immobile corner of the house and a distant, immobile outside. Yet the story of the itchy girl also evokes the tenacity of a mother's relationship with her daughter. The mother runs after her daughter, despairing as she floats over the ridge, having her hopes lifted as she glimpses her over the next range, extending her love as a lifeline along branches she ties together to reach up the cliff. For married daughters, the bond between mother and daughter is the "fragrance" that continues to link affinal kin after a daughter floats away to a distant household.

Cross-Sibling Intimacies

Gender emerged from the practices and representations of domestic space as differential relations of adolescents to the houses of their parents. Each anticipated social trajectory—marrying out of a house or staying within—was coupled to another across the intervals between fire pit and cistern, courtyard and cliff, mountain pine and field radish, squash vine and scattered cedar. Each relation reflected another through displacements or transpositions, making it possible, for instance, for bride and groom in a uxorilocal marriage to switch ritual positions in a wedding ceremony with a minimum of social dissonance, the groom performing in every detail the role ordinarily played by a bride. In the view from the parents' courtyard, then, relations between brothers and sisters were an asymmetric dyadic opposition. But another prominent series of poetic and gestural techniques opened up a different perspective, from which these relations were not an opposition but a generative union, out of which emerged a sister's productive relations with her husband.

Infants in Zhizuo rarely touched the ground in their first year or so of life. They were carried around on someone's back during the day, and they slept with their parents or siblings at night. Elder daughters shared their mother's burden of raising younger siblings; girls as young as five bore infant siblings on their backs. Younger siblings relied on elder sisters for nourishment and care when their mother was busy caring for an infant or working in the fields. When siblings were slightly older, sisters—even younger sisters—were expected to cook for their brothers and feed them. Cross-sibling relations were built on this foundation of care flowing from female to male siblings. In childhood, sisters bore (*bùù*) their brothers; after marriage, brothers were to reciprocate by helping bear (also *bùù*) their sisters and their children. Relations between brothers and sisters were imagined to bear the productive unions of husbands and wives.

These relations shored up sisters' unions at every stage of their married lives. Directly after marriage, brothers were expected to visit their married-out sisters frequently, take their sides in quarrels with husbands or other members of their new households, and encourage them to return home if they were treated badly (Yang F. 1990, 55). When sisters accumulated enough wealth to build a house, brothers were expected to contribute labor to its construction, building the two outer walls of the house that shored it up from the sides. This labor was split between generations of brothers: the husband's mother's brothers built the upstream wall, and the wife's own brothers built the downstream wall. Brothers were also crucial participants in rituals to encourage the growth and health of their sisters' offspring. In the early 1990s, Zhizuo residents commonly practiced three such rites. First, three days after a child's birth, one of its mother's brothers gave it a milk name in a naming ritual. Second, after three years, if a child was in poor health or unable to walk, its mother's brothers sponsored an offering to a spirit of health and long life (the *menè*). Pine branches used in this ritual were hung permanently on the outside back wall of a house as a reminder of the mother's brother's support for the child. Third, in cases where sisters had repeated difficulty giving birth, brothers unwittingly participated in the *mæho* ritual described in chapter 2: the beak of the treadle pounder, representing the fetus or infant, was lifted surreptitiously from a brother's house or courtyard.

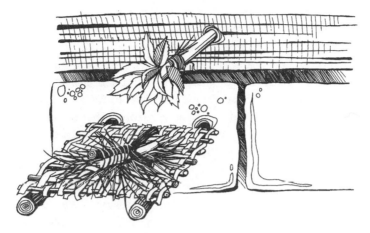

Figure 3.3 An ancestral effigy.

The techniques of death ritual focused concentrated and repetitive attention on the relations of living brothers (or their sons) to the productive unions of their dead sisters and their descendants. Among the most evocative of these techniques was the art of constructing ancestral spirit effigies (*nèts'ɿ̀*) for the houses of the deceased's agnatic descendants. On the eve of a "dawn to dusk offering" (*nihèpi*) held seven days (for a woman) or nine days (for a man) after a death, a brother of a dead woman (or a brother of the dead man's wife) guided the deceased's youngest son up the mountain and shot an arrow into the pines. The son uprooted the sapling nearest to where the arrow landed and bore it home on his back. From this pine, the brother carved a round rod representing his sister's husband; from a chestnut branch, he made a forked figure representing his sister. He bound the pine into the fork of the chestnut with colored thread, seven strands (if the woman died first) or nine strands (once her husband died). He represented his own relationship to the couple in a small, square, plaited bamboo platform, which he attached to the back, upstream wall of the house's upstream room. He placed the pine and chestnut figure on this bamboo platform with the heads pointing slightly upstream—the conjugal pair coupled forever on a plaited bamboo bed (shown in Figure 3.3).

This effigy diagrammed the trajectory these social relations were anticipated to take in the process of mourning. Husband and wife were to lose their individual identities, merging into a single form, a ceaselessly generative coupling of phallus to crotch. Brother and sister were plaited into the supporting form of a bed, the interwoven bamboo strips attesting to the intimacy of their union. And these two forms of relation merged into one: the triadic shape of brother, sister, and husband, from which the fertile energies of a household would henceforth flow. Ancestral spirit effigies did not merely memorialize an "ancestor," representing an ideology of agnatic descent passing from father to son to grandson. They did not even memorialize a relation between two parents. Instead, they gathered and fixed a relation between two forms of social relation, of spouses and of cross-siblings.[14] In life, these two forms of relation came together repeatedly in ritual and daily routine to bear and nourish children. In death, these remembered relations were woven into the wood and mud-brick fabric of a house to lend it their fertile energies.

The mute tableaux of ancestral effigies remind one of the secret inscriptions of childhood memory Bachelard found to reside in house images: "Except for a few medallions stamped with the likeness of our ancestors our child-memory contains only worn coins. It is on the plane of the daydream and not on that of facts that childhood remains alive and poetically useful within us. Through this permanent childhood, we maintain the poetry of the past. To inhabit oneirically the house we were born in means more than to inhabit it in memory; it means living in this house that is gone, the way we used to dream in it" (1964, 16).

Most ethnography finds childhood worlds opaque; mine is no exception. But occasionally adults told me stories that seemed to capture echoes of childhood voices. One close acquaintance whose childhood was "alive and poetically useful" to her was Luo Lizhu, the ritual specialist who performed Li Qunhua's *mæho* ritual. Her kin and neighbors still told stories of her pranks of fifty years past—a tale of her cross-dressing as a boy who was cross-dressing as a girl at a wedding was a favorite—and in her seventies she retained a relish for childish escapades. She spent several afternoons in my room entertaining a group of children and adults with tales of two elderly female heroes who bridged adult and childhood sensibilities: Jimìabamo, a trickster who appears to human eyes in the guise of an old woman, and Grandmother Wosomo, a version of the popular goddess Guanyin Laomu.[15] Grandmother Wosomo assigns souls waiting to be reborn to human wombs. One of Luo Lizhu's stories was a tale of a flood, in the capacious genre of flood stories told by non-Han peoples throughout China's southwest.[16] After a flood wipes out human civilization, a brother and sister procreate to re-populate the world.

> There are floods, fires, and windstorms, but it is not easy to know why. This is the story of the great flood.
>
> Two brothers and two sisters opened up a buckwheat field. They worked all day, and they went home at night. The next morning, they found the bushes and grass had grown again, as if they had never plowed. Before going home, they made a snare out of their lead rope. An old woman came by and got caught in the snare. Perhaps she could have freed herself, but she didn't; she just sat and waited. When the brothers and sisters came back, they saw the old lady sitting on the ground. They wondered why she didn't free herself.
>
> The elder brother and elder sister said, "It seems that the ghost [*nè*] who made the brush grow back on our field is this old woman. Let's kill her."
>
> The younger sister and younger brother said, "She looks like our mother. We mustn't kill her."
>
> The old woman said, "You, big brother and big sister, go work copper and make a copper house to live in. Work iron and make an iron house to live in. Work wood and make a wooden house to live in. Work stone and make a stone house to live in. Little sister and little brother, you go plant squash and live in a squash house. Plant gourds [*bɔ*] and live in a gourd house."
>
> The two little ones planted gourd vines, and the vines grew gourds. They made the biggest one their house. When the sun shone, the gourd split open, and they came out to work. When the sun set, they went back inside the gourd to sleep, and it shut itself up.
>
> After a while, the dragon [*cilù*] blocked the water's tail. The water backed up, and there was water everywhere. It flowed from the knife handles, it flowed from the salt bowl, it flowed from the cinders in the fireplace. There was no place to live, no place to husk grain. As the water flowed, the gourd vine grew. The water rose higher, the vine grew longer; finally the gourd bumped against the sky. The water receded, the gourd floated down; finally it settled to the ground. Everything else below the sky, all that was living, died. The only ones living were these two, the brother and younger sister, and the honeybees, for honeybees can fly.

After the flood, Grandmother Wosomo goes out to look for the brother and sister. She asks a mule, a wasp, and a bumblebee if they have seen the couple. They respond with bad-tempered threats, and she punishes them. Then she asks a honeybee, who tells her where they are. She rewards the honeybees by making them domestic partners of humans. Then she locates the siblings.

> Grandmother Wosomo found her descendants, her seeds, her family, her grandchildren, her great-grandchildren, this brother and sister. She led them back; she told them to farm grain; she told them to raise sons and daughters.
>
> But elder brothers and younger sisters are ashamed together.
>
> So from that slope he rolled the male part of the millstone [*nǐp'ɔ*], from this slope she rolled the female part [*nǐmo*], and at the river they came together face to face. From that slope he rolled a sieve, from this slope she rolled a winnowing basket, and at the river they came together face to face. So brother and sister became a family, because they were the only ones left.
>
> On the fifth month, when the rainstorms came, they carried home leaves of the droop-leafed plant.
>
> "Ah, we're ashamed together," said the brother, "so let's cover your vagina with these and just do it a bit together. Good for heaven and earth, good for humans and tigers." So, because there were no other people, they covered her vagina with a leaf and played around. But the leaf broke, and they became man and wife. The sister became pregnant. After she carried for three years, she gave birth to a chunk of meat. It was lean meat, round as a straw basket. After it was born, they sliced it up with a knife on a cutting board. As they cut off each slice, they tossed it away, and the animal it landed on turned into a person. When there were no more animals left, they tossed the slices into the trees and the grass, and this is how the hundred surnames were created.[17]

Hidden like seeds in their gourd house, brother and sister live out a dream of contained and self-sufficient cross-sex union. Their gourd is a *bɔ,* small with a bulbous base and long neck, of the kind used to make musical instruments called *balɔ,* "gourd-pipes" (shown in Figure 3.4). Five or six bamboo pipes are fitted with fire-hardened bamboo reeds, inserted through holes in the bulbous end of the gourd, and sealed with beeswax. Zhizuo residents associate gourd-pipes with Lòlop'ò ancestry. Of all the musical instruments—bamboo flutes, mouth harps, double-reed horns (Ch. *suona*), and two-stringed fiddles (Ch. *erhu*)—only gourd-pipes are played indoors and among mixed generations or genders. In wedding and mortuary rituals, they are associated with the values of the residential building—its interior, productive stability beneath the miniature beds of the ancestors. Seed-bearing vessels penetrated by airy bamboo rods, they are houselike models of stable and harmonious cross-sex union. As the siblings' gourd opens and closes with the rising and set-

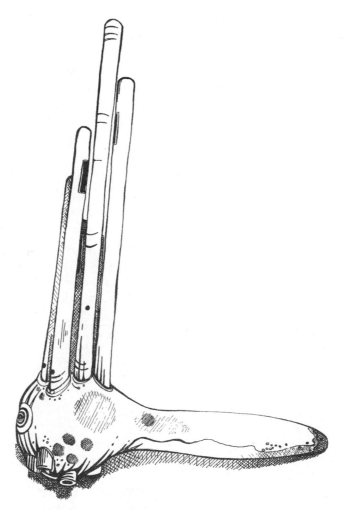

Figure 3.4 A gourd-pipe.

ting sun, they alternately broadcast themselves outward and return to their nest, truncating the cycle of birth and death to revolve only within their self-contained sphere. Seeds that return to the fruit after being sown, they hold close the promise of fecundity without ever giving in to growth, decay, and death. Their gourd skin encloses a model of society; once the world has been wiped clean by the flood, this model *is* society. Wosomo calls the siblings her descendants, seeds, grandchildren, and great-grandchildren, but in the interval between the flood's recession and her discovery of them they have neither ancestors nor descendants.

Their pairing matures into a productive union when Wosomo leads the siblings back and tells them to farm grain and raise sons and daughters. They test her command to commit incest against the natural order of domestic materials. In Lòlop'ò houses, millstones usually occupy one end of the porch that runs the length of the residential building. Two round stones rest one on top of the other on a stone or wooden rack. Grain is poured through a hole in the upper stone, and this stone is turned with a rod to grind the grain against the lower one. Upper and lower millstones (níp'ɔ and nímo) are tagged as male and female, respectively, with the suffixes p'ɔ and mo, commonly used to indicate the sex of animals. Bamboo sieves and winnowing baskets too are male and female, the smaller sieve used always in combination with the larger winnowing basket placed beneath it. In contrast to the harmonious union of bamboo and gourd in gourd-pipes, millstones or sieves and baskets come together with the halting rhythms and harsh grinding or shaking motions that Lòlop'ò poetics associate with the pain and exhaustion of labor, as in these lines, repeated many times in a long lament[18] that describes the labor of producing rice, buckwheat, and hemp offerings for a deceased mother:

3.7

fill a bamboo winnowing basket	mò cæ o mo jè do go
fill a bamboo sieve	mò cæ ò jɔ jè do go
shake and shake again	jì và jì và và do go
toss and toss again	jì o jì o o do go

Seeds are being sieved and winnowed here, in preparation for sowing. Generative union emerges from cross-sibling relations only at the cost of a separation that takes one sibling with his millstone or sieve up "that slope" and the other, with her stone or basket, up "this slope," and joins them again in the valley in a harsh, difficult union that presages a life of labor. The siblings repeat this gesture of separation with the droop-leafed plant, which ruptures at the right moment for the union to bear fruit. And, finally, a grotesquely extended pregnancy produces no easy issue, but rather a chunk of meat, which must be subjected to the further labor of chopping before the world may be repopulated.

In ancestral effigies and in the gestures and poetics of mortuary ritual, cross-sibling relations, imagined as the perfect and original cross-sex union, are represented as "bearing" (bù) productive relations of union and descent. Like Bachelard's poetic images of houses, these resources retrieve a particular, stereotyped adult dream of childhood—of tranquil and self-sufficient generative unions, brother and sister in their gourd house after the flood. Such dreams are not uncommon across cultures, as James Boon (1990, 94–114) brilliantly demonstrates; in Zhizuo, they are implicit in nearly every representation of domestic space. In the lament quoted at the beginning of this chapter, for instance, daughters and sons mirror the successful and stable unions of their parents, sons sitting below fathers on one bed, daughters below mothers on the other, grandsons and granddaughters repeating the reflection one step down, each generation of paired siblings moving up to fill the place of the older generation as it passes away. Descent produces union within the embrace of a house's walls, erasing the distinction between agnate and affine. The story of the gourd house and the plaited and bound materials of ancestral effigies bring this dream to bear on the generative unions of husbands and wives. In these representations, such unions, achieved at the cost of sending one sibling across the courtyard or up the other mountain, continue to draw procreative force from the original intimacy of brother and sister.

Despite a provision of the 1981 marriage law forbidding marriage between first cousins, many parents still dreamed of marrying their offspring to their mother's brothers' children or father's sisters' children—preferred forms of marriage in many Yi areas. Determined parents could overcome the legal obstacles to cross-cousin marriage with gifts to the clerks responsible for recording household and marriage registrations. Working with evidence from Eastern Indonesia, where varieties of indirect marriage exchange proliferate, James Fox has suggested that ideologies of cross-cousin exchange may take their force from "the idea of a return or reunion of life: the 'life' that a brother and sister share can be restored only by the marriage of their children or descendants of their children" (1980, 12–13, quoted in Boon 1990, 104). Parents in Zhizuo spoke of cross-cousin marriage as a way of keeping their daughters within their families: "Because this child is so smart and so able, it would be best to keep her in the family. When it works out, there is nothing better, a tighter and tighter family, a daughter and a daughter-in-law both," as one parent put it. But parents also admitted that their children rarely found such alliances as attractive as they did, and this could make the marriage a disaster for the entire group of siblings and their children. "If they don't get along, there is nothing worse," said the same parent. "Everyone loses face, and it breaks up the unity of the whole family." Cross-cousin marriage reversed the gesture that divided sister from brother across a courtyard in preparation for her marriage out. It retrieved the dream of a contained and autonomous house, where sibling relations were allowed to mature into generative unions. For parents hoping to arrange such marriages for their children, the distance between generations was like the droop-leafed plant, the necessary gesture of separation that created a "return to life" in the fruitful union of siblings.

The Bed's Head: Embracive Descent

For many in Zhizuo, upstream rooms were the final point of circulation through a house's spaces. Some, such as eldest sons and their wives, arrived within a few years after marriage when they built their own houses. Others, such as youngest sons or daughters with uxorilocally resident husbands, did not arrive until after their parents' deaths. And still others, such as those who never married or who lost their spouse and children, never arrived, spending their lives in downstream rooms or barn lofts. Even in the most severely overcrowded households, senior men and women were rarely displaced from upstream rooms before their own deaths: widows or widowers often occupied these rooms alone for many years while other household members competed for the remaining space.

This room was a house's ritual center and the residence of several kinds of household spirits. Life in this highly structured space, among this density of signs of death and renewal, descent and affiliation, imposed requirements of bodily comportment and linguistic propriety that many, Li Zhiwu among them, found onerous. Li Zhiwu and Li Qunhua arranged their room in a singular way, sleeping together in a bed against the downstream wall. Twice a day, they cooked for their household on a fire pit, centered near the opposite, upstream wall. A cabinet stood against the back wall, next to a ladder leading to the attic; water cisterns and piles of greens or radishes occupied the front wall, by the door. By contrast, a proper upstream room contained two beds: a man's bed against the back wall, opposite the door (where Li Zhiwu and Li Qunhua kept a chest), and a woman's bed against the front wall (where this couple kept their water cisterns). Between the two beds was a fire pit with a three-legged iron cooking stand. Below the foot of the man's bed,

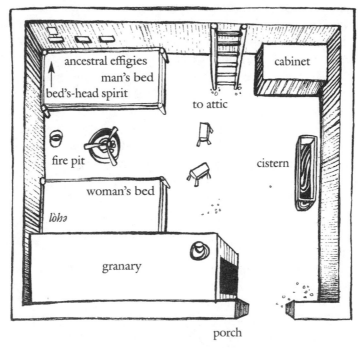

Figure 3.5 An ideal upstream room, properly arranged.

a ladder led up to the attic; below the foot of the woman's bed, near the
door, sat a water cistern of a single hollowed log or several large clay
pots (see Figure 3.5). This was the arrangement described in the mourning chant quoted in fragment 3.1, a perpendicular intersection of a gendered differential (across the fire pit) and a generational one (from the
beds' upstream heads to their downstream feet).

An upstream room afforded little privacy; the entire household was
in and out day and night. One night, Li Zhiwu told me, his eldest son
burst in for a midnight snack, found his parents in a single bed, and
scolded them for an hour for behavior unbecoming to the elderly. That
was bad enough; were they to build another bed, he and his wife would
have no excuse at all to sleep together, for children are far less tolerant of
their parents' intimacies than parents are of their children's. Still, Li
Zhiwu said, the two beds in most upstream rooms are a sham. During a
visit to a neighbor's house, he nodded at the man's bed against the back
wall, piled deep with clothing and utensils. "Only people with very thick
skin dare leave clothing all over that bed like that," he whispered. I asked

him why. "Because ninety percent of those men's beds are just for show. Everyone knows that the man doesn't sleep there; he sleeps in his wife's bed. You want to make the bed up nice with blankets so it looks like you do sleep there, or people laugh at you. Especially as you get older—then they laugh harder." Were he to move his wife's and his one bed to the front wall, where a woman's bed would properly go, he said, people would never stop laughing. In its present place, it was neither clearly a woman's bed nor clearly a man's, and for all other people knew, he or his wife slept in another room. One thing I would never find in Zhizuo, he insisted, was a couple sleeping together on a man's bed, against an upstream room's back wall. This was not only embarrassing; it could even be dangerous. In most upstream rooms, ancestral spirits and their guardian, the "spirit at the bed's head" (*gɜwúdenè*), resided above this bed. To have sex there would be as offensive as to give birth or menstruate there.

Even in Li Zhiwu's upstream room, the corner where the back and upstream walls met was called the *gɜwúdɛ,* or "bed's head." Though their bed was nowhere near this corner, Li Qunhua frequently uttered instructions such as, "Hand me that pot, there at the bed's head," or "Come up here to sit, closer to the bed's head." (The actual head of the bed was called the same thing, and I sometimes blundered about the room in confusion when told to find a pot or a sitting place.) For the crucial communal acts of cooking and eating, household members oriented themselves to this corner, taking seats on small, mobile stools around the fire, as though on opposite beds. Li Qunhua sat near the upstream wall with her back to the water cisterns by the door. Her daughter and elderly kinswoman sat downstream of her. Li Zhiwu sat near the "bed's-head" corner, as though at the head of the man's bed, with spaces for his sons and male guests downstream of him. In this house, the beams above the bed's-head corner were empty. In most other houses, this space was the home of a bed's-head spirit, represented by several sheets of paper, stacked one on top of the other and tacked with a bamboo bar to the back wall (shown in Figure 3.6). A small wooden shelf above it protected the paper from falling soot; another below supported offerings in bowls. Twelve chestnut leaves tied to a twig stuck into the wall on the upstream side of the paper formed a "flower" (*wudɜ́*) for the spirit's enjoyment. On the first dawn of the lunar new year, the family refreshed their bed's-head spirit by tacking a new sheet onto the paper stack and replacing the "flower" with a new bundle of leaves. Most people felt that the presence of a bed's-head spirit necessitated the conven-

Figure 3.6 A bed's-head spirit.

tional arrangement of furniture that Li Zhiwu eschewed. Offerings to this spirit should be placed on a bed beneath it, it was agreed, and any bed located there should be a man's. With the man's bed placed there, the natural place for the woman's bed was against the opposite wall — and so on with the fire pit, chests, and cisterns. The unusual arrangement of Li Zhiwu and Li Qunhua's upstream room was possible because their bed's-head spirit and ancestral effigies resided in another house, vacant and deteriorating, which Li Zhiwu had inherited from his parents.

From this corner, the bed's-head spirit presided over the ancestral effigies, which it protected and domesticated. Ancestral effigies were positioned in a line proceeding downstream from the bed's-head spirit, with a twelve-leafed "flower" identical to that for the bed's-head spirit above each. People spoke of the bed's-head spirit as an official who exercised jurisdiction over the ancestral effigies, coordinating their energies, moderating their whims, and preventing them from unjustly harming their descendants. To bring a deceased soul within the house was to place it under the influence of this spirit, and living souls also cohabited this space with the dead, under the eye of the bed's-head spirit. Ritualists explained that living persons, like dead ones, had three souls: one stuck with the body, one stayed in the grave site, and a third hung about the house near the bed's head.[19] The souls of those working, traveling, or studying away from home were especially likely to be lingering there, basking in the protective embrace of the bed's-head spirit. Li Zhiwu, who had spent years wandering the province during the Cultural Revolution, was fond of this idea. "Bed's-head spirits are like guard dogs," he told me.

"One evening I was in Wanbie, preparing to cross the Jinsha River, on my way back home," he related. "As I was about to board the ferry, I remembered that a dog bit me on the leg in my dream the night before. So I stayed on the bank while the boat pulled away. When it reached the middle of the river, I saw it sink, and I saw several people drown. That dog was my house's bed's-head spirit, warning me not to cross the river that day." The spirit had kept watch on him through his soul that had lingered at home while he traveled, he said, warning him of danger through his dreams. Others affirmed that dogs were a reliable dream sign for bed's-head spirits but cited the principle that dream signs stood for their opposites. Dream dogs often warned that the house's protector was about to turn on its inhabitants. When bed's-head spirits were neglected, molested, or otherwise insulted (say, by eating dog meat in their presence), they could cause madness, illness, or sudden death.[20]

Ancestral effigies were lined up according to generation in *reverse order* to that in which living generations slept in the rooms of a house or sat on the beds of the upstream room. The youngest generation of ancestral spirits was just downstream of the bed's-head spirit, the next eldest generation downstream of the youngest, and so forth, down the wall. This was the order of their propitiation on feast days, beginning with the bed's-head spirit and ending with the eldest deceased generation. People in Zhizuo spoke of this hierarchy as an expression of the nature of memory and grief. One kept closest the spirits of those whom one could remember in life: siblings, parents, and grandparents. As memory faded, so did the power of an ascendant to do harm or confer benefit. And so did kinship. "How can you say my great-great-grandfather is still kin to me, if no one living remembers who he was?" as a man of about twenty put it to me. "My kinship with those I remember is close, but when I don't remember them, and I don't grieve for them, I have little feeling of kinship with them." Ancestral effigies were preserved and recognized as kin for only three generations. The oldest ancestral effigies in any house represented the eldest living household member's great-grandparents' generation. Many houses had rows of ancestral effigies containing four or more generations, but these always included effigies for members of the oldest living inhabitant's generation or the generations of her descendants. After three generations, ancestral effigies were destroyed and their kinship with the living ritually terminated.[21] At the funeral (*kukedo*) of the last representative of a household's eldest generation, the senior generation of ancestral effigies was removed from the wall, placed on the lid of the coffin, and allowed to fall to the ground and be trampled in the procession to the grave site.[22]

The corner at the bed's head was thus a kind of pivot between a household's living and its dead. Ideally, living generations progressed from downstream to upstream seats and rooms as children gradually took their parents' places. Dead generations progressed from upstream to downstream, passing out of house and memory as they reached the end of the row of effigies. Bed's-head spirits and ancestral effigies diagrammed a distinctive variation on the ideologies of memory and descent described in the literature on kinship and lineage in rural China.[23] This literature emphasizes agnatic descent groups focused on a common ancestor, in whose name a corporate landed estate was often founded. Lineages and sublineages were distinguished externally and unified internally through worship of a founding ancestor. Ancestors were worshiped both in "domestic" settings, corresponding to a single household or a compound of a few agnatically related households, and in "hall" settings, corresponding to multiple households; the literature stresses forms of memorialization in both that valued founders and exclusive continuity. Even studies of smaller and shallower agnatic descent groups who did not necessarily hold property in common describe related men as finding corporate identity in an exclusive genealogical line linking present generations of males to ancestors and descendants.[24] In each case, memory of the dead was seen to draw its significance from a point of origin in the distant past, from which emanated the unbroken and exclusive line that connected present, past, and future.

In Lòlop'ò households, however, the point of origin for memory was in the recent past: the grief and affection one felt for the newly deceased. This origin was embedded in space at the bed's head, where the bed's-head spirit formed a pivot between living and dead. From this origin, memory attenuated in force and significance as it reached down the line of ancestral effigies. Like a lineage founder, the nameless bed's-head spirit granted unity and structural coherence to the line of descent. This unity did not memorialize only agnatic ascendants; it involved wives, mothers, and mother's brothers as well, but agnatic descent was nevertheless at its core. Given their memorial focus on the newly dead and their active efforts to forget distant ancestors, one might assume that Lòlop'ò would find it difficult to form large descent groups. But bed's-head spirits, which occupied the position of a lineage founder without actually participating in a chain of agnates, were flexible resources for creating unities of descent. Chapter 4 shows how Zhizuo residents used the bed's-head spirit's jurisdiction over the agnatic and affinal dead as a model for a common founding ancestor (Agàmisimo) to whom all who resided within a specific territory could lay claim.[25]

Granaries: Womb Economies

The furniture in his upstream room had assumed its present arrangement in 1958, Li Zhiwu told me. Before that memorable year, nearly a quarter of the room's space had been occupied by a granary of planks built into the corner opposite the bed's head. Grain was stored in baskets there, secure from rats and dogs. Li Zhiwu's mother's bed had leaned against the granary's wall, opposite her husband's. Above its head, where the granary met the upstream wall, she had inserted a single three-forked pine branch into the wall; below the branch, she had set up a small wooden shelf, where she kept a plaited bamboo box containing grain seeds and an egg. This was a household spirit called the "granary lòhɔ" (níka lòhɔ). By 1956, when agriculture was collectivized, granaries in Zhizuo stood empty; in 1958, most were dismantled and burned for firewood in the collective mess halls of the Great Leap Forward.

Only two of the Zhizuo households I visited had preserved a granary. One belonged to my friend Luo Lizhu. Her granary had escaped destruction in 1958 because her husband, now long dead, had been a production team leader who used it to store collective grain. In the three decades that followed, it had held the team's grain, stored hempen yarn and cloth, or stood empty. In 1980, with the revival of household cultivation, Luo Lizhu had filled it again with grain. Sleeping beside the granary, with the key to its padlocked door on her person, she controlled her household's daily finances, deciding how much grain went into the pot and how much money left a clay urn within the granary. For help with these tasks, she relied on the little lòhɔ spirit on the granary's outer wall. This spirit, she explained, regulated the flow of grain from the granary through the digestive tracts of her family. "Some people are always hungry," she said. "There's a woman living below us who can put away six kilos of rice a day. They eat all their grain up before the second month [leaving six or seven months before the next harvest]. But with a good *lòhə*, your family will eat and drink little and still stay healthy; I boil two kilos every meal for the six of us, and everyone is satisfied after a bowl or two. People from the city don't understand this; they think the more they eat, the longer they live, and they never know where all their wealth goes."

Luo Lizhu believed that the Great Leap famine had been precipitated in part by the destruction of granaries and *lòhə*. In the autumn of 1958, the new collective mess halls had served up a year's worth of grain and meat in a few months. That year's harvest flowed uselessly through commune members' digestive tracts, Luo Lizhu said, leaving them only leaves and wild herbs to eat. Before the granaries were burned, skillful female household managers had worked with their *lòhə* to sustain a delicate regulative balance between the economies of bodies and granaries. Destroying the *lòhə* and handing over control of household economics to male collective leaders such as her husband, she said, naturally ended in disaster.

In addition to the womanly virtues of skillful household economy, granary and *lòhə* had been associated with a ritual vocabulary of germination and childbirth. This was a favorite topic for Luo Lizhu, who delighted in the dynamics of ritual form. The shelf below the *lòhə* held a granary in miniature, she said, a plaited bamboo rice box, containing seeds of every form of grain planted and an egg. Beside the box one placed a wedding flower, made of a split bamboo chopstick and a paper streamer. These offerings were renewed yearly at the fall harvest. Among the skills a senior woman should cultivate, was the capacity to determine which portion of each type of grain should be kept for seed. She still kept her own seed in hempen bags in her granary, as most senior women had done before 1956; in this respect she was like Grandmother Wosomo (or Guanyin Laomu), said to store souls preparing for rebirth and to distribute them to the wombs of women. In her ritual practice, Luo Lizhu had once treated granaries as wombs. Performing the *mæho* ritual, she had mimed the act of childbirth by pulling an effigy of a fetus from beneath a bed. The bed was a substitute for a granary, she said; before 1958, she had pulled such fetus effigies out of the granary's small, square entrance.

As womblike repositories for seeds, granaries and *lòhə* were invested with an awesome and sometimes frightening power. In mythology, granaries appeared in close association with fearsome natural forces, like female tigers (the syllable *lò* in *lòhə* is the word for tiger). One day, as Li Zhiwu and I walked through a heavily forested part of Zhizuo, where people had once frequently spotted leopards and wildcats, he entertained me with a story of a tigress (*lòmo*) who gave birth in a granary:

> A family from Chezò had a seasonal house up here a long time ago. One year, before they moved here from their house in the village, a tigress made a nest in the granary. She had a litter of cubs there. When they came back, they built a fire and started to cook some rice. The cubs in the granary cried out, and the tigress returned. She clawed at the door, but she couldn't claw it down. When her cubs cried out again, she turned around and battered the door with her buttocks until it cracked. One of them was more clever than the rest. He heated an axe in the fire and shoved it through the crack in the door. The tigress smashed her buttocks into the door, impaled herself on the hot axe, and ran away. Then they opened the granary and killed those cubs.

This tale suggests that the forces of conception nestled in the granary had a wild power to threaten a house's integrity, which might be countered with punitive male sexuality. Like bed's-head spirits, granary *lòhə* had a collective counterpart. A spirit called, simply, the Lòhə guarded Zhizuo's common granary, the collectively held ancestral trust once used to finance the *ts'ici* system. Rituals for this spirit employed a threat of aggressive masculine sexuality to control the feminine sexual power that senior men feared would blossom out of control during the rice-transplanting season (as discussed in chapter 5). This Lòhə "went wild" two years before the Cultural Revolution, precipitating a crisis of germination and conception that still afflicted Zhizuo in the early 1990s.

Several ethnographers and historians have noted that the dangers of pollution widely associated with birth and menstruation in rural China are evidence of a wary respect among men for the social power of feminine reproductive capacity (Ahern 1974b; Seaman 1981; Martin 1988; Furth 1986). Most of this work has emphasized the potentially disruptive effects of this capacity to male ideologies of agnatic descent. In places where men idealized families that grew from generation to generation without disruption or division, women learned to nurture affective bonds with their children to press for another goal: neolocal households where they could be independent from the exacting authority of their mothers-in-law (Wolf 1972; Ahern 1974b). In Zhizuo, where most men were deeply ambivalent about the idea of two or more married brothers living under the same roof, and where family division was more often seen as the positive birth of a new household than the diminishment of an older one, women's affective bonds with their children were less of a danger to male aspirations. But feminine reproductive capacity still directly and potently shaped the future of every household for good or ill. In poor regions like this, where productive resources were severely limited, an excess of children (especially of boys) created immense difficulties for parents, and a dearth of children (again especially of boys) deeply threatened their future security. The proper management of birthing was as crucial to a house's future as the skilled oversight of limited grain and seed. Before 1956, the corner of the upstream room that held their beds, granaries, and *lòhɔ* helped senior women attain a formidable capacity to establish practical authority over their households' affairs. They used the granary and its guardian spirit to nurture an association between germination and conception, making it seem natural that, as the power to regulate birthing lay in their hands, so should the authority to manage grain, seed, and money. The locked door of the granary was an obstacle to senior men who wished to assert their own influence over the balance of productive and reproductive capacities cultivated there. Given the crucial importance of this balance to the future of every household, it is no wonder that stories like that of the tigress should depict the granary's association with feminine reproductive capacities as frightening and potentially destructive.

The houses Zhizuo residents remembered inhabiting in the first half of the twentieth century had shaped two perspectives on life and death across an upstream room. The corner of the bed's head framed a view of life and death as a line of transmission, embracing multiple relations in each generation but preserving a solid core of agnatic descent. The corner of the granary framed a view of life and death as a cyclical regenerative economy, in which granaries and wombs sheltered the seeds from which new life would spring. To inhabit one position was both to face the place of the other gender and to see oneself from the perspective that place engendered. One could occupy the opposite bed for a time in one's daily routine, perhaps pausing to imagine the capacities and attributes granted another by that side, only to be drawn back across the room by habit and social expectation. One might even absorb attributes from the other side, combining them in one's person with the capacities one's own side granted—as Luo Lizhu did with the powerful spirit familiars (*mɛlònè*) she inherited from her father.

Nor were this side and that side mutually exclusive: each inflected the other across the few feet of the house's most intensely inhabited room.[26] We can glimpse these inflections most clearly as they materialized in the house's form. The generative cycles of the granary were echoed on a longer scale in the line of descent above the bed's head, as it faded after three generations, only to return as new life when ancestors were transformed into descendants in a final mortuary ritual (*likáduhè*). As miniature embodiments of the walls that embraced and domesticated the entire agnatic line, bed's-head spirits were the granaries for this regeneration, storing the agnatic seeds that would eventually germinate in new life. The cycles of life and death sheltered in the granary were likewise inflected with an aspect of the transmissive lines concentrated at the bed's head. Granaries were not only storage places for grain and seed but also hiding places for wealth that women inherited from their parents, especially their mothers. In the granary, women sheltered both the sense of a powerful and dangerous feminine reproductive capacity and their own muted transmissive lines of descent.

Attics: Andocentry and the State

After losing control of the granary in the late 1950s, most women never recovered it. With collectivization in 1956, the state reached into households to take command of the crucial regulative economy of eating, spending, and saving grain. In Zhizuo, as throughout China, collectives were led almost exclusively by men, sometimes loosely organized as agnatic descent groups (Croll 1981; Diamond 1975). Scientific discourses about agriculture and human biology, generated at higher, invisible levels of state organization, took the place of the *lòhɔ* in deciding how much grain would be eaten, spent, or saved. Cadres calculated daily figures for proper grain consumption according to shifting demands from above and the scientifically determined needs of bodies, male or female, laboring or not laboring, youthful or elderly. Collectivization of grain production and distribution stretched and distorted the links between germination and conception. In retrospect, people in Zhizuo judged these dislocations to have been devastating; many shared Luo Lizhu's sense that they were at the root of the Great Leap famine.

After household cultivation was revived in 1980, granaries were not rebuilt. The attics of residential buildings had always been central to grain production: threshed grain was spread over a layer of tamped earth on the attic floor to dry slowly for several months. In the 1980s and 1990s, the dried grain was simply collected in baskets and pots and stored in the attic. Rats were more troublesome there, but cats and poison could check their depredations.

Like granaries, attics stored wealth and secrets. But in contrast to granaries, they were, with few exceptions, off limits to women. Li Zhiwu entered his attic through a trap door near the upstream room's back wall. This was where he kept meat from the single pig he killed every autumn, salted, arranged neatly on beds of clean pine needles, and preserved by the smoke from the cooking fire below. Here Li Zhiwu's father had kept the portion of the household's wealth that he had inherited or accumulated working as a porter along the salt trading route that passed through Zhizuo. Li Zhiwu also hid treasures here: some old titles to land his family had once owned, some silver jewelry his mother had passed on to him (in lieu of passing it to a daughter). In other households, attics were residences of a variegated class of inherited spirits of the professions: teachers set up tablets representing Confucius there; carpenters erected shelves for Lu Ban, the ancient founder of their art; hunters made offerings to effigies for hunting spirits (*luubanè*); and diviners kept their spirit familiars (*mɛlònè*). Like the inherited wealth kept in attics, the skills these spirits represented were passed from father to son. In contrast to the ancestral effigies in the room below, cast away as their kinship with the living grew distant, attic spirits were repositories for an undecaying patrilineage.

Daily, Li Zhiwu climbed the ladder to his attic to bring down a bit of meat or fat and the next day's portion of rice. His decisions about daily consumption were informed by the science of human metabolism that had guided collective management. Using a piece of chalk on the wall boards, he added up 1 kilo per day for the laboring bodies of his household and ½ kilo for his youngest daughter and the elderly kinswoman. Li Qunhua never entered the attic when Li Zhiwu was around or when I was present. Other men in Zhizuo objected strenuously to women passing above their heads, especially in a room where food was cooked and eaten. The pollution associated with menstruation and birthing, one man explained, passed from women's bodies downward, through their feet. He didn't care about all that, Li Zhiwu said, and it wasn't his objection that kept his wife out of the attic. "These women are afraid of attics," he declared. His wife refused to cut or handle any meat. "These women are afraid of offending life. They hide inside the house when you slaughter a pig, and they won't even help butcher or chop the pork." "It's mostly women who want to bear children who pay attention to these things," Li Qunhua said. "They want to make life; they want to give birth; they shouldn't kill or offend life. But for me it has become a habit." She let Li Zhiwu control and apportion the household's grain, she admitted, because she didn't like walking around in the attic, among the dead pigs' heads and slabs of meat.

While collectivization had transferred control of the economies of spending, eating, and keeping seed into the hands of male managers, the economic policies of the reform era further weakened the authority of senior women over their households' practical affairs. During the Mao era, the state had encouraged hempen cloth production in upland Yunnan by supporting hemp prices in relation to prices of grain and cotton. Already a significant source of cash for most Zhizuo residents before Liberation, hempen cloth production was crucial to every family's survival between 1952 and 1978. Hemp production was never fully collectivized: production teams grew hemp and distributed it to member households depending on their number of able-bodied women. Women processed, spun, and wove hemp individually and sold cloth or thread to the collective. In most households, the senior woman kept the resulting cash on her person or near her bed, using it to buy extra grain, cotton cloth, and other necessities and distributing it to other household members. As the reform era began, the state raised grain prices (in 1978) and then instituted floating prices for hemp and hempen cloth (in 1980). As a result, hemp lost 33 percent of its value in relation to grain between 1978 and 1981. By 1981, most women in Zhizuo had abandoned hempen cloth production.[27] Searching for new means to generate cash, men in Zhizuo began to harvest timber illegally from the mountainsides, sawing it by hand into boards, which they hauled by mule to the lowlands for sale. Though some men turned over the cash they generated to their wives and mothers, most I surveyed did not. They spent it on alcohol and gambling or saved it to build tombs for their parents or houses for themselves or their sons.

By the time household cultivation was revived in 1980, then, houses and the gendered relations they helped sustain had been thoroughly transformed. Most men made use of the sacrosanct space of the attic, redolent with patrilineal associations and difficult for women to access, to capture control of grain. In this, they were encouraged by the state. With few exceptions, a household's senior able male was designated as the official household head (Ch. *huzhu*),[28] who served as a liaison to local authorities and as their arm of intervention in family life. Household heads were responsible to the state to oversee this basic level of production and resource management. This responsibility and the attic's associations with patrilineal inheritance coincided to give senior males like Li Zhiwu the feeling of a natural right to manage the daily economies of their households. In Li Zhiwu's house, the values once associated with the granary reinforced the gendered antiphony between the attic and the room below, as Li Qunhua avoided the attic to save herself from contact with dead meat and its "offense to life." In this transaction, Li Qunhua and other senior women lost a space dedicated to nurturing the values of feminine reproductive capacity.

In her pathbreaking study of gender and power in rural North China, Ellen Judd argues that informal relations of power in daily life and minute operations of state power intersected in the reform era to produce a social field profoundly fractured along the lines of gender (1994, 250). Households, officially defined, became the foundational level of production, to which land was allocated and in which labor was managed, opening control of the basic resources of the political economy to "customary andocentry." Making senior males the persons through whom households and the state hierarchy interacted, a diffuse state power revitalized and reinforced the pervasive devaluation of women and the deeply gendered asymmetry of power that had long permeated the cultural field. Domestic space in Zhizuo provided resources for gendered social relations that diverged substantially from those of the North China villages that Judd studied. Before 1956, many senior women had wielded resources like the granary and *lòhò* to control their households' practical affairs; even during the collective period, most were able to retain substantial influence over the value that women in their households produced by working hemp. The cumulative effect of state interventions in households in the collectivist and reform periods was to selectively disable such resources that favored the authority of senior women and fortify those that favored that of senior men. In this process, the gendered asymmetries of state power did not merely reflect and encourage a "customary andocentry"; they actively reshaped the foundations of gender relations. State power reconfigured relations nurtured in upstream rooms to resemble more closely the andocentric gender relations that were the norm in most of rural China.

Conclusion

Houses were practiced, conceived, and lived as technologies for producing differential social relations. The poetry, rituals, and built space out of which houses were fashioned rarely allowed any position or relation to rest securely in itself. Each took form within an intersection of relational differentials that opened it up toward another, inflected it with the attributes of another, or proffered to it the image of another. These transactions brought forth possibilities for envisioning a house as a dense and unified condensation of social relations. Ancestral effigies and the myth of the gourd house encoded two among many such visions: in ancestral effigies, relations between spouses and between cross-siblings were woven together into miniature house forms; in the gourd house, a dream of cross-sibling unity absorbed all social differences into a single, self-sufficient house form that stood in for society as a whole. Each such dream of unity was a foundation for further generative relations: the fertile energies condensed in ancestral effigies nurtured household reproduction; the union of brother and sister in the gourd house repopulated the world.

Such dreams of unity emerged vividly in house representations that confronted loss, such as the mourning song quoted at the beginning of this chapter (fragment 3.1). That song offers a nostalgic vision of a stable, nourishing unity, a family seated around a fire pit "like toadstools around a pine." This unity is framed by the empty places where the mourned one once slept or ate. The song goes on to compare the wooden door frame within which the deceased mother once stood to the empty frame of her body:

3.8

bamboo hat frames	mo pé là ho kʼa
wooden door frames	sị pe á dù kʼa
mother is an empty frame	su mo kʼa mú do jɔ
no heart in her abdomen	cì ka ni m vɔ̀
no breath in her torso	gɔ ka cɔ n hò du̱ va

Through the empty frame of her mother's corpse, the singer views the long history of relations that have fixed her own position in the upstream room. The song laments each such relation, beginning with the birth of the singer and her siblings:

3.9

mother gave birth to a son	su mo zò ho t'ù
she gave birth to a daughter	su mo né ho t'ù
her womb at the arrow's point	cè pæ che t'è do
her head in heaven's hands	wú ka mù ne do
in its hands	do ne ho
mother gave birth beside the bed	mo jɔ né ho ko tɔ che
bore a daughter beside the bed	né ho ko tɔ che
as a dog grabs a bone	á nò wù kɔ kæ̧
father grabbed his son	p'ò jɔ zò ve kæ̧
father lifted his daughter	p'ò jɔ né te kæ̧
wrapped her in his apron	né kæ̧ p'à pí t'ɔ tu lɔ
as honeybees love the bitter herb	yi k'ù bò ni ga
your love sprang forth	ni ni kà du lɔ ga
as a hawk spots a chick	tsɔ mɔ ye zò ma
as a bat spies the torch	bæ̀ tí à do ma
you beheld your daughter emerge	né ho ma du næ
beheld your son emerge	zò ho ma du næ
mother's bitter love sprang forth	su mo shó ni kà du lɔ ga

Continuing, the song catalogues each significant passage in the mother's relation with her daughter. Three days after the birth, with no hen to kill for the naming ceremony, the mother borrowed a name at a horse market. She was "so poor she wiped her daughter's shit with her hands, so poor her trousers were in strips, so poor her back was in tatters." She bore her daughter on her back and made dolls of *lȩ* leaves for her to play with. As the child grew, she learned to herd and then to farm, and the granary gradually filled with grain, the courtyard with chicks, the corral with goats, and the barn with oxen. The house became a sea of wealth, and the mother began to age: "unwilting flowers of the ghost world, we never thought mother might wilt; wild persimmons of the forest, we never thought she might drop; mother's carrying strap has snapped, her breath has faltered." Contemplating her mother's empty place takes the mourner through each of the social relations that had nurtured her passages through a house's ranked spaces. As she sings, she shifts points of view from that of her mother bearing the child, to her father watching it emerge "as a hawk spies a chick, as a bat spies the torch," to that of herself and her siblings watching their parents wilt and die. Through the frame of her mother's empty place in the sequence of sibling union, parental union, and descent, the singer gains partial access to each position in the upstream room.

This representation of the mutually enveloped and enveloping frames (*k'a*) of house and body made an appeal similar to that of the *mæho* ritual. Both looked to a moment when, from within a particular, circumscribed position, a person found all the social relationships that circulated through a household available to her—a moment when nothing was out of reach. If loss emptied these frames, it also gave people opportunities to take on, partially and imperfectly, the perspective of another. In this way, houses could be a kind of material foundation for an inclusive ethics through which their inhabitants could share each other's burdens and responsibilities, despite the many differences of power and perspective that divided them. Chapters 4 and 5 show how the intricate differentials of household space served as models for a larger house, the territory of Zhizuo's rotating headmanship system. In memories of this *ts'ici* system, a box of ancestral bones circulated through the valley, expanding relations of descent and affinity to figure this place as a house, retrieving the dream of unity expressed in laments, ancestral effigies, and gourd houses on a larger scale. As we shall see, this dream eventually gave birth to a deeply conflicted ethics of inclusion and mutual responsibility with which Zhizuo residents responded to the pressures and devastations of the socialist state.

CHAPTER FOUR

The Valley House

In 1953, a team of ethnographers, taking part in a nation-wide ethnic identification project, visited the village of Yijichang in Yongren County.[1] Their report analyzed patterns of land use, relations of exploitation, and local government structure in this area before Liberation and identified its people as members of the newly constituted Yi nationality. The pre-Liberation local state hierarchy, the report stated, had here, as elsewhere, been an instrument of direct oppression, designed to extract wealth from the people through taxes and corvée labor. In the late Qing and Republican years, the first level of this oppressive hierarchy had been an institution unique to this part of Yunnan. It was called a *huotou,* and it administered a small group of Yi villages. Of the Yijichang *huotou,* the report declared:

> It is said that in Yijichang in the late Qing and early Republic, the positions of *huotou* and so forth [in the hierarchy of local government] were dominated by local tyrants and evil gentry. After the county reform [in 1925], corvée and grain taxes gradually increased . . . and the *huotou* seized every opportunity to blackmail the people. After 1935, corvée and grain taxes grew ever deeper. . . . The suffering of poor laborers and peasants was extremely heavy. Each change or continuity at this basic level of the puppet state followed its need to oppress and exploit the peasants. (YSB 1986, 109)

In the 1990s, thirty years had passed since the last remnants of *huotou* in northern Yunnan had been dismantled. Yet in Zhizuo, a long day's walk from Yijichang, recollections of the *huotou* remained at the heart of a prolonged and complex struggle over collective memory. Party and government cadres in Yongren still held to the view that the several *huo-tou* systems in the county had been the lowest level of an oppressive administrative hierarchy dominated by "local tyrants and evil gentry," their chief purpose the extraction of corvée, taxes, and military conscripts from an unwilling populace. But many in Zhizuo vigorously protested this characterization. They spoke of their *huotou* (called the *ts'ici* in their own language) as their ancestors' cleverest invention, designed to insulate their community from the worst caprices of local officials and state agencies.

In northern Yunnan, *huotou* were found where concentrations of those who spoke the Central dialect of Yi resided along important trading routes or in close proximity to administrative centers. Officials and soldiers who traveled through these areas frequently descended on relatively affluent households to demand their most lavish hospitality. In mountain communities, where even the wealthiest had few resources, such hospitality could well ruin the host. *Huotou* systems apportioned the responsibility for hosting outsiders, rotating it yearly among the community's most prosperous households. Host households also took on other tasks, such as feeding and clothing prisoners, delivering letters, repairing roads, burying unclaimed corpses, and sponsoring communal agricultural rituals. As Zhizuo residents remembered it in the 1990s, their *ts'ici* system had drawn them into a domestic community similar to that of a house. It had made a common residence of their mountainous landscape, created a common ancestry for people of diverse origins, involved them in common financial and ritual enterprises, and passed on techniques for dealing with the powerful and troublesome visitors that any house must occasionally entertain. While their *ts'ici* could not diminish the force of the local state's demands, it could at least distribute them evenly among those best able to bear them.

Despite harsh judgments of the *ts'ici* by ethnographers and land reform work teams, the socialist government did not immediately do away with it after gaining control of northern Yunnan. The new township government arrogated the host household's administrative responsibilities, but it allowed Zhizuo residents to continue to elect *ts'ici* each year and to use the harvest of the land in their ancestral trust to support public rituals. Most of this land was collectivized in 1956, but a portion of about 1 *mu* continued to rotate with the title of *ts'ici* among production teams. This diminished *ts'ici* system lasted until 1965, when political activists seized its central emblem and polluted it with menstrual blood. In the years that followed, it became clear to many in Zhizuo that this act had transformed a family of apical ancestors into a cabal of "wild ghosts." During the Cultural Revolution, these ghosts methodically killed off those who had governed Zhizuo through the disastrous Great Leap famine, and they continued to prey on cadres and peasants through the early 1990s. Chapters 6, 7, and 8 show how people used stories of these depredations to distribute responsibility for the wounds and losses suffered in the Great Leap Forward and the Cultural Revolution between the imagined state, with its distant centers of power, and their own neighbors and kin. Talk of the *ts'ici* ghosts, I argue, helped people reconstitute an agonistic sense of community in the face of their own shared responsibility for past violence.

This chapter and the next set the stage for this discussion by representing a vision of the *ts'ici* system that ritual experts and members of former host households presented to me, an outsider. Their specialized knowledge was at the heart of struggles over memories of the *ts'ici* after 1965. It gave such memories continuity and coherence, kept alive the possibility that the *ts'ici* might be reconstructed should local officials accede, and created a foundation for the politically sensitive claim that the area once administered by the *ts'ici* should be the territory of a distinct nationality. This knowledge formed the ground on which many in Zhizuo continued to nurture the ideal of a single, embracive domestic community, despite the deep conflicts that divided them.

This chapter explores talk of the responsibilities, ideal moral character, proscribed activities, and prescribed compensation of host households and their staff of five. Such accounts employed metaphors of procreation and moral ideas about speech, sexuality, and sociability to create an imagined unity under the former *ts'ici* for all who claimed to be Lòlop'ò. They made use of extended temporal and spatial homologies to associate the *ts'ici* with procreative force. In temporal terms, they drew parallels between giving birth and nurturing children and the communal work of farming rice to pay for the *ts'ici*'s social and ritual obligations; in spatial terms, they compared the bounded territory of Zhizuo to the *ts'ici*'s house, centered on a productive unity of ancestral spouses and troubled by a crowd of honored but potentially threatening guests. As Lévi-Strauss pointed out, house images frequently display the capacity to integrate diverse or mutually contradictory ideas and principles (1983, 1984; see also Carsten and Hugh-Jones 1995). Following this suggestion, I argue that recollections of the *ts'ici* system used a series of interrelated house images—a reliquary box, the *ts'ici*'s house, the houselike valley—to fashion an inclusive domestic unity imagined to embrace all

Zhizuo residents and to exclude from household matters the powerful outsiders the system ostensibly served.

Re-Membering a Corpse

My own position as an outsider with putatively powerful connections to state agencies inevitably seemed to bring to mind the *ts'ici* system for my hosts in Zhizuo. The first to mention it to me was Qi Degui, a schoolteacher in his late forties. During my first week in Zhizuo, Qi Degui offered me a guest room in the elementary school. "Had you come before Liberation, we would have carried your luggage, feasted you every day, and gotten you drunk every night," he told me. "Now I can only give you a hard bed and a bowl of stale rice." Qi Degui was a frustrated intellectual. Although his education in the county's only middle school had been cut short by the Cultural Revolution, he still dreamed of scholarly accomplishment. He showed me his pride and joy: an article he had published in a single-issue journal on the history of Yongren County. Titled "The *huotou* system of the Yi of Zhizuo," it succinctly outlined the process for choosing a *ts'ici* household, sketched out the responsibilities once shared by this household and its staff of aides, and briefly mentioned the decline and demise of the *ts'ici* system. During my first weeks in Zhizuo, Qi Degui showed up at my schoolhouse room every morning to lecture me on the *ts'ici*. I had come to study religion? If I wanted to understand this nationality's religion, he said, I must begin by studying the *ts'ici*.

As my circle of acquaintances expanded, I found that my difficulties in explaining my purpose in Zhizuo often dissolved when I mentioned the *ts'ici*. Many regarded it as the feature that made Zhizuo Lòlop'ò noteworthy, the most obvious object of interest for an outsider. "Though it was destroyed a long time ago," a man of Qi Degui's generation asserted, "the *ts'ici* still exists in people's hearts. It is the heart of our nationality." A budding entrepreneur, who would have made an excellent candidate for *ts'ici*, was more explicit: "If the Communist Party were serious about restoring national customs, it would allow us to reinstate the *ts'ici*. After all, it is our nationality's most important custom." In the 1980s, the post-Mao regime had granted new legitimacy to such terms as "nationality" (Ch. *minzu*), "nationality religion" (Ch. *minzu zongjiao*), and "nationality customs" (Ch. *minzu fengsu*). By the early 1990s, some in Zhizuo had begun to assert that their official nationality should be Lòlop'ò rather than Yi. Such claims were always founded on statements about the old *ts'ici*. The territory of the "Lòlop'ò nationality" was the region that had been governed by the *ts'ici*, its language was the dialect spoken in this region, and its distinguishing "religion" and "customs" were the rituals once associated with the *ts'ici*.

Most adults in Zhizuo were happy to talk about the *ts'ici* in these general terms, but they deferred specific questions to a small group of "experts." These were men (and a few women) who had served as *ts'ici*, whose parents had served as *ts'ici*, or who had aided *ts'ici* with their ritual duties. In time, I had frequent conversations with these elderly people, who seemed to share the conviction that if Zhizuo had anything to offer a scholarly outsider, it was quite naturally knowledge of the *ts'ici* and the ritual obligations associated with it. In the biographies of many, the *ts'ici* system and its destruction had played an extraordinary, sometimes cataclysmic, role.

I came to know three of these experts particularly well. Li Yong's parents had served as *ts'ici* in 1929, when he was a child of nine. He recalled with relish the fanfare generated by officials and soldiers who came and went from his parents' courtyard. His father had belonged to a lineage of ritualists on whom other *ts'ici* relied to perform a cycle of communal rituals. In adolescence, Li Yong had trained with his father to learn the chants and gestures that gathered health and fertility from the surrounding valleys and towns and deposited them in the jewel-bright valley of Zhizuo. Li Yong considered Liberation to have been the abrupt finale of the *ts'ici* system. He refused to talk about the institution's post-1950 existence, saying only that it had been "hollow" (*kɔ*), devoid of meaning or interest. Li Yong was also diffident about his personal history, but I learned its bare outline from others. In the 1950s and 1960s, he had been assigned to a special production team reserved for rich peasants and former ritualists, who were given the worst food and the most difficult and degrading labor. In 1966, as the Cultural Revolution began, he was imprisoned and beaten daily by Red Guards for being a purveyor of superstition. Eloquent, arrogant, and alcoholic, Li Yong was proud of his precise and beautiful ritual chants. He insisted that he alone of all ritualists in Zhizuo remembered full and correct chants for the *ts'ici* spirits. For more than two months, he spent several afternoons a week with me, recording and explicating chants and outlining "rules and procedures" (*cìpe mope*). Perhaps more than any of my other informants, Li Yong seemed to regard the *ts'ici* as a closed system of rules, poetry, and gestures, a bounded body of knowledge that could be passed on in full to an apprentice. After we recorded and discussed the last of his chants, he said he had nothing more to impart, and our discussions of the *ts'ici* ended, though we continued to meet to talk about other topics.

Qi Bao'en was in his mid-eighties, about ten years older than Li Yong. He was the gentlest of men, with a subtle wit. When I knew him, he could no longer navigate Zhizuo's steep paths, and we met in his courtyard or sat in the sun against a wall by his house. Qi Bao'en too was an accomplished ritualist, of another lineage patronized by *ts'ici*. His family had been classified as poor peasants during the land reform movement. In the decades preceding Liberation, service as *ts'ici* had been reserved for the wealthiest; in the 1950s, only those who were secure in the political legitimacy afforded by the label "poor peasant" or "agricultural laborer" volunteered for service. Qi Bao'en had served as *ts'ici* in 1954. In the years that followed, his household avoided the persecutions that wealthier former *ts'ici* suffered, and his son advanced to a position in the township government. Although Qi Bao'en himself was not persecuted during the Cultural Revolution, this son committed suicide. Qi Bao'en retained a living commitment to the rituals of the *ts'ici* system, a commitment forced on him by the ghosts the *ts'ici* spawned after its destruction. In 1980, his household contracted a parcel of land abutting the ancestral trust land. When the wild ghosts of the *ts'ici* began to kill off those who dared plant this land, Qi Bao'en protected his family by secretly propitiating its guardian spirit (the Lòhə). In the early 1990s, village cadres, caught up in a political crisis engendered by these killings, began to pay him to continue his propitiations.

The youngest expert on the *ts'ici* system was Qi Chun, in his late forties. His parents had been Zhizuo's last *ts'ici* couple, in 1964 and early 1965. Labeled "poor peasants," they had done well: Qi Chun's elder brother, Qi Lin, had graduated from middle school and become chief administrator of the People's Court in the county capital. In early 1965, under intense pressure from a work team of the Socialist Education campaign, Qi Lin had denounced his parents as the ringleaders of a "superstitious sect." This act quickly led to the final demise of the *ts'ici* system. Qi Chun kept the hempen costume his father had worn as *ts'ici,* and he donned it when an illness he attributed to the *ts'ici* ghosts flared up. His neighbors said that among the symptoms of his periodic possession was a compulsion to talk through the formal cycle of rituals the *ts'ici* had once sponsored. Qi Chun scoffed at this, but he admitted that he did like to talk about the *ts'ici* system to anyone who would listen. In our conversations, he carefully described the ritual cycle, beginning with rites performed at the new year and proceeding methodically through the calendar.

In remembering the *ts'ici* system of the 1930s and 1940s, individuals such as Li Yong, Qi Bao'en, and Qi Chun exhibited a "virtuosity in self description" that, as Webb Keane (1995, 102) notes, seems to characterize societies in which ritual oratory and formal discourse are strongly valued. Much of their speech about the *ts'ici* was formalized, consisting of lists of rules and procedures, poetic phrases from ritual chants, and reflexive exegetical commentary. Like many anthropologists blessed with highly articulate informants, I often listened to this discourse with a sense of unease. It seemed to refer to a timeless, bounded world that could have had no real existence in the violent, conflict-ridden, and rapidly changing context of early twentieth-century China. With only a few exceptions, my ritualist teachers did not admit to disagreement about ritual procedures or the roles of the *ts'ici* household and its staff; and, in the face of their authority, others rarely raised alternative views. In this talk, the *ts'ici* system took on a textlike legibility, eminently readable but divorced from the confusion and ambiguity of daily life. Still, the more I listened to these experts, the more evident it became that their passion for talking about this institution—and especially for talking about it with an outsider—did not emerge from simple nostalgia for a more ordered past. Discussions of the *ts'ici* were often occasions for other kinds of talk. Each of these individuals frequently dropped into their lists of rules or descriptions of rituals certain oblique references to the wounds and losses they and their families had suffered in the state campaigns that had shaped rural life over the past four decades.

It was not until many months into my stay that I began to understand the crucial connection between this talk of a lost past and the present concerns of people in Zhizuo. My circle of acquaintances widened, and I was invited to occasions such as funerals and exorcisms that people tried to shield from the eyes of most officials from outside. I fell ill with hepatitis, left Zhizuo for three months, and found on my return that many people took my reappearance as a sign of loyalty to my friends there. Perhaps crucially, I returned alone, no longer accompanied by the young research assistants from my sponsoring agency, whose presence had made some of my informants uneasy. People began to tell me, piecemeal, stories of the *ts'ici* system's destruction and the ghosts it had engendered. If recollections of the *ts'ici* of the 1930s and 1940s displayed the crystalline symmetry of a dead form, I realized, this was because it was, emphatically, dead. It was a corpse, and talk about it was arranged with the same care given to aligning the limbs of a corpse in a coffin, shrouding it with new hempen and cotton clothing, and ritually smoothing away the blemishes of pain, hunger, wounds, tears, and grief that life had given it. But this corpse had not died well. It had been violently killed and, like the many souls killed by hunger just a few years before its death, it had returned. Stories of this return inflected nearly every aspect of the complex relationship between this always reemerging community and the socialist state.

The violently dead were double beings. On the one hand, they returned as wild ghosts to afflict their descendants with pain and death; on the other, like any other ascendant, they were released as ancestral souls, gathered from mountain slopes, and given a place at the bed's head, where they became sources of fertility and domestic unity. Memories of the *ts'ici* system of the 1930s and 1940s were similarly double. On the one hand, they made possible ghost stories through which Zhizuo residents patched together a conflicted common sense of their place as a living community in the landscape of the socialist nation. On the other hand, these recollections preserved a compact, formal diagram of social relations, like an ancestral effigy, which, it was hoped, might be a source of health and unity for a domestic community. In both senses, talk of the *ts'ici* amounted to a powerful strategy of self-representation. The *ts'ici* had once been a means of mobilizing common productive resources to represent Zhizuo as a coherent, united, houselike community both to its members and to powerful outsiders. Thirty years after the *ts'ici*'s demise, people in Zhizuo reengaged this strategy. Their talk about the *ts'ici* was an effort to retrieve control over collective self-representation from the state agencies who had been charged with promoting and distributing the official revitalization of "nationality customs" and "nationality religion."

Those Who Can Bear It

In the last two decades of the Republic, about fifteen hundred people lived in Zhizuo's villages and hamlets. The largest villages formed a rough oval around the central valley, with its stretch of irrigated rice paddy land. A footpath, paved with stone in the steepest places, followed the stream into this valley from the south, skirted the large villages on the sunny side, and exited through a steep canyon to the north. This path linked two county centers, the towns of Dayao and Yongren (see Figure 4.1).

A variety of armies traveled these mountains, forcibly recruiting soldiers and requisitioning grain, money, livestock, and corvée labor. Between 1915 and 1929, warlord armies from Sichuan and Yunnan passed through the tiny county of Yongren on Zhizuo's northern border at least eight times, requisitioning nearly 2 million yuan and grain worth over 800 Ch. *liang* of silver. The People's Liberation Army passed through twice on its Long March, attacking and briefly occupying the town of Dayao early in 1935 and returning in 1936. In 1938, the Burma Road became South China's only conduit for supplies from the West to keep alive the Guomindang's resistance against the Japanese. This road passed far to the south of Zhizuo, but a branch road was built through Dayao and Yongren Counties to link the Burma Road to the Guomindang bases in Sichuan. The heavy military, administrative, and civilian traffic on this road often spilled onto the footpath through Zhizuo. In the 1940s, the Nationalist government's forced military conscription bore heavily on both counties, and groups of soldiers passed through Zhizuo to hunt down youths who sought to evade the draft. Finally, in 1948 and 1949, the Communist Party underground carried out a series of armed rebellions in the area, and "Communist bandits," Guomindang regulars, and militia units fought pitched battles in Zhizuo and the surrounding mountains (CYZZ 1993, 148–151).

In addition to this formidable military traffic, local officials and police stopped in Zhizuo to oversee conscription and tax collection, recruit corvée labor, settle disputes, arrest criminals, or rest on the road between county towns. Zhizuo was located in Dayao's northernmost district (*qu*). In the period of instability that preceded the fall of the Qing dynasty in 1911, an ethnically Han merchant named Xia had seized control of this district and had given himself the title of Ch. *tusi. Tusi,* who were hereditary officials in regions inhabited by non-Han peoples, maintained varying degrees of independence from provincial and central state bureaucracies.[2] Until 1949, the Xia family controlled their mountainous realm through the Ch. *bao-jia* system of local administration.[3] Under this system, the district was divided into units called *bao,* for which the Xia family selected Ch. *baozhang* to conscript soldiers and collect taxes and levies. Zhizuo formed a single *bao,* and its *baozhang* appointed a Ch. *jiazhang* (until 1938, Ch. *luzhang*) to take responsibility for each small village (or each neighborhood, in the larger villages). The Xia family allowed

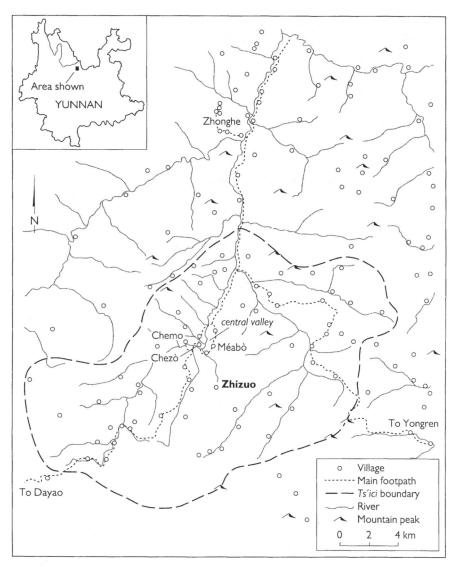

Figure 4.1 The Zhizuo *ts'ici* and surrounding area.

baozhang to retain about 2 Ch. *dan* of the tax grain they collected as a yearly salary, while *jiazhang* drew pittances of about .26 *dan* a year for their thankless task of convincing their fellow villagers to pay their taxes (YSB 1986, 109). In the 1940s, the power of the Xia family in Zhizuo was rivaled by that of the *bao*'s militia commander, Luo Guotian, who sold guns to men in Zhizuo and organized them into a formidable fighting force. Tensions with Luo Guotian, the pressing need to keep an eye on revenue collection, and Zhizuo's convenience as a rest stop on the road to the county capital frequently brought members of the Xia family to Zhizuo, with retinues of guards, servants, and runners.

Each year, Zhizuo residents selected a *ts'ici* household from among the community's most affluent families. The title of *ts'ici* rotated around the oval of villages in Zhizuo's central valley "toward the right hand" (counterclockwise), falling each year on a household in a different village. The most expensive and time-consuming obligation incurred by this household was to lodge, feed, and entertain the stream of soldiers, officials, police, merchants, and other influential visitors who walked the stone path through the valley. In addition, the host household and its staff of five maintained a prison cell for locals who were arrested for crimes or who were being held to await forcible conscription. The *ts'ici* carried letters from the district center to the next group of villages on the route to the county seat, maintained the stone footpath that made this route easier to travel, and buried all outsiders who died within Zhizuo and had no nearby kin. They managed a common fund, loaning it out each year to a family who, in lieu of interest, built a giant swing used in New Year's celebrations. Finally, the host household and its staff organized a yearly cycle of communal rituals intended to draw fertility, wealth, and good health into Zhizuo and drive away poverty and disease.

Unlike *baozhang* and militia commanders, host households in the *ts'ici* system were not appointed by the Xia family; they were elected by the community's most influential men. Foremost among these were the *baozhang* and, in the 1940s, the militia commander Luo Guotian. Representatives from the other relatively wealthy families of the area, *jiazhang* from each of the villages, and former *ts'ici* also participated. Two of Zhizuo's most affluent families had long identified themselves as Han. Despite their wide influence in the community, they were explicitly excluded from these meetings, which were open only to Lòlop'ò. This restriction applied also to the Xia family, who were Han and outsiders. The group of men met yearly on the lunar New Year day, as much of Zhizuo's population gathered in the courtyard of the previous year's host household to celebrate the transfer of the title of *ts'ici*. The outgoing *ts'ici* ushered these most important of his guests—between twenty and thirty in number—into the barn loft of his house. Cleared of hay and furnished with two low beds and a fire pit, this room was the cell kept to hold those arrested by agents of the local state. The *baozhang* and the militia commander took seats at the upper ends of the beds, and the others crowded in next to them. Those who did not wish to assert a claim of status or participate in the discussion squatted on the floor at the foot of the beds or near the door. The guests were served a meal of rice, meat, and alcohol, with service proceeding from the beds' heads to the door. They then reviewed the names of two households chosen the year before to serve as hosts for the next two years and added a third name to the list.

Because the title was to rotate around the valley "toward the right hand," households of only one village were considered for each year. Zhizuo residents insisted that the *ts'ici* household should have been free of deaths for the year previous to its service (except for miscarriages and deaths of infants without teeth). If the household scheduled for the following year had experienced a death, another choice was made. Households with widows or widowers of any generation were unacceptable. Most important, the household had to have a healthy, resident elderly couple who could take on the ritual duties of the *ts'ici*. This couple must have raised several children to adulthood and must have preserved the habit of wearing old-style Lòlop'ò clothing: hempen sandals rather than the more common straw ones, hempen shirts and trousers, and robes that buttoned down the side instead of the front. Finally, and crucially, the household had to be wealthy enough to bear the financial burdens of the *ts'ici*.

The formula "give it to those who can bear it [on their backs] or carry it [in their hands]" (*bù dù vé dù ká su t'è gò*) was supposed to guide the selection of the *ts'ici*. Every year, the host household drew an income of about 30 *dan* of grain from a 10-*mu* parcel of land that rotated with the *ts'ici*, but it often expended as much as 60 *dan* of grain and forty to fifty goats. The hundreds of soldiers and officials who traveled through the valley could plunge the host household into serious debt. For this reason, prospective *ts'ici* were said to be desperate to evade the responsibility. A staff member from the outgoing *ts'ici*—the *lòra*, chosen for his ability to speak and entertain—attended the meeting to persuade candidates to accept the position. Face to face with the most powerful members of the community, most of those selected found themselves accepting. Yet after the meeting, they would often seek a patron among the meeting's most influential members; the militia commander Luo Guotian and a certain former *baozhang* were said to have been favorites. Borrowing from kin and calling in their debts, the newly selected would offer the patron a massive bribe of money and livestock, following this up with a chicken or young goat every month for a year. If the bribes were sufficient, the patron would speak for the family at the next year's meeting, claiming that its situation had changed and that it could no longer bear the burden. A daughter of a former *ts'ici* commented that having one's name mentioned at the meeting might easily mean ruin, either from the expenses of the *ts'ici* or from the bribes paid to avoid it.

Though few willingly took on the burden of the *ts'ici*, this service compensated a household's members with prestige they could obtain in no other way. Selection was public affirmation that a household had attained the most enviable of states. Relations between its eldest husband and wife were harmonious and fruitful, attended by neither deaths nor quarrels; they had produced several sons and daughters, and their fertility had blossomed into wealth. A passage from a mortuary lament, in which a daughter sings of happy times before her parents' deaths, describes this ideal state of fortune:

4.1

like rings on a buffalo's horns	wú nì k'ɔ pé̱ zò
our fields widened	kà dù mɪ pé̱ wo
our pastures expanded	ló dù mi pé̱ wo
every kind of livestock grazed for us	jí lu jè ja ga
every kind of grain grew for us	kà lu tso ja ga
our sons raised a sea of wealth	zò ho né yi t'ù jɔ ga
our daughters filled the granary	né ho lò je ka̱ jɔ ga
our bowls overflowed with grain	tsò mi sɿ zò jɔ du̱ lɔ
our cups filled up with broth	dɔ mi ló zò jɔ du̱ lɔ

Those who selected such a household expected that, if it fulfilled its ritual obligations correctly, its harmonious productivity would spread throughout Zhizuo. Having served as *ts'ici* also made one a lifelong member of the inner circle that controlled the *ts'ici* system and, many insisted, ensured a couple a long and healthy life.

In some ways, Zhizuo's *ts'ici* system bears comparison to Mesoamerican cargo systems. Eric Wolf once suggested that service in such systems tended to impede the mobilization of wealth as capital within a community in comparison to capital mobilization in the outside world (1955, 458). This suggestion stimulated a debate about whether cargo service tended to level a community economically by creating an incentive for the most prosperous to expend their wealth within the community or to stratify it socially by creating avenues for the rich to accumulate social prestige.[4] While Zhizuo residents' reminiscences are not sufficiently detailed to decide whether the *ts'ici* system impeded the mobilization of wealth as capital, they do allow for some informed speculation.

Of the four Zhizuo households classified as landlords during the land reform movement, one was Han and thus had been excluded from service, and another was in a hamlet far from the oval of large villages from which *ts'ici* were chosen. In the mid-1940s, the Han family opened a hostel in Zhizuo for travelers with mule trains. With its profits, the family purchased land to farm with hired labor and mules to haul salt, sugar, and opium, expanding its fortunes considerably. The two Lòlop'ò landlord households whose location made them eligible for *ts'ici* service were those of the militia commander Luo Guotian and a former *baozhang* whom Zhizuo residents considered to be "gentry" (Ch. *shenshi*). These were the only households powerful enough to forestall their own selection as hosts in the *ts'ici* system, thereby avoiding the enormous drain on their resources that service would have entailed, and to receive flows of bribes from other families wishing to evade service. By the end of the 1940s, both of these households were heavily engaged in the salt, sugar, and opium trades, while most Zhizuo residents benefited from these trades only by hiring out as porters or muleteers. One might speculate that the *ts'ici* system helped free a few of the politically and militarily most influential to make use of Zhizuo's location along a trading route, even as it limited the capacity of many prosperous community members to mobilize their wealth for trade.

A Productive Embrace

The titles of *ts'ici* and *ts'icimo* (*ts'ici*'s wife) were granted to the household's eldest married couple. A staff of aides and other household members shielded this pair from the mundane duties of hosting visitors, carrying baggage and letters, guarding prisoners, and burying unclaimed corpses. The husband and wife were expected to live a life of quiet seclusion in the service of a group of ancestral spirits, the souls of a mythological family believed to have founded Zhizuo. This family was said to have been not Lòlop'ò but Líp'ò—Central dialect speakers who lived in the adjacent mountains. Each account of the *ts'ici* system included a tale about how these ancestors, a father and his sons, traveled every year from their home in the villages of Vèlí and Laba higher in the Baicaolin Mountains to Zhizuo's wide, pleasant valley in search of wild pigs. At the center of the valley was a marsh, where they drove the pigs into the mud to be clubbed to death. On one occasion, as Li Yong told this story, the father looked around him and liked what he saw:

> At that time, the forest was very thick, and water gushed and spurted from the spring down there. One of them dropped his knife sheath to drink water, and two rice grains rolled out. He shook more seeds out of the sheath. "Can one plow and plant in this place? It looks like a fine place to live. If this is a good place to plow and plant, let the heads of these rice plants grow as long as horses' tails; let the rats not eat them or the insects climb them; let them be truly excellent." After saying this, he sowed the seeds in three places.

Father and sons then went home. They returned nine months later to see (*hɔ*) the rice growing tall and thick, untouched by rats, birds, or insects. Understanding that this was indeed a fine place to live, they brought their families (*chì*, literally "houses") to settle. Initially, Li Yong said, all the obligations of the *ts'ici* fell on a single house in the center of Chemo called Ts'icizò, "little *ts'ici*." After several generations, as the numbers of visitors to the valley increased, this family found its burdens too heavy, and it created an ancestral trust of a large parcel of the valley's best land to rotate from village to village with the obligations of the *ts'ici*.

Upon their deaths, the father from Vèlí and Laba and his wife were united in two locations, one mobile, another fixed in the living landscape. The mobile site was a wooden reliquary box, passed with the title of *ts'ici* from one household to another. This box was rectangular, a little larger than a shoe box, with a protruding, scalloped rim on its lid (see Figure 4.2). It held, according to different accounts, two, six, or twelve ox, tiger, or human bones; a few seeds of buckwheat; six or twelve copper coins; and the legal title to the 10-*mu* ancestral trust that supplied the *ts'ici* household with its income. The box was shaped like the earth of Lòlop'ò mythology: a rectangular valley, surrounded by mountains (the lid's scalloped rim), beneath which were seeds, buried wealth, and the bones of ancestors.

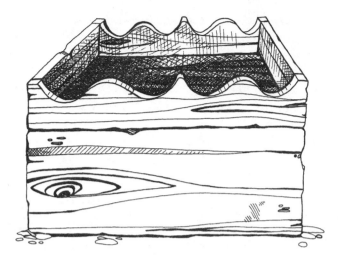

Figure 4.2 The reliquary box, shaped like the earth of Lòlop'ò mythology, which was passed with the title of *ts'ici* from one household to another each year.

The fixed resting place of the father and his wife was on a hilltop behind Chemo. Even in the 1990s, many mountain villages in Líp'ò and Lòlop'ò areas had preserved a patch of old-growth forest on a mountain slope behind and above the houses (CYZZ 1993, 137). One large, old tree was a Misi, said to govern the earth, weather, crops, animals, and all other living things in the area around the village. Others were sometimes Mijù (or Mitsɿ), the spirit of "earth veins," which governed weather; Shɿmògù (or Amùt'anè), a lightning spirit; and Lebùnè, a hunting spirit. Properly called Agàmisimo, "great earth spirit behind the house," Zhizuo's Misi embodied the souls of the founding ancestral couple. It inhabited a giant pine tree on the peak of a hill several hundred yards higher than Chemo's highest house but much lower than the surrounding mountains. This tree was separated from the dense forest around it by a low stone wall. From the top of this hill, Agàmisimo could survey the entire central valley of Zhizuo, although its influence was said to extend much further, to all the villages and hamlets of the *ts'ici*.

The souls of this founding couple's children inhabited other places in the valley. Ritualists disagreed as to the sex of these children; some claimed, for instance, that the eldest was female, others that it was male. As spirits, however, all were double gendered, a spousal pair, bound together in permanent conjugal union, like an ancestral effigy. The eldest child and his or her spouse (Lòhə) occupied a small round stone beside the ancestral trust fields. This spirit was propitiated yearly, when rice seedlings were transplanted into the ancestral trust land. Another couple (Lɔmælòhə, or "Lòhə at the river's tail") resided in a small stone shaped "like a little person," or fetus, curled up inside a close, stone shelter just below and outside the valley. The *ts'ici* sponsored propitiations for this spirit whenever drought threatened the rice. A third (Cha) rested on a small wooden shelf within the doorway of a private house in Chemo and was propitiated yearly in the spring to counter the threat of epidemic disease. A fourth (Mijù) occupied a giant pine on a hilltop across the valley from Agàmisimo's tree and regulated the weather, especially on the valley's drought-prone eastern side. A fifth, no longer propitiated in the 1930s and 1940s, rested in another stone on the valley floor.

These spirits remained a lively conversational topic in the early 1990s. "Here's what some people say about Agàmisimo," Qi Degui once remarked. He and I were sitting outside the school gate, looking out toward Agàmisimo's hill and the village of Chemo before it, where the ever-diligent Li Zhidong was planting walnut trees. "He has a head, up there near the top of the hill, a stomach in the center of Chemo, and arms, legs, and feet down by the river. Families on the head, like the Pu family, produce lots of college students. Those who live on his stomach never go hungry. And people who live on his feet, like Li Zhidong, are always running about busy, wishing they were on the stomach or the head." Poking fun at Li Zhidong's industry, Qi Degui imagined Agàmisimo to be like the ox (or tiger) of Lòlop'ò mythology, distributed over the land at the creation of the world, his intestines becoming the rivers, his abdomen the seas, his hair the forests, his ribs the roads, his teeth the cliffs, his lice the goats, and his dandruff the sparrows.[5] Agàmisimo's body, sprawled out over the village of Chemo, could as well be said to cover all of Zhizuo, encompassing its spirit progeny like its own head, stomach, and feet.

Qi Haiyun, a man in his late twenties who was soon to become Zhizuo's Party secretary, used a different set of idioms to describe the relationship between Agàmisimo and Mijù, one of Agàmisimo's spirit progeny, who occupied a pine tree on the opposite hilltop:

> Mijù is over there on the shady side because he is only a branch of Agàmisimo. Agàmisimo sits where the sun shines first because he is like the king of a country. He governs Mijù and all the rest, including the little spirits at the mountain passes who are like customs officials guarding

the doors; you have to have their permission to pass, or things go badly for you.

But why are they on opposite sides?

It's like in a house, where older and younger generations don't sit together. Spirits are like that, too; if they sat together, they would be equal. Agàmisimo takes the best seat. Analyzing it with modern thought, we could say that Agàmisimo is like a township [Ch. *xiang*] government, and Mijù is an administrative village government [Ch. *cungongsuo*] in the township. Or, better, it's as though Mijù is the land-management office [Ch. *tudi guanlisuo*] of the township government: the territory they govern is the same, but Mijù has more specific duties. He manages the rain and the insect infestations, while Agàmisimo governs everything.

A body divided among head, stomach, and feet; a country with customs officials at the borders; a household where the elder generation takes the upstream seats; a township government organized bureaucratically into departments—each metaphor evokes an entity with a definite boundary, internally differentiated into organs encompassed by and subordinate to the whole. From its anchorage on the hill above Chemo, Agàmisimo's presence saturated the territory of Zhizuo to its boundaries.

Because Lòlop'ò actively forget their forebears after three generations, destroying ancestral effigies and keeping no written or oral genealogies, Agàmisimo did not participate directly in any line of descent. This founding ancestor was available to all who inhabited the territory it embraced. Many Lòlop'ò did imagine themselves to be descendants of the group of Líp'ò immigrants from higher in the Baicaolin Mountains—though without citing any genealogical evidence. But many speculated about other, more distant, origins, including ancient forebears from Nanjing[6] or more recent Han immigrants from Sichuan.[7] Still, only a few families who had insisted on their Han identity for generations could not add to these speculations the assertion that Agàmisimo was their own ancestor. When finer distinctions were made, they were based on residence rather than on genealogy. Thus, a group of households along the line of sight from Agàmisimo's giant tree to the valley's center claimed a particularly intimate relationship with the founding ancestors. They marked this intimacy at funerals with unfinished coffins rather than the black lacquered coffins used by most, and some suffered unusually at the hands of the ghosts created by the destruction of the *ts'ici*.[8] Despite such distinctions, however, no single family could assert exclusive rights to the inheritance bequeathed by these common founding ancestors: the titles, ancestral estate, and benefits of health and fertility associated with the *ts'ici* system. Like a bed's-head spirit in a house, Agàmisimo was the sign of a domestic unity that included all inhabitants in its sprawled and differentiated embrace.[9]

Agàmisimo's pine shared its hilltop with a tree of equal height and girth. In 1912, the year after the fall of the Qing dynasty, Agàmisimo's tree was struck by lightning. This was interpreted as an omen of disaster, acutely confirmed in the chaotic decades to come, and a claim by the lightning spirit Shìmògù on Agàmisimo and its descendants. As in other parts of China, death rituals in Zhizuo depicted an underworld modeled on the bureaucratic state.[10] Shìmògù was said to occupy the vastness of the empty sky, but it was also associated closely with the underworld bureaucracy. When, having consulted his written ledgers, the fearsome underworld king Yama (or Yàlǒwú) determined that someone was to die, he ordered Shìmògù to send down his police, Cánìshunì, to manacle the soul and escort it to the underworld. Zhizuo residents described these minions with precision—they carried manacles and chains exactly like those used by the men employed by the *baozhang* to capture youths for the Guomindang armies and lead them away to war. Lòlop'ò performed a brief ritual immediately after a death to plead with Shìmògù's hired hands to depart to the sky with their single captured soul and leave the living be. After the lightning strike of 1912, Zhizuo residents gave the pine beside Agàmisimo's to Shìmògù and began to initiate all offerings to Agàmisimo and his spirit progeny with a sacrifice to this spirit. Shìmògù was a permanent feature of the cosmos, present since the formation of sky and earth. But its claim on Agàmisimo was historical, associated with the fall of the Qing and the chaotic increase in demand for human fodder to swell warlord armies. Shìmògù's giant pine fissured Agàmisimo's unity at its source with a sign of the calamitous death that higher, bureaucratic powers could so easily bring. Always eating first at Agàmisimo's feasts, this spirit was a reminder that no living community could persist without paying these powers their due.

Warden, Speaker, and Bearer

Ritual experts spoke of the elderly *ts'ici* and *ts'icimo* primarily as servants of these ancestral spirits: hosts to the reliquary box and sponsors of the cycle of rituals for Agàmisimo and its spirit progeny. The union of this couple was imagined to enfold all of Agàmisimo's descendants, like the skin of that spirit's extended body or the walls of a parental household. Like the conjugal but asexual coupling of the founding ancestors, this union was a source of procreative force for all those it embraced. In service of this force, the *ts'ici* couple was expected to strictly avoid everything associated with their influential visitors from the lowlands. Instead of wearing cotton, they were to wear the hempen clothing thought to have been worn by the original ancestors. They had to eat and drink from wooden bowls and clay jugs rather than from factory-made ceramic bowls, and they could eat no meat of dogs, horses, cattle, or any animals that had died without being slaughtered, all of which were associated with lowland Han and considered filthy and insulting to ancestors. They could not drink anything but homemade wheat beer and were not allowed to smoke. They were to be restrained in speech, never referring to death, violence, or conflict; and they could speak no Chinese for their year of service. It was understood that, as an elderly couple, they would not sit or sleep on the same bed or have sex. The *ts'icimo* was required to be past menopause so that menstrual pollution would not compromise her ritual purity. And they were to be socially restrained, stepping outside their upstream room only rarely and letting their staff and other members of their household serve as intermediaries between themselves and their important guests.

Nevertheless, the household's influential visitors brought within its walls everything the *ts'ici* couple was constrained to avoid. A staff of kin and friends, selected by the *ts'ici* a few days after the lunar New Year (on the year's first day of the tiger), managed these threats. This staff had five positions: *bòjə, k'ələ, lòrə, fumo,* and *fuzò.* In the recollections of ritual experts and members of former *ts'ici* households, the prescribed duties and ideal personal qualities of these staff members exploited ideas about speech, sociability, sexuality, and procreation to manage the margins of the host household and negotiate the boundaries of the *ts'ici* territory. This staff protected the center of ancestral procreative force in Zhizuo by expediting the smooth passage of potentially threatening outsiders through and away.

Those who described the *ts'ici* system to me compared the *bòjə* to a prison warden. He helped the household with its least pleasant duties, which involved caring for prisoners arrested by the *tusi*'s guards or by police from the county town. In keeping with its role of host for troublesome guests, the *ts'ici* household kept, clothed, and fed all such prisoners until they were led out of the valley in chains. Prisoners were kept in a room in the barn loft, which was furnished with a pair of low beds, a strong lock, an iron collar, and chains. Most prisoners spent only a few days in this cell, since all serious cases were tried at the residence of the Xia *tusi* or in the county seat. Minor cases such as livestock theft and disputes over field boundaries were handled in the *ts'ici*'s courtyard. In such cases, the offended party made a formal complaint to the *baozhang*, who forwarded a written report to the *tusi*, who then decided whether to order a hearing. To conduct a hearing, the *tusi* traveled to Zhizuo and summoned the *baozhang* and the militia commander. After eating a full meal at the host household's expense, the *tusi* sent the *bòjə* to bring in both parties to the dispute. These individuals knelt in the courtyard while the *tusi* and the militia commander sat on the elevated porch to question them and deliver judgment. Zhizuo residents claimed that the host household paid the fees associated with hearings, though additional fees were probably exacted from the accused parties. In contrast to most agents of justice, some in Zhizuo maintained, the warden and the *ts'ici* treated prisoners as guests, feeding them adequately and neither beating nor cursing them. In the last decade of the Republic, many prisoners were local youths arrested in order to be forcibly conscripted into the Guomindang armies, and most of these young men would have had ties of kinship with both the warden and the host household.

Zhizuo residents recalled that the *ts'ici*'s cell was put to its final use in May 1949, after a battle with a "Communist bandit" named Ding Zhiping. According to official histories, Ding was a Communist Party member and a staff officer in the People's Liberation Army, serving in the Eighth Route Army. Six years previously, he had returned to his hometown in nearby Huaping County to begin underground work. By 1949, he had gathered an army of several hundred, which he called the People's Liberation Army, Western Yunnan Column. In March, he attacked the Huaping County town and then marched on Yongren. There, the numbers in Ding's column grew to more than ten thousand, as the Yongren militia and troops of sympathetic local military commanders from Sichuan and northern Yunnan joined it. From Yongren, the column divided to attack the northern Yunnan towns of Yuanmo and Dayao (CYZZ 1993, 190). Reports of the battle at Dayao that drifted to Zhizuo described it as a terrifying cataclysm, in which tens of thousands of Guomindang soldiers, accompanied by tanks and cannon, defeated Ding's army. Telling this story, Li Yong quoted a brief passage from a chant used to exorcise the ghosts of those who had died violently. The words of this passage refer to Ding's battle for Dayao, he said. (The first stanza of this fragment is in Chinese.)

4.2

Outside the north gate of Dayao town	Dayao xian bei men wai
outside the south gate	nan men wai
outside the east gate	dong men wai
outside the west gate	xi men wai
every day they shoot each other	pi ni pa lè la rò
every day they stab each other	pi ni cì le jɔ rò
go to where your stabbed friends are	ni cì chɔ̀ jɔ dù yi
go to where your slashed companions are	ni cì pe̱ jɔ dù yi
your best-loved friends are there	ni chè chɔ̀ nó ka jɔ
your best-loved companions are there	ni chè pe̱ nó ka jɔ
every day they stab each other	pi ni cì le jɔ
every day they knife each other	pi ni da lè jɔ
every day they die from gunshot wounds	pi ni pa lè sr̠ jɔ rò

More terrifying still, Ding's forces fled Dayao back toward Yongren on the mountain road that passed through Zhizuo. Ding and more than a hundred troops holed up in the massive new house of the militia commander Luo Guotian, threatening to burn it down if attacked. Unable to stomach the idea of his new house in ashes, Luo offered Ding peaceful passage out of Zhizuo. After the "Communist bandits" filed out his front door, Luo and his Zhizuo militia attacked them, killing more than twenty and sparing none of the wounded. For the next few months, Guomindang troops hunted those who had escaped through the surrounding hills, locking them up in the host household's prison cell until they could be taken to Dayao for punishment.

Stories of this battle were also the occasion for recollections of the host household's most onerous of duties, burying outsiders who died within Zhizuo's boundaries and who had no kin to care for their corpses. Ordinarily, such burials were the *bòjɔ*'s responsibility. Yet people in Zhizuo strongly believed that to handle the corpses of those who had died of violence was to incur the grave danger of violence or affliction descending on one's own head. After the battle with Ding Zhiping, the *bòjɔ* and the other staff members who ordinarily shielded the *ts'ici* from contact with outside, polluting influences hid in their homes while more than twenty corpses lay rotting in the sun. Finally, the *ts'ici* and his son dragged them one by one into a gully and buried them. For forty years after this incident, people passing this mass grave reported spotting the ghosts of Ding Zhiping's defeated army wandering headless about the rocks, with bullet holes in their bodies or bayonets through their chests.

Another member of the *ts'ici* staff, the *lòrɔ*, or speaker, was expected to help the household with its formidable task of feeding and entertaining important visitors. Former members of host families spoke of enormous trouble and expense. "These days, officials come in groups of two or three, stay a day, and leave," recalled a woman who had been twelve when her household was *ts'ici*, "but back then, they came in groups of twenty or thirty. They came in litters with bearers and someone out front to wave the flies away." These processions of soldiers, officials, clerks, and runners would sometimes stay for days, demanding meat, bean curd, and alcohol at every meal. The worst years in living memory were 1935 and 1949, when soldiers from both the People's Liberation Army and the Guomindang armies visited Zhizuo in quick succession. Residents of the large village of Chemo recalled that in the summer of 1949 four hundred soldiers of the Guomindang's Twenty-Sixth Division lodged in the host household's courtyard for a month, hunting down the remnants of Ding Zhiping's troop of Communists and eating meat every day. Later that year, soldiers of the People's Liberation Army stayed with the same host household for several weeks. This family, among Chemo's most affluent, was financially ruined just in time to be classed as lower-middle peasants during the land reform movement and to enjoy the relative safety from persecution this status afforded for the next thirty years.

These powerful outsiders rarely showed the civility that hosts could expect from local guests. Another child of a former *ts'ici* remembered that on one of his frequent trips through Zhizuo the Xia *tusi*, dissatisfied with the quality of his dinner, beat the *ts'ici* with a board. Other officials also beat *ts'ici*, cursed them, or threw things at them. The speaker's job was to employ skills of wit and conversation to prevent such incidents. During his year of service, he lived in the host household, at its expense, with the sole duty of eating, drinking, and chatting with the guests. The ideal speaker needed to be a gregarious personality, a good drinker, and an accomplished conversationalist. He had to be fluent in Chinese, dress fashionably, and possess cosmopolitan manners that would not draw the scorn of sophisticated guests. The speaker was required to greet the guests as they entered the valley, lead them to the host household, seat them, and call for food and drink, allowing the *ts'ici* and *ts'icimo* to make only a brief, welcoming appearance before retiring again.

Another aide was the *k'ɔlɔ*, or bearer, whose main responsibility was to carry the luggage of visiting officials as they left the valley. Since most officials traveled with more belongings than one man could carry, the bearer often pressed his kin or that of the *ts'ici* to help. He and his crew accompanied officials twenty-five kilometers south to the next group of villages with a *huotou* system on the way to the county capital,[11] or twenty kilometers north to the district seat, residence of the Xia *tusi*. Once on the road, officials sometimes pressed the bearer and his company into service for the journey to the county capital or even beyond. The bearer also saw to it that letters arriving in Zhizuo were carried onward south to the next group of villages or north to the district seat. Because the bearer himself was so busy, this task frequently fell to the younger members of the *ts'ici*'s own household. Li Yong recalled that during his father's year of service in 1929, he delivered letters after school. He was only nine years old and shoeless, but when a letter came, he packed it in his school bag and carried it more than twenty kilometers, returning in the dark. The bearer also had a ritual obligation: at the New Year, he carried the reliquary box from one host household to the next. This duty required of the bearer a ritual purity similar to that of the elderly *ts'ici* couple. Li Yong insisted that the best candidate for bearer was unmarried; he could wear only clothing associated with the original Líp'ò ancestors; and he had to be an "honest" man, who spoke seldom and displayed little agility of wit. Qi Bao'en put it more bluntly. The ideal bearer, he said, was an idiot (*bomi*) who spoke slowly, if at all, and was naive about sexual relations.

In addition to warden, speaker, and bearer, the staff of the *ts'ici* included two assistants, *fumo* and *fuzò* (combining the Chinese word *fu*, "deputy" or "assistant," with the Lòlongo suffixes *mo* and *zò*, "big" and "small"). Several villages in Zhizuo selected responsible men to greet and host important people passing through from other villages or regions. Those selected in the host household's village became general assistants to that household and helped organize and prepare food for rituals. At most, they expended several days of labor and two chickens, and their only compensation was the prestige of their jobs.

The Price of Horse Feed

The rules and procedures recounted by ritual experts and former members of *ts'ici* households gave warden, speaker, and bearer the right to collect recompense for their duties. In exercising this right, they extended the personal qualities associated with their practical responsibilities to participate in the imaginative work of constituting Zhizuo as a house. Some of these rules were listed in chants performed during rites for Agàmisimo and his spirit progeny. Li Yong performed part of one such chant for me to illustrate the warden's right of compensation:

4.3

receive from the village's head and tail	che wú nì mæ sho
from all who live in Zhizuo [Júzò]	Júzò chì lɔ jɔ
all who live in this *ts'ici*	ts'i ci chì lɔ jɔ
who breed fine horses	mò jí mò tsæ ga
who breed horses smoothly . . .	mò jí mò go lɔ gɔ . . .
from one family	chì vɛ sho chì ni
take two *sheng*	nì shɔ́ ngo lɔ sho
from three families	sá vɛ sho chì ni
take six *sheng*	cho shɔ́ ngo lɔ sho
take no more	mò lu ngo n sho
take no less	ní lu ngo n sho
from the sky's creation	mùi ni chì hæ jí
from the earth's origin	me ne je wò jí
fathers and sons have bred horses together	p'ò jɔ zò jɔ jí dó ngɔ ngɔ
thirty generations of fathers	p'ò p'ò sa ts'r je
thirty generations of sons and grandsons	zò lí sa ts'r je

At the end of his year of service, the warden visited every household in Zhizuo that owned a brood mare to collect the "price of horse feed" (*mò tsò sho*). Each family with a productive mare was expected to contribute 2 *sheng* of grain. In this mountainous region, horses and mules were the sole mode of transport other than human backs. They were especially valuable along the salt and sugar trading route that passed through Zhizuo, and their price was very high. Mules were particularly prized as the strongest and most agile of pack animals. Zhizuo residents estimated that just before Liberation a decent horse cost 200 to 300 yuan and a good mule up to 500, whereas cattle cost only 40 to 50.[12] Raising horses and mules could be lucrative for those who could afford a brood mare, and residents estimated that in the late 1940s Zhizuo had a population of about five to six hundred horses, concentrated in the most prosperous households. An enterprising warden might thus collect 1,000 to 1,200 *sheng* of grain after his year of service. The "price of horse feed" was a sort of tax, people recalled, but unlike the taxes collected by the *baozhang,* it was levied only against the most prosperous.

As a tax on the fertility of horses, the "price of horse feed" was appropriate remuneration for the warden, whose duties became increasingly associated with compulsory military service in the Guomindang armies. A military conscription law was instituted in 1933. Initially, it stipulated that only sons would not be drafted; in a family with two to three sons, one would be drafted; in a family with three to five, two would be drafted. But as the Guomindang struggled to prosecute the war against the Japanese, military conscription in rural Yunnan expanded dramatically in scope and intensity. Conscription quotas for the nearby county of Yaoan, for instance, increased from 120 men in 1935 to 800 in 1942.[13] During the civil war, the military conscription law was revised to stipulate that one son would be drafted from a family with two sons, two from a family with three sons, and three from a family with five sons (CYZZ 1994, 298). The words from Li Yong's chant, "from one family, take two *sheng,* from three families, take six *sheng;* take no more, take no less," seem to mimic this harsher injunction, which Zhizuo residents chanted thus:

4.4

of two sons, harvest one	nì zò chì zò sho
of three sons, harvest two	sa zò nì zò sho
of five sons, harvest three	ngó zò sa zò sho

Youths were drafted from their villages in October and November of each year, so their official term of service could begin in January. Each autumn of the Republic's last decade, Zhizuo's *baozhang* employed two local men to capture conscripts. Carrying guns, iron neck bands, and chains, they apprehended youths, chained their necks, and led them to the prison cell of the *ts'ici,* where it was the warden's responsibility to guard them. These two men were roundly despised by their neighbors, who called them "dogs' legs" (*ánò chì*) and sometimes spat on them when passing on the paths. When these police were spotted near their villages, youths from poor households fled or went into hiding. Some ate a wild fruit that produced a permanent goiter or amputated two joints of their trigger finger. Wealthier families paid the *baozhang* a bribe when their sons reached the age of sixteen and followed this up with more bribes each autumn. After being gathered in the *ts'ici*'s house, recruits were chained together and led from the valley at gunpoint. War and the execrable conditions suffered by ordinary soldiers in the Guomindang armies ensured that few returned. The warden's chanted words "from the sky's creation, from the earth's origin, fathers and sons

have bred horses together, thirty generations of fathers, thirty generations of sons and grandsons" clearly associate a line of agnates with the
procreative potential of brood mares. The warden taxed the fertility of
horses just as the Guomindang taxed the fertility of fathers with forced
conscription.

The warden's price was governed by the same principle of reciprocity
that organized the *ts'ici*'s duties as host. To associate the "price of horse
feed" with his job of smoothing the way for the hated "dogs' legs" was
to acknowledge that higher powers would always demand tribute. In
the case of forced conscription, this price was sons, on whom the future
procreative potential of any family depended. While the burden of
forced conscription could not be distributed equitably, the warden's
chanted insistence on taking only from those who had mares was an assertion that the analogous tax on the fertility of horses, at least, should
be distributed among those who could bear it best.

The Speaker's Price

The idiom of procreative potential also informed the rules
for compensating the speaker and the bearer. A few hundred yards upstream of the ancestral trust fields, where a bend in the river on one side
and terraces on the other formed a warm, protected corner, was another
plot of land, of about 1 *mu*. This was the seed bed in which rice to be
transplanted into the larger fields grew for its first fifty days. Like the ancestral trust fields, it rotated with the *ts'ici*, and it was farmed communally
by workers organized by the host household. It was called the *lòrʒmi*, the
"speaker's field." A tenth of the rice seedlings grown in this field were
transplanted back into it, and the speaker received their harvest.

In many contexts, Zhizuo residents compared growing rice to raising
children. Sowing rice was likened to insemination; uprooting and transplanting seedlings to giving birth; hoeing, weeding, and fertilizing the
growing plants to feeding and clothing children; harvesting rice plants
to the labor of helping people die; and storing rice seeds to keeping ancestral souls in preparation for their rebirth.[14] Men from the households of the *ts'ici* and their brothers lavished attention on the womblike
speaker's field, fertilizing it with ashes from nitrogen-fixing tree species
and several applications of manure and soaking, plowing, and harrowing it repeatedly until the earth blended into a thick, nutritious mud.

After smoothing the bed with a wooden dressing bar, the *ts'ici* himself chose a time when no women were nearby to hang a bag of seed on his belt and scatter it over this warm, sheltered earth. Fifty days later, female kin and friends of the *ts'icimo* pulled up the seedlings and transplanted them into the larger fields, replanting about a tenth into the *lòrᶎmi,* on a festive occasion in which this work was explicitly associated with giving birth (described in chapter 5).

One afternoon, as he was talking about the speaker's compensation to a group of men gathered in my room, Li Yong abruptly switched topics. In Zhenamo, nearby, he said, people do not replant any rice seedlings back into their seed beds after pulling them up. Instead, they spend the entire year intermittently tilling and fertilizing their seed beds to prepare them for the next year's seeds: "Every time a Máchìp'ò [a derogatory term for Zhenamo residents] has spare time, he is out tilling his seed bed. They are very stubborn people. That's what Máchìp'ò means, stupid, stubborn people. They never learn anything new; they always sow the same fields their ancestors sowed. Even now the Party can't convince some to transplant back into their seed beds. They say the seed bed is the mother and the seedling the son, and to replant the seedling in the seed bed would be like the son fucking the mother."

Those listening laughed as though he had told an off-color joke. People in Zhizuo do transplant seedlings back into their seed beds. Not to do so in a place where every inch of irrigable land is precious would make one as stupid as a Máchìp'ò. I never heard anyone explicitly deny that "the seed bed is the mother, the seedling the son," but saying it out loud disturbed the neat homology Zhizuo residents habitually make between procreation and rice production. As he told how Zhenamo residents extend the logic of procreative metaphor one step further than Lòlop'ò usually care to, Li Yong's implication was clear: by accepting the harvest from seedlings transplanted back into the seed bed as his due, the speaker consumed the issue of a son's sexual relations with his mother.

The Price of Grass

If someone had to eat this scandalous by-product, the speaker was an appropriate choice. I came to understand this as those who had been members of *ts'ici* households repeatedly contrasted the offices of speaker and bearer. The speaker had a famous time eating, drinking, and chatting, while the bearer's job was a heavy burden. The speaker needed to be a sophisticate, while the bearer was preferably an idiot. The speaker wore stylish "Han" clothing that buttoned down the front, while the bearer dressed in old-style hempen clothes that buttoned down the side. And the speaker accepted every opportunity for social intercourse, while the bearer rarely spoke and was ideally celibate. In these recollections, the opposite orientations of speaker and bearer toward eating, speaking, sexual activity, and signs of Lòlop'ò ancestry were of a piece with their opposite relations to the boundaries of the Zhizuo *ts'ici*.

In collecting his compensation, the bearer was a boundary maker. His recompense for his year of service was called "the price of grass" (*cí p'ù sho*). At the end of the year, he undertook a tour of the small high-mountain settlements on the *ts'ici's* borders, collecting money or grain from those living outside who grazed their goats and cattle on land within. There was no common understanding of how much this fee should be, and what the bearer collected depended on his own industry and the thickness of his skin. The chant quoted earlier in fragment 4.3 also mentions the bearer's tour and names some of the boundary villages from which he bore back his compensation. Chanted in the bearer's voice, it evokes his ideally childlike character.

4.5

Where do I receive the price of grass?	cí p'ù à lí sho
I bear it back from Lík'ɔ̀	Lík'ɔ̀ bù k'o ga sho kò lɔ
back from Yík'ùti	Yík'ùti k'ò ga
the valley's head and tail	jɔ̀ wú jɔ̀ mæ
Tàbǽgòmo and Jɔjɔmo	Tàbǽgòmo Jɔjɔmo
I receive and all goes well	sho tsǽ go tsǽ ga
I feed my entire family	bo lɔ ngo chì jo
my grandchildren laugh	ngo lí gɔ sɔ ga

In negotiating which hamlets should pay for the right to graze their animals on what land, the bearer established the territorial boundaries of the *ts'ici*. As he hauled visitors' baggage out of the valley and carried letters through it, he worked to preserve these boundaries by facilitating the movement of outsiders through and away. His hempen clothing, monolingual speech, and presumed celibacy reproduced in his person this boundary-making status. His clothing signaled his intimate connection with the original Lòlop'ò ancestors, his laconic speech and celibacy that he eschewed an excess of social relations with people other than close kin.

The ideal speaker, in contrast, specialized in boundary traversals. His job of cultivating and enlivening relations with powerful outsiders was centrifugally oriented. His Han clothing, multilingual facility, conversational skills, and indulgence in food and alcohol all directed his person toward promiscuous and facile sociability, especially with outsiders. His task was to take on the qualities of those who most directly threatened the community in order to deflect part of that threat. Indiscriminate in his social relations, the speaker may have been thought indiscriminate sexually as well: his personal qualities precisely fit the stereotype of a successful adulterer in Zhizuo. And in Zhizuo, as in many places, the forbidden indiscrimination par excellence was incest between mother and son. The speaker too reproduced his boundary-traversing status in his person. To pay him with the issue of an unavoidable sexual relation between mother and son was to recognize the social promiscuity with which he helped preserve Zhizuo's boundaries by continuously transgressing them.

Recollections of the speaker's transgressive character illuminate the proscriptions applied to the *ts'ici* couple. At the house's center, in the upstream room, this couple combined all the most powerful signs of Lòlop'ò ancestry with restricted speech, sociability, and sexuality as well as abstention from everything associated with Han outsiders. At the house's margins, in the courtyard, porch, and outer rooms, the speaker stoked the fires of hospitality with everything the *ts'ici* and *ts'icimo* were enjoined to avoid—a specialist in scandalous unrestraint managing the unrestrained speech, sociability, and sexuality that transgressed the house's walls from without. As designated hosts for the entire territory of Zhizuo, the *ts'ici* couple made it possible to imagine this territory similarly as a household, sheltering both a powerful productive union and potentially troublesome guests, who must be fed, flattered, and hurried on their way.

Zhizuo residents' insistence on the bearer's contrasting character participated in this imaginative constitution of a houselike territory in a different way. The proscriptions that were applied to the bearer's diet, speech, clothing, and sexuality were identical to (if not as strict as) those applied to the *ts'ici* and *ts'icimo,* because of his association with the reliquary box they served. In their relation to this box, the *ts'ici* couple acted as a conduit through which the procreative power of the ancestral union it represented descended on the valley-house of Zhizuo. In *his* relation to the reliquary, the bearer made this union move, passing it like a bride from one village and one household to the next, treating it as the sister and wife that bound each Zhizuo household to others. In this way, Zhizuo residents could imagine bearer and *ts'ici* couple to combine in their persons the principles of descent and affinity on which all relations of kinship were built, extending these principles to saturate the house of Zhizuo to its outer boundaries. As they recollected the rules and procedures of the *ts'ici* system, people used these ideas about the fluidity and fixity of speech, sexuality, and sociability to imagine Zhizuo as, at once, a household descended from a single set of ancestors and a circle of households connected through marriage alliances.

Conclusion

The ethnographers who in 1953 bravely set out to classify the inhabitants of thousands of mountain villages like Yijichang and Zhizuo learned to be flexible in applying Stalin's four criteria for defining nationality—common territory, common language, common economic base, and common psychological makeup (Stalin 1956, 294–295)—tempering them with older associations with origin and inheritance that the term *minzu* ("nationality") had gathered since its adoption into Chinese around 1900 (Dikötter 1992, Liu Y. 1963). To these ethnographers, Zhizuo residents clearly shared a territory, language, economy, and historical origin with the speakers of the Central dialect of Yi who surrounded them (if only more problematically with the far-flung groups also labeled "Yi" in other parts of the southwest). Even in the 1980s and early 1990s, county and prefectural officials frequently invoked these criteria to dismiss Zhizuo residents' claims to a separate *minzu* status as ignorant or delusional.

People in Zhizuo, however, took advantage of associations of *minzu* with origin, inheritance, and descent to link the problem of "nationality" to a large and systematic body of expert knowledge about the past. Their accounts of the *ts'ici* system used moral ideas about speech, sociability, and sexuality to craft an imagined unity for all those who claimed to be Lòlop'ò. Creating terms of comparison between agricultural cycles and life cycles, and the spatial arrangements of households and those of the territory of Zhizuo, these recollections compounded mutually contradictory ideas about descent and affinity into a single institutional container (Lévi-Strauss 1983, 185). Zhizuo was a single productive unity, a household descended from a single set of ancestors, or a series of households bound together through marriage exchanges and mutually involved in the intimate processes of household reproduction. From within this imagined unity, Zhizuo residents could deal with powerful outsiders as a household would, flattering them with the honors and privileges of guests while excluding them from internal household affairs.

Ethnographers and administrators could easily pass off this self-consciously formal and reflexive talk about the past as innocuous nostalgia for a defunct "nationality custom." But under the cover of its formality, it created a forceful strategy of self-representation, in which spatial descent and symbolic affinity took the place of the historical genealogies that preoccupied those who created and defended *minzu* classifications. Claims that the *ts'ici* is "the heart of our nationality" and "our nationality's most important custom" employed the troubled political potency of the term *minzu* to give this self-representational strategy force in the present. Much has been written about how colonizing regimes create ethnicities for their subjects. Studies of ethnicity and nationality in China, especially, have repeatedly shown how local identities are forcefully produced or molded by state policies (Harrell 1990, 1995; Mackerras 1994; Gladney 1991, 1994). These accounts of the rules and procedures of a long dead but fondly remembered institution point to another side of this dialectic, in which older local self-representations engage or absorb state discourses about ethnicity to create new possibilities for struggle and self-definition.

CHAPTER FIVE

Digested Words

On what authority were my interlocutors' memories of the rules and procedures of the *ts'ici* founded? This was a persistent concern for me as my tapes and notebooks filled. My efforts to retrieve and inscribe memory were implicitly guided by a common-sense, "Western" understanding of memory as a species of representation. In this view, past events are inscribed on a surface or stored in a repository in the form of words and images that may be brought back again and again to the present (Wyschogrod 1998, 174). In China, a somewhat different scriptic model of memory has long been closely associated with special respect for the authority of written communication. As Chad Hansen (1992, 40) has shown, (Han) Chinese folk theories of language, drawing on a long tradition of scrupulous philosophical writing about language, tend to privilege writing as bearing closer relation to the authentic past than speech, making it possible for historical realities to be directly inscribed in writing without first being diverted through speech. Li Yong, Qi Bao'en, and Qi Chun all seemed to eye with considerable ambivalence my efforts to inscribe their speech. Li Yong mixed his show of respect for my rapid scribbling with amusement and perhaps a little contempt. It was typical of Han (Cep'ò) like me to rely on such aids to memory, he told me.[1] This was one regard in which Lòlop'ò ritualists differed considerably from Han ritualists and officials—and apparently from scholars as well. Did I know the story of the origins of *nèpi*, the speech used to address ghosts and spirits? I did indeed, having heard it from nearly every ritualist in Zhizuo. Perhaps they had told it badly, said Li Yong, and he repeated it:

Long ago, two men, one Lòlop'ò and one Han [Cep'ò], learned of an old man who knew how to speak to ghosts and spirits. They journeyed nine days and nine nights to meet him, and he taught them all the *nèpi* chants we now use. They both wrote them down. The Han used a brush and paper, but the Lòlop'ò was too poor to afford paper. He wrote on a flat buckwheat cake. It was a long walk home, and this was the only buckwheat cake he had, so he ate it. Since then, Lòlop'ò ritualists have held their *nèpi* chants in their stomachs, ready to speak at any time, while Han ritualists have no memory and have to read theirs. Unless they have a book, Han cannot perform even the simplest of rituals, while Lòlop'ò have all their words right here [patting his abdomen].

Nèpi is the quintessential form of authoritative speech. It commands attention from those whose attributes and intentions are most unlike one's own: inhabitants of an alien world separated from this world by the gulf between life and death (compare Keane 1995, 106). It is effective speech, which bends the most evil, malicious, and recalcitrant forces to one's will. This story recognizes the existence of a scriptic model of memory at the foundations of this authoritative speech and grafts onto it an alternative model—let us call it "digestive."

Scriptic and digestive memory diverge in this story with the opposition between paper and buckwheat. In *nèpi*, and in ordinary speech as well, Zhizuo residents associated paper and writing with displays of wealth by visiting officials. The following passage of one *nèpi*, for instance, describes the Han officials who crowded the *ts'ici*'s courtyard, eating and drinking their fill as they lettered official documents:[2]

5.1

squatting on golden stools	si cæ bà tsr ti̱
lounging on cushioned chairs	ró tsr p'æ t'ệg ti̱
sitting at the table's corners	jó tsr ngɔ̀ t'ệ ti̱
they write books, practice calligraphy	su sú và sú bo jɔ
they blow flutes of bamboo	su mo pe̱ mo t'ệ tsɔ
strum *erhu* of precious wood	sr pe̱ sr t'ệ tsɔ jɔ bɛ
fill the courtyard with incense smoke	su shú j'ɔ mǽ k'ò yi
beat drums with heads of thunder	ku dǽ nǽ mǜ lɔ̀
drink with heads of fog, oh!	ji dɔ nǽ mǜ ḱɔ dɔ le
kill goats and eat goats	su p'æ sr̀ p'æ tsò lɔ̀
pour barrels of sweet wine, oh!	su wú chò wú dɔ le

A sign of wealth, refinement, and bureaucratic power, writing was also a currency for communication across the cultural and linguistic di-

vides that separated visiting Han officials from Zhizuo residents. Like
other Chinese, educated Lòlop'ò could use writing to communicate
with literate people when spoken language failed—usually by tracing
characters with their fingers against their palms. With or without writing, paper was a currency for communicative exchanges across the even
deeper divides that separated the living from spiritual entities. Every exchange with ghosts or spirits included offerings of paper streamers (tied
to the pine branches of effigies), named in *nèpi* as gifts of silver. Additional paper in the form of miniature flags or money stamped out of the
bulky toilet paper women used to absorb their menstrual flows marked
the filthier entities with Han identity.

Too poor to afford the soiled, silvery currency of paper, the Lòlop'ò
man in Li Yong's story inscribes his *nèpi* on a buckwheat cake. Grown
only on swidden land, buckwheat was closely associated with mythical
ancestral origins in the heights of the Baicaolin Mountains. Like paper,
buckwheat was a currency for transactions between worlds, but gifts of
buckwheat went to deceased kin rather than to ghosts. Too, it was ten-
der for modest accumulations of wealth, as durable as silver and far
steadier than paper money. It borrowed the mysterious capacity of
money to grow in value (a capacity that only a few Lòlop'ò were ever in
a position to experience) without involving one in the dangers of mon-
etary investment and trade. As Li Zhiwu explained: "Buckwheat never
sours or rots, so you can pile it up forever. This is why we call a wealthy
Lòlop'ò an 'old buckwheat' [*kòmà*]. You can pile it up for thirty years.
The longer you keep it, the more you have, since its husk gradually
swells. So if you give me five *sheng* this year, I will have seven *sheng* next
year and a *dou* [ten *sheng*] the year after. And pigs grow faster eating
buckwheat, too." As currencies of accumulation and exchange, paper and
buckwheat were appropriate media for words that were authoritative or
persuasive enough to cross the ontological divide between the inhabitants of the living world (*ts'mni*) and those of the world of ghosts and
spirits (*nèmi*), or the social divide between peasants and visiting officials.

Eating his buckwheat cake as he walks, the Lòlop'ò man in the story
transforms scriptic memory into digestive memory, making the words
his body's own. Buckwheat is, I was often told, the most digestible of
grains, never swelling the abdomen like lowland grains and blessed with
the power to clear a blocked or balking digestive tract. In the digestive
model of memory, the most authoritative words have been ingested
fully, infusing the body like the life energies of good food, flowing from

it in an unbroken stream. Ritualists who pause, stutter, or appear to exert effort to bring forth their words are inferior.[3]

Unlike scriptic memory, which may be alienated and exchanged with ease, digestive memory may be transmitted but not alienated and may be exchanged only through a kind of perversion: some Lòlop'ò ritualists have been known to buy spirit familiars, usually from Han ritualists (Ch. *duangong*), to help them remember and speak, but such transactions are fraught with dangers and pollutions. Li Yong and Qi Bao'en were both careful to insist that the *nèpi* for rituals sponsored by the *ts'ici* had never been bought or sold; rather, they had been transmitted along several lines of descent, of which they themselves were the final representatives. The origin of this memory, its pre-text, is writing. The Lòlop'ò man digests his written *nèpi* on a walk of nine days and nights, the precise length of the journey to the underworld, the ground *nèpi* are intended to traverse. This ideology of memory builds on the intertwinings of body and landscape effected by walking on a journey. Writing—the original composition of *nèpi*—is what is forgotten on the journey and, being forgotten, is also what lends digestive memory its authority. Still, what some forget, others remember. Remembering writing grants others exceptional powers—the fabled powers of Han ritualists, for instance, who can tread on coals or glowing plowshares; or the violent powers of visiting officials, whose documents and seals allow them to seize land, wealth, and bodies. The difference between Lòlop'ò and Han is a difference not merely in language and dress but, more fundamentally, in the ways they remember and forget their most powerful words. It is a moral difference.

This chapter explores the words about the *ts'ici* system that ritualists held most dear. These words were seen to participate in a mode of memory that differentiated Lòlop'ò morally from their Han neighbors and held the potential to unite Lòlop'ò into a living community. Among the most indispensable responsibilities of the *ts'ici* were yearly public rituals for Agàmisimo and its spirit children. Li Yong, Qi Bao'en, and Qi Chun had all presided over these rituals. Each devoted most of his time with me to carefully elucidating their forms: the roles *ts'ici* and staff were to play, the construction of an effigy particular to each spirit, and, especially, the lengthy and elaborate *nèpi* devoted to each. They described these rites in calendrical order. Agàmisimo, in its hilltop pine, was propitiated in the first lunar month (on the day of the tiger). The Lòhə, in its stone by the ancestral trust fields, was feasted in the fourth month (the day of the dog) during rice-transplanting season. Mijù, in its pine across the valley from Agàmisimo, received offerings in the fourth month (the day of the horse). Lɔmælòhɔ, in its stone shelter at the river's tail, was propitiated in the fourth and fifth months as needed when drought threatened. Cha, on its shelf in a private house, was offered sacrifices in the fifth month (the day of the horse), when disease tended to spread. And Agàmisimo was propitiated a second time in the sixth month (the day of the tiger), when insect infestations were common. This chapter touches on the ceremonies ritualists emphasized as crucial for the health of the *ts'ici*—those for Agàmisimo, the Lòhɔ, and Cha.

These ritual specialists found that their capacity to chant the *nèpi*, for these rites lent authority to all their utterances on the *ts'ici* system. Li Yong was particularly apt to sprinkle his discourse with well-chosen phrases from his vast hoard of *nèpi*, citing them to underline his description of the compensations of warden and bearer, for instance, or to illustrate his tale of Ding Zhiping's battle for Dayao town (related in chapter 4). For Li Yong and his fellow ritualists, the heart of the *ts'ici* system and the core of what, with mixed feelings, they expected me to inscribe, lay in this poetry. They had digested these words over many years of apprenticeship; the words were so much a part of their bodies and persons that they remained still available, though some had not been voiced for nearly thirty years. It was their possession of (and by) these words that caused others to defer to them as the true experts on the *ts'ici* system. Their memory bridged the rupture caused by the *ts'ici*'s destruction, participating in an unbroken line of transmission from the original ancestors. These words recalled the origins of community and the principles of its constitution, principles through which, despite the many devastations it had endured, it might still be re-membered. At the same time, these words created an authoritative foundation for a particular interpretation of memories of violence. They made it possible for others to systematically associate the violence of the Great Leap Forward and the Cultural Revolution with the destruction of the *ts'ici* system and the revenge of its ghosts. Although they seemed on the surface to be politically innocent descriptions of past ritual forms, these words were thus resources for double-edged memory work. This work remembered Zhizuo as a longed-for place, morally distinct from the lowlands and inhabited as closely and densely as a house. But it also re-membered Zhizuo as a wounded place, devastated by violence from without and within, and in need of healing.

A Fertile Spiral

The first rite of this yearly cycle, Li Yong and other ritualists recalled, was the feast for Agàmisimo. It was held in the first lunar
month as men began to soak and harrow their rice seed beds in preparation for sowing. This was an occasion for senior men. Women did not
participate; men below the age of fifty were discouraged; visitors from
outside were never invited; and members of Zhizuo's few Han families
were not welcome. It commemorated the insemination of Zhizuo's fertile valley bottom by the original ancestor with rice seeds from his knife
sheath. In the absence of genealogical records, this ritual was a crucial
means of distinguishing between those included in a community of descent and others and a means of imagining a common domestic residence for this community. As the rice-growing season progressed, the
granary and commensal fire pit of this houselike place would be cele-
brated in other rituals. But this first rite commemorated the house's institution under the inseminating gaze of a common ancestor.

The ceremony began with a procession. Sixty to eighty senior men
gathered at the *ts'ici*'s house at dawn on the day of the tiger. They left at
home the cotton shirts, light jackets, and short-billed green cotton caps
that came into style in this region in the 1940s and 1950s, wearing only at-
tire they imagined the original ancestors to have worn: hempen aprons,
hempen sandals, wide-bottomed trousers, hempen shirts with buttons
down the side, and goatskin or sheepskin capes. Speaking Chinese was
forbidden. With the elderly *ts'ici* and a ritualist of his choice leading the
way, these men left the courtyard to ascend in single file through the village of Chemo and up the hill behind. Since officials, soldiers, or merchants from outside were likely to be living in the *ts'ici*'s house, this was a
sensitive moment. Members of the *ts'ici* household distracted the visitors
with food and drink. If a persistently curious outsider followed the procession, the *ts'ici* had no recourse but to cancel the ritual and reschedule it
twelve days hence, on the next day of the tiger.

Arriving at the two great pines on the hilltop, a few men would begin
to build fires and boil water. Beside the pines, the *ts'ici*'s ritualist constructed an effigy for the lightning spirit Shìmògù: a triple-forked fir
branch with a miniature ladder leading up its trunk. He killed a cock for
this effigy and performed a *nèpi* chant intended to send it up the ladder
to its home in the sky. He created a second effigy for Agàmisimo: six unforked pine boughs decorated with paper streamers and planted in the

earth, each representing two of the year's twelve months. He slit the throat of a ram chosen for the full circle of its horns and offered six bowls of wheat beer, offerings donated by the *ts'ici* household. As he performed the *nèpi* chant for Agàmisimo, others butchered and boiled the meat. The ritualist offered the cooked meat again to both spirits and performed both *nèpi* a second time. The men passed the meat around and drank the wheat beer. A tall ladder was erected against the trunk of Agàmisimo's tree, and the ram's horns were tied high to the trunk, where there was an unobstructed view of the valley. The men then scattered for home, and the *ts'ici* made a private offering to the reliquary box in his own house.

As in all Lòlop'ò rituals concerned primarily with remembering or forgetting, most participants contributed only by walking, eating, and digesting.[4] In contrast to the ritualist's intricate material and verbal creations, these actions seem passive and bare of meaning. Nevertheless, in the myth of origins quoted in chapter 4, the play of remembering and forgetting that instituted a community of descent in this valley had involved precisely walking, eating, and digesting. On their mythical walking journey, the original ancestors had found gendered relations to emerge from the landscape like the rice "as long as horses' tails" blossoming in the fertile valley bottom. Back home in Vèlí and Laba, the men distributed and digested the meat of wild pigs, remembering and renewing their ties to their "families" (*chì*), with whom they would create a new society. But journeying back nine months later, they forgot their origins—their descent—like the man who forgot the written origins of *nèpi* by eating his inscribed buckwheat cake on a nine-day walk. And this forgetting established the original ancestor as their sole collective progenitor, the source of their new society and the authoritative words on which it would be founded.

Walking, eating, and digesting, the men who participated in Agàmisimo's feast performed a similar poetics of remembering and forgetting. Ascending, they wound through their own villages, approached the site where the original ancestors had built their house, and then traversed the forgotten ground, bare of inhabitants, between the last houses of Chemo and the pines on the hilltop. This was the narrative of their own descent traced in reverse, step by step. Beyond the hill's crest, there was nothing left to living memory, only that which, to live, one must struggle to forget: the landscape dropped and then ascended again to the White Chalk Mountain, the domain of wild ghosts. Above was only the sky, playground of Shìmògù, who had marked the bark of Agàmisimo's tree with the writing (Ch. *wen*)[5] of lightning and whom the ritualist had ordered back to the imperceptible depths of the heavens. Eating beneath Agàmisimo's pine, the men commemorated the distribution of meat that had established a new community in the space opened by forgetting previous ascendants. Descending and digesting, they reaffirmed the patrilineal authority and fertile potency their descent had granted them. They retraced the digestive transmission of the words and principles that gave this new society its shape and coherence.

The *nèpi* chanted before Agàmisimo's pine suggests that in addition to walking, eating, and digesting these men were preoccupied with *looking*. Indeed, they could hardly have resisted gazing off into the valley—its entire sweep from the river's head to its tail lay open to their view. They could examine each village and its cultivated fields; they could pick out their own homes and retrace the paths that had led them to this hilltop. According to Li Yong, the first ancestor had stipulated on his deathbed that this should be so: "Give me a high place, where I can see [*hɔ*] everything," he had said. His descendants had given him this great pine on its hilltop, and twice a year they tied a pair of ram's horns high to its trunk to serve as eyes, playing on the metaphor of eyes as testicles, common in both Lòlongo and colloquial Chinese. As it opens, the *nèpi* for Agàmisimo, here chanted by Li Yong, commemorates the inseminating effects of this gaze:

5.2

great-grandfather Misi behind the house	a gà a pʉ́ Misi ni
spirit from Vèlí and Laba	ni k'o Vèlí Laba nè
spirit from T'ɛsò and Lɔvɛ	T'ɛsò Lɔvɛ nè
powerful, auspicious one	go wò lɔ́ te su
who feeds all the earth's creatures	mé ne jè wò tɔ́ te su
who sows an even rain	mʉ̀ ho dɔ mʉ̀ ho te su
look over the sky	mʉ̀ wú hɔ chì ni
the sky improves	mʉ̀ wú tsæ te su
look over the land	mi mæ hɔ chì ni
the land flourishes	mi mæ go te su
great-grandfather Misi behind the house	a gà à pʉ́ Misi ni
you who makes our food tasty	su ni tsò wú tsæ te su
who makes our drink delicious	dɔ mì tsæ te su

The verb *hɔ* ("to look" or "to see") is repeated often in the myth of origins to which this chant refers. When the ancestral group of agnates came to the valley hunting pigs, they saw (hɔ) the land, which became fertile under their eyes. They looked (hɔ) at the swamp at the valley's center and sowed rice seeds there. In the ninth month, they came to look (hɔ) again and saw (hɔ still) that each stalk had become ten. The view from the hilltop collected the temporal sequences of ascent and descent into an encompassing spatial frame. It provided an apical perspective on one's own descent, gathered it with the descent of others into a single field, and infused this visible field with masculine fertile potency.

As the chant progresses, this emphasis on seeing is joined with an equally insistent sense of movement, of driving (kà) and circling (jɔ). Agàmisimo is imagined as circling sky and earth to capture their nourishing qualities and drive them inward toward the valley below:

5.3

as you see the sky	mùi ni hɔ chì ni
drive the sky back here	mùi ni kà k'ò lɔ
as you see the earth	me ne hɔ chì ni
drive the earth back here	me ne kà k'ò lɔ
oh, as you drive the sky	ye sà, mùi ni kà chì ni
circle the sky's four corners	mùi ni lí ngɔ̀ jɔ
as you drive the earth	me ne kà chì ni
circle the earth's four sides	me ne lí p'æ jɔ
the grain's heads spring up here	jo wú hé ká do
let them spring up here	hé ká do gɔ̀ lɔ
the grain's roots grow here	jo mæ hé ká go
let them grow here	hé ká go gɔ̀ lɔ
bring gentle wind and steady rain	mùi hé tɔ fù hé ká ho gɔ̀ lɔ

The fertile power of this gaze, then, is associated with its mobility. From this high place, a moving gaze could discriminate here (hé ká) from there (ru ká or ju ká), drawing a visible boundary around Zhizuo, into which fertility and good weather might be driven and from which insects, hailstorms, and infectious disease might be expelled.

Several versions of this chant circulated in Zhizuo. In the village of Méabò, on the valley's drought-prone shady side, ritualists associated pests and contagions with ghosts of indeterminate or alien kinship who wandered the ridges and gullies beyond the inhabited river valleys. Their nèpi appealed to Agàmisimo to expel these influences and bar their return.

5.4

oust the wild ridge ghosts	sa ká ni bò lɔ
thwart the wild gully ghosts	sa bùi ni t'i lɔ

drive bugs to the river's head	bùù ka̱ lɔ wú ho
drive insects to the river's tail	bùù ka̱ lɔ mæ ho
let no insects come chew the seedlings	ju̱ chi bùù zò t'à k'ò lɔ
let no bugs come eat the green grain	ju̱ ngɔ bùù zò t'à tsò lɔ
let no great winds come	ho va hé t'à lɔ
let no stinging hail come	mùù bò lo ho hé t'à lɔ
let no typhus or encephalomyelitis come	no̱ ká shr yi hé t'à lɔ
let no coughs or colds come	ts'o no̱ jí no̱ hé t'à lɔ
oust the wild ridge ghosts	sa ká ni bò yi
thwart the wild gully ghosts	sa bùù ni t'i yi

It was not enough simply to drive good influences into the visible, cultivated lands below and discharge the bad to the wild, unseen mountains beyond. A lengthy section of the *nèpi* called "driving over sky and earth" (*mùts'r mits'r ka̱*) extended this dynamic to the nearby towns and cities. Agàmisimo was to drive the good food, excellent drink, and rich soil of these places to Zhizuo along a specific path, a spiral path "toward the right hand" (counterclockwise), beginning in the nearby county center of Yongren.

5.5

over there in Yongren	Yongren ju̱ ká ngɔ
let no food sit there	tso mè ju̱ t'à ti̱
no drink rest there	dɔ mè ju̱ t'à ti̱
no earth for sons	zò jɔ mi n ngɔ
no land for daughters	né jɔ mi n ngɔ
no earth for feet to sink into	chì t'o chì hé mi n ngɔ
no soil for fingers to plunge into	lè jé̱ lè hé mi n ngɔ
let no food sit there	tso mè k'ó t'à ti̱
no drink rest there	dɔ mè k'ó t'à ti̱
no earth for plows to turn	lɔ lɔ ju̱ do mi n ngɔ
over there in Yongxing . . .	Yongxing ju̱ ká ngɔ . . .

This refrain is repeated many times, each repetition beginning with a new place name. In this performance, the names describe a spiral through the towns and cities of northern Yunnan, from Yongren to Yongxing, Wanbie, Panzhihua, Yanfeng, Dayao, Chuxiong, Kunming, and finally back to Zhizuo. Returning to Zhizuo, the negative particles *n* and *t'à* are dropped from each line, transforming it into an affirmative demand:

5.6

here in our Zhizuo [Júzò]	ngo Júzò hé ká lɔ
let food come sit here	tso mè hé ti̱ lɔ
let drink come rest here	dɔ mè hé ti̱ lɔ

earth for feet to sink into   chì t'o chì hé mi ngɔ
soil for fingers to plunge into   lè jé̱ lè hé mi ngɔ
earth for plows to turn   lɔ lɔ̀ hé do mi ngɔ

Qi Wenping, the ritualist from Méabò who chanted this version for me, used Chinese names of towns and county centers that he knew I would recognize. Other performances used Lòlongo place names to trace a more elaborate route. Most paths twisted through Líp'ò villages in Dayao, descended to the plains of Yaoan, climbed east through the Chuxiong plateau, headed north up the river valley of Yuanmo, and finally ascended again to Zhizuo. However tortured, each route formed a circuit "toward the right hand" leading away from Zhizuo and back.

In daily life, Zhizuo residents traveled two experientially and conceptually distinct networks of paths and roads. One was a web of mountain paths that crossed the ridges to communicate between high-mountain villages of Líp'ò and Lòlop'ò kin. These were paths of mutual visits, reciprocal gift exchange, and shared participation in funerals, weddings, and festivals. The other network was the branched structure of paths, roads, and trunk roads that followed the river valleys from these high villages down to township centers, market towns, district centers, and provincial capitals.[6] These were primarily paths for market exchanges and bureaucratic transactions. Together, these networks traversed a difficult landscape, dissevered into kinship-oriented and market-oriented routes, fragmented by gullies and mountain ridges, splintered into days and hours by the arduous labor of walking.

Sweeping over this fissured terrain in spiral circuits, Agàmisimo's chanted spiral journey overcame the obstacles of time and fatigue to draw the landscape together into an embracive domain view. This was a specific form of memory; it was *commemoration,* an act of power, a deliberate distancing from the world of paths and narratives that must be walked and digested one step at a time. It contemplated a landscape that had been transformed forever by the ancestral act of insemination, freeing ancestors and humans of their historicity, their embeddedness in time (Munn 1970, 144). It unified and bounded the visible world, excluding what lay beyond sight. Near the end of the *nèpi*, Agàmisimo was exhorted to "whirl about this place" (*hé chì vá vá*). The verb *vá vá*, "to circle" or "to whirl," was used most frequently in connection with water, to describe whirlpools funneling particles from a stream's surface into a deep center or water bugs dancing quick circuits of their territories. The gaze of senior men, given force by the values of patrilineal descent, united the visible world. Like a whirlpool, this inseminating gaze drew food, drink, fertility, and good weather from the towns and cities beyond toward the deep valley below. Like a water bug, it circled this territory, defending it from wild ghosts, hailstorms, and infectious disease.

On a visit to Agàmisimo's hilltop, Li Zhiwu pointed out to me an extraordinary feature of the valley's built topography, clearly arranged with great care by his forebears. From Agàmisimo's pine, a perfectly straight line of sight intersected nearly every ritual site of the *ts'ici* system. Looking down into Chemo, one could see the roofs of Ts'icizò, where the first ancestors were supposed to have settled. A bit farther along this line of sight was the house where the spirit Cha resided. On the mountain slope below the village was a mimosa tree used in the ritual for the Lòhɔ, guardian of the ancestral trust land. In the center of the valley floor, and lined up precisely with each of these places, was the white stone of the Lòhɔ. And on a hilltop across the valley, at the terminus of this line of sight, was the giant pine of Mijù. This line gave the valley a houselike architecture. From the perspective of residents of the sunny side, the spirits along this line were homologous with three of the most deeply resonant locations of a house. Agàmisimo was modeled on a bed's-head spirit, the Lòhɔ on the little *lòhɔ* in charge of a house's granary, and Mijù on a spirit that guarded the barn and regulated the health and fertility of the animal inhabitants of a house's shady side (*lócimìci*).

Agàmisimo's feast was an opportunity for Zhizuo's senior men to view this entire line of sight from their hilltop, finding it to be unified in a domestic community of patrilineal descent and infused with male fertile potency. As we saw in the case of houses, however, Lòlop'ò tend to see every unity of place as a provisional moment in a world shot through with difference. Like a house, the valley had been arranged so that the view from each ritualized place might be reflected from another. On other ritual occasions, Zhizuo residents gathered to look back up at Agàmisimo from other points along this line. From there, Zhizuo's senior men found other perspectives—of women and younger men—to obscure the transparency of their seminal gaze.

Curb Their Lust!

Shortly after the first feast for Agàmisimo, men in Zhizuo sowed rice in their seed beds, scattering it from hempen bags attached to their belts. Some fifty to sixty days later, depending on the altitude of the seed beds, women and girls uprooted the seedlings and transplanted them into the rice paddies. In Zhizuo's central valley, the first fields transplanted were the twelve contiguous fields of the ancestral trust—the *yilɔmi*. At dawn on the chosen day (the fourth lunar month's second day of the dog), the *ts'icimo* and her closest kin and friends gathered at the speaker's field to uproot the seedlings. They separated out a tenth to be transplanted back into the seed bed and bore the rest in back baskets to the ancestral trust fields. There, from eighty to one hundred young men and boys, each with a team of oxen, crowded into the ancestral trust to plow and harrow in preparation for transplanting. The margins of the fields filled with groups of men and boys boiling rice and maize to feed the laborers. On the hillsides above, hundreds of women and girls looked on, dressed to the nines in festive embroidered clothing. It was a beautiful sight, said Li Yong, reciting a fragment of *nèpi* performed on that day:

5.7

this valley of Zhizuo [Júzò]	Júzò chì lɔ jɔ̀
our great *ts'ici* house	ts'i ci ngo chì vɛ
see the fine plow oxen	lò mò lò tsæ̠ hɔ chì ni
three hundred pairs of oxen	lò mò sa ho tsɛ
three hundred pairs come	sa ho tsɛ ne lɔ
see the cooks and plowmen	kà mo kó mo hɔ chì ni
throngs of thousands come	tú bɔ bɔ ne lɔ
crowds of hundreds come	ho kɔ kɔ ne lɔ
see the *yilɔmi* over here	yi lɔ mi hé ká hɔ chì ni
the plowmen begin to work	kà mo pé tu chì ni
like the road of stars	mùu lɔ kǽ shṟ wo lu cí ne jɔ
a hive of yellow jackets	bò du tsǽ k'u lɔ
babbling as they labor	lùu lùu chì ni go̠ tu lɔ
a mud nest of wasps	bò hɔ ní k'u lɔ
laughing as they work	sɔ sɔ chì ni go̠ tu lɔ

This was the view from a smooth, white stone on the margin of the uppermost field of the ancestral trust. A group of senior men including the *ts'ici* and his staff gathered at this stone before the plowing to sacrifice to the Lòhɔ, the senior child of Agàmisimo. The *ts'ici*'s ritualist built an effigy of three unforked pine saplings to represent Agàmisimo and three chestnut boughs to represent the Lòhɔ (illustrated in Figure 5.1). He offered both spirits bowls of alcohol and tea, chanted Agàmisimo's *nèpi* as he killed one goat, and then chanted to the Lòhɔ as he killed another.

Figure 5.1 An effigy for the Lòhɔ.

Later, the *ts'ici*'s deputy and assistant (*fumo* and *fuzò*) would direct volunteers to cook the goat meat and distribute it to the crowd.

Li Yong had assisted his father in this rite several times, looking on with the senior men from the margin of the field. But his fondest memories were of wading in the mud with his oxen, jostling the other youthful plowmen, and showing off to the young women looking on. Often, he said, so many ox teams were packed into the fields that each could plow only a row or two. Plowing remained relatively orderly, since the furrows had to be deep and straight. But harrowing was a chaos of galloping oxen and flying mud. In preparation for harrowing, the fields were flooded to their brims. Each youth stood on a tough, wooden rake pulled by an ox or a buffalo, using the lead lines for balance. Since, in harrowing, the rake tended to sink and wallow if the animals moved too slowly, younger men often whipped up their animals to career around the field at an uncontrolled gallop. At the ancestral trust fields, youths raced each other diagonally across the furrows, riding their rakes like racing sleds as curtains of mud covered them from head to foot. Danger added excitement to the contest, for falling in the mud on this day was an omen of death. This was no joke, men of Li Yong's generation insisted. Li Peiwu, also from Chemo, recalled that in 1946, when he was ten, his classmate fell head first off his rake. Li Peiwu comforted him and cursed those who whispered that he would die within a year, but the next spring he did die, of abdominal pain. This, Li Peiwu claimed, was clear evidence of the Lòhə's power to kill, which would manifest itself in abundance in the 1980s. Still, these men remembered the contest with delight as the high point of their year. Li Peiwu looked forward to it all winter, fattening his oxen carefully and refusing as many early requests for labor exchanges as he dared, so that the animals would be fat and strong for the fourth month's day of the dog.

After harrowing, the fields were dressed with a straight plank set perpendicularly on the end of a long handle. With the exception of irrigating the growing rice, this was the last contribution men made to rice production until after the harvest. Dressers waded into the paddies and bent over the dressing bar to sight along the level field, their faces close to the mud. Their posture imitated that of women transplanting rice seedlings, which men viewed as demeaning and physically dangerous for their own relatively inflexible bodies. Inverting their bodies into a feminine position and drawing close to the earth—a womb for seeds and a nurturing house for seedlings, saturated with connotations of female sexuality— dressers worked the transition from male to female labor. Dressing was like cleaning and sweeping out a house that would receive a newborn child, a task usually left to the expectant husband. In the ancestral trust fields, it was carefully ritualized. The first few passes with the dressing bar were performed by either the *ts'ici*'s bearer (*kələ*) or a married man with several healthy offspring and a smooth relationship with his wife. After smoothing the topmost field, this man made two offerings of a green bamboo branch, a boiled egg, and a goat's foreleg to a "spirit of field dressing" (*yidəbùunè*) at two mimosa trees located one above the other along the line of sight between Agàmisimo's hilltop and the rock of the Lòhə. He then returned to transplant the first seedling. Facing east, he inserted the seedling into the mud and, out of earshot of any female onlookers, quietly voiced some variation of this simple chant:

5.8

let the green rice grow long as horses' tails	che ngə mò mæ ci gɔ̀ lɔ
let the rice stalks grow long as horses' penises	che vɔ̀ mò tæ li gɔ̀ lɔ

Perhaps nothing marked the central importance of the feminine labor of transplanting in the analogic practice that associated rice production and procreation better than this male attempt to ritually appropriate it.[7] In this practice, rice seedlings were like newborn children. Comparing them to penises as transplanting began was a provisional attempt to arrogate this labor to the sphere of male fertility, as though it were merely another version of sowing. Immediately after this first seedling was planted, however, hundreds of women who had been sitting on the terraces above gathered bundles of seedlings and fanned out across the paddies. Beginning on the eastern edges, they worked stooped over and walking backward, quickly inserting seedlings into the mud in lateral rows.

The male youths withdrew to the hillside terraces above. As the afternoon drew on, they sang taunting, ribald songs to the women below. Working in clusters with their friends, young women and girls answered with songs of their own, matching the men's wit with wittier replies. Sometimes a group of friends on the hillside designated a singer and fed him lines addressed to one young woman, while her friends put their heads together to think up retorts. These songs threatened the girls' close male kin with severe embarrassment. In most families, when an unmarried girl waded into the field, her father, brothers, and male parallel cousins (whom she was prohibited from marrying) went home to avoid seeing her in this charged atmosphere.

Party officials discouraged this tradition of competitive singing in the 1950s, and after 1965 youths in Zhizuo abandoned it altogether. Though many men of Li Yong's generation described the scene of singing with gusto, they claimed to have forgotten the actual songs. This was the linguistic play of youth, not the serious speech to ghosts and spirits that ritualists digested and passed on. Still, some variants of the *nèpi* chanted that day incorporated metaphors and phrases from men's songs (pointedly excluding women's replies). I recorded three versions: Li Yong had chanted his version during public rituals for the Lòhɔ in the 1950s; Qi Bao'en had performed his publicly in the 1950s and 1960s and secretly in the 1980s and 1990s; and Qi Wenping, from the shady side's village of Méabò, had learned his version from his father, whom *ts'ici* from his side of the valley had patronized in the late 1940s.

Each variant began by asserting that this was the correct day and month for the sacrifice and describing the offerings: a goat with broad horns, a yellow-mouthed sheep, the best grain, and the best wheat beer. They mentioned sowing grain in the marsh where the first ancestors had dropped seed from their sheaths. In passages such as the one quoted in fragment 5.7, they described the plowmen packed into the round, central river bottom around the ancestral trust "like the road of stars" (the Milky Way). They told of how one man, using all his strength, dresses the field, plants the first seedling, and offers a chicken's egg and a goat's foreleg to the spirit of field dressing. Li Yong's rendition continued:

5.9

twelve flowers bloom	yi tsʻȑ nì ga
I speak of twelve	ngo lɔ tsʻȑ nì tu lu ngɔ
see in the first month	kʻò cì hɔ chì ni
the first month's paper flower blooms	kʻò cì ju lò yi
see in the second month	bɯ sɔ̀ hɔ chì ni
the second month's *læmo* tree blooms	bɯ sɔ̀ læ mo yi
see in the third month	sa nga hɔ chì ni
the third month's cypress blooms	sa nga tè mò yi
see in the fourth month	lí ho hɔ chì ni
the fourth month's mimosa blooms	lí ho jɔ mo yi

The "paper flower" of the first month refers to flowers of bamboo and paper exchanged during the festive transfer of the *tsʻici* from one household to another on the first day of the lunar year. Another flower blooms in each succeeding month: the *læmo* tree, the cypress, and the mimosa, followed by fire grass in the fifth month, bitter buckwheat in the sixth, sorghum in the seventh, oats in the eighth, sweet buckwheat in the ninth, the funeral flower[8] in the tenth, the plum tree in the eleventh, and the camellia in the twelfth.

Qi Wenping objected to this section of Li Yong's chant (fragment 5.9). It had been drained of content, he claimed, for the sake of squeamish Party members. His own version mimicked the taunting tone of competitive singing, in which blooming flowers were metaphors for feminine sexual arousal:

5.10

twelve flowers bloom	yi yi tsʻȑ nì ga
the first month's paper flower blooms	kʻò cì ju lò yi
the golden bamboo rice box blooms	mò cæ kà bò yi
yellow rice blooms on this bank	ti go nà cæ yi
black rice blooms on that bank	te pʻæ nà ne yi
the boar's fatty meat blooms	ve pú hò bò yi
fine blooms tempt	yi wú yi pʻà pʻo
if honeybees don't call	bò lɔ yi n je
flowers wilt and topple	mí mo kʻù tʻè lò
what bee visits?	a tsa bò lɔ je
flies and sawflies visit	rɔ mù hi mo je
wasps and horseflies visit	bò mo ná mo je

Yellow jackets visit the *lemo* flowers of the second month, yellow wasps the cypress flowers of the third. In the fourth month, ugly mimosas stoop over the mud:

5.11

what flower is ugly?	a tsa yi n tsæ
the mimosa is ugly	jɔ mo yi n tsæ
its leaves dangle	jɔ p'è ná la la
its petals pucker	jɔ yi dɔ lɔ lɔ
what dares visit?	a tsa lɔ je yé
stinging mud-daubers come	vè chì bò mo tà lɔ je
poison bumblebees come	bò mo bò tí go lɔ je
the fifth month's fire grass blooms	ngo ho kǽ mæ̀ yi

As it continued, Qi Wenping's chant played with the verbs *yi* ("to bloom") and *t'a* ("to be sexually aroused"). *T'a* (which I have translated rather inadequately as "to lust," "to arouse," and "to excite") ordinarily refers to animals in heat; when applied to humans, it is frankly obscene, as are the violent references to vaginas (*dubò*) and wombs (*bòdò*):

5.12

twelve flowers bloom	yi yi ts'r̀ nì yi
twelve bees buzz	bò mo ts'r̀ nì mo
don't bloom, don't bloom!	t'à yi t'à yi ve
daughters of the fourth month, don't bloom!	lí ho mæ̀ ne t'à yi tu
donkeys lust in the third month	sa nga mò bó t'a
aroused by the scent of green wheat	[yɔ] ngɔ́ vè ne t'a
dogs lust in the seventh month	shr̀ ho á nò t'a
what odor arouses them?	a tsa vè ni t'a
every odd scent arouses	chì sa vè ni t'a
sons of heaven lust in the first month	k'ò cì mù̈ zò t'a
what odor arouses them?	a tsa vè ni t'a
rice cakes and green pine needles	che p'ui t'a ci ngɔ vè ni t'a
daughters of the fourth month, don't bloom!	lí ho mæ̀ ne t'à yi tu
what odor arouses them?	a tsa vè ni t'a
the scent of muddy water!	yi na vè ni t'a lɔ bɔ
don't bloom, don't bloom!	t'à yi t'à yi ve
daughters of the fourth month, don't bloom!	lí ho mæ̀ ne t'à yi tu
plug their vaginas with mud!	yi na du bò pè lɔ do
stop them up with green seedlings!	do lo go ba ngɔ lɔ do
pinch their wombs with fire tongs!	a tsɔ bò do yi lɔ do

don't lust, don't lust!   t'à t'a t'à t'a ve . . .

  we offer a pine branch   t'à zò ji do gɔ̀
  a green bamboo stalk   mo ngɔ cha do gè
  paper like silver   t'a ye p'ɔ́ do gɔ̀
  a granary of grain   lò chì ká do gɔ̀
  that you curb their lust   t'à t'a mó gɔ̀ lɔ

What really arouses men in the first month, Qi Wenping commented, is the scent of alcohol. There is no work to do, and there are many weddings to attend. During the day, young men sit around drinking and eating fatty meat; at night, they go courting. Women, however, are aroused by the scent of muddy water, and in the fourth month, when the mud of rice transplanting is everywhere, they can grow truly shameless. The men who had gathered in Qi Wenping's barn to hear him perform this chant—all in their forties and fifties—regaled me with tales of women's seasonally recurring sexual aggression. When girls and married women assemble to plant rice, the men claimed, they talk incessantly, and most of their talk is of men. After a day of transplanting, gangs of women tour the houses of widowers and unmarried youths, sometimes even breaking down the doors of men who prefer to be left alone. During the day, the best-looking youths are badgered wherever they go, and at night they are not safe even in their own homes. Muddy water, fire tongs, and the extra bundles of green seedlings left to die on the margins of a transplanted field, Qi Wenping noted, are instruments a man can use against a woman who has gone too far in pursuing him.

I do not know whether some men might have engaged in the sexually violent acts Qi Wenping's chant mentions; the metaphorical intent, however, is clear. In the line "plug their vaginas with mud!" (*yi na du bò pè lɔ do*), *yi na* is the muddy water that flows between women's legs as they transplant rice. *Yi*, "water," also puns on *yi,* "to bloom." Men refer to female orgasm as *du yi lɔ; du* denotes female genitalia, *yi* is water, and *lɔ* is the common verb for "to come" (here taking on a double meaning much as the equivalent verb in English can do). In this context, *yi na* connotes the waters that flow from women's genitalia. To plug a vagina with *yi na* would be to turn that flow back on itself. The next line, "stop them up with green seedlings!" (*do lo go ba ngɔ lɔ do*), alludes to the bundles of excess seedlings left to die on a field's margins after transplanting is completed. In the analogic practice that associates transplanting rice with birthing, these bundles are like stillborn fetuses or dead infants, left to be scattered by passing feet. Here, the chant moves from turning the flow of sexual desire back on itself to blocking the organ of reproduction with its own failed product, an image full of evil resonances, above all as the ultimate origin of wild ghosts. Finally, the fire tongs (*a tsə*) mentioned in the next line are carved from tough, flexible wood and bent by being heated in the fire until they retain a tweezerslike shape. To "pinch their wombs with fire tongs!" (*a tsə bò do yi lə do*) would be to assail the cool and damp of wombs with the heat and dryness of fire itself, attacking the flow of sexual energy and reproductive power at its source.

Qi Wenping's chant excited controversy among other ritualists. Li Yong asserted that the only lineages of ritualists that *ts'ici* should have legitimately consulted were from his own village, Chemo; Qi Wenping's father had belonged to an upstart lineage, which a couple of *ts'ici* from villages on the valley's opposite side had patronized illegitimately in the late 1940s. Qi Bao'en claimed that the *nèpi* should not mention twelve flowers at all: unscrupulous ritualists had imported this section into the chant from love songs in the 1940s. Qi Wenping countered that both these ritualists had diluted their versions in the 1950s for fear of official criticisms. His father's chant, not performed in public since the late 1940s, was the only authoritative version. Still, all three agreed that the *nèpi* was an appeal to the Lòhə to curb the desire of women in its most volatile season.

After the disputed section, each ritualist's version told of how the Lòhə took form during a prior stage of society, in which women had actively pursued men. Li Yong's chant continued:

5.13

none offered to Lòhə	Lòhə k'o m pi̱
there was such a day	k'o ne chì ni ngɔ
as the sky took form	mù ni jé ne cì
as ritual began	p'è wú k'o chì ni
as creation began	cì wú k'o chì ni
women pursued men	mæ̀ lɔ ro lɔ jo̱
so it went that day	k'o ne chì ni go
men looked around	ro lɔ hɔ chì ni
and found no place to hide	vɛ dù vɛ kæ k'o n sa
so it took form	k'o ne chì ni cì tu̱ lɔ
the eastern Lòhə formed	bi do Lòhə cì gɔ
could not but form	n cì n go
once Lòhə took form	bi do Lòhə cì chì ni
men pursued women	ro lɔ mæ̀ lɔ jo̱
pursued and caught them	mæ̀ lɔ jo̱ tu̱ lɔ
men embraced women	ro lɔ mæ̀ lɔ zr
embraced and held them	mæ̀ lɔ zr tu̱ lɔ

so things reversed   mí kʼɔ hɔ chì ni
  men's strength grew   ro lɔ wò væ̀ tu̠
  men began to drive women   ro lɔ mæ̀ lɔ kà̠ tu̠ lɔ
so it began that day   kʼo ne chì ni go
  on such a day it began   chì ni go tu̠ lɔ
twelve flowers bloomed on that day   tsʼɽ̀ nì yi chì ni
  and thus lust followed   chɔ chì ni jɔ du tu̠ ngɔ

    oh, you eastern Lòhɔ   pi do Lòhɔ ni a

Since the sacrifice to the Lòhɔ is now performed only sporadically, Li
Yong said, the situation today resembles that distant time when women
pursued men. Women no longer have thin skins. In some villages,
groups of young girls actually go about knocking on boys' doors; in his
own, widows looking for mates chase off the wives of married men.
Worse still are the widows of Méabò, who will open your door, walk
right in, and sit down. "Some men have to hide behind locked doors," he
continued. "Before, a widower could choose to remarry or to sit in
peace. But now as soon as a wife is under ground, widows appear from
everywhere, and the husband has no choice but to remarry." (Li Yong
was a widower of long standing.)

These verses and the talk of feminine sexual aggression they inspired
can best be understood in the context of the labor exchanges that dominated the rice-transplanting season. Zhizuo residents strictly divided the
labor of growing rice by gender. As we have seen, men from individual
households prepared seed beds and sowed rice seed. When the seedlings
were ready for transplant, men and boys plowed, harrowed, and dressed
the fields, while women and girls uprooted and then planted the seedlings. Before collectivization in 1956, and again after 1980, a system of
labor exchanges throughout the *tsʼici* enabled each household to transplant all its rice quickly, in one or two days. The differences in altitude
between Zhizuo's high, outlying stream bottoms and its lower central
valley meant that rice could be planted on a staggered schedule, with
the higher or shadier terraces, where the grain would take longer to
reach maturity, planted earlier in the season, the lower or sunnier fields
later.

As the season began, each household set a date for its own planting
and calculated the labor it would need. An average household farmed
about 2.6 *mu* of rice land in 1955 (by 1984, population growth had reduced this to 1.6 *mu* per household, according to official brigade statistics). Each *mu* required eight or ten men with four or five oxen to prepare

it in a single day. Men and boys began early in the season to offer their labor and their household's ox or buffalo to kin and neighbors in the higher valleys, who later reciprocated in kind. Those who owned no oxen would exchange two days of labor for one day's work by an ox-man team. In households short of draft animals or male labor, men might work many more days than in others, but their own land could still be prepared in one or two days.

Women also began early to accumulate enough labor to transplant their household's land in one or two days. Each *mu* required twenty or more women or girls to complete in one day, so women worked for others about twice as many days as men. During this season, most women spent every day almost exclusively in the company of women. They left for the fields early in the morning and returned after dusk, leaving domestic chores such as cooking and feeding animals to men. When working in distant fields, they sometimes slept in their hosts' courtyards rather than endure the long walk home. Many planned their season's work with small groups of friends who migrated among fields together and worked side by side.

Men in Zhizuo seemed to find these gatherings of women and girls both exciting and threatening. Groups of youths in nearby fields showed off for the women, whipping up a buffalo to run through the mud or bathing a sleek ox in the river. But if a man of any age ventured near the crowds of laboring women alone, he provoked taunts and laughter. Not even outsiders were spared. Ordinarily, when I encountered women or girls on village paths or at the edges of fields, they were extremely circumspect, offering at most a quick smile or a brief word before hurrying on. But the same women, when transplanting rice, would stand up as I walked by and shout taunts or jokes, laughing with their companions. Even little girls absorbed the atmosphere. A ten-year-old girl once overturned everything I thought I had learned about the daylight demeanor of girls and women in Zhizuo. Knee deep in the mud with several small companions, she smiled broadly as I approached, lifted her skirt, and pointed to herself, dissolving into giggles as I hurried by, shocked to the core. Other men often went far out of their way to avoid a field where women were transplanting, especially if their own daughters, sisters, or parallel cousins were present.

Several observers of rural China have commented on the overlapping, informal alliances that women create as they gather to wash clothes on a riverbank or pare vegetables at a communal pump (M. Wolf

1972; Martin 1988; Judd 1994). Margery Wolf noted that in rural Taiwan such women's communities often accumulated great power to influence the decisions that men made; public opinion about men and their actions took shape in women's gatherings, and this talk could easily shame men or cause them to lose face (1972, 40). In 1970s Taiwan, such power was muted and subversive, exercised almost entirely behind the scenes. In 1990s Zhizuo, women often exerted it publicly, sometimes with the specific intent of shaping official policies. (Chapter 9 describes one such occasion, when women's gatherings brutally shamed the local Party secretary and forced the county government to reverse a birth planning policy.)

Though many men were cautious of these gatherings for the public humiliation they could exact, most of their expressions of anxiety were reserved for the sexual capacities on display. In chapter 3, I mentioned that the sexual freedom accorded unmarried youth made it difficult for parents to manage their children's marriage choices. The scene of the ancestral trust planting, where clever sexual banter rang out between youths on the hillsides and girls below, must have aroused parents' deepest apprehensions. As Li Zhiwu recalled dreamily, "Many marriages were made on that day." Moreover, parents had every reason to fear a state of affairs in which "women pursued men" and men "had no place to hide," especially if the constant companionship of their girlfriends did make some young women bolder during rice-transplanting season. A father could negotiate with his son over which girls the son would pursue, but if women were to do the chasing, the father would have no say over who might come knocking at his son's door.

The specter of aggressively promiscuous crowds of women likely also raised fatherly anxiety about losing daughters to those not interrelated within the Zhizuo ts'ici. We have seen that parents encouraged their daughters to marry their cross-cousins, with limited success. When this was not possible, parents wished at the very least for their daughters to marry other Zhizuo Lòlop'ò. In this way, they could retain many forms of attachment to their daughters, from casual visits to the dense array of ritual obligations that fell to daughters in mortuary ceremonies. In the 1990s, during the bright winter months that preceded the transplanting season, bands of mostly Han youths from lowland villages walked to Zhizuo to visit the barn lofts of local young women. And during the first lunar month, a "clothing competition festival" was the occasion for hundreds of youths from outside to flood Zhizuo to watch local girls dance in their festival finery. A *nèpi* for a ghost called *srkanè,* who preyed on beautiful young women who loved to talk, dance, and wear nice clothing, hints at the resentment these invasions caused. In these verses, Han youths, "greedy as wild dogs," watch gorgeously clothed local girls laugh and wiggle on riverbank stones. The youths are called "Kúju," a derogatory term for poor Han of low education and morals.

5.14

seven beloved daughters	ǽ mæ̀ né shɨ̀ ro̱
seven loved ones over there	shɨ̀ ro̱ k'o ka jɔ
sewing and embroidering	chi bo vɔ̀ sè jɔ
clowning and laughing	væ cí væ ha jɔ
on that slope lively ones	k'o bò cæ̀ cæ jo
on this slope noisy ones	hé bò cæ̀ nì jo
Kúju greedy as wild dogs	Kú ju æ ve ngò
Kúju laugh like fools	Kú ju læ sì ji
Kúju watch and drool	Kú tæ̀ læ mì ro
they love bells, breastplates, and earrings	pe kó pe jɔ to nó tu
dangling earrings, they perch on stones	pe bò jà ha ló mo ti̱
embroidered leggings	chì t'ù chí næ tsæ̱
shoes with spotless soles	chì næ bò n kæ
leggings against the stones	chì t'ù ló mi je̱
leggings with spotless hems	chì t'ù bò n kæ
they spread clean leaves to lean on	p'è k'a wú lɔ je̱
spread rows of leaves to sit on	p'è k'a jɔ̀ tà ti̱
wiggling waists and buttocks	p'ì shɨ̀ jo lɔ jɔ
mobs of Kúju	Kú pe Kú chɔ̀ jɔ
clown and laugh	væ cí væ ha jɔ

Local youths stood little chance of marrying Han women from outside, and many found Líp'ò women from higher in the mountains ugly and uncultured. Most thus aspired to marry local girls, but too many bees were buzzing around these flowers for youths to view the collective display of feminine productive and reproductive force during the rice-transplanting season with equanimity. If young women did gather courage from daily mutual companionship in the rice fields to make more independent sexual choices, they imperiled *ts'ici* endogamy. And this threat menaced both the youths who sang taunting songs from the hillsides and the elderly men gathered about the Lòhɔ to ritually promote the community's reproduction.

    The gendered division of labor called attention to the extended analogy between sowing rice and insemination, transplanting, and birthing.

Gathering in talkative crowds to transplant seedlings, women displayed the sources of their influence in household and community affairs—their productive and reproductive labor. The men who verbally attacked this community of women and girls were expressing fears about women's sexual independence and their powers to subvert the interests of their husbands, fathers, and brothers. But they were also granting backhanded recognition to this impressive display. From the heights of Agàmisimo's hilltop, senior men engaged in a fantasy of communal reproduction structured as descent from male ancestor to male heir.[9] From the Lòhə's stone, however, these same men encountered another version of reproduction in which women and girls controlled granary and womb and shaped the future of the seeds and heirs they produced. This encounter drew coherence from the generative differentials of household space. If Agàmisimo was the bed's-head spirit of the valley, the ancestral trust fields were its granary, and the Lòhə was the little spirit hanging above the beds of senior women, their *lòhə*. The appeal of senior men to the valley's Lòhə to regulate the community's crucial reproductive resources was modeled on this little *lòhə*, which smoothed the flow of rice and seed through a household. Admonishing the Lòhə to curb women's lust, these men envisioned the astonishing exhibition of youthful sexual energies arrayed before them as a force that must be contained to reproduce an extended house.

They Vomit Lying Words

The hot season—the sixth, seventh, and eighth lunar months—was the time of pestilence in northern Yunnan. With no pesticides in use until the late 1970s, insects feasted in clusters on the rice stalks. Women spent their days in the fields sweeping long, plaited bamboo scoops over the rice plants, trapping the pests, and packing them into tightly woven carrying baskets to burn. It was also the time of epidemic contagion. Meat spoiled quickly, and fly, louse, and rat populations were at their peaks. Zhizuo residents called the most common epidemic forms *nokà* and *shryi;* in the early 1950s, "barefoot doctors" translated *nokà* as typhus and typhoid fever (Ch. *shanghan*) and *shryi* as epidemic encephalomyelitis (Ch. *liunao*).[10] The terms could also be combined in a single phrase, *nokà shryi,* to designate all infectious disease.

Older people remembered seasons when epidemics of infectious disease swept through the mountains, killing as many as eight or nine people
in a village. During epidemics, people avoided visits to infected houses or
villages. Mortuary rituals were sparsely attended, and many were post-
poned until the tenth lunar month, when the danger of contagion receded. N̠oká and shryi were thought of as entities with specific attributes—
malevolent ghosts or spirits. The ghost of n̠oká was said to "hear but not
see," to be blind with extraordinarily sharp ears. One could enter an
afflicted house without danger as long as one did not speak. Men and
women in their fifties and sixties spoke of sneaking silently about their villages as children, fearing that the ghost of n̠oká would hear anything
louder than a whisper and attack from the stricken, shuttered houses. The
ghost of shryi was said to "see but not hear." To be overheard was safe
enough, but to be visible from an afflicted house was to be vulnerable. The
vectors for these infections were glances and overheard words. Contagion
was a matter of speech and visibility, hearing and seeing.

In anticipation of this season, the ts'ici sponsored a sacrifice to another of Agàmisimo's offspring, Cha, who warded off pestilence and
contagion. This was the first ritual of the cycle to be abandoned, and, unlike the rites for Agàmisimo and the Lòhɔ, it was never revived. It
sparked little controversy among the ritualists whom I asked to remember it: all deferred to Li Yong, the only ritualist alive to have presided
over it personally and the only one who could perform its nèpi.

For as long as anyone could remember, Li Yong told me, Cha had
resided on a small shelf just within the upstream doorway to a house in
Chemo. On the fifth month's first day of the horse, families from that
village and other parts of Zhizuo gathered in this house's large courtyard. In contrast to Agàmisimo's hill or the Lòhɔ's stone, one could see
nothing of the valley from there, only the mud-brick walls of house and
courtyard. Each participant arrived carrying his or her own bowl and
chopsticks. The ts'ici arranged for a household in the village of Chezò to
bring a goat. Each household brought a sheng of grain; a portion of this
was reserved to pay for the goat, another to feed the participants. The
ts'ici household brought two chickens, and each of the five members of
the ts'ici staff brought a cock.

In the courtyard, before the house's raised porch, the ts'ici's ritualist
built an effigy for each entity to be propitiated: a miniature corn-drying
rack for Shr̀mògù, spirit of lightning and bringer of death;[11] a row of six
unforked pine saplings for Agàmisimo; six groups of sticks carved with
claws, ears, and eyes for Cha.[12] Before each of these effigies, the ritualist

placed offerings of wheat beer, grain, and salt. He killed the two chickens for Shìmògù and Agàmisimo, the goat and five cocks for Cha. Men of the *ts'ici* staff cooked the grain and butchered, chopped, and boiled the animals; spread a bed of pine needles over the ground; and counted out hundreds of small, individual piles of meat onto this bed. Each participant received a pile of meat and a ladle of grain in his or her individual bowl. This was an extraordinary procedure. In the other rituals of the cycle, food was passed fluidly from hand to hand and eaten on the spot; here, it was divided meticulously into individual portions before being served. These procedures denied, and in denying drew attention to, the social adhesions along which traveled the glances and words that bore contagion.[13]

Li Yong treasured the intricate *nèpi* for Cha, his exclusive possession. He cited it frequently when he lectured on the obligations and compensations of the *ts'ici* staff. (Fragments 4.3 and 4.5, in chapter 4, are from this chant.) The rules and procedures of the *ts'ici,* this *nèpi* stated, originated with the formation of the cosmos: "who made these rules? great-grandfather Misi made them." They came into existence as the black clouds formed, as the great lightning spirit Mùwòhætə (another name for Shìmògù) took shape, as Cánìshunì (the police who descend to arrest dying souls) came into existence, as sky and earth took form. And then, sometime later, the evil of infection arrived: "see the fields, see the pastures, evil, such evil, strange diseases arrive, coughs and colds, *noká* and *shryi* . . . see Chezò and Méabò, see this Zhizuo *ts'ici,* our entire *ts'ici* house; strange diseases arrive." For each cock killed, the chant had a few lines for the member of the *ts'ici* staff who had contributed it. It mentioned the speaker's compensation, the warden's "price of horse feed," and the bearer's "price of grass." Six times, the ritualist called on Cha to drive disease and pestilence from Zhizuo. Like Agàmisimo, Cha was to encircle the region, expelling contagion and bringing back fertility. "See the *noká* and *shryi;* drive them away; drive the insects upstream, drive them to the river's head; chase the pests downstream, drive them to the river's tail; coughs and colds, strange diseases, diarrhea and stomach pains, drive them away."

Li Yong called my attention to a few verses in the middle portion of the *nèpi.* These portrayed the scene in the *ts'ici'*s courtyard, he said, where famous Han officials and miserable criminals were housed and fed. He laughed over the depiction of officials and criminals both gorging on meat and wine at the *ts'ici'*s expense. These verses associated epidemic infection with the style in which officials and criminals ate, drank, and, especially, spoke.

5.15

on such a day	kʼo ne chì ni hɔ
the *tsʼici* speaks	tsʼi ci pi̱ chì ni
some eat their fill	tsò bo̱ tsæ te su̱
some get drunk	dɔ bo̱ tsæ te su̱
thus he speaks	kʼo ne chì ni pi̱ te su̱
some fall ill as work begins	kà wú no̱ te su̱
some fall ill as work ends	kà mæ no̱ te su̱
comes such a day	kʼo ne chì ni ngɔ
Han come and go	ce yi hé lɔ jɔ
thus some fall ill	kʼo ne no̱ te su̱
on such a day	kʼo ne chì ni hɔ
they vomit lying words	tà pó tà yì jɔ
thus is the *tsʼici*'s house	tsʼi ci kʼo chì ni jɔ
criminals at the *tsʼici*'s house	tsʼi ci hɔ̱ lɔ̱ te su̱
on such a day	kʼo ne chì ni gɔ
he feeds them meat	tsò mi ju̱ chì ni gɔ
some stuff themselves with meat	tsò mi ju̱ bo̱ te su̱
he gives them drink	dɔ mi hɔ chì ni gɔ
some get drunk on wine	dɔ mi dɔ bo̱ te su̱

Here, parallel constructions frame and contrast two styles of speaking. The first style is the *tsʼici*'s speech, mentioned in the second line of this passage, introduced by the phrase "on such a day." The *tsʼici*'s speech is *pi̱*. Zhizuo residents employed several words to formally designate offerings or propitiations to nonhuman entities. *Ho* was to make a simple offering of food; *və̀* was to make a temporary offering, involving a simple effigy and a few verses; *pi̱* was the most serious and delicate kind of offering, a negotiation with the most powerful or inimical of nonhuman forces. To *pi̱* was to speak formally in the presence of a nonhuman entity gathered into the material form of an effigy. It was to use speech to convey offerings of food and words across a divide, conventionally framed in terms of ontology (the divide between the world of the living and the world of ghosts). *Pi̱* was digestive speech, which nurtured a ritualist on the long journey of his apprenticeship, and which he carried in his stomach to pass on at these crucial moments of negotiation with nonhuman forces. The *tsʼici* of this verse transforms a social divide into an ontological one. He uses *pi̱* to transmit offerings of meat and drink to the criminals and Han officials who crowd his courtyard, just as a ritualist uses *nèpi̱* to convey offerings to the entities he wishes to placate or drive away.

A repetition of the phrase "on such a day" introduces a second mention of speech, that of the officials and criminals at the *ts'ici*'s house: "they vomit lying words." Li Yong fixed on this line as being in need of explication—it is a metaphor whose meaning is not immediately transparent. It might be translated more literally as "they vomit like the sow." As a sow eats, she takes great mouthfuls; and as she chews, her feed falls from the corners of her mouth to pile up beneath her jaws. The phrase captures this action precisely. It is used here to evoke the speech of Han officials. This is the opposite of digestive speech: the words are regurgitated before they are even swallowed; they reverse in the mouth. This verse is an excellent example of metaphorical "turning speech" (*mèkò: mè* means "mouth," *kò* means "to turn" or "to return"), of which, Li Yong reminded me, the best *nèpi* makes ample use. *Mèkò* turns in the mouth to reveal several meanings, the choice of which depends on the listener's knowledge and acuity. But these words of officials and criminals are not *mèkò;* they do not turn so much as *reverse*, like vomited food. *Mèkò*, like *nèpi* in general, is true speech because it is transmitted from ancestral sources through the long journey of corporeal absorption. In contrast, the words of officials and criminals fall from the mouth and pile up; they carry no gifts or offerings; they are lying words.

Thus the *ts'ici* offers food and drink with digested speech; officials and criminals stuff themselves, vomiting words as though drunkenly regurgitating their meat. We shall see this scenario evoked in exorcisms to describe relations between humans and wild ghosts, who gorge themselves on offerings without ever becoming satisfied and whose evil essence is captured in the image of a blocked digestive tract. I have referred to the divide across which offerings are transmitted alternately as ontological (differences among kinds of beings) and social (here, differences of role and hierarchy). It is more precisely the interfusion of these—a *moral* divide. It is a difference in the way speech interleaves memory and the body. *Pi*, or *nèpi*, inhabits the body, and this is how it is remembered; the body is the route through which its authority is transmitted. The speech vomited up by Han officials short-circuits the body. In this, it is like the writing that founds their authority, which passes too easily into the eye and out of the mouth.

Li Yong's *nèpi* for Cha associates the style of speech of Han officials with infectious disease. This association is deeply overdetermined; it brings together many of the concerns that animated the experts' speech about the *ts'ici* system. We have seen that epidemics of the most feared contagions were thought to depend on sight and hearing for their transmission—speaking too loudly or being too visible left one vulnerable. This idea is consistent with a view expressed often among Lòlop'ò that gaudy dress or loud speech exposes one to harm from inimical entities of every character, from those who attack flashy young women (*srkanè*) to those who descend on people who argue loudly (Ch. *zhoushen*).[14] The expensive dress and cultivated language of the *ts'ici*'s powerful visitors from the lowlands made them flamboyant and loquacious in local eyes, regardless of their actual behavior. They were vulnerable to contagion, then, and already beginning to vomit—words, but perhaps food and drink as well. Being vulnerable is but a step short of being a *cause:* the ghosts of *nokǎ* and *shryi* who hear and see variably, but with such terrible effect, do so through the senses of those already lying ill.

But the *style* of the speech of officials and criminals was also at issue. Their vomited words were of a piece with the other kinds of orality that depleted the *ts'ici*'s resources. As it made the *ts'ici* a burden to be avoided, their overconsumption threatened the reproduction of *ts'ici* households and the *ts'ici* system itself. As we have seen, the speaker on the *ts'ici* staff was expected to adapt a similar style of speech as he ate and drank prodigiously with the guests. His glib and promiscuous speech associated him with sexual promiscuity and a perverse reversal of the productive and reproductive processes that sustained this domestic community. The scene at the ancestral trust planting raised an analogous concern that throngs of women, with their free-flowing talk about men, would imperil the community's endogamous reproduction; this threat was given back to them in muttered verses about blocking and reversing the flow of their reproductive force. In talk about the *ts'ici* system, dreams of reproductive self-sufficiency, desires for communal endogamy, and fears of epidemic infection all turned on this distinction between styles of speaking. The rules and procedures of the *ts'ici* system were commemorated and transmitted in measured, digested speech, which adhered to ancestral forms and avoided the Chinese language. Remembering these procedures, senior men such as Li Yong, Qi Bao'en, and Qi Wenping defined their digested speech against other forms: the uncontrollable chatter of women planting rice, the glib wit of the *ts'ici*'s speaker, the vomited speech of criminals and Han officials. The humor with which my ritualist friends explicated these forms did not hide the menace they were seen to carry. Each was characterized by a too-facile transmission of words that brought a threat to communal

reproduction—of reproductive perversions, lust-driven women, predatory youths, and epidemic infection.

Conclusion

I asked each of those with whom I discussed the rules and
procedures of the *ts'ici* system to walk with me to the ritual sites we were
talking about. Li Yong scoffed at me. "Why do you want to go up
there?" he asked, barely inclining his head toward Agàmisimo's hilltop.
"There's nothing up there anymore; it's hollow [*kɔ*]." Qi Bao'en said he
was too old and couldn't walk well enough, Qi Chun had business in the
county town, and Qi Wenping had irrigation to attend to. Describing
the rites and *nèpi* connected with these places, these men recalled them
in the full light of their most public moments, when they were packed
most densely with life and meaning. Now, Agàmisimo's trees had been
deliberately felled; the Lòhɔ's stone lay by haunted fields; and the house
where Cha resided was derelict.

Talking of these places as they had once been was a form of mourning. Like mourning, this talk attempted to reshape the boundaries of a
living soul in the dead's absence (Rose 1996, 35). To remember the valley's most central places, to invoke the powerful entities that still inhabited them (if only in the form of wild ghosts), and to recite the digested
words that structured them was to appeal again to place as the foundation of a domestic community. This conscientious memory work used
the echoes of ritualized words to reenvision social relations emerging
from these places. It drew on a ritualized poetics of place to center and
bound a domestic community—to refigure a house. Here, the themes of
descent and affinity, production and reproduction, mutual nurturance,
the exchange of substance, and the long debts of flesh, with which ordinary domestic space was invested, were reconstituted as ocular, aural,
and kinesthetic. They were magnified through the visual and auditory
spaces of this embracing valley, refracted through the seeing, hearing,
speaking, walking, and digesting that were the persistent concerns of all
this talk. These made possible the intertwining of word, body, and place
with which people inhabited this landscape. They were the means by
which persons extended themselves over inhabited space and constituted it as mutually enveloped and enveloping.

Talking of the lost *ts'ici,* then, was a way of thinking about community as more than the social relations of production and reproduction to which any house gives rise, more than concrete networks of exchange of talk, goods, and labor among kin and neighbors. It was a way of reimagining a community as an embracing place, a common dwelling that one shared even with those whom one barely knew—or whom one knew all too well—who had once done terrible things to oneself or one's family or friends. This talk took shape against a background of other talk, which Li Yong, Qi Bao'en, Qi Chun, and Qi Wenping preferred not to recite, at least in my presence. The pauses in their stories seethed with other stories: of the death of the *ts'ici* system and the evisceration of community. The silences in their *nèpi* chants echoed with other *nèpi,* performed to evict from body and house the wild ghosts of those who had died of hunger, suicide, or other violence. To understand what motivated these efforts to re-member community, we must now attend to this background of other, more troubled, words.

CHAPTER SIX

A Spectral State

Chinese peasants had a number of difficult lessons to learn as they awakened into the new national order brought by Liberation.[1] The most crucial concerned "class struggle": peasants were required to absorb the Maoist concept of class, with its overwhelming emphasis on relations of exploitation within hierarchies of power (Dirlik 1983). A key forum for learning about class struggle was oral performance in the genre of "speaking bitterness" (Ch. *suku*). In public "speaking bitterness" sessions, peasants were trained to render their experiences of poverty, powerlessness, and exploitation in the old society into narrative form, working them into the national story of liberation from past injustice (Anagnost 1997).

When Zhizuo was liberated in 1950, most adults there were already accomplished in the oral performance of chronicles of release from poverty and powerlessness. When called upon to "speak bitterness," they drew on the vocabulary of mourning songs (such as the examples that open chapters 2 and 3). As "speaking bitterness" narratives were reworked throughout the Mao era, reinvoking the past and repeating the story of its annihilation (Anagnost 1997, 17–44), Zhizuo residents wove this trope back into these songs. "Speaking bitterness" narratives were no longer performed in public by the 1980s, but their traces remained in verses sung upon the deaths of loved ones. In the following passage of a lamenting song (*xchəngə*), a woman in her seventies, singing at a funeral for a nephew, tells of how her own parents' poverty was lifted as their children grew, Liberation arrived, and land reform caused their fields, pastures, and wealth to expand:

6.1

hungry flapping bats	mù̀ ngá tu mì zù
not a day without hunger	m mì lu̠ n jɔ
bitter ribbed oxen	lò bə lò shó zò
not a day without bitterness	n shó lu̠ n jɔ
no land for farming	kà dù mi n jɔ
no land for herding	ló dù mi n jɔ
trousers worn out at the knees	mæ̠ ji̠ dɔ gò va ne shu̠
shirt backs tattered	mæ jù̠ p'a ká bù̀ ne shu̠
poverty like grass	n shu̠ ci n je
poverty like water	n shu̠ yi n je
and then	à pá he chì po̠
our sons grew fat	zò ho zò væ̀ tu̠
daughters grew tall	né ho né mo tu̠
the bitter herb spread	yí k'ù lè mo kæ
and Liberation came	kæ fáng lɔ chì ni
our fields grew	kà dù mi pé wo
our pastures increased	ló dù mi pé wo
we gained land for herding	ló dù mi jæ̀ ci tu̠ lɔ
gained land for farming	kà dù mi sho væ̀ tu̠ lɔ
livestock of every stripe	jí lu jè ja ka
grain of every flavor	kà lu tso ja ka

The song reverses the narrative layering of "speaking bitterness": instead of refashioning personal experience to accord with the narrative of national transformation, it domesticates the national annihilation of the past, drawing it into service of the singer's gratitude to her parents for the labor of raising her, absorbing it into the familiar flow of social reproduction. Mentioning Liberation, the song makes self-conscious reference to "speaking bitterness":

the bitter herb spread	yí k'ù lè mo kæ
and Liberation came	kæ fáng lɔ chì ni

The "bitter herb" is *yík'ù,* a tough, ground-dwelling perennial of acrid flavor. But *yík'ù* is also a pun on a familiar Chinese phrase for speaking bitterness, *yiku sitian,* "recalling past bitterness, savoring present sweetness." The pun is reinforced in this couplet by the parallel positioning of *yík'ù* at the beginning of the first line and the Chinese loan word for "Liberation" (*kæ fáng,* from Ch. *jiefang*) at the beginning of the second. The couplet blurs distinctions between memories of living the national transformation and memories of speaking it. And in so doing, it invokes a shadow of menace. The herb *yík'ù* grows everywhere on the disturbed earth of field margins and overgrazed mountainsides. It appeared suddenly and spread rapidly during the Great Leap Forward of 1958 and 1959, as hillsides were deforested to allow experiments in large-scale swidden agriculture and to feed copper and iron furnaces. In the 1990s, older people in Zhizuo remembered its abrupt and ubiquitous appearance as a portent of the unforgettable disaster that followed the Great Leap. And they drew this memory into the service of describing further personal disasters: the phrase "the calamity of *yík'ù* from heaven" (*yík'ù amùu wò*) was commonly used to speak of the sudden and inexplicable descent of misfortune on a person or family. The song recalls Liberation and land reform fondly, as coinciding with a sudden change of personal fortune. But it also conceals a reflection on the vast social changes Liberation portended and the terrible calamity in which these changes culminated at the end of the decade.

The spread of the "bitter herb" in both these senses—as a prescribed narrative style for shaping personal biographies to national transformations (*yiku* in Chinese) and as a material invasion of the landscape's every corner (*yík'ù* in Lòlongo)—is a potent metaphor for the thorough transformation in state power that Liberation brought. In the early 1950s in northern Yunnan, the socialist state rapidly deposed or executed the old elite, created new institutions of government throughout the rural landscape, and instituted a thorough inversion of old class hierarchies. This onslaught disabled Zhizuo's *ts'ici* system. It became clear that this new state power could be neither managed nor understood through the old regime of hospitality, which had welcomed the Republican state's agents into the community's center in order to mitigate their most devastating effects. Zhizuo residents struggled to envision the state in transformed terms. Their stories of this period, explored in this chapter, show the new state spreading through their lived landscape, excavating its most meaning-laden places, and building them over with its own institutions. In response, the affects and memories embedded in these places detached and became animate, frustrating state projects in ways that were often ironic or even comic.

In the mid-1950s, the state initiated another series of profound social transformations. Relations to the land on which the old vision of community had been built were overturned as land and labor were collectivized. People in Zhizuo found the state itself replacing ancestral authority as a generative force for production and social reproduction. But this vision hollowed out during the Great Leap Forward, as production faltered and social reproduction failed. In their stories of the Great Leap

and the devastating famine that it precipitated, Zhizuo residents drew
on exorcism rituals to develop a new mode of envisioning state power.
In this vision, the state was likened to a spectral chain, a predatory bureaucracy of wild ghosts, dominated by the fury and resentment of the
unmourned famine dead. For more than thirty years after the famine,
people in Zhizuo would continue to develop this vision in ghost stories,
eventually elaborating it into an efficient mode of subverting local state
authority. This chapter traces the struggles Zhizuo residents underwent
to reenvision the state of the 1950s through their stories of land reform,
collectivization, the Great Leap Forward, and the famine. These stories
culminate in the bitterest recollections that any in Zhizuo would ever recite to me, memories that fissured social life for decades to come.

Excavations

Episodic killings punctuated the first years after Liberation, as the People's Liberation Army (PLA) campaigned against counterrevolutionaries. The Communist Party gained control of Yunnan at
the end of 1949 and the beginning of 1950, setting up People's Governments in every district and county. In early 1950, the new provincial government found itself desperately short of grain to feed the urban population and the burgeoning masses of PLA soldiers entering the province.
The first act of the new local governments, then, was to requisition grain
by force from the rural populace. Thousands of cadres and soldiers were
sent to the countryside to collect grain, concentrating on the most
influential sector of the rural population, those who owned the most
land. By April, disgruntled local elites had raised armed rebellions
throughout most of the province's mountainous districts, killing grain
collectors and seriously disrupting requisition (DZY 1991, 1:86–88). In
Dayao County, a Líp'ò man named Pu Guancai raised an army of
nearly two thousand, which he called the Western Yunnan Youth Anti-
Communist Grain Resistance Army. Pu Guancai's army attacked a district government just south of Zhizuo, taking hostage twenty-seven
cadres who were meeting there (CYZZ 1994, 108). By December, the
PLA had regained control of the mountainous regions and mounted a
vigorous mopping-up campaign, arresting more than sixty-two thousand people (DZY 1991, 1:88). The Xia *tusi* and his son Xia Jian, an officer
in the Guomindang army, were arrested as ringleaders of another armed

rebel movement. An army firing squad executed the *tusi* in a low-lying field near his house before an audience of thousands. Further executions virtually wiped out the powerful Xia family and its closest allies.

In 1951 and 1952, executions continued on a wider scale. In the summer of 1951, the Party launched a nationwide movement to suppress counterrevolutionaries, in which hundreds of thousands were accused of being foreign spies, having undisclosed ties to the Nationalist Party, or being involved in counterrevolutionary conspiracy. By the end of the year, more than seven thousand had been executed in Chuxiong Prefecture alone (CYZZ 1994, 114). In early 1952, the PLA captured Luo Guotian, Zhizuo's richest landlord, former militia commander, fearsome bandit fighter, and local rival to the Xia *tusi*. He was brought to Zhizuo for a struggle session, accused of organizing counterrevolution, taken back to Dayao for further struggle sessions, and shot. After his death, Zhizuo's new leaders made his treasured house, which he had defended from Ding Zhiping's "bandit" army with such wily success, into the headquarters for the government of the new Zhizuo township (*xiang*). One of the Xia family's houses became the seat for the neighboring Zhonghe township government. Another was made the seat of the Zhonghe District (*qu*) government, which administered both townships.

Of all the killings, Zhizuo residents remembered most vividly those of the three landlords Zhang Wenxin, Li Yinke, and Qi Guoxing. Zhang Wenxin was Zhizuo's most prominent Han personage. Beginning with mules borne by two brood mares that had been given to him by his first wife's parents, he had built a thriving business hauling salt, sugar, and opium. He lived in a large house in Chemo with two wives and a son and had developed a reputation for stinginess among his Lòlop'ò neighbors. Zhang was accused of covert participation in the Xia *tusi*'s rebel organization. He was hauled before a crowd of his employees and neighbors, who were encouraged to vent their grievances against him. One of his former workers swore that shortly before Liberation he had seen Zhang burn a note from Yunnan's underground Communist Party asking for his support. This accusation ensured his death. Li Yinke and Qi Guoxing were also fingered as counterrevolutionary associates of the Xia family. Both Lòlop'ò, they were the only people in Zhizuo apart from Luo Guotian and Zhang Wenxin to be classified as landlords, although they owned relatively little land and employed only two or three workers each. On a cloudless day in the twelfth lunar month, shortly after Luo Guotian's execution, two PLA soldiers bound the three men, marched them to the schoolyard, and shot them before an audience of hundreds gathered on the terraces above. More than forty years later, many who had been children then could still mark with a tossed stone the precise spots where the three men had stood: Zhang on the right, Qi in the center, Li on the left. Their ghosts were the first of many that would accumulate at this site through the 1950s and 1960s.

These executions decimated the elite group that had selected the *ts'ici*. Of the elites who had been powerful enough to avoid service as *ts'ici*, only one escaped death—by fleeing to the provincial capital, Kunming. With the most influential community members out of the way, land reform went smoothly. A land reform work team from Dayao classified the population into rich, middle, and poor peasants and agricultural laborers. About 20 percent of households in this area were labeled "middle peasants," 70 percent "poor peasants," and 9 percent "agricultural laborers"; the remaining 1 percent were "rich peasants" and "landlords" (YSB 1986, 102–103). The team confiscated the lands, houses, and agricultural implements of the landlords and all land that rich peasants rented out or worked with hired labor. These lands and goods were divided evenly among the poor peasants and agricultural laborers. After the executions, the remaining members of the circle that had selected the *ts'ici* were mostly classified as rich or middle peasants. Further reforms continued to close off opportunities that these classes might have had for advancement. Some were soon made members of special punishment production teams, where they did the heaviest and most degrading labor, earned fewer work points, and were assigned quotas of unpaid labor.

Nevertheless, yearly meetings to select *ts'ici* continued. The participants were now mostly former *ts'ici*, seeking to restore some of their lost prestige and to soften the humiliation they now suffered. As before, *ts'ici* were selected during a New Year's gathering of Zhizuo's population. Members of Zhizuo's nascent Party organization and cadres of the new township government often attended the festival, but most did not participate in the meeting. Many of these officials had grown up in Zhizuo, and they were deeply ambivalent about the *ts'ici* system. On the one hand, it was an embarrassment to those who had to explain its continued presence to district and county leaders. On the other hand, its festivals and rituals remained so popular that no local official dared prohibit them outright.

Still, criteria for selection of *ts'ici* were sharply altered. A *ts'ici* household no longer required wealth; it needed only to be headed by an elderly couple with a smooth marriage and a history of bearing healthy children. Influential outsiders now lodged in Luo Guotian's roomy house, and the government took over maintaining roads, holding prisoners, and judging local disputes. The only responsibility left to the *ts'ici* household and its staff was to organize the yearly cycle of rituals. Former *ts'ici* now chose their successors from among former poor peasants and agricultural laborers in order to borrow the legitimacy of these classes. To become *ts'ici* in the 1950s was to join a group of the officially discredited, but it was also to be assured a quiet prestige among kin and neighbors and a long life under the protection of Agàmisimo.

National land reform regulations required the requisition and redistribution of lands belonging to ancestral halls, temples, monasteries, churches, schools, and other organizations. Sobered by the armed resistance to its grain requisition policies in regions inhabited mainly by minorities, however, Yunnan's provincial government issued special regulations for "mountainous minority nationality districts." Work teams were to conduct land reform without "wounding nationality feelings," with "respect for nationality customs," and with an eye to "fostering unity among nationalities." The instructions stated that "minority nationality spirit mountains, spirit lands, and burial grounds must not be disturbed. Common lands related to religious belief may also be preserved in whole or in part" (CYZZ 1994, 118; DZY 1991, 1:99). Zhizuo's land reform work team thus made no attempt to redistribute the 10 fertile *mu* of ancestral trust land. People continued to gather in the fourth month to plow and plant these fields communally. The township government appropriated the harvest, returning a small portion to the *ts'ici* household to support the ritual cycle.

Party and government cadres gradually increased their criticism of the *ts'ici* rituals and took steps to reform their content. In the early 1950s, a few politically ambitious Zhizuo residents joined the Party. One spring, one of these new members sat next to the ritualist Li Yong as he chanted to the Lòhə in preparation for planting the ancestral trust fields. The Party member reported to the land reform work team that part of the chant was obscene and offensive to Party morality. The team publicly criticized Li Yong, and the next year's *ts'ici* selected a different ritualist to perform an expurgated chant.

The only *ts'ici* ritual abandoned in the 1950s was the sacrifice to Cha, the spirit that protected the community against contagious disease. In 1953, a serious typhus epidemic struck the area. Several in Zhizuo recalled with precision that the epidemic had been halted by a phone call. A cadre walked to Zhonghe and made a call to Dayao on a newly constructed phone line. The call was received by a Zhizuo native, Li Zhang, who had just been appointed deputy county head. Li Zhang immediately ordered a medical team to Zhizuo. The team inoculated the entire population against typhus, halting the epidemic with stunning efficiency. Li Zhang made the most of this victory: now that the revolution had brought modern medicine to Zhizuo, he announced, there would be no need to propitiate Cha. Given the success of the inoculations, few were disposed to argue, and the *ts'ici* of 1954 eliminated the sacrifice to Cha from the ritual cycle. With this event, the category of "feudal superstition" began to fill out for Zhizuo residents. The contrast between a dynamic trajectory toward a scientific future in which phone calls and injections would be commonplace and the superstitions of a discredited feudal past was drawn clearly for the first time. Li Zhang pushed the point home by personally selecting a site for a new state medical clinic. It would be built on a hillside where hundreds still gathered nearly every day of the tenth lunar month to perform the tenth-month sacrifice for kin who had died during the previous year.

With land reform, the new state had begun to dismantle and reformulate social relations in the countryside. Killing off the old elite in campaigns against counterrevolutionaries had given land reform work teams a crucial opening to carry out procedures developed through years of experimentation in other parts of China: redefining and codifying class divisions among the population; pitting rich peasants against middle and poor peasants and agricultural laborers; and redistributing land, houses, livestock, and implements across this divide. Still, these procedures could be effective only when backed by the authority of the new state. It was essential that locals be made to feel the state's solid presence in new institutions with tangible contours.

Setting up local government centers in Luo Guotian's house in Zhizuo and in the Xia *tusi*'s houses in Zhonghe began a long process of excavating intensely meaningful places and reoccupying them with signs of the new regime. This process was episodic and piecemeal, characterized by missteps, surprises, and setbacks and by the uneven rhythm of advance and retreat, excess and rectification, that characterized local politics in the Mao era. Forty years later, however, Zhizuo residents narrated it as though its intent had been clear and its logic meticulous: it had reworked the landscape of their valley to produce a new kind of state power.

In these tales, cadres chose with unerring instinct to build new institutions in places where the productive unities of households had resonated with a larger communal unity. These were places where people had turned the temporal spiral of life and death into a reaffirmation of productive and reproductive relations; where negotiations with the forces of the cosmos were carried out; where gates opened between this world and the other. These ritualized operations had all required active engagement with images of state power. The moment of death was marked by a bureaucratic ruler from the sky and his feared police; the underworld was ruled by bureaucratic officials who required payments of bribes and fees; the maintenance of life and health required a delicate ritual palaver with the forces of spirit officialdom to protect life from their "lying words." Imagined in this way, state power was always on the outside. Creating and nourishing life were a matter of clearing a communal space within, where officialdom could be kept at a distance.

Now the new institutions of the state advanced through these places as tangible, material presences, like the fingers of the bitter herb. As township cadres arrogated the harvest of the ancestral trust fields and censored the songs and chants performed there, they replaced the nuanced play of reproductive metaphor with the alien logic of production for the sake of production. As the same cadres took over the duties of the *ts'ici,* they overturned the dynamic in which the *ts'ici* household had managed the dangers of the outside to become the center of a common domestic unity. Now the local government would direct all productive unities from within, by virtue of its ties to outside state powers. As county deputy head Li Zhang substituted injections for the sacrifice to Cha, he excavated its meaning from the courtyard where that spirit had been propitiated and overturned the association of disease and contagion with the "lying words" of official visitors. Health would now be managed through scientific progress, guaranteed by the socialist state. Each such act of occupation was seen to bring the state within, to the center of life and death, the organizing center for production and social reproduction.

This emerging imagined shape of the state can best be discerned through the resistances it inspired. Zhizuo residents' tales of state institutions occupying meaningful places were tales of darkly comic disaster. Markets failed; buildings collapsed; cadres living on these sites died or went mad; ordinary peasants farming or building on such locations found illness and death descending on their houses. The values, affects, and memories embedded in these places became animate—first as disgruntled spirits, later as vengeful ghosts. Although this resistance was subtle, diffuse, and without identifiable human agents, it required an extraordinary level of agreement among Zhizuo residents. It required that the meaning and value of these places emerge clearly and that a distinct image of the state arise in contrast. The first tales of this agentless subversion were set in the early 1950s, around the time of Li Zhang's signal victory over the spirit Cha. These stories give hints of how the strategies of subversion that were to grow in coherence and force for the next four decades might have originated. Among them were stories of a key institution in the new state's developing structure: the network of supply and marketing cooperatives.

Supply and marketing cooperatives were well entrenched in most of the country by the early 1950s. Until 1953, they were voluntary: peasants gained membership by paying a flat entry fee to purchase one share. The cooperatives purchased agricultural products and handicrafts from their members, advanced them credit, and sold them products of other regions in retail shops. As more and heavier restrictions were gradually imposed on private merchants, the cooperatives became the only secure markets for agricultural products (Shue 1980, 203–208). In the autumn of 1951, Zhizuo was chosen as one of the first four sites in northern Yunnan for the establishment of a supply and marketing cooperative (CYZZ 1994, 124). Despite its remote location, Zhizuo was an important trading center for hempen cloth. A periodic market had been established in the schoolyard there in 1935, at which Líp'ò and Lòlop'ò from the surrounding mountains sold their hempen thread and cloth to agents from a large hemp-buying corporation with branches all over northern Yunnan. The new cooperative sought to supplant such private merchants in the hemp trade. To attract mountain residents, the state set the price paid for hemp and hempen cloth well above the market price. Nationally, state hemp-purchasing prices rose 33 percent between 1950 and 1952, far outstripping prices for grain and cotton (Zhang 1984, 10). By selling their hemp to the cooperative, poor peasants and agricultural laborers could make enough cash to buy cotton cloth for the first time in their lives. Cotton was a luxury item in these mountains, but even the poorest aspired to wear embroidered cotton garments at weddings and festivals.

The supply and marketing cooperatives instituted a new system for the procurement and rationing of grain in late 1953. Called "unified purchase and supply," this system required peasants to sell quotas of surplus grain to the cooperatives at prices set by the state. It was intended to overcome an immediate serious shortage of grain in state granaries and to create conditions for quicker progress toward socialism in the countryside. The new system virtually eliminated private grain markets. Peasants were free to sell any grain they produced in excess of quota, but only at government-supervised markets and only to working people and grain-short peasants, not to grain dealers (Shue 1980, 214–227). In Zhizuo, where virtually all households had been defined as grain-short and exempted from the requirement to sell grain to the state, the most important effect of this system was to make it impossible for residents to continue to buy their grain from dealers. Cooperatives were encouraged to establish grain markets on the sites where traditional periodic markets had once flourished. Thus the Zhizuo cooperative planned a grain and hemp market. It would occupy the space in the schoolyard that had been used by the pre-Liberation market, and it would take place every ten days, as before. Zhizuo residents would sell hemp to the cooperative and buy grain, alcohol, and cloth from it and from private sellers under the watchful eyes of government regulators.

The market failed almost immediately. After two sessions, locals stopped attending, and the cooperative called off the venture. Li Gao was only a child at the time, but he remembered his mother's comic tales of vats of alcohol spilling all over the schoolyard, dogs upsetting pots of bean curd, and rolls of hempen cloth unfurling in the mud: "They said that maybe it was Agàmisimo making trouble. A diviner in Chemo said that Agàmisimo was revolted by the Han who came to run the market and that he would not allow it to happen. I never believed it when my mother said Agàmisimo didn't like the market. Why? There was a market there before. But maybe it's true. People just had a feeling that the new market wouldn't be packed and lively, so they didn't come."

Others scoffed at such theories. "The reason that market didn't work had nothing to do with Agàmisimo," said Qi Degui, a schoolteacher about Li Gao's age. "The cooperative cadres didn't know what they were doing, and they managed it badly." Indeed, few state-run grain markets were successful in 1953 and early 1954. Vivienne Shue's explanation for this failure is similar to Qi Degui's. After the unified purchase and supply system was implemented, the supply and marketing cooperatives came under increased pressure to meet state quotas for grain purchases.

State-run grain markets made it more difficult for cooperatives to meet these quotas, for the markets were an arena where peasants could sell their grain directly to other approved purchasers (Shue 1980, 225). For this reason, cooperative cadres delayed setting up the markets and advertised them poorly. It was not until late 1954 that state-run markets were finally widely established.

As supply and marketing cooperatives expanded rapidly in scope and importance in late 1954, cadres of the Zhizuo cooperative decided to build a permanent store where peasants could market their hemp. The schoolyard was the most obvious site, as it remained the only land in Zhizuo, apart from Luo Guotian's former house, that was formally owned by the state. Nevertheless, made wary by the previous year's failed market, the cadres chose a different site—a level, empty commons in the center of Chemo. Before 1950, this had been a place of collective delight for children. On the first day of each lunar year, one household built a gigantic swing for children on the site, as interest on the loan of a common fund managed by the *ts'ici*. When the revolutionary government canceled all debts in 1950, that year's recipient had kept the fund, and no more swings had been built. In 1954, the site lay empty, used by children as a playground and youths as a dancing ground. The cooperative hired local carpenters to build a large, tile-roofed structure on the site. Reaching for symbols of progress, the builders smoothed the mud bricks over with a layer of mud plaster and whitewashed the walls. For the windows, they transported panes of glass from Dayao by mule. The only other building in Zhizuo with plastered walls and glass windows was Luo Guotian's former house.

Chemo residents remembered that rumors floated about even as the building was going up. "A geomancer said the site was no good," Li Gao recalled. "It was too close to Ts'icizò [where the original ancestors were supposed to have settled] and an insult to Agàmisimo. Then a diviner, maybe the same one as before, said that Agàmisimo didn't approve of the building because it had plastered walls and glass windows. She said [in Agàmisimo's voice], 'The building is ugly, in front of my door; it looks like a Han house.' The people who ran the cooperative were Han from outside, and Agàmisimo was disgusted by them living there, right in front of Ts'icizò."

When the building was finished, the cooperative announced that it would once again sponsor a periodic market at Zhizuo, this time in its own front yard. Zhizuo residents could use revenues from hemp sold to the cooperative to buy cloth, meat, and alcohol from private traders.

This second attempt at a market failed as badly as the first. "On the first day, those who had brought meat couldn't sell it, and those who had brought alcohol couldn't sell it, so ten days later, no one bothered to come." Frequently renovated mud-brick houses often stood more than a hundred years, but this store fell down after four. The cooperative eventually divided up the lot and sold it as house sites.

Over the next twenty-five years, the cooperative store was rebuilt twice more. In 1958, a new store was built on an old burial ground, with tombstones from the graveyard and trees from a site where a mortuary ritual called "sleeping in the wild" (*likáduhè*) had been performed. People in Zhizuo told stories of how each of the cadres who lived in the building went gradually mad and died as they were "crushed" between the tombstone foundation below and the graves on the hillside above. In 1978, the building was dismantled and rebuilt in an empty maize field. Another market for hemp, grain, and vegetables was opened in front of the new building, only to fail immediately. These failures were narrated in series, each episode confirming the logic of the previous ones. Yet the first stories still retain a trace of the origins of a developing strategy of subversion. A single, unnamed diviner, using the voice of a spirit instead of her own, set in opposition Agàmisimo, the spirit of productive community, on the one hand, and the state-sponsored market and store, on the other. It was an assertion that, with this apparently harmless initiative, the state was bidding to replace ancestral authority as the center of productive unity. The same claim, voiced in increasingly strident tones, would underlie the development and elaboration of agentless subversive tactics over the next four decades.

Practical Superstitions

After the land reform campaign was completed in the fall of 1952, peasants in China were drawn in overlapping stages through several successive forms of collectivization. This process began with the formation of mutual aid groups in 1952 and 1953, continued with the creation of what were called "low-level agricultural producers cooperatives" from 1952 through 1955, and gathered speed from 1955 through 1957 as these ventures were combined into the much larger high-level agricultural producers cooperatives.

Mutual aid groups were voluntary organizations, sometimes temporary or seasonal, in which peasant households managed their land individually but pooled much of their labor. In the winter of 1952, Líp'ò and Lòlop'ò in Dayao and Yongren Counties were among the first peasants in northern Yunnan to create mutual aid groups (CYZZ 1994, 123). These farmers had long experience in negotiating systematic labor exchanges to accomplish the labor-intensive, gender-specific tasks of preparing rice fields and transplanting rice. The new mutual aid groups formalized and expanded these customary systems of labor exchange. At the end of 1953, under mounting pressure from higher levels of government, local officials spearheaded a first drive for collectivization. Still, the process went slowly; it was not until November 1955 that mutual aid groups in this mountainous region were finally amalgamated into cooperatives, with an average size of about twenty-eight households (CYZZ 1994, 124). Each household contributed its land to a new agricultural producers cooperative in return for a share in the cooperative and work points for labor. Households were often also required to contribute livestock or money. In Zhizuo, households were asked to contribute 32 yuan for each member. This sum could be paid in cash or in livestock, but animals were valued at absurdly low prices: 20 yuan for a mule, 10 for a goat.[2] Like many peasants in China, people in Zhizuo became fearful that their newly gained land and other types of property were disappearing overnight with little compensation.

In less than a year, another wave of collectivization swept China. In late 1955, Mao made speeches calling for a "high tide of socialist transformation." Provincial leaders responded quickly by setting new targets for bigger and more fully "socialist" collectives. In the spring of 1956, following the trend throughout the country, a work team was sent to Zhizuo to combine all its cooperatives into a single, large high-level agricultural producers cooperative. The most significant difference from the former cooperatives, some in Zhizuo recalled acerbically, was "more talk." The Han visitors of the collectivization work team held continual meetings and criticism sessions to urge people to work harder. The team also created special punishment production teams for "landlords, rich peasants, counterrevolutionaries, and bad elements." Work in these teams earned only about two-fifths as many work points as work in ordinary production teams.

These transformations are commonly understood as many successive rewritings of contracts between individual peasant households and the state. But it is clear that in Zhizuo they were far more: each reconfiguration of relations to the land reworked the foundations of domestic community that had been produced through the rites and metaphors of the *ts'ici* system. Collectivization, in fact, began a forty-year-long struggle over a central emblem of that community, the ancestral trust fields. This struggle turned on the mundane problem of rice-transplanting schedules. Lying on the wide, sunny bottom of Zhizuo's central valley, these fields were surrounded by the richest rice land in many kilometers. Strong prohibitions attached to transplanting any of the surrounding land before the trust was planted; it was disrespectful to the Lòhɔ, inviting harm from the spirit. When agricultural producers cooperatives were formed, locals had warned that dividing up the trust fields among cooperatives might make the rich lands surrounding the trust impossible to transplant. Collectivization cadres compromised. The lower ten paddies of the ancestral trust were granted to a Chemo cooperative. The two upstream paddies rotated each year to the cooperative of that year's *ts'ici* household. When the cooperatives were merged into a single high-level cooperative in 1956, this arrangement was preserved, the representative fields rotating with the title of *ts'ici* among the cooperative's production teams.

As an unintended consequence, the economic responsibility for *ts'ici* rituals now fell to the cooperatives' production teams. The *ts'ici* household continued to set dates, arrange for ritual specialists, and organize rituals, but since it no longer received any direct income from the ancestral trust, it was up to the cooperative or team to supply sacrificial animals and grain. Production team leaders began to participate in the meetings to choose the *ts'ici* and to negotiate the rotation of duties from team to team. These negotiations were often delicate. Team leaders risked their members' strong disapprobation if they refused to sponsor the *ts'ici* rituals, and they risked accusations of engaging in "feudal superstition" if they did. Production teams reduced the sacrifice to the Lòhɔ from two goats to two chickens and, from 1958 through 1960, to two eggs. But they continued to contribute two rams a year to Agàmisimo through the mid-1950s and early 1960s.

Production teams on the valley's sunny side soon dropped sacrifices to two minor *ts'ici* spirits, Mijù and Lɔmælòhɔ. These spirits were directly concerned with regulating the rain, and their propitiations were most important to residents of the drought-prone shady side. Mijù resided in a giant pine on this side of the valley, above the village of Méabò. The rice lands for this village were fed by a small stream that often slowed to a trickle or dried up altogether during the planting season. Shortly after collectivization, the single production team on the shady side began to sponsor a sacrifice to Mijù. In 1962, this slope's team was split into three, and these teams rotated among them the responsibility for organizing the rite and contributing a sacrificial goat. Team leaders kept this arrangement quiet, knowing that it could draw harsh criticism. But they worried that without it their teams would run an unacceptable risk of drought.

Lɔmælòhə was the only *ts'ici* spirit with no fixed customary date for propitiation. After the rice was planted, at times when rain was needed, the *ts'ici* would supply a ritualist with two chickens and send him to the winding canyon at the river's tail. There he would kill the chickens before a stone that was shaped like a fetus and was enclosed in a tiny stone womb. "Sky father, earth mother, every root is parched," the ritualist would chant. "Every stalk is dying of thirst, the fish in the river are dying of thirst, the shrimp in the ravine are dust, every crawling thing and every flying thing is dying of thirst; grant us three days of rain, give us five nights of rain." After collectivization, each production team assigned one or two workers the duty of regulating the flow of irrigation water. In dry weeks, this task became much more difficult, as the workers had to painstakingly irrigate one paddy at a time with a minuscule flow of water. Irrigators for several teams might pool private resources, buy two chickens, find a ritualist who knew the right *nèpi* chant, and walk down the river to make the sacrifice. After eating a meal of chicken soup, the irrigators would go home and hope for rain, earning their work points the easy way. Even as people learned to repeat denunciations of such practices as false, harmful, wasteful, and superstitious, they continued to act on practical realities: sometimes sacrifices to Mijù or Lɔmælòhə were the only ways to bring rain. Indeed, some in Zhizuo noted that these spirits were treated better and fed more often during the Mao era than before, when the residents of the shady side could also rely on Agàmisimo.

Tales of the mid-1950s focused on the compromises that the enduring fragments of the *ts'ici* system forced on those who carried out collectivization policies. These struggles were, in part, about how the new state would be imagined. To what extent would visions of a communal productive unity, focused on the rites and festivals of the *ts'ici* system, be allowed to endure as land and labor were reorganized to serve the state's social and economic goals? To what extent would it become necessary to imagine the state itself as the generating center of production and social reproduction, and what shape would that center take? Tales of struggle and compromise around the *ts'ici* give the sense that these questions were unsettled during this time. Yet they also appear as episodes in what was seen in retrospect as an onrushing process; they are now overshadowed by memories of the calamitous time to come. In the years of the Great Leap Forward, the shape at the center would be revealed as a fearsome emptiness (*kẓ*), a ghostly and endlessly demanding mouth.

A Spectral State

A slogan attributed to Kang Sheng, who would later become one of Mao's closest advisors, circulated through rural China during the Great Leap Forward in 1958 and 1959. It communicated a millenarian vision of the years to come: "Communism is paradise; the People's Communes are the bridge [to it]" (*Gongchanzhuyi shi tiantang, renmin gongshe shi qiaoliang*).[3] "Paradise," *tiantang,* translated into Lòlongo literally as *mùchìkà,* "sky hall," the realm of the thunder spirit Shrìmògù and his spirit police.

Li Zhiwu once recounted to me a fever dream he had as a youth of nineteen, lying in bed during the famine precipitated by the Great Leap, his limbs heavy with edema: "I saw two villages, one on this side, one on that side. The one on this side looked like Chemo. There was a bridge from this side to that side, a single log, narrow and slippery. I had to walk across to that side, but I was afraid, and halfway across I fell off. I woke up alive. If I had made it to the other side, I would have died then or soon afterward, for the other side was the underworld [*mómi*]." Li Zhiwu's village of Chemo was divided by a deep ravine from the hill to its south, where a village of gravestones formed portals to the underworld. His dream bridge arched over such a gulf, passing through the sky from whence Shrìmògù's police descended with shackles to lead away expiring souls.

When the paradise of the People's Communes, created in the autumn of 1958, turned into the hell of severe famine a few months later, souls were released not into the just, orderly bureaucracy of the underworld (*mómi*) but into the gulf—the chaotic world of wild ghosts (*nèmi*), from whence they descended in parti-colored, birdlike flocks upon the heads of their living kin. Those like Li Zhiwu who slipped from the bridge into life found themselves floating in an alien space, where for at least three decades social life would be shaped by the unvoiced fury, greed, and anguish of the famine's dead.

⌒⃝

The vision of the Great Leap Forward emerged from the highest level of national leadership in late 1957, as China's leaders discussed development strategies for the Second Five-Year Plan and after. Collectivization had created a foundation for agricultural development, but it had solved few of China's economic problems. From the Third Plenum of the Eighth Party Congress in September, a strategy emerged that abandoned plans for balanced growth and emphasized mass mobilization of China's five hundred million peasants to expand rapidly in both industry and agriculture toward a fully socialist utopia.[4]

In the winter of 1957–1958, more than one hundred million peasants were mobilized for large-scale water conservation projects. In Yunnan, by January of 1958, more than two million had been recruited to build reservoirs and canals (DZY 1991, 1:136). Hundreds of men from Zhizuo traveled to Dayao's large Baihe reservoir construction site, where they lived in tent encampments. Over the next two years, laborers from Zhizuo participated in building canals and reservoirs throughout the prefecture, including vast engineering projects such as the 12,500-kilowatt Dahaibo electric station and the giant Kangyun Canal (CYZZ 1994, 134). A drought in the winter of 1957 and the spring of 1958 increased the urgency of these projects. Hundreds of thousands of additional workers were recruited, and laborers were required to work up to fifteen hours per day (DZY 1991, 1:140). Every person who stayed behind in Zhizuo—man, woman, and child—labored on a road from Zhonghe and a long canal through the central valley. At the same time, they participated in a provincewide drive to collect human and animal waste for fertilizer. In Zhizuo, as in many of Yunnan's minority nationality regions, human waste was viewed as filthy and dangerous and had not been used on fields. Zhizuo residents built their first outdoor toilets in early 1958, one for each production team. Punishment teams collected the waste in buckets and carried it to the fields.

The water conservancy campaign required the organization of labor on a massive scale that far transcended the resources of China's collectives. In April 1958, acting on a suggestion from Mao, the Party's Central Committee decreed that the agricultural producers cooperatives (which had an average size of about 164 households) should be combined into much larger collectives in order to mobilize labor more efficiently and to anticipate the scale economies of mechanized agriculture. The large collectives that emerged almost immediately were lavishly praised by the media and widely emulated. In August, the *People's Daily* reported that Mao had approved of the large collectives and dubbed them "People's Communes." A few days later, an enlarged Politburo conference in the seaside resort of Beidaihe called for the formation of People's Communes throughout the country, and, very quickly, cooperatives in every province merged into communes. Yunnan was the slowest to complete the transition, but even there by the end of October the province's 18,934 cooperatives had become 833 communes, with an average size of 3,000 to 5,000 households (DZY 1991, 1:144).

In Chuxiong, the prefectural Party Committee had already begun to extoll the benefits of communes in a July telephone meeting:

> People's Communes are sprouts of communism and a transitional stage to its fullest form. Creating People's Communes will resolve every problem, and inequalities will gradually disappear. The People's Communes will include industry, agriculture, commerce, study, education, and the military. Each commune will have its own factories, its own economic center, its own university, middle schools, and elementary schools. . . . Old people will enter nursing homes, children kindergartens, the ill hospitals. Eating will be done in collective mess halls. (CYZZ 1994, 130)

After the Beidaihe conference, this committee ordered five of Chuxiong's counties, including Dayao, to communalize before the beginning of September. To prevent chaos, communalization proceeded by a method described as "moving the top without moving the bottom." The leadership of each district reorganized itself to lead the commune, but the existing distribution of production responsibilities did not change until after the fall harvest. Zhizuo merged with five other agricultural production cooperatives in the Zhonghe area to form a commune of about 4,200 households. After the fall harvest, Zhizuo became two management districts (Ch. *guanliqu*) of six in the Zhonghe Commune.

Almost immediately, the commune created collective mess halls in the courtyards of production team leaders. Parades of elementary-school students marched through every team collecting kitchen utensils, grain, and small domestic animals such as pigs, chickens, and pigeons. Schoolchildren were encouraged to keep watch on their neighbors' households and report those who secretly retained pots or grain. When a holdout was discovered, a band of schoolchildren raided the family's house and beat their pots loudly as they marched them to the mess halls. All large livestock and agricultural tools such as plows and harrows were turned over to the commune. After the fall harvest, accounting was moved to the commune level. The commune, not the production team, became responsible for assigning its members' labor, providing for their consumption, and handing up procurement quotas of grain. The commune assigned food and pay across all management districts, regardless of their previous income, the quality of their land, or the labor of their members. This amounted to a transfer of wealth from richer to poorer management districts and from richer to poorer teams within the districts. Zhizuo's two management districts, especially in their outlying hamlets, were by far the poorest in the commune. In the spring of 1959, after Mao directly criticized commune-level accounting as excessively egalitarian, accounting was moved to the level of the management district, but until then Zhizuo residents ate the fruit of the lower, warmer valleys around Zhonghe.[5]

Indeed, for the first few months of the commune, people in Zhizuo ate as never before or since. Unimaginably, food was free in the mess halls, and people could eat as much as they wanted. "Every day was like a wedding banquet," a resident of Chemo recalled. "The women and young children ate on one side, the men on the other, and twelve dishes were served twice a day." As at wedding banquets, round "tables" of fresh pine needles were laid on the floor of the courtyards that served as mess halls. The weather was dry and bright in these months after the harvest; it was the time of the year for courtship, for weddings, and for eating. People squatted at the tables in groups of six or eight, the propitious numbers for wedding feasts. Some women began to wear to daily meals the clean, elaborately embroidered shirts, trousers, aprons, and hats they reserved for festive occasions. With a kind of astonished nostalgia, some recalled that each team's mess hall was open to any member of the commune, encouraging feats of epicurean endurance: "Here in Chemo, they made one huge mess hall to feed everyone. You could eat your fill in Zhonghe, walk up to Chemo and eat again, cross over to Chezò and eat another meal, then walk up to Lɔwú [about two hours away] and eat once more. And the mess halls competed with each other to serve the most delicious food. You could spend the whole day eating feast after feast."

The feasting was accompanied by a dream of millennial superabundance. Communism would bring the end of scarcity, transforming life into a continuous enjoyment of the pleasures of modernity. This dream circulated through the countryside in Great Leap rhetoric, trumpeted in the press and echoed by local cadres. In November or December, Tan Zhenlin, a close associate of Mao and a major architect of the Great Leap policies, articulated this vision in vivid language:

> After all, what does communism mean? . . . First, taking good food and not merely eating one's fill. At each meal one will enjoy a meat diet, eating chicken, pork, fish, or eggs. . . . To be sure, delicacies like monkeys' heads, swallows' nests, and white fungus will be served to each according to his needs. . . . Second, clothing. Everything required will be available. Clothing of various designs and styles, not a mass of black garments or a mass of blue garments. In the future, ordinary cloth will be used only for making working outfits. After working hours, people will wear silk, satin, and woolen suits. . . . When all the People's Communes raise foxes, there will be overcoats lined with fox furs. . . . Third, housing. Housing will be brought up to the standard of modern cities. . . . Central heating will be provided in the North, air conditioning in the South. All will live in high-rise buildings. Needless to say, there will be electric lights, telephones, piped water, radios, and televisions.[6]

For a few months, this dream seemed to enrapture many in Zhizuo. Communism would explode all the careful regulative economies whose goal was a smooth (but boring) flow of grain and meat through a digestive tract and a smooth flow of generations through a household. Life would be a perpetual wedding feast.

Meanwhile, however, everyone in Zhizuo was working very hard. In April 1958, responding to pressures from the center, the Chuxiong People's Congress had vowed to increase agricultural production by 25 percent. In May, the Party secretaries of five of Chuxiong's counties met to answer Mao's call, voiced in a recent speech to the Eighth Party Congress, to "lift the lid, break down superstition, and let the initiative and creativity of the laboring people explode!"[7] The Party secretaries published a "Friendly Socialist Competition Battle Manual" to be distributed to every locale. The five counties, it announced, would "cooperate in death-defying labor" to increase grain production five- or sixfold, guarantee 825 kilos of grain per *mu,* and battle for 1,000 kilos per *mu.* The manual stated, "In order to fulfill the requirements of an extensive shock assault, we will organize a great socialist cooperation in each county, township, commune, and team, to engage three hundred thousand people in savage battle, to eat, sleep, work, hold meetings, and decide on work points, all in the fields" (CYZZ, 1994 135).

"Shock battalions" were organized for the spring rice-transplanting season. Zhizuo's elementary school emptied as the schoolchildren marched to work in the fields with their grandparents. From May through July, some two hundred thousand cadres formed agricultural inspection teams and fanned out throughout Yunnan, pressuring local officials to carry forward the goals of the Great Leap by quadrupling 1957 grain production totals over the next five years (DZY 1991, 1:140). More inspectors from the prefectural and commune levels flooded the countryside, admonishing team leaders to keep close records of how much time each person devoted to working, sleeping, eating, and attending meetings. As Li Zhiwu's brother, Li Zhilin, described it:

> People had to work all day and then keep on working all night just to plow the land. Strange! Now we just plow during the day and get it all done. During the Great Leap Forward, we had to plow during the day, plow at night, transplant rice during the day, transplant rice at night. Sometimes at night we had to hoe or dig canals. But there was no electric light, and most often no pine torches, so no one could see what he was doing. Sometimes people were wounded by the hoes of others who couldn't see them. Stupid! Old men, old women, and children not yet a meter high were the workers. All the young men and women had been sent away to work at mining and reservoir building.

The laborers ate and slept in the fields rather than waste the few minutes it would take to climb back to the villages. Workers were ordered to work in rank-and-file formations like soldiers: when hoeing, men were told to spread out across a field in a straight line; when transplanting rice, women were supposed to back up across the paddy in concert. In the July rice-planting season, this military-style discipline was extended to the seedlings themselves. Li Zhiwu recalled, "Even when people from Chezò were working in fields directly below the village, where it is only several hundred meters from the fields to the houses, they were not allowed to go home at night. When they were transplanting rice, they had to stretch a string across the field and plant the rice along it, making perfectly straight rows and columns. If all the seedlings did not line up when they were finished with a field, they had to pull them up and start over."

Rice seedlings, like workers, were concentrated in great numbers to accomplish incredible tasks. Following a nationwide emphasis on close planting, provincial authorities issued an order to plant five thousand to ten thousand seedlings in excess of the seedlings per *mu* planted the year before (DZY 1991, 1:140). In the autumn, the fields themselves were disciplined in a similar style. Mao, Tan Zhenlin, and other central leaders looked forward with great optimism to the benefits of agricultural mechanization. In September, the Yunnan Party Congress called for a fundamental transformation of the face of the province, through "industrialization, agricultural mechanization, and technological and cultural revolution." Vowing to "mechanize agriculture to create a great surplus of grain, self-sufficiency in cotton, and the export of great quantities of other economic crops and livestock products," it declared mountainous, impoverished Dayao County a "red banner county," which would take the lead in agricultural mechanization (DYZ 1991, 1:141). Throughout the county, battalions of peasants labored to tear out the terraces, which followed the contours of the mountain slopes, and straighten them to prepare for tractors and combines. Many terrace walls were higher than an adult's head, and some had taken decades to build. This task absorbed nearly the entire labor force remaining in the villages in the dry seasons of 1958 and 1959. Zhizuo's cadres decided to begin this work on the ancestral trust fields, the most visible sign of superstition among the Lòlop'ò masses. Teams of elderly and adolescent laborers attacked the fields, reshaping them into ten orderly quadrangles with precisely straight borders. This work was not finished until the winter of 1959, when the county abandoned further efforts to discipline the fields. The ancestral trust fields remained the only rectilinear terraces in the valley.

All this work was accomplished by women, children, and elderly men, for all the younger men had been recruited for a second wave of mass mobilization, this one to produce steel and copper. Mao himself had made iron and steel production a central priority of the Great Leap Forward in the second half of 1958, deciding that steel would be the foundation of the great leap in industry and that by producing steel in rural locations using indigenous methods China could double its 1957 production of steel in one year. In August, the Beidaihe Politburo conference endorsed Mao's target and launched a nationwide "great leap forward in iron and steel." In Yunnan, the country's foremost copper-producing province, the provincial Party Committee called for a "great battle for steel and copper." Thousands of small, backyard furnaces were built in towns and villages throughout the province, all elementary and middle-school students were rallied to collect scrap, and volunteer teams were organized to search the mountains for mining sites. By October, nearly four million people were working full-time on copper and steel production in Yunnan, and in many locales more than 80 percent of long-distance transportation was devoted to hauling ore and scrap

(DZY 1991, 1:143). In Chuxiong Prefecture alone, more than two thousand small blast furnaces were built, and a hundred thousand peasants were recruited to scour the mountains for wood to burn into charcoal for the furnaces (CYZZ 1994, 136). Zhizuo residents built an iron furnace and a sulphur foundry at home, and they traveled to Dayao and Jianhua to work in copper mines and to Wanbie to work in an iron foundry. At each mine or foundry, laborers were organized into residential groups according to their home village; people from Zhizuo built makeshift dwellings together and worked in the same teams. The work was exhausting and dangerous: sulphur workers grew ill from the fumes, reservoir workers were crushed in landslides or blown up by dynamite, and iron workers gradually starved when food supplies grew scarce.

By the summer of 1959, the drive to produce steel and copper had absorbed 40 to 50 percent of the labor force, creating acute shortages of agricultural labor. Policy planners were pushing to increase production while using less labor and less land. In July 1959, responding to calls to devote land to experiments in high productivity, Chuxiong's prefectural Party Committee held a mass meeting to celebrate "heroes of production." One hero had weeded 330 *mu* of rice in a single day; another had plowed 31 *mu*. After the meeting, the committee published and distributed a 108-page pamphlet called "Fresh Deeds" (*Xinxian shi*). The pamphlet collated and commended hundreds of extraordinary feats of production accomplished in Chuxiong's communes—rice production of 10,000, 31,000, and 40,000 kilos per *mu;* maize production of 100,000 kilos per *mu;* tobacco production of 3,000 kilos per *mu;* twelve ears of maize from one seed (CYZZ 1994, 135).

By September, a nationwide movement, called the "Sputnik Field Movement" after the Soviet satellite launched the year before, was in full force. "Destroy superstition, create miracles, and release the suppression of sputniks throughout the land!" demanded Chuxiong's Party Committee (CYZZ 1994, 135). Specific goals were set for certain communes in each of Chuxiong's counties. None would be exempted; those local leaders who failed would be accused of "planting white flags." The lowland counties were to launch "sputniks" of 80,000 kilos per *mu* of rice. Some communes were singled out to launch "sputniks" of 250 million kilos of maize per *mu,* 10,000 kilos of tobacco per *mu,* 300,000 kilos of potatoes per *mu*. In Chuxiong County, in the prefecture's center, the local Party Committee vowed to launch four "sputniks," each of 100,000 kilos per *mu* of winter wheat on waste land. And it specified exactly how this would be accomplished: "Plant closely, arrange the fields in wavelike mounds of earth, and develop every empty space into a three-dimensional planting. In each *mu* plant 1,000 kilos of seed. Each kilo has 10,000 seeds, making 10 million in total. Each seed produces two ears, making 20 million ears per *mu*. Each ear, on average, bears fifty grains. Thus, the production per *mu* will reach 100,000 kilos" (CYZZ 1994, 135).

This plan concisely encapsulated the hyper-real logic of the Great Leap Forward. All the figures added up: fifty grains per ear times 20 million ears made a billion grains, or 100,000 kilos at 10,000 grains per kilo. Even the requirement that each seed produce two ears was not outlandish: winter wheat could be encouraged to sprout double stalks by grazing it after the first few weeks of growth. Given the will to struggle and the proper style of mass organization, the energies of millions of seeds together would accumulate in a miracle of production. For Zhizuo residents, such instructions redefined procreative metaphor, presenting a forceful vision of the nation as a vital, organized mass of millions of productive souls struggling toward a common goal. In this new order, productive activity required an overarching agency that simultaneously individuated each seed and depersonalized it. This was the agency that counted the seeds in a kilo of grain (a blind guess: in Chinese, "ten thousand" (*wan*) is a conventional expression of hyperbole) and transformed those who farmed the earth into numbered masses—even when the numbers themselves were clearly fictions. Thus the new procreative metaphor presented a vision of the state as well as of the nation. The state was the force that made possible the crucial transition between the minuscule energies of an individual seed and the combined effects of millions.

Zhizuo launched several "sputniks." One was a wheat field, planted on the model outlined by the Party Committee's plan. Another was a field of sweet potatoes. Zhizuo and the surrounding mountains had been transformed in 1958 and 1959 by an order to "revolutionize buckwheat," applied to Yunnan's highest, coldest mountains (DZY 1991, 1:145). Lĭp'ò and Lòlop'ò had customarily planted buckwheat on high swidden land, unsuitable for terracing. To "revolutionize buckwheat," local cadres prohibited its cultivation, ordering peasants to plant sweet potatoes and Irish potatoes instead. At the same time, management districts in the mountains of Dayao County carried out a vast expansion of swidden acreage. In Zhizuo, teams of laborers spread out over the hill-sides to cut down the forests, haul the wood to the collective mess halls to burn, and liberate the land for sweet potatoes. The sweet-potato "sputnik" was launched on a swidden field on the valley's dry eastern side. Li Zhilin offered vivid description:

> All the women had to cut off their hair to use as fertilizer. Everyone had to kill their dogs and make them into fertilizer. We had to collect all the manure from the animals and pile it with the hair and chopped dogs in one field, so it would produce several thousand times the usual. In fact, it produced nothing, and the yield was poor on the wheat fields, because all the fertilizer had already been used up. They planted sweet potatoes in that field, then every day they dug them up, weighed them, and recorded their weight. Then they planted them again and dug them up the next day. They did this every day, so an official could arrive and say, "This sputnik field has produced tens of thousands of yuan worth of sweet potatoes!"

Here Li Zhilin answers his own earlier question about the "strange" quality of labor during the Great Leap Forward. Why did working all day and all night produce so little food? Because the goal of labor was not to produce food—it was to produce words. In such recollections, the state was an empty mouth crying out in hunger for words and grain, driving men and women to labor ceaselessly to satisfy its exacting and mutable palate. It was a spectral state.

On a stream bank near the river's tail, Li Wenyi showed me how to carve flaps in the black bark of a willow twig to serve as ears for the black *gu*, the wild ghost officials. One must distinguish black *gu* from white *gu*, he told me—wild ghost officials from their wild ghost victims.

> Those who can't speak to ghosts [*nèpi*] don't often separate the two clearly. The black *gu* are sent down from the sky. They are the wild ghost officials [*chè ts'ř mà*] who kill live, healthy people, destroying them with hunger or suicide. Their victims are the white *gu*. These are ordinary wild ghosts who wander the earth with no power to kill; they afflict with illness, but they don't kill. When you speak to them, you address first the black *gu*, then the white *gu*, one after the other, like that.

Li Wenyi was preparing to exorcise the ghosts of Li Xiong's grand-parents, who had for many years afflicted their grandson with lethargy and swollen limbs. Both grandparents had died during the Great Leap famine. A few hours later, he spoke for a long time to the wild ghost officials, as Li Xiong and his family sat on the riverbank nearby. In his speech, Li Wenyi offered the ghost officials heaps of grain and meat. Near the end, he offered them also all the words he had spoken:

6.2

speech as sharp as chicken's claws	hæ̀ pi̱ ye pæ̀ mo
I have gone on all day without end	su ngo m mæ̀ chì ni mo
I have spoken until my mouth hurts	ngo pi̱ le bà bo ka
spoken everything clearly	pi̱ ne je̱ tsr ka
I give all this speech to you	ngo pi̱ ne pi̱ t'è̱ gò

These are the greediest of all beings, Li Wenyi told me:

They consume everything you offer them, all your sharpest words, and still they want more. They are greedy, corrupt, and nasty. When you offer them grain, you mustn't take a single seed back with you, and you must offer them every kind you can find. You must boast to them, "I give you heaps of boiled grain. *If you don't believe this, count the grains.*" They count the grains in a sea of grain like the sand on a beach. Though there are so many different kinds, they count every grain. But you fool them; you mix mustard seed in with all the other grains because mustard grains are so small that they are uncountable. As you burn the effigy with all the ghost's possessions, you sow grain in the fire. You sow it only in the fire, so not a single seed will take hold in the earth and grow. [My emphasis]

Labor shortages, calamitous agricultural innovations, and natural disasters led to precipitous declines in food production throughout China from 1958 through 1960. At the same time, vastly exaggerated reports of grain production encouraged the state to increase procurement to unprecedented levels. Central planners believed in a vast superabundance of grain that would allow them to swell the industrial labor force with a "human sea" (Yang and Li 1980). Between 1958 and 1960, around thirty million peasants were allowed to migrate to the cities, requiring some 6 million tons of additional grain per year (Bernstein 1984). During the same time, the central leadership sped up exports of grain to purchase capital goods needed for heavy industrialization. In Yunnan, the provincial Party Committee reported a 1958 grain harvest of 24 billion kilos, doubling the 1957 harvest, and planned for a harvest of 30 billion kilos in 1959. (Later reconstructions of grain production figures found that the

1958 harvest was 8 billion kilos, 6.7 percent smaller than the 1957 harvest, with the 1959 harvest declining an additional 6.8 percent [DZY 1991, 1:145].)

During a period of limited national retrenchment in the spring of 1959, provincial leaders encouraged a struggle against the "boastful wind" (Ch. *fukua feng*) of wildly inflated figures. Yunnan revised its reported production of iron and copper down by half, but it retained the 30 billion kilo figure for grain. On this foundation, the province increased net grain procurement 6.8 percent in 1958 and an additional 27 percent in 1959 (DZY 1991, 1:145). By 1960, central planners had become aware that the harvests were smaller than had been reported, but throughout the summer and fall grain procurement continued at rates influenced by the earlier figures (Bernstein 1984, 351). In Chuxiong, the reported harvest for 1960 was 1.6 billion kilos, 2.7 times the 1957 harvest of 602 million kilos. (Adjusted figures later estimated the harvest to have been 31 percent smaller than that of 1957 [CYZZ 1994, 136].) Local cadres in Chuxiong frequently set procurement targets even higher than those demanded by the center and the province. Some communes competed to launch "grain procurement sputniks," leaving peasants with little or no grain (DZY 1991, 1:145).

In December 1959, the Chuxiong's People's Congress vowed to press ahead in the Great Leap with renewed energy. Many communes had allowed their members to retain small private vegetable plots. These were now communalized. Cattle, horses, and pigs were confiscated from production teams and concentrated in large communal farms. In Zhizuo, private vegetable plots had never been assigned, since there was no tradition of growing vegetables in garden plots separate from the grain fields. And livestock production had already been collectivized in 1958. Li Zhilin recalled:

> Here in Zhizuo, they made pig farms and goat farms. All the goats were taken up to Henilɔ and grazed together. We had to try to haul all the goat manure twenty kilometers from Henilɔ down here to fertilize the rice fields. They had a pig farm just below the school there, where they could feed them with waste from the mess halls. But they had an epidemic of gastric disease in the horse farm, and all the horses and mules died. The goats all caught goat fever and died. When there was no longer any waste from the mess halls, the pigs all starved to death.

After February 1959, the "eight guarantees" policy under which food had been free in the mess halls was rescinded. Months before, the mess halls had run out of meat, as the last remaining chickens, pigs, and goats were slaughtered. A severe grain ration was instituted in June.

> For the first few months of eating in the mess halls, we killed cattle and goats to eat. But after two months, the cattle had all been killed, and the goats had all been killed, and there was no meat to eat, especially because the goats were dying off fast. Then they rationed the grain and gave each person six *liang* [about 10 ounces] of cooked grain to eat. Three in the morning, three in the evening. Hungry! Children got only four *liang* [7 ounces], old women four or five. People got very hungry. They all got edema [Ch. *zhongqan bing*, literally "swelling, dry sickness"]. That is, some swelled up, and some dried up.

As the 1959 wet season wore on, the men and women assigned to cook in the mess halls searched the hills for edible wild plants to cut up and boil with the grain. Chuxiong's official gazetteer estimates that in 1960, in production teams with a serious deficiency of grain, people ate on average 5 *liang* (about 9 ounces) of grain per day (CYZZ 1994, 139). In Zhizuo, people remember eating only a scant handful of grain thrown into a thin porridge of sweet potatoes, radishes, and wild herbs.

Overconsumption in communal mess halls, overprocurement of grain, and disastrously reduced food production combined to precipitate both a mortality crisis and a fertility crisis of unprecedented proportions throughout China. It is not clear how each of these factors contributed, especially given wide regional disparities. Recent arguments have tended to look for explanations that assign a single chief cause for the catastrophe. One influential proposal gives the decline in agricultural labor productivity as the main cause of the crisis, tracing this decline to a policy that deprived peasants of the right to withdraw from collectives in the fall of 1958 (J. Lin 1990).[8] Another emphasizes the role of mess halls, proposing that excessive food consumption was largely responsible for the rapid depletion of grain in 1958, the most prominent cause of mass starvation (Yang 1996, 54–55).

Nor do demographers agree on the famine's severity. Official vital statistics from the period have proven difficult to interpret. Even in the years preceding the Great Leap, China's vital registration system was not adequate to record all deaths, and in the frenzy of the campaign, vital registration was likely to have been even less accurate (Banister 1987, 85).[9] Following official data closely, Ansle Coale (1981) estimated 16.5 million "excess" deaths from 1958 through 1961.[10] By contrast, John Aird (1982) and Xizhe Peng (1987) independently arrived at figures of about 23 million. Judith Banister (1987) found that official mortality statistics implied 15 million excess deaths from 1958 through 1961. Her reconstruction of population trends, assuming underreporting of deaths both before and during the famine, estimated 30 million excess deaths in the same period. Cong Jin (1989) derived a similar figure for excess deaths, adding about 10 million in reduced births to arrive at a total demographic impact of about 40 million (Yang 1996).

The severity of the crisis varied widely by region. The worst-affected area was a belt of provinces stretching across China from Sichuan and Guangxi in the southwest to Henan and Anhui in the east. In Sichuan, official statistics show that mortality rates rose from 12.1 per thousand in 1957 to 38.9 for the 1958–1961 period, peaking at 54.0 in 1960. In contrast, in the relatively mildly affected province of Shanxi, mortality rates did not rise much from the 1957 level of 12.7 per thousand during the 1958–1961 period, reaching only 14.2 in 1960 (Yang 1996, 38). Although Yunnan was badly affected according to any measure, its official mortality rates show that the famine there was not nearly as severe as in the worst-affected provinces. In 1957, Yunnan already had the highest mortality rate in China (with the probable exception of Tibet, for which data are not available). Mortality rates there rose from 16.3 per thousand in 1957 to 19.5 in 1958–1961, peaking at 26.3 in 1960 (Zou and Miao 1989, 172).

Throughout China, mortality rates were significantly higher in the countryside than in the cities. In Yunnan, mortality rates in Kumning city remained an average of 3.3 per thousand lower than in the province as a whole. By contrast, in certain regions of the province, especially remote mountainous areas such as Chuxiong, the famine's effects were far worse than in the rest of the countryside. And mortality in Dayao was higher than in any other county in Chuxiong, perhaps because Dayao had been declared a "red banner county" that was to take the lead in the Great Leap. In a rare mention of famine deaths, the official prefectural gazetteer makes laconic reference to the situation in Dayao in the fall of 1958: "After fulfilling grain requisitions, the masses were hungry. Edema and other illnesses developed in close succession, and in many places people died. Dayao County was among Yunnan's 'red banner counties.' There the situation was most serious; the 'five winds'[11] flourished, and

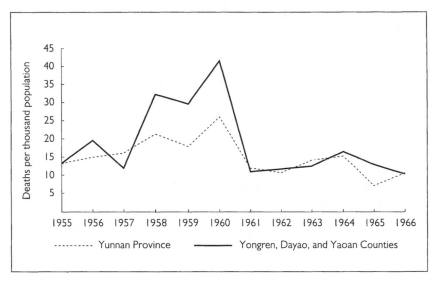

Figure 6.1 Crude death rates (per thousand), 1955–1966. *Source:* YSTRB 1990.

the phenomena of edema and death were most prominent. . . . At the time, the words 'right deviationist' were feared, and few dared oppose the state of affairs. . . . The number of people who died of hunger or disease was very great" (CYZZ 1994, 135).

Mortality rates in Dayao[12] rose from 12.2 per thousand in 1957 to 40.6 in 1958. In the winter of 1959, after the first frenzy of procurement competitions and "sputnik" launchings had subsided, the mortality rate declined again to 19.5 per thousand. But at the end of 1959, as the Great Leap campaign was renewed and overprocurement continued, famine deaths again increased. Dayao's mortality rate peaked in 1960 at 41.8 per thousand (YSTRB 1990, 380–395). Despite the likely underreporting of deaths, official mortality statistics alone make it clear that the famine in Dayao was devastating—far worse than in either the province as a whole or the nation in aggregate. (See Figure 6.1.)

The few in Zhizuo who would speak to me of hunger and death in the famine voiced contained fury at the avarice, stupidity, and corruption of local officials. Zhizuo's leadership had remained intact when communes were created in 1958. The district officials of Zhonghe became the new leaders of the Zhonghe Commune, and the cadres of Zhizuo's township inherited leadership of its two management districts. These leaders were nearly all locals, with extensive local ties of kinship and friendship, but they became increasingly isolated during the famine. Commune and management district cadres spent most of their time behind the massive walls of government buildings. Hungry locals imagined that what they did there was eat:

> Here in Chezò, so many people were starving to death. There were children, the small ones who couldn't work, who got only three *liang* of rice a day. After eating like this for a long time, you starve. But the officials didn't die. They ate well, damn it! The district leader at Zhonghe was named Qi Jianhe. People in Zhonghe were hungry too, even though they were hungrier here in Zhizuo. But Qi Jianhe ate chicken, pork, ham, eggs, and sticky rice. They couldn't eat it all, those people.
>
> There was this cart driver in Zhonghe. Cart drivers had Sundays off. Peasants had no Sundays; we had to work seven days a week and work in the evenings as well. Every day we worked seventeen to eighteen hours. And we were hungry! Anyway, this cart driver would drive to Dayao and rest a day, then drive back to Zhonghe and rest a day. But once he got a fishhook stuck in his throat, with the line coming out of his mouth. They took him to Qi Jianhe, who yanked on the line and said, "What are you up to! This is the Great Leap Forward! You've been eating fish?" There he was, caught like a fish on a line. Qi Jianhe and his wife—oh, they ate very well. All the work teams had beehives, and during the Leap they gathered them all together in one place, so only the officials could eat honey. Sometimes they got as much as two hundred to three hundred kilos of honey, and they ate it all.

Some residents of Chezò estimated that more than seventy-five people in their village of about six hundred died of hunger, while the cadres ate meat, eggs, and honey.

One image surfaced more often than any other in these narratives, seeming to sum up all the horror and stupidity of the famine. As the wet season of 1960 dragged on, large numbers of people began to swell with edema from protein deficiency in communes throughout Chuxiong. The prefectural Party Committee chose to regard edema as a disease. In the final months of the year, it launched a major campaign, ordering each county and commune to assign cadres to build clinics and treatment stations for edema sufferers. Each important Party and government official at every level was to be involved personally in this effort (CYZZ 1994, 139). Zhizuo's edema treatment station was a massive steamer:

> They built a huge pot down there by the stream and made a giant steamer of wood to put on top of it. Four people could sit inside. They built a fire underneath, put a lid on top, and steamed the people until they were hot and soft. They steamed them like rice. One of the doctors they sent from Dayao to help with the steamer said, "These people are pitiful. Edema is easy to cure. All you have to do is give everyone a kilo of grain a day, and no one will get sick from edema." They locked him up as a right deviationist and held struggle meetings against him until he killed himself with poison.

Zhizuo residents lined up along the stream bank to be steamed in their clothes, on the theory that this would draw out the excess water causing their swelling. As they exited, soaked to the bone, they received an exit card that, depending on their condition, allowed them a few hours of rest each day.

Qi Deyi's house was directly below the school gate. From there, one could look down into his courtyard and watch the old man arrive home bareheaded, bearing loads of firewood, or see him sitting in the sun, splitting bamboo stalks to weave into baskets. I met with Qi Deyi only once, and though we saw each other nearly every day, he never spoke to me again. It was early in my stay. I had not yet gained independence from those assigned to monitor me—a young ethnographer from the Chuxiong Yi Culture Research Institute and a clerk from Zhizuo's government. We sat together in a deserted schoolroom, drinking the two bottles of clear grain alcohol I had bought for the occasion and posing stumbling questions about ritual. If I wanted to study religion, I had been told, this old man would be a crucial informant: he was a former ts'ici and Zhizuo's most accomplished ritualist. Sitting on a high chair in this fireless room, faced by three baldly inquisitive youths, and surrounded with the paraphernalia of interrogation—desks, pens, notebooks, a tape recorder—Qi Deyi was clearly uncomfortable, perhaps afraid. He drank quickly, and after he was quite drunk, he left off formulating answers to our questions. I turned off my tape recorder, and Qi Deyi told a story for which we had not asked and which we did not welcome. It was a confession and a plea to leave him in peace.[13]

He had been famous as a ritualist, he said, but that was a long time ago. Before 1958, he and his brother Qi Dezhong had spent every autumn performing tenth-month sacrifices, rites that were required for all who had died the previous year. In the tenth month, every family, rich or poor, who had suffered a death held a ceremony on one of three outdoor sites in Zhizuo. The rite lasted an entire day and required hundreds of participants to make contributions ranging from a rice cake or a handful of grain to an entire sacrificial goat, depending on their relations with the dead and the obligations incurred in earlier mortuary rites. Many in Zhizuo spent the entire tenth month fulfilling mortuary obligations. The main site was a hilltop where a grove of old-growth trees had been preserved, just below the hill of graves between Chemo and Chezò. After 1953, when Li Zhang built the medical clinic there, tenth-month sacrifices continued behind the clinic, a little farther up the hill. In the mid-1950s, this site was in such demand that two eight-hour rites were sometimes held in one day, the first ending around five in the afternoon, the second proceeding into the night.

Many local cadres harshly criticized tenth-month sacrifice as superstitious and wasteful. Still, as Qi Deyi succinctly put it, "officials die too." Local cadres were deeply enmeshed in mortuary obligations, and they found it difficult to mount serious attacks on mortuary rites, especially when they might affect rituals for their own close kin. The ceremony required a ritualist to perform a chant that lasted from six to eight hours. Qi Deyi and Qi Dezhong were masters of this chant, the only true masters in Zhizuo's central valley. Their services were in high demand, and they made a good living each autumn from the goat's foreleg and *sheng* of grain paid for each performance.

This chant was the most difficult of all feats of memory, Qi Deyi said. It had forty-six sections, which told of the origins of everything, the earth and sky, all living things, every kind of spirit, ghost, and strange being. It sent the dead off on their journey over earth and sky toward the underworld. It cleansed the corpse of its wounds, pain, wildness, bitterness, hunger, and death; and it told of swaddling it with its spouse in layers of silk and quilts and leaving it suspended pure and high, head to the west and feet in the stars, like a cocoon in a tree.[14]

The year 1957 was a busy time for tenth-month sacrifice. Zhizuo had been united into a single cooperative for two years. Individual households used grain allocated for household consumption for the gifts of raw grain and rice cakes, and the production team of each deceased's household donated the minimum sacrificial animals required for each rite, three goats and a piglet. But in 1958 it all ended. All the grain went to the mess halls, all the goats and pigs to commune farms. By the tenth lunar month (in December), grain rationing had begun, and people were living off sweet potatoes and radishes. In the absence of individual stores of grain, tenth-month sacrifice was impossible. The two other major mortuary rituals still held for every dead soul were also abandoned: the night vigil (*kukado*), in which souls were conducted to the underworld and given stores of grain and animals to sustain them there; and the day vigil (*nihèpi*), in which the recently dead passed on gifts of grain, alcohol, words, and tears to other dead kin. These rites had involved every household in a dense network of deferred obligations to tens or even hundreds of others. This network collapsed entirely in the autumn of 1958. People simply hauled their dead to the graveyard and buried them as best they could.

In the winter, as people started to starve and die, Qi Deyi and his brother Qi Dezhong were arrested.

> Yang Guowen arrested us. He was the boss of Zhizuo [the leader of one of its two management districts]. He tied us up and made us build [an addition to] that clinic up there at the tenth-month sacrifice site. We had nothing to eat, and we had to build that clinic ourselves, with our hands, as thought reconstruction [Ch. *sixiang gaizao*]. No one helped us. After my brother died, I built that clinic alone. While I was building it, I forgot the tenth-month sacrifice *nèpi*. I don't remember it, don't ask me to sing it, no one remembers it now.

When Qi Dezhong died of hunger and overwork while laboring on the clinic, Qi Deyi buried him without ceremony.

Hauling bricks for the state medical clinic to the tenth-month sacrifice site, Qi Deyi forgot the words of this *nèpi*, which his body had absorbed over many years of apprenticeship and which founded his social identity as a brilliant ritualist and a powerful conduit of ancestral wisdom and authority. Digestive memory shattered, and another form of memory, given over to the economy of repetition and return that we call trauma, took its place. Not long before I left Zhizuo, Qi Deyi held an exorcism for the ghost of his brother. He had performed many such exorcisms over the years. Qi Deyi could no longer remember the exorcism chant, so he hired another ritualist, Li Wenyi, to perform the ceremony. As he chanted to the black *gu*, the wild ghost officials who descend from the sky to afflict their victims with violent death, Li Wenyi inserted the name of Yang Guowen, who had arrested Qi Deyi and his brother.

Qi Deyi's brother Qi Dezhong was a particularly vicious wild ghost, Li Wenyi told me on another occasion; Qi Deyi had gone mad after his brother died and had been intermittently mad ever since. But *all* those who died of hunger or thirst in the famine became wild ghosts. None had been properly admitted to the underworld; none had been given stores of grain and herds of goats to sustain them in death:

> They wander the fields and paths; they waylay their descendants and demand gifts of grain and meat; they are always starving, always greedy. These days, we perform exorcism after exorcism, far more than ever before. But few exorcisms are successful for long; those ghosts keep coming back, and their descendants keep falling ill. That is why some call this the age of wild ghosts.

The reversal of the policies that had driven the Great Leap Forward and recovery from the famine those policies had precipitated involved complex interaction between local initiatives for reform and policy adjustments emanating from the center (Yang 1996, 75; MacFarquhar 1997). In Yunnan, as elsewhere, two rectification movements, in the winters of 1960–1961 and 1961–1962, set the political tone for policy liberalization. In each movement, cadres were encouraged to criticize each other for promulgating the "five winds" of excessive communism, commandism, boastfulness, blind orders, and cadre privilege. After an investigative trip to the countryside in the spring of 1961, Yunnan's governor composed a letter to Mao suggesting a wholesale policy adjustment, including making mess halls voluntary, returning plow animals and large agricultural implements to production teams, and adjusting the size of the teams to better suit local conditions. He proposed that in the province's many mountainous districts production teams should again be made the basic unit of production and distribution and that, in some teams, contracting production to households (Ch. *baochan daohu*) should be permitted (DZY 1991, 1:158–159). Mao had received many similar promptings from elsewhere, and his written approval of this letter accelerated the pace of policy liberalization in Yunnan.

The first adjustment was in the scale of communes, which were reduced from the size of a former district to the size of a former township. In September, Zhizuo became an independent commune, responsible for its own production, procurement, and redistribution. At the same time, collective mess halls were abandoned, and grain was allocated directly to peasant households. Supply and marketing cooperatives redistributed thousands of iron pots and ceramic bowls to peasant households, which no longer had the means to cook their own food. Exaggerated production reports and procurement targets were revised drastically downward, and limited supplies of relief grain were given to the worst-affected production teams. In December, private vegetable plots were redistributed to peasant households throughout Chuxiong Prefecture (CYZZ 1994, 139). For the first time, Zhizuo residents began to grow radishes and leafy vegetables in private garden plots rather than on the margins of grain fields.

Finally, in the summer of 1962, production teams again became the basic units of accounting, production, procurement, and redistribution. Communes and counties were prohibited from forcibly recruiting labor from the teams. Agricultural implements and surviving livestock were redistributed to the teams. Pigs were distributed to individual households, which were allowed to eat half of each pig they raised after selling half to the state. In mountain districts, the size of production teams was adjusted to reflect the size of a "natural village." In places where households were widely scattered, such as in Zhizuo's outlying districts, a production team might be only three to five households, as compared to the average size of about twenty (CYZZ 1994, 133, 139). Remote, single households were allowed to plan their own production and consumption (Ch. *dan'gan*), with limited guidance from neighboring teams.[15] Grain production recovered in 1961 and 1962, approximating the pre-Leap levels of 1957. In addition, the central leadership increased procurement prices for grain and meat by about 25 percent and began to import grain (Yang 1996, 77). Mortality rates for Dayao County in 1961 followed those of the province and the nation in returning to 1957 levels (see Figure 6.1). After falling to an unprecedented low in 1960, birth rates surged dramatically in 1961 and peaked in 1963, evidence that the years of mass starvation were over.

⌒⤳

In Zhizuo, the Great Leap Forward had profoundly disordered time itself. In the language of mourning, the time of life and death through which generation passed into generation had been imagined as a stream flowing past the measure of a stationary rock. The Great Leap blocked and reversed the currents that gathered to form this stream. It unbalanced the digestive flows of grain and meat through houses and bodies, causing them first to erupt into unsustainable excess and then to dry up altogether. It inverted the nature of labor: useless work that produced nothing but hunger was transformed into heroic feats of production; all labor became foremost the production of wild words for the state's insatiable mouth. The flows of grain, meat, alcohol, tears, and words from the living to the dead and among the living through the dead ruptured, and the tissue of funeral obligations so crucial to social relations was torn through. The work of mourning became impossible, and the famine dead returned to afflict their descendants with psychic and physical pain. They would keep returning for many years, as social relations among the living fragmented further. During the Socialist Education campaign and the Cultural Revolution, the wild ghosts of the famine would exacerbate the social schisms generated during the Great Leap, lending their force to a developing oppositional practice of time.

Conclusion

Zhizuo residents' tales of the 1950s are evidence of a profound transformation in their imagination of state power in relation to person and community. A resource employed by many rural Chinese to envision the broad shape of the Imperial and Republican states was mortuary ritual. The rich ethnographic and historical literature on the rituals and literatures of mourning describes detailed spirit realms, where hierarchies of spirit officials oversaw the dead, conducting tribunals, dispensing justice, ordering tortures, collecting taxes, circulating documents, engaging in corruption, and receiving honors and chastisements in ways that mirrored the activities of officials of the Imperial and sometimes even the Republican bureaucracies.[16] In their own mortuary rites, Zhizuo residents also imagined such a realm: the *mómi,* a just bureaucracy, where Yama (Yàlɔ̀wú), king of death, ruled over hosts of hierarchically ordered officials, who extracted bribes and other tribute from the dead. Outside the borders of this realm was the chaotic *nèmi,* world of ghosts, where the disturbed and homeless souls of the violently dead wandered like bandits and criminals. The most conspicuous feature of this underworld realm was that it lay elsewhere. Most daily activity went on apart from it, and its intersections with the world of the living were across a distinct ontological divide. Exchanges of words, gifts, bribes, or tribute across this divide required rule-bound procedures, formalized languages, and highly restricted vocabularies.

For people in Zhizuo it was this divide, more than any feature of the underworld's internal bureaucratic organization, that was most salient for envisioning the Republican state. Officialdom, represented most vividly by the Xia *tusi* and his servants, was separated from the living community by a similar divide—at once social and moral. Managing transactions across this boundary also required special, delicate procedures of ritual and language, for which Zhizuo residents employed experts: the *ts'ici*, his speaker (the *lòrɔ,* a witty, multilingual sophisticate), and his bearer (the *k'ɔlɔ,* mute and stupid enough not to give offense). Though state forces were very much present within the community—extracting taxes and corvée, regulating markets, judging disputes, arresting wrongdoers, and drafting youths for cannon fodder—the *ts'ici* system worked to exclude the state from its sustaining vision of generative unity. As it drew officials who descended from outside into the community's very center in order to send them quickly on their way, the *ts'ici* used hospitality to maintain the moral and social boundaries between inside and outside and to manage the threats to community that boundary transgressions entailed. The generative force nurtured in the *ts'ici* system's rites, envisioned as sustaining a contained, houselike reproductive community, was the moral opposite of Han officialdom—the inside to the state's outside.

In the early 1950s, the social and moral boundaries that had kept the state at the margins of the community dissolved. The institutions of the new state spread over the intimately lived landscape like the "bitter herb." They excavated and reoccupied the places where people had gathered to negotiate with the forces of life and death and to reaffirm their productive and reproductive relations. The agents of the state were recruited from among kin and neighbors; the local government, now lodged within the community, sought not to hold the state at bay but to place it at the center of daily life. By the mid-1950s, when land and labor were collectivized, the state was seen to be bidding to replace the ancestral authority of the *ts'ici* spirits as the generative origin of communal reproduction. This was state power of another shape entirely: an intimate power, radiating from the community's center and requiring of every subject intensive efforts at personal transformation. Mortuary ritual and the "Imperial metaphor" of a separate, bureaucratic realm were no longer useful resources for envisioning its shape or understanding its effects. Chinese socialism was fluid and experimental in the mid-1950s, and it is likely that people in Zhizuo saw various possible models for understanding state power emerge and collapse. Yet in retrospect their stories give the effect of a swift and inevitable onrush of events toward the cataclysm that would color every vision of state power for the next three decades. In their stories of famine, Zhizuo residents mobilized another powerful set of ritual resources to envision the shape of state power. The generative center of communal reproduction hollowed out (k_2); the state became an empty mouth, voicing ceaseless demands to be filled with words and grain—an avaricious wild ghost.

Unlike the ordered bureaucracy of the underworld (*mómi*), the world of ghosts (*nèmi*) was understood to be intimately interfused with the world of the living. Wild ghosts (*chènè*) did demand from the living special and elaborately complex ritual and linguistic procedures, but they were by no means bound by such procedures themselves: they were everywhere present on paths, in houses, and in bodies; they were always already within, unseen but malignant, the cause of the most chronic and incomprehensible physical and mental afflictions. And they were neither Han nor strangers:[17] they were one's own kin and ascendants, capable of the worst predations precisely because they had once been the most intimate and beloved. Even the humblest, driven to violent death by more powerful wild ghost officials, were caught up in a kind of predatory bureaucracy: behind them and the afflictions they brought stretched a long chain of ghost officials, clear across the national landscape to Beijing. Most famine dead were not buried correctly or mourned properly until 1978. Instead, they roved the intimately lived spaces of paths, fields, houses, and bodies. In the chaotic period to come, from the arrival of the Socialist Education campaign in the spring of 1965 through the end of the Cultural Revolution in 1976, these crowds of ghosts would lend their weight to a vision of the state as an intimate spectral entity, the hollow center of a devastated community—a vision darkened by acts of revenge, unanswered demands for justice, and traumatic returns of loss and devastation. To understand the power of this vision in shaping post-famine events (the subject of chapter 8), we must first investigate the ritual resources from which it borrowed its form: the rites of exorcism.

CHAPTER SEVEN

A Geography of Pain

Ascending to Zhizuo, one emerges from between the high walls of a gorge. The valley widens, villages appear on the hillsides above, and the path crosses a tile-roofed bridge. Here where road and river intersect is a stretch of ground bare of growth and black with ash. Half-burned bits of contraptions survive: an arched willow branch, a plank with painted eyes. The ground is littered with charred pots, knives, baskets, and bits of blackened cloth. These are the belongings of people who have died badly and returned to prey on their kin. From here, these wild ghosts and those who killed them are sent away, through the valley's excretory aperture, down roads and rivers, across the breadth of the nation, to attend markets and hold meetings in the great cities of the east.

Exorcisms (*chènèpi*) of wild ghosts gained unprecedented significance in the era my ritualist friends called the "age of wild ghosts," the period between the famine and the present. These rites were crucial resources for understanding personal grief and pain in the context of the profoundly transformed vision of state power consolidated after the Great Leap Forward. Exorcisms had been a central form of ritual practice in these mountains for a long time. The complex ideas and intricate idioms they employed gave evidence of lengthy development, in which notions and techniques of diverse origins were absorbed and synthesized. Yet those who specialized in their unpleasant and dangerous performance believed that in recent years their frequency had increased manyfold. One ritualist estimated that two or three exorcisms were held each week in Zhizuo, whereas before the famine only three or four had been necessary each year. An exaggeration, perhaps, but all insisted that in this age the air was thick with wild ghosts and that the techniques used to send them away had supplanted many of the myriad other arts of ritual healing.

In the first two decades after the famine, exorcisms were performed in secret. People bore the effects of the violently dead to new sites in secluded canyons and burned them at night, away from the eyes of local officials. In 1978, however, as central and local governments relaxed their vigilance against ritual practice, exorcisms began to burgeon openly. Their growth was encouraged by the revival of funeral ritual, especially the rites of *kukædo* (the night vigil) and *nihèpi* (the day vigil).[1] In the late 1970s and early 1980s, many in Zhizuo performed these mortuary rites for kin who had died during the famine or the Cultural Revolution and had never been properly mourned. To enable these rituals to proceed smoothly, exorcisms were sponsored for those who had died of hunger, suicide, or other violence. Openly remembering that siblings or ascendants had died badly allowed people to trace recurrent physical or psychic ailments to them, and many were exorcised repeatedly. Through the 1980s and 1990s, the numbers of exorcisms grew, as each rite to send away the ghost of an ascendant encouraged other kin of the afflicted to identify the same entity as the root of their own difficulties.

Intended to enable forgetting, exorcism rituals also compelled remembering. By the early 1990s, possession by wild ghosts (*chènèt'æ*) was the most common diagnosis for difficult, chronic, or recurrent ailments, many of which might once have been attributed to other entities.[2] And it was by no means only those who had lived through the famine or the Cultural Revolution who were troubled by wild ghosts. Like their parents, youths consulted elderly diviners to discover the causes of their symptoms. These diviners had long personal memories of past violence, and they often traced physical or psychic troubles to violently dead ascendants the youths had never known. Many exorcisms thus transformed the afflictions of youths into the returns of past violence of which they had no direct experience. Each ritual of forgetting worked personal afflictions into a common historical consciousness, structured by the recurrent returns of the past. By repeatedly purging bodies, houses, and the intimate landscape of the famine's returning effects, people insisted that this cataclysm be remembered in corporeal and psychic pain. Eventually, exorcism rites became the foundation for a subversive practice of time. They were worked into a coherent narrative strategy, which generated tales of the bad deaths and ghostly returns of local officials thought to have shared responsibility for the famine. These tales were attempts to apportion responsibility for past violence between the national center and the kin and neighbors, who were the state's local agents. They defeated state efforts to leave past injustices behind along a linear "socialist road" toward the future.

Chapter 8 examines this temporal practice in detail. As a prelude to that discussion, this chapter investigates exorcism rites as healing practices. These were by far the most complex of the ritual practices of healing in Zhizuo. They involved sculpting the most elaborate effigies and chanting one of the lengthiest and most difficult *nèpi*. In this chapter, I treat these intricacies as more than merely empty proliferations of ritual arcana (though they were that, too!). Exorcisms were efforts to create concrete effects upon the most difficult and elusive forces. Their intricate material and verbal vocabularies assembled models or diagrams of a constitutive moment of social personhood. This was a moment in which time and place turned back on themselves. In place, the interlayered habitations of body, house, and landscape became entangled or congested, blocking or reversing flows of substances, relations, and affects. In time, the layered transitions of days, seasons, and life cycles reversed to infect the present with anguish from the past. Exorcisms attempted to untangle or unravel these congested flows in time and place. Their principal means for doing this, I argue, was coincidence between the referential and formal aspects of their material and verbal languages. As healing practices, exorcisms encouraged transactions between language and the body—language as a coincidence of sensual and referential effects, the body as an interfusion of social and material relations. And in healing individual bodies, they became resources for attending to communal wounds, repeatedly reopened by the returning pain and injustice of the past.

I spent much time in Zhizuo working to understand exorcism rituals and the difficult ideas that surrounded them. I attended ten separate exorcisms, in whole or part. In stark contrast to mortuary rites, exorcisms were viewed by Zhizuo residents as unpleasant and dangerous. To attend and eat was to help bear a burden of pain; it was to implicate oneself in the returning evil and to risk contamination by it. My closest friends did not approve of my running off to exorcisms. They felt it was unhealthy—and when I contracted infectious hepatitis, they suggested that it was from eating goats sacrificed to wild ghosts. But I always felt welcomed by the rituals' sponsors, who seemed to accept that I too might help. Baffled by the rites' complexity, I apprenticed myself to Li Wenyi, a ritualist in his early eighties, much in demand across Zhizuo to perform exorcisms. Li Wenyi taught me how to construct the difficult effigies for wild ghosts and instructed me on the significance of each of their parts. I recorded his exorcism chants and those of three others. To transcribe and translate them and to learn about wild ghosts and their effects, I consulted with many others, both ordinary participants and skilled ritualists. Two of the ritualists were women; two were from Líp'ò villages outside Zhizuo. For all, exorcisms were the most serious of topics, deserving of precise and extensive exegesis. This chapter begins by briefly discussing the ideas of reversed flows, contagion, and entanglement with which wild ghosts are associated. It then tells the story of a single exorcism, a rite for a nineteen-year-old girl possessed by the ghost of her dead baby brother and troubled also by her grandfather, who had been a prominent local official during the famine and who had committed suicide during the Cultural Revolution. The last part of the chapter touches on the formal properties of the poetic language used during exorcism rites. How might poetic language heal? I suggest that this poetry's affective force and potential for healing emerge from the ways its formal properties and its semantic message coincide in the bodily motions of walking.

Wild Ghost Genealogies

Among the crucial tasks for ritualists and diviners called on to diagnose a chronic physical or psychic ailment was to establish a lineage for pain. Pain was traced to an intermediate root or cause (*ju*), the death by violence of a spouse, sibling, ascendant, or other closely related person. This cause tied the pain into an interminable causal chain; each identifiable violent death was rooted in others, caused by more indeterminant forces erupting into the world. Ritualists sorted through the links of this chain by dividing convergent evil forces into white *gu* and black *gu*—white *gu* were named ascendants, dead of violence; black *gu* were wild ghost officials. In a few cases, wild ghost officials were identified with actual historical actors: chapters 6 and 8 mention the wild ghost official Yang Guowen, who led Zhizuo through the Great Leap and the resulting famine; this chapter describes how Li Wenyi's exorcism chant named Lin Biao and Jiang Qing, both prominent leaders of the Cultural Revolution, as emperor and empress of wild ghosts. In general, however, wild ghost officials were unnamed and indeterminate, imagined as a host of bright entities swirling about the blue sky like flocks of noisy and colorful parakeets. Black *gu* were thought to be the root causes of violent death; yet without named white *gu* to act as channels, these wild ghost officials were powerless to afflict. This chain of wild ghosts was not a simple or straightforward metaphor, employed to trace the determinate cause of all violent death to actual state officials—some violent deaths clearly had little to do with social forces extending beyond a single household or village. Rather, it was a flexible tool for apportioning the responsibility for pain or grief between known kin or ascendants and other forces, social or "natural," whose shape was less clear.

Confronted with a chronic or recalcitrant physical or psychic ailment, ritualists and diviners examined the histories of known ascendants for deaths of specific kinds. To distinguish clearly between bad and ordinary deaths, ritualists referred to a list repeated often in exorcism chants:

7.1

some die bearing sons or daughters	t'à mo zò ho né te shr
some die with blood-dyed clothing	t'à mo p'á chì sì tí shr
some die with blood-soaked groins	t'à mo p'á dɔ sì k'ɔ̀ shr
some die crushed by trees or stones	t'à mo cì tí lo lɔ shr
some die of hunger or thirst	t'à mo mi cì hæ̀ cì shr
some swell and explode	t'à mo p'è cì jɔ́ cì shr
some hang and explode	t'à mo chæ̀ cì jɔ́ cì shr
some are stabbed or slashed	t'à mo cì lè dɔ lè shr
some trip and crush their heads	t'à mo chì t'i wú bæ shr
some die of loud shouts or big words	t'à mo cè ká dà và shr
some are roasted by fire	t'à mo à dó bo̲ lɔ shr
some are swept away by floods	t'à mo yi và vé ká shr
tile-roofed houses burn	ngæ̀ mo t'a he p'e
thatch-roofed huts burn	cí mo lì he p'e
at work on the road	mà gà di do yi
they step on mating snakes	cæ lc cæ bo t'o
at work on the mountain	mà gà wò mó te
crushed by falling trees	dɔ mó cí mo tí tu lɔ
some have intestines ruptured by poison	t'à mo hì chi wu kɔ jɔ́

The first item on every list was death in childbirth. Lòlop'ò spoke of this as the original and paradigmatic form of evil death. Luo Lizhu, the elderly female ritualist introduced in chapter 2, spent many afternoons helping me to translate exorcism chants. On one occasion, she told me a myth of the origins of exorcism ritual. It was about a young woman named Pi̱mæ̀menè, the first person to become a wild ghost.

> As sky and earth were being formed, there was a family of two parents with a single daughter. Soon after she married, the daughter died bearing a child. The fetus turned around and lodged in her birth canal. Because at that time there were no wild ghosts, her parents didn't know how to perform an exorcism [*chènèpi*]. She was not admitted into the underworld and was in terrible pain. She wandered the world with the infant stuck in her birth canal. Every day she returned to harm her parents. They were full of grief, but they could do nothing. Every day they went to the riverside to weep, and they often bore offerings for their child down to the river. Finally, they bore all her belongings to the riverside and burned them. After this, she no longer returned to harm them. But she killed her husband, who also turned into a wild ghost.

The image of Pi̱mæ̀menè wandering the world with an inverted fetus lodged in her birth canal brings together many of the associative threads that make the idea of wild ghosts flexible and powerful enough both to permeate mundane aspects of daily life and to preoccupy people during the most painful tragedies. The most prominent and durable of these threads have to do with reversed flows, contagion, and entanglement.

In the first thread, wild ghosts are imagined as blocking or reversing flows. Like the fetus stuck in Pi̱mæ̀menè's birth canal, wild ghosts simultaneously interrupt the flows of substances through living bodies and the temporal flows of life and death. White *gu* obstruct bodily flows to make their victims ill; black *gu* bring forms of death that bar their victims from the underworld, rendering them incapable of rebirth. The term *chènè*, "wild ghost," is not only used to refer to discrete supernatural entities; it is also employed to describe states of affairs in which flows are reversed. For instance, as people set up ancestral effigies on the wall of an upstream room, they pay strict attention to ranking order. Placing one's grandparents closer to the head of the bed than one's parents is *chènè:* it reverses the proper flow of generations, producing illness and trouble. Placing the figures to point downstream instead of slightly upstream is also *chènè*, as is cutting them with the grain of the tree running in reverse so that their heads point toward the tree's roots, or cutting their faces from the west rather than the east side of a twig. As chapter 3 described, carpenters pay similar attention to the orientation of every beam, post, and rafter in a house. Pointing the head of a post or beam toward the earth, downstream, or downhill when building a house is *chènè*.

Obstructions or reversals in flows through the landscape are also *chènè*. Luo Lizhu sometimes spoke of *chènè* as an evil potential in the vital flows that animate the landscape, always ready to cause calamity:

> Wind and water both have some *chènè* in them; so does fire. If the wind is blowing as you approach a dangerous place in the road, the *chènè* in the wind might cause it suddenly to swell up, blow you off the path, and kill you. Or when you cross the water, it might suddenly well up and sweep you away. Or the river bed might collapse under your feet. This is called "water surging" [*aye yì*]. Or you might look at the water swirling around and grow dizzy and fall in. This is also *aye yì*. Wind, water, and fire all have *chènè* following them.

Like swelling in a body, a sudden welling up of wind or water is caused by a reversal of flow. Wind in Zhizuo usually follows the valleys and streams from south to north, but the most vicious winds blow from the north. Li Zhiwu confessed to me that such winds always made him afraid: "For one thing, they are omens of *chènè*—people say that the sound that wind makes is the sound of *chènè*—and for another, wind is what blows a spark up into a fire and sweeps it from house to house." A fire that burns down a house is always attributed to *chènè*; its sudden, fierce spread is like the welling up of wind or water that kills travelers.

The image of wind blowing a spark of fire from house to house contributes to the most fearsome thread of ideas about wild ghosts: they are violently contagious, and they can spread along the relational links that connect each person and each house to others with terrible speed. This notion of contagion is linked to ideas about death in childbirth and about pollution caused by menstrual and postpartum discharge. In Zhizuo, as in much of rural China, menstrual blood is considered offensive to spirits and ancestors.[3] My informants claimed that almost all non-human entities, from the most evil to the most benign, "love cleanliness" and despise menstrual blood. Spirits thought to be ethnically Han (particularly *mæ*, which kill infants, and *mɛlònè*, spirit familiars owned by some diviners and ritualists) are the only exceptions. During rituals of all kinds, women are warned to beware where they sit so as not to pollute the materials from which effigies are constructed. Menstrual pollution of coffins or tombstones can spell disaster for the dead's kin. Ritualists insisted that the *ts'ici* spirits were particularly offended by menstrual blood. The most common rationalization for excluding all women from rites for the collective ancestral spirit Agàmisimo was that all were polluted by their association with menstrual blood and postpartum discharge.

Menstrual blood, it was argued, also endangered the health of those exposed to it. The idea that bodies, houses, and the landscape were composed of directed flows made this aspect of menstrual pollution particularly menacing. Women were careful not to climb ladders or trees in the presence of men, who feared that menstrual pollution would follow the flow of gravity and drop on their heads. Men took offense at women who unthinkingly stepped over carrying poles left out on the path, for menstrual pollution could flow from a pole placed on one's shoulder down into one's body. Men often treated menstrual pollution as though its effects proliferated to block or reverse the flows of other influences. This was particularly explicit in house building. Builders kept careful watch on their tools and on the timbers they prepared to build houses to make sure that women past puberty did not sit or step on them. Any woman might be menstruating, one never knows, carpenters said, and a timber stepped on by a menstruating woman would be like a timber with its head where its tail should be, causing death and misfortune in a house for as long as it stands.

Men were also quick to point out that sex during menstruation, though risky for men, was even more dangerous for women. Sex reversed the flow of menstrual blood, forcing it back up into the uterus (*dolomo*), where it could cause itching, foul odor, and difficulty in urinating. According to local herbalists, the backed-up menstrual blood could also cause uterine cancer (Ch. *zigong ai*) and other ailments that harmed a woman's reproductive capacity. Women were enjoined to avoid bathing while menstruating, since the water could carry the unclean blood back up into the uterus. It was best for the body to rid itself of menstrual blood as fully and quickly as possible. Because walking or heavy labor could slow or stop the flow of blood, menstruating women tried to stay at home and do only light tasks whenever possible. Menstrual cramps were thought to be the effect of a reluctant flow of menstrual blood; the blood remaining in the body wreaked havoc on it.

Postpartum discharge was similarly dangerous. After a birth, mother and child remained in a polluted state for the first sixty days, a period called *hojo,* "in the month." All the ritual restrictions on menstruating women applied also to *hojomo,* "mothers in the month"—indeed, when speaking of ritual pollution, men often mentioned menstruation and the pollution of birth in the same breath. Postpartum pollution seriously endangered men who came into contact with it. A man who had sex with a mother in the month was likely to develop an affliction called *hojono*: he became feverish, his body swelled, his eyes blurred, and his testicles hardened, dried up, and stank. These symptoms could last for years. Even sleeping under the same blanket with a woman in the month could give a man a mild form of *hojono*, afflicting him with bouts of fever, dizziness, and headaches. Like sex during menstruation, sex during this period was also seen as particularly harmful to women: it could destroy their capacity to give birth and could lead to slow, feverish death after three to five years. Local herbalists explained that during both menstruation and birth, a woman's body was extremely "hot," as the result of a temporary accumulation of *cè*, "breath" (similar to Ch. *qi*). This accumulation made new life possible, but it also made the body vulnerable to the pollution of menstruation or birth. The most direct way pollution could be carried back into the body was bathing. A new mother should not bathe until the end of the sixty-day period, when a bath should be prepared from the boiled leaves of three fragrant trees, and the mother should wash herself and her infant from head to foot. Some herbalists spoke as though the polluting agent were not the actual postpartum fluids but the overheated state of a woman's body after birthing. Sex could pass this heat from the mother to her partner or prolong it dangerously in the mother.

The vulnerability of menstruating and postpartum bodies is key to why these states were regarded as contaminating. Men saw birthing as a strategic pass (Ch. *guankou*) through which most women must travel, during which they were most susceptible to misfortune. Menstrual blood and postpartum fluid indexed the potential for the horrible and painful death at a young age that accompanied the capacity to give birth. The list of deaths in fragment 7.1 speaks of bodies swelling (*p'ècì*) and exploding *jác̀ì;* death in childbirth was imagined as a swelling and explosion of the body as a result of obstructed flows. For men, the most alarming aspect of both forms of pollution was their quick and invisible contagion. The potential to infect bodies or substances at a distance distinguished these forms of pollution from other kinds of filth, such as human feces or dog meat. The heated, vulnerable qualities of menstruating or postnatal bodies were milder forms of the dangerously swollen state of a woman bearing a child; the contagious qualities of menstrual and postnatal pollution were less deadly versions of the contagion of death in childbirth. When a woman did die in childbirth, ritualists counseled her family to take extraordinary precautions to protect her house from pollution. Luo Lizhu listed them thus:

> You must go up to the barn loft and shoot three arrows out the window into the sky. You must go down to the mill and grind three times backward, toward the left hand. To take the corpse out of the house, you must make a hole in the wall; you must not take it out the door. You must give the corpse no night vigil [*kukædo̱*] or day vigil [*nihèpi*]; you must carry it out and bury it without coffin or tombstone, far from your burial ground. And then you must perform her exorcism, the full exorcism for white *gu* and black *gu*.

Ritualists and ordinary people alike spoke of the pollution of death in childbirth spreading from house to house like a fire spread by the wind. Before the Socialist Education movement of the early 1960s, when a woman died in childbirth within Zhizuo's inner valley, most families sealed their houses until after her exorcism. They scattered ashes before the doors, placed branches of thorns and Sichuan pepper in the door frames, stuffed all cracks with straw, and stayed inside night and day except for absolutely necessary tasks such as drawing water. In the early 1990s, only close neighbors sealed their houses after a death from childbirth, but most others avoided traveling or performing heavy labor. Nearby neighbors were also careful not to wash or process hemp; wash, make, or repair clothing; mill or pound grain; or chop wood—all said to attract wild ghosts.

The description of an exorcism that follows illustrates how this rite employed images of entanglement to combine ideas of blocked or reversed flows with notions of contagion. Exorcisms invoked a moment of social personhood in which the multiple intersections of social relations that produced persons gathered and intensified to confusion. It was a point at which memory and forgetting began to interfere with each other, where that which should have been forgotten recirculated through tangled social relations to return repeatedly to the present. Like a whirlpool in a river or a knotted intestine, these social tangles generated blocked or reversed corporeal and temporal flows. And by short-circuiting the directional flows that kept social persons minimally separated, giving them their own identities and ensuring that one person's illness or trouble didn't become everyone's, entanglement also generated contagion. After invoking such a tangled moment, exorcisms performed a disentanglement, seeking to restore multiple directional flows in lived space and time.

Hauntings

Shortly after she gave birth to her first child at the age of nineteen, Li Jie began to speak in the voice of her baby brother, dead for five years. Talking over her illness, her neighbors noted her troubled lineage. Li Jie's mother's father was Li Zhong, a name associated with the most painful events of the recent past. He had been an official of the Zhonghe Commune during the Great Leap Forward, and, like many former officials, he had been driven to suicide during the Cultural Revolution. Li Jie's dead grandfather might well be involved in her baby brother's return, it was said, but this depended on whether the infant, eight months old at death, had grown teeth. Had he died without teeth, his soul could be considered a *ma* and treated as casually as the soul of a domestic animal. Two full pairs of teeth, however, one above and one below, would have entitled him to a small-scale funeral, with siblings and fathers' sisters' children playing the roles of orphaned son, orphaned daughter, and wife's brother. Li Jie's parents had chosen to treat the baby as a *ma,* burying it without funeral or coffin downstream from their family burial plot and upending an earth-carrying basket over the tiny grave. Had he been fully human, as teeth would have indicated, this casual treatment would have made his soul a wild ghost, allied with his notorious dead grandfather, wandering starving and greedy, preying on his kin.

Li Jie's troubles coincided with a difficult shift of residence. A year earlier, she had moved out of her parents' house to join her husband in a room at the school where he taught. Soon after, she moved again, to her husband's parents' house, where her mother-in-law could help with the birth of her child. Confined with her new baby in a strange house and village, Li Jie seemed to have found the first sixty days after the birth profoundly disorienting. She quarreled frequently with her husband's parents and wept alone with her baby in the courtyard. Her weeping eventually turned to high-pitched babbling, the babbling to words and sentences. Through her mouth, her dead brother asked for goats, chickens, grain, and a wife. He demanded a house and clothing. He stated the precise amount of his father's salary and insisted on a lavish funeral.

Li Jie's husband's parents protested that she was spouting nonsense. But she persisted, and they gave in. After several rounds of negotiations, her husband's parents and her own agreed to split the cost of a funeral. Her parents found a family with a recently dead infant girl, who agreed to marry her soul to the dead baby boy. Together, Li Jie's natal and affinal households bought a tiny coffin, filled it with silk clothing, and bought three goats to kill. Nearly four hundred of their kin and friends attended a night vigil (*kukædo̱*), bringing grain, chickens, young goats, or rice cakes, depending on what obligations to the two households they had incurred at previous mortuary rites. Nine days later, the two households sponsored a day vigil (*nihæ̀pi̱*), during which they fashioned an ancestral effigy for the souls of the dead boy and his infant wife, placing it with the effigies of Li Jie's ascendants on the wall of her parents' house. On both these occasions, Li Jie played the role of orphaned daughter (*zòmæ̀*). During the night vigil, she poured round after round of alcohol for the guests; during the day vigil, she ladled water into a hole in the ground and sang mourning songs. The funerals did not cure Li Jie's trouble. She continued to fight with her husband's parents, and she would not stop weeping. A diviner was consulted. He reminded her husband's parents that behind the dead baby stood other, more fearsome wild ghosts, most particularly her notorious dead grandfather. A few days later, the household sponsored a full-scale exorcism to drive away both Li Jie's baby brother and the violent inheritance unearthed by his return.

Gatherings

As the story of Pi̱mæ̀menè makes clear, exorcism was conceived at its simplest as disposing of the personal effects of the violently dead. Prior to 1958, people in Zhizuo had carried a dead person's most transportable belongings—clothing and jewelry, knives and favorite pots and pans—to the top of a mountain that towered over Agàmisimo's hilltop, before burning larger items such as furniture at the river's tail. This was the tallest peak in the area, pale with white clay, where the rim of the world met the blue sky from whence wild ghosts descended. Up there, the ritualist Li Wenyi claimed, he had seen wild ghosts celebrating: "You can see them dancing with babies on their backs, dancing without heads, dancing with spears through their bodies, with bloody cloths about their brows. They all wear rings and bracelets." During the Great Leap, this journey to the mountaintop had become impossible. It was exhausting for painfully overworked and underfed bodies, and to be seen openly making offerings to the famine dead was dangerous. After the famine, people held exorcisms in secluded canyons and at night when necessary, adding the clothing, utensils, and jewelry they might once have carried up the mountain to the effects they burned by the riverside.

Li Jie's infant brother had owned nothing. Still, her husband's parents had heard many stories of wild ghosts returning repeatedly to demand more gifts. "No matter who the ghost is, you have to burn a lot of stuff," a more experienced neighbor had told them. As Li Wenyi, whom Li Jie's husband's parents invited to perform the ritual, explained, this was a result of the deadly bureaucratic chain in which a bad death entangled a soul: "You burn things for your own wild ghost, but it must hand them over to the wild ghost officials. They examine the loot and send your ghost back to bite you again if it is not enough." Li Jie's in-laws prepared for the exorcism by carefully selecting some baby clothing, some old dishes, and a few small baskets to burn in place of items the baby might have come into contact with in his natal house.

Li Wenyi walked to Li Jie's house on the morning of the chosen day for a preliminary rite (*chènèvè*). Its purpose was to appoint a time and place for the offering and to designate clearly everything that would be offered. Li Jie's agnatic kin and I arrived late, but Li Wenyi later told me that the rite had not gone smoothly at all. Li Jie had been lying on a bed, playing with her baby, as Li Wenyi prepared an effigy and began to chant. After chanting for a few minutes, Li Wenyi asked Li Jie's mother-in-law what items were to be burned. As Li Wenyi pointed to each object, assigning it to the ghost, Li Jie sat up in her bed, baby on her lap, and let out a wail. She pointed at a chest and exclaimed, "I want this!" Standing up and marching around the room, she pointed out the best pot, a box full of embroidered clothing, and a set of new baskets, saying, "I want this! I want this!" "It was all their best things," Li Wenyi reported. "I pretended to get angry. 'Do you want me, or can you do this yourself? If you don't want me, I'll go.' She said, '*Nə! Nə!* [I want! I want!].' The parents thought it was the dead baby speaking, so they had me assign all those nice things to the ghost. If it *was* the baby, that was a *very* greedy ghost!"

With pots, chests, gourds, knives, baskets, teapots, and clothing loaded into giant carrying baskets and strapped to their backs, the members of Li Jie's husband's household walked to the exorcism site. At the last minute, Li Jie's in-laws had decided to kill two goats instead of just one. Her husband's younger brother led a goat and carried a kid in a basket. Li Jie trailed behind, bearing her baby on her back and carrying a live sparrow, tied with a string. Until the Great Leap, all exorcisms in

Zhizuo's central valley had taken place at the "river's tail," the winding gorge where the river leaves the valley. In subsequent years, other sites had been created in hidden gullies. Lɔwú, where Li Jie lived, had its own site, directly below the village. Like the other locations, it was near an intersection of path and stream where the creek flowed into a forested canyon rather than past houses or fields. Li Jie's parents, siblings, and other kin from her natal village had already begun to gather beside the river when her affinal household arrived. Some gathered firewood from the hillsides, built three fires, and started scrubbing a very large pot. Others sat in the sun and chatted. Li Jie sat by the stream, her baby on her lap, a bit apart from her mother and several other women from her natal village.

With five or six other men, the ritualist Li Wenyi scoured the hillsides for materials for an effigy. As the most evil of nonhuman entities, wild ghosts required the most complex representation. From the surrounding slopes, the men gathered pine, fir, cedar, willow, and sequoia branches as well as vines, bamboo, grass, pine needles, and the leaves of two kinds of fragrant deciduous trees. Li Wenyi had brought other materials, including raw hemp and straw. With a knife as his only tool, he cut and marked twigs, branches, and straw, while others watched or talked quietly around the fires. With the first strokes of his knife, he split a long willow rod into two flexible arches. He used these arches (called *guve*) to delimit the gathering site for ghosts and people. One arch he planted downstream. This was the doorway for the black *gu,* the wild ghost officials from the sky, who would enter the site against the flow of the stream and leave it by the same route, traveling downstream. The second arch he planted upstream. This was the doorway through which the white *gu*—Li Jie's dead baby brother and the crowds of violently dead who were now his associates—would enter the site and through which the living would leave.

The two arches made reference to a doorway Li Wenyi had built that morning as he made the appointment with the wild ghost inside the house. There, he had taken two pine trees, each as tall as he was, stripped the bark from one, twisted a rope of straw to tie them together, and leaned them against the wall near Li Jie's bed. "The one without the bark is the white *gu,*" he explained later, "and the one with the bark is the black *gu.* You tie them together so you can negotiate with them both at once. Outside, you separate them, so you can give each what belongs to it." These trees were also used in other rites, Li Wenyi pointed out, where the tree stripped of bark alluded to the white, cloudy sky and the world of people, while the tree with black bark intact alluded to the blue, cloudless sky and the world of ghosts. By tying the two together with a straw rope, Li Wenyi indicated that white and black, the living and the dead, the intimacy of the white clouds and the unimaginable distance of the blue sky were tangled together in Li Jie's house, as the wild ghost tangled itself in her body. The tactile reference to entanglement was reinforced with nine bundles of straw that Li Wenyi knotted together in three bunches of three and hung on the twisted straw rope. At the riverside site, the two arches split this single doorway in two, delimiting a space in which they were still entangled but giving it two distinct directions into which it would eventually cleave: upstream and downstream. The upstream arch, Li Wenyi said, was the door into the world of people (*ts'ɔmi ádù*), while the downstream arch was the door into the world of ghosts (*nèmi ádù*). The arches marked off a space between, like the house or body of the possessed, where living and dead were mixed together. Once they smelled the cooking meat from the animals to be sacrificed, Li Wenyi said, wild ghosts from everywhere would gather at this site to sit with the kin and neighbors who had come to lend their support. "Sometimes you can see them gathered here; you don't see their bodies, just their hands warming themselves around the fire."

This sense of gathering a complexity of materials from uninhabited and unbuilt wild spaces into a provisionally delimited place where a multiplicity of beings, living and dead, sit together was reinforced by the opening lines of Li Wenyi's chant to the wild ghosts. These lines described how an inheritance of pain descended from the indeterminate reaches of the sky through a savage lineage. Nurtured by the deathly sky spirit Mùgòhædɔ (or Shr̀mògù), verified as wild ghosts by Pìmæmenè (the first wild ghost, dead in childbirth), and sent down by the spirit police Cánìshunì, the black *gu* dropped on the heads of wild animals on the earth. These were eaten by other wild animals and transformed into wild ghosts as they were digested. Finally, the wild ghosts descended on a "green pigeon's son," a Lòlop'ò man.

7.2

who nurtured you, ghost?	ni à sà chè jí su
Mùgòhædɔ nurtured you	Mùgòhædɔ chè jí su
who verified you, ghost?	à sà chè tsɔ su
Pìmæmenè verified you	Pìmæmenè chè tsɔ su
who sent you, ghost?	à sà chè p'ɔ su
Cánìshunì sent you	Cánìshunì chè p'ɔ su

you, ghost, were sent to the earth	ni chè p'ɔ̀ mi ji jɛ̠
you descended from the sky's four corners	ni mù̠ mi lí ngɔ̀ jɛ̠
you descended to the earth's four sides	ni mé ne lí p'æ jɛ̠
you fell on antelope and musk deer	ni chi p'ɔ shò p'ɔ wú t'ɛ̠̀ jɔ̠
you fell on leopards and tigers	ni zɤ̀ mo lò mo wú t'ɛ̠̀ jɔ̠
you fell on rabbits and weasels	ni t'à lò hɔ lò wú t'ɛ̠̀ jɔ̠
you fell on a green pigeon's son	ni a gɔ̀ zò wú jɔ̠
you came to bite and claw him	ni rɔ̀ t'ɛ̠̀ kɔ̀ lɔ chí lɔ bɔ
came to entangle and madden him	ni ví lɔ là lɔ bɔ

The lines in fragment 7.2 describe both a descent (*jɛ̠*) through space and a genealogical descent (also *jɛ̠*) from the spirits that nurtured, verified, and dispatched the black *gu*, through the digestive tracts of wild animals, to human victims. At the same time, in reference to white *gu*, Li Wenyi's chant repeatedly invoked relations of affinity. The following refrain, for example, connects the steps of the white *gu* as it travels toward Beijing, where the ghosts of those who die of violence congregate:

7.3

go to where your ghost friends live	ni chè chɔ̀ jɔ dù yi
go to where your ghost companions live	ni chè pɛ̠ jɔ dù yi

Black *gu* are an inheritance, descending on their victims' heads from outside and above in the form of sudden disaster; white *gu* emerge from one's own experience, the affinities one develops in life with kin and friends. This distinction had an analog in the play of filiation and residence that coincided with Li Jie's "madness." Li Jie's troubles had begun with her move from her parents' house to that of her husband's parents. Her dead brother reawoke as she was establishing new relations with her husband's unfamiliar family and as distance transformed her old relations with her natal family. The negotiations among her affinal and agnatic kin over her baby brother's belated funeral had brought the ambiguities of descent and affinity to the fore. Did the ghost (as a black *gu*) properly belong to Li Jie's agnates, an inheritance of the violence that had killed her grandfather? Or was it (as a white *gu*) more particular to Li Jie's own person, springing from her own experiences of caring for her now-dead baby brother? If the first, to what extent should Li Jie's new household take on responsibility for the difficult memories of her former household? If the second, was the ghost Li Jie's sibling or ascendant (for she took on the role of its orphaned daughter at its funeral) and thus the responsibility of her natal household? Or was the ghost tied to her child (for she had carried her baby brother when he was an infant, and his ghost had appeared when she gave birth to her own infant) and thus the responsibility of her new household? All these relational ambiguities came together within the arches that delimited the upstream and downstream boundaries of the ritual site: the inherited black *gu* who had killed her brother and the acquired white *gu* who distressed her, the parents who had nurtured her and the parents she lived with, the conflicted living and the restless dead.

Entanglements

The ritualist's knife gradually transformed piles of leafy branches, vines, grasses, and straw into a populous interweaving of spectral presences. At the feet of the upstream and downstream arches, Li Wenyi placed a pair of crossed fir sticks, each split at one end, with a tuft of dried grass stuffed into the crack. On top of the arches, he hung knotted bundles of straw. The effect was to transform the simple arched doorways into guarded passages, hung with complex, bristling, cruciform presences (illustrated in Figure 7.1).

Below each arch, the ritualist planted a triple-forked branch, hung with paper streamers. Pine branches were the most fundamental ingredient in the material vocabulary of ritual effigies (*nègu*). The simplest of healing rituals used a single three-forked pine branch to gather and locate a ghost. In other rites, pine branches or saplings were multiplied into twos, threes, and sixes and were paired with the branches of other trees to reflect a spirit's multiple aspects. Li Wenyi gave these branches faces by planting before them small pine slabs, carved with flaps for ears and horizontal slashes for eyes, a nose, and a mouth (shown in Figure 7.2). With these, he told me, the ghosts would hear the offered words, see the presents of clothing, utensils, and furniture, and taste the offerings of grain, meat, and alcohol. The pine branches were unnamed ghost officials who guarded the arched doorways, he said; later he would kill a chicken for each.

Between these bristling, guarded doorways, the ritualist created representations of white *gu* and black *gu*. The act of locating a nonhuman entity in an effigy always tends to fragment that entity into several aspects. Even the simplest effigy, a single triple-forked pine branch, marks this tendency to multiply, with three branches splitting out from the stem and hundreds of needles from the branches. In this most complex of effigies, Li Wenyi planted three triple-forked pine branches each for

Figure 7.1 The arched gates to the exorcism site and their guards.

Figure 7.2 A wild ghost official, with its carved ears, eyes, nose, and mouth.

Figure 7.3 The wild ghost's body and its senses.

white *gu* and black *gu*. "It used to be that we used nine if the ghost was male and seven if it was female, but ritualists have gotten lazy, so now we use only three," he said.[4]

Around this proliferation of bodies erupted more bodily segments and organs. Within each group of three pine branches, Li Wenyi planted three fir branches, a pine face marked with a double set of ears, and a cluster of five willow sticks carved with conventional symbols—"a single set of ears, a double set of ears, a tiger's claws, a dog's claws, and a limit of three days, three months, or three years" (see Figure 7.3).

Arching over these groups of interlaced bodies, claws, faces, and ears, Li Wenyi placed three willow "rafters." "With the rafters, you are building the ghost a house," he told me. Over the rafters was laid a roof of crisscrossed branches of a fragrant tree (*cá*) used for wedding arbors; a leafy bamboo staff floated above the entire structure like a flag (as shown in Figure 7.4). "It's an arbor, like the arbor at a wedding," Li Wenyi explained. "You build an arbor for the ghost as its house." Two houses or arbors had been built, enclosing bodies branching into more bodies, with multiple ears, eyes, mouths, and claws. Li Wenyi offered these houses to the ghost branch by branch in direct exchange for the head and torso (and, in other versions, the feet) of the patient. Indicating each part of the structure with a staff, he chanted these words:

Figure 7.4 The arbor of rafters that arched over the wild ghost's body.

7.4

now, her head is not worth thousands	æ mæ ngo rɔ̀ wú tu̱ m p'ɔ̀
I bring out thousands to offer	ngo tu̱ cì do jo pi̱
her torso is not worth hundreds	rɔ̀ gə ho m p'ɔ̀
I bring out hundreds to offer	ngo ho cì do jo pi̱
I offer a new growth of pine	ngo t'à p'ò gu do pi̱
I offer willow branches	ngo bæ̀ tí gu do pi̱
I offer a green arbor of cedar	ngo tsǽ pu k'ə ngə t'ù ne pi̱
I offer a silver arbor of *cá*	ngo cá pu k'ə p'u t'ù ne pi̱

As rafters arching over the pine core made the body a house, and branches piled on rafters made the house an arbor, further elaborations made the arbor a body. Li Wenyi completed the effigy for the black *gu* by wrapping it in cloth—three turns of white hemp, then three of black cotton (see Figure 7.5). Later, Li Jie's husband's parents would drape the effigy for the white *gu* in baby clothes. As he bound each structure with loop after loop of the malodorous dog vine, Li Wenyi's chant left no doubt that he was binding a body:

Figure 7.5 The wild ghost's body/house, wrapped in cloth and bound with dog vine.

7.5

I stab your ghost torso with green bamboo	mó ngɔ chè gɔ ngó̱ gɔ̀ bɛ
bind your ghost neck with a dog-shit vine	á nò chì n ji li chè li p'ɛ gɔ̀ bɛ
prick your ghost eyes with fir needles	chá p'é chè me t'ɔ gɔ̀ bɛ
bind your feet with a straw rope	cí p'a chì lɔ p'ɛ

Clothing the effigy completed the process in which a dispersed force—the wild and unstable element in wind, water, and fire—was gathered into a house, an arbor, and then a body. Like a human body, the effigy was made up of a dense interleaving of the material and the social, and, like a human body, it was situated within a mutually enveloped and enveloping domestic place. It contained multiple senses for interacting with the variegated social world constructed around it; its cloth skin enveloped the enveloping form of a house, containing other, branched bodies, with their own sensory equipment and the multiple social relations this equipment enabled.

To this point, Li Wenyi had marked off a section of the stream with two bristling, arched doorways; created pine branch ghost officials to

Figure 7.6 A bird of prey with a sparrow, representing a parakeet, dangling from its beak.

guard each; built two more sets of pine branch effigies for white *gu* and black *gu* within the doorways; given these effigies mouths, ears, eyes, and claws; and built a house, an arbor, and a clothed body around each. Now he constructed two bird models of crossed sticks, drew a bird's eye on each one, and planted them within the doorways. He dangled a smaller cruciform bird from the beak of one with a strand of hemp and used another strand to tie the live sparrow to the beak of the other (see Figure 7.6). The bird models were birds of prey, black *gu* preying on the white *gu* sparrows, which stood in for parakeets, thought to be material manifestations of wild ghosts. "The ghost likes it best if you can capture a real parakeet for it," Li Wenyi commented, "but they are hard to catch." Finally, the ritualist constructed a wand. He marked nine leafy willow branches with eyes, noses, mouths, and ears and tied them together. He carved another, larger, face with horizontal slashes for eyes, nose, and mouth and double flaps for double ears and lashed it to the willows. This collection of eyes, ears, mouths, and faces would be a conduit for the words and offerings Li Wenyi would direct at the ghost.

Assemblages

Several features of the effigy Li Wenyi created stood out, even for those who knew little of ritual esoterica. Ordinary participants at exorcisms, making no claims to ritual expertise, drew my attention to two in particular. The first was its multiplicity. Within the two bristling doorways proliferated manifold spirit beings, none represented as unitary subjects or objects. Like a needled, triple-forked pine branch, each named presence contained possibilities for endless further proliferation. The branched bodies of these beings were not organized according to the bodily hierarchy repeated so often in Lòlop'ò ritual language (head, torso, feet). Instead, they were splintered into parts and organs, especially organs that sense (faces, ears, eyes) and organs that pierce and wound (claws, beaks). Nor were these bodies self-contained. Body, house, and landscape each slid easily into the others: the landscape was marked by an upstream mouth (for people to enter and leave) and a downstream anus (for ghosts to enter and leave); pine branch bodies became houses, then arbors (delimited areas of the landscape), and then again clothed bodies.

In this respect, the effigy resembled what Gilles Deleuze and Félix Guattari (1983, 1987) would call an "assemblage." Rather than describing persons as subjects in relation to objects, Deleuze and Guattari trace lines of flow and intensity that circulate among corporeal fragments. They investigate assemblages of parts—bodies, acts, passions—caught up in mobile relations with other parts. One illustration is mutual corporeal and affective involvement of mother and newborn infant, the state that Lòlop'ò call *hojo,* "within the month." Deleuze and Guattari cite the infant psychology of Melanie Klein (1975), who argued that a nursing infant does not perceive its mother as a totality; instead, it establishes relationships with the parts of the mother's body with which it comes into frequent contact, the most important being the linkage of mouth and breast. Deleuze and Guattari write as though persons were composed of assemblages similar to that of the infant's mouth and the mother's breast: body-part relations of part subjects and part objects.

We might imagine Li Jie, in need of exorcism, as involved in many such assemblages. One infant suckled at her breast; another spoke through her mouth; neither was a whole subject for her. The one suckling was not yet even unquestionably human; the one speaking was but one soul of a dispersed, three-souled being. It had already been sent away, but part of it remained, entangled among the other relations that constituted her person. Its emergence while she was confined in her husband's parents' house with her new baby signaled the heightened complexity of the relations that constituted her as a newly married daughter-in-law, relations among her parents, her husband, and her husband's parents. Within the household, new connections among persons, or parts of persons, were formed and dissolved. In her village and along the stream that ran past the larger villages of Zhizuo, linkages founded on previous funeral obligations were negotiated and transformed. Each of these connections effected a particular stance toward the past: toward obligations sustained and released, toward the violent death of Li Jie's grandfather, and toward her dead baby brother's short life. These stances intersected to determine Li Jie's future.

A related feature of the effigy that many participants pointed out to me was its textured complexity. "You can tell that this is the most evil of all ghosts, because its effigy is the most complex," observed Li Zhiwu, who was just learning with me the differences between white *gu* and black *gu*. Each part of the effigy entangled dissimilar objects from widely separated areas of the landscape. The house/arbor/body figures were piles of interlaced branches from various tree species, growing on different parts of the mountainside. The cruciform branches and straw guarding the doorways were deliberately tangled. Birds dangled from the beaks of birds, invoking parakeets, painted in twelve painfully varied colors. Even the swathes of hempen and cotton cloth that wrapped these tangles were complex. I once asked Li Wenyi why ritualists counseled people to avoid weaving, sewing, or washing clothing in the days after someone has died badly. He answered obliquely, with a phrase from his exorcism chant:

7.6

eleven ridges intersect	ts'r tí gɔ̀ chè
twelve gullies intersect, so it is said	ts'r ni gɔ̀ li chì mi jo

Like knots of ridges and gullies, cloth—especially hempen cloth—is a convergence of threads. Mourning songs tell of how hemp is grown in "eleven gullies" and soaked, peeled, washed, and pounded in a tangled mass in "twelve streams" to clothe living children and dead parents.[5] Clothing the effigy in hemp and cotton was like making into social flesh the child one bears, gathering multiple linkages, alignments, and associations within flexible and provisional boundaries marked by mouth and anus, the front and back doors to a courtyard, or the passage of the river into and out of an inhabited valley. Yet, like eleven ridges converging, the effigy's clothing also indicated the possibility that this gathering might become so intense, so complex that all movement might cease. The effigy represented the material grounds of personhood—bodies, houses, and the delimited landscape—as fields of entanglement. Its manifold, interlaced texture invoked a congestion of the mobile relations out of which social persons were fashioned. This was a state in which no relation was smooth (*go*), in which everything bristled and grew stagnant. It was the dark side of that dense interpenetration of intimately inhabited spaces that (as I argued in chapters 2 and 3) shaped domestic life for Zhizuo residents.

For her husband's parents, the return of Li Jie's baby brother doubtless invoked such a thicket. As chapter 3 discussed, Lòlop'ò often view cross-sibling relations as the archetypal form of generative relations. In the myth of the flood, for instance, a brother and sister inhabit their gourd house as Grandmother Wosomo's "seeds" from which all living things on the earth spring. The generative intimacy cross-siblings enjoy, especially when elder sisters bear, nourish, and raise younger brothers, is transformed as sisters grow up, move to their own room in the barn loft, and then marry out. In affinal relations, cross-sibling intimacy becomes a support for generative relations between wives and husbands, a support that operates across a differential between separate households. For Li Jie's kin, her baby brother returning to speak through her mouth as she was carrying her own baby was a sign that the relations involved in her shift of residence had reversed and congested at a crucially transformative stage. This obstinate memory of cross-sibling intimacy threatened to entangle itself in her new relations with her husband and child rather than supporting them across a distance as relations between brothers and married sisters should do.

At stake, then, were entanglement and disentanglement across boundaries that engaged and disengaged persons as material and social beings. What were the nature of these boundaries? Given the fears of birth pollution that infused talk about wild ghosts, Li Jie's kin had doubtless found the delicate state of *hojo,* within which she and her infant were intertwined, to weigh in favor of putting on a full-scale exorcism. In a suggestive reading of Mary Douglas's *Purity and Danger* (1975), Julia Kristeva (1982) elaborates and sharpens themes common to much Freudian thought about the interleaving of material and social in the constitution of persons. For Kristeva, the delimitation of a "clean and proper" body and the expulsion of the improper, the unclean, and the disorderly from within bodily boundaries are conditions for subjectivity.

Bodily fluids such as feces, saliva, menstrual blood, and postpartum discharge are evidence of the body's permeability, the dependence of its interior on its exterior, and the potential for the boundary between them to collapse. Kristeva extends Douglas's argument that the unclean is what threatens individual and social existence by moving out of its proper place. She asserts that bodily fluids are unclean because they attest to the impossibility of a clear bodily order, which is nevertheless a requirement for subjectivity. Horror of bodily fluids is a refusal of the always impure, always disorderly materiality of corporeal existence. The task of symbolic relations is to cover over the fluid mobility that makes bodily boundaries ambiguous in order to protect a subject's autonomy and identity.

I cite Kristeva to illuminate by contrast the interaction of corporeal boundaries and bodily pollution in exorcisms. The boundaries at stake in divining and exorcising wild ghosts were not limits; they were regulated passageways. Boundaries did not delimit distinct subjects; they enveloped assemblages of body parts and relational linkages. If there was horror at the passage of bodily fluids through boundaries, it was a horror of blockage and reversal, of self-pollution, swelling and explosion, expelled wastes backing up against the flow, the dead backing up onto the living, officials and soldiers from the lowlands flooding the mountain valleys. At stake was not the integrity of boundaries but the relative mobility of that which flowed through or accumulated within them. The unclean was not that which was not in its proper place but that which was either immobile or too mobile, that which obstructed movement or flowed in improper directions. The effigy on the riverbank evoked this horror by portraying a bounded dwelling place in which all flows had ceased, in which the thresholds were blocked with crossed branches of straw, and in which multiplicities of beings and part-beings were congested in a hopeless tangle. The intent of exorcism was to unravel such tangles.

Eating and Speaking

Most participants in the exorcism that day seemed to pay little attention to Li Wenyi's elaborate constructions. Li Jie sat on the riverbank entertaining her baby with the live sparrow, until Li Wenyi took it away. Clusters of women and children sat together talking and keeping an idle eye on the proceedings. Groups of men fed the fires, boiled water in a huge pot, and prepared the animals for slaughter. Li Jie's husband and his brothers helped Li Wenyi slit the throats of a goat before the white *gu* effigy, a kid before the black *gu* effigy, and a chicken each for the ghost officials guarding the doorways. They cleaned the animals in the stream, cut them into small pieces, boiled all the pieces together, counted out ninety-three piles of pine needles, and laid a handful of meat onto each of the piles. One handful was distributed to each of the ninety-three participants.

People chewed their handfuls of meat silently and rather uneasily. Some speared chunks with sticks and roasted them on the fire to render them more edible. Li Jie's husband's parents boiled together in a single large pot a portion of every kind of grain they produced and distributed it in a similar fashion, scooping out individual portions into the bowls that each participant had brought. Most people found eating these separate portions of meat and grain distasteful. Some claimed that the ghost had already taken the food's essence, leaving it flavorless, others simply that it was unsanitary. At some exorcisms, people glanced at me apologetically as I chewed chunks of goat meat and said quietly, "Just leave it if you can't eat it." I soon learned, however, that leaving any part of one's portion was a breach of manners in which few indulged, no matter how tempting.

Eating together in Zhizuo was, of course, a means of creating communities, either relatively stable ones like households or relatively fluid ones like a gathering of friends. A special emphasis was placed on sharing meat: when slaughtering a pig, one carried three ribs apiece to each daughter who had married out and gave the delicate tongue and eyeballs to parents with whom one had split a household. Similar but more elaborate procedures were observed with goats at weddings and mortuary rituals. The flow of meat through a digestive tract could be traced back to its origin in the whole corpse of an animal; to eat meat was to find one's person emerging from a whole social body. It was a body in continuous disassembly, but in each dissevered part one nevertheless tasted a memory of prior unity. One eats separate portions of meat and grain at exorcisms, Li Wenyi told me, because you are splitting the household with the ghost, giving it a portion of all household goods, including the food. Eating at exorcisms inverted the ordinary significance of eating together, deliberately denying community and temporarily isolating each person from the networks of social relations that produced him or her, for these were the links along which contamination traveled.

While the others ate, Li Wenyi chanted, using his speech to gradually sever relations with the ghost. Ritualists divided exorcism chants into five sections. The first section told of the origins of the black *gu* in the sky and its descent to the earth; fragment 7.2 is from this opening section. The second section described the ghost striking the ill or dead person like a bolt from a crossbow, using language nearly identical to that quoted in fragment 2.2 (chapter 2), which was used to drive away the *mæ*. The third section enumerated the offerings, including all the parts of the effigy; portions of Li Wenyi's version appear in fragments 7.3 and 7.4. In the fourth section, the ritualist extracted himself from the relations of exchange and communication he had so painstakingly established with the wild ghost, denying that he had spoken or offered to it. These first four sections were repeated four times, twice each for white *gu* and black *gu*, a first time as the animals were being slaughtered, a second time after they were butchered and cooked. The fifth section sent the ghost on a long journey. It was chanted only once for white *gu* and once for black *gu*, after the cooked offerings had been made. While the first three sections traced the accumulation of ghosts, people, animals, grain, branches, and vines within the two willow arches, sections four and five, described in the fragments that follow, effected the return of the ghost to its wild origins.

As he began his final repetition of the fourth section, Li Wenyi untied the live sparrow from where it had been hanging on the bird of crossed sticks and tied it to the white *gu*'s house/arbor/body. He began to guide the ghost in reverse along a route he had already described once, the route from the sky, down to the dispersed heads of wild animals, and finally onto the head of its victim:

7.7

parakeets are your ghost friends, it is said	ni t'à jò lí jo chè chɔ̀ bɛ
leopards and tigers are your ghost friends	ni zɹ̀ mo lò mo chè chɔ̀ bɛ
go to where your ghost friends live	ni chè chɔ̀ jɔ dù yi
go to where your ghost companions live	ni chè pe jɔ dù yi
musk deer and antelope are your ghost friends	che p'ɔ shɔ́ p'ɔ chè chɔ̀ bɛ
where wild ones turn their faces	ní p'à à tí hɔ
there turn your ghostly face	ni chè p'à à tí hɔ

leopards and tigers are your ghost companions	zɨ̀ mo lò mo chè pɛ bɛ
where wild ones cast their eyes	ní me à tí hɔ
there cast your ghostly eyes	ni chè me à tí hɔ
where wild ones step with their claws	ní bùɨ à tí t'o
there step with your ghostly claws	ni chè bùɨ à tí t'o

In the chant's previous sections, speech had been the vehicle that bore offerings from the ritualist's hands to the ghost's mouth. As Li Wenyi concluded the fourth section, however, the ordinary utility of speech as a means for social articulation was inverted: like the food consumed during the rite, speech became a cutting tool. Li Wenyi inserted his long chopping knife into his wand of nine tangled branches with its many ears, eyes, and mouths. He slashed at the white *gu*'s house/arbor/body with the concealed knife as he chanted. One by one, he named the wild animals with which wild ghosts were said to run and mimicked their inarticulate sounds:

7.8

I am not the one who speaks	pi̱ su̱ ngo n ngɔ
the tiger is the speaker, *goo!*	pi̱ su̱ lò mo ngɔ, goo!
I am not the one who speaks	pi̱ su̱ ngo n ngɔ
the leopard is the speaker, *ɔ́ɔɔ!*	pi̱ su̱ zr mo ngɔ, ɔ́ɔɔ!
I am not the one who speaks	pi̱ su̱ ngo n ngɔ
the bear is the speaker, *wdaa!*	pi̱ su̱ vɔ ngɔ́ ngɔ, wdaa!
I am not the one who speaks	pi̱ su̱ ngo n ngɔ
the boar is the speaker, *eóoo!*	pi̱ su̱ vè pɔ́ ngɔ, eóoo!
I am not the one who speaks	pi̱ su̱ ngo n ngɔ
the wolf is the speaker, *góoo!*	pi̱ su ni so ngɔ, góoo!
I am not the one who speaks	pi̱ su̱ ngo n ngɔ
the wild dog is the speaker, *wáaa!*	pi̱ su̱ à vi ngɔ, wáaa!

Li Wenyi went on to imitate the sounds of antelope, musk deer, weasels, rabbits, crows, grouse, golden pheasants, common pheasants, blue hill pigeons, green pigeons, and parakeets, in that order. His animal cries followed a clear trajectory, beginning with the sounds of heavy, earthbound carnivores, moving on through progressively quicker and lighter beasts, to ground birds, and finally to swift flyers such as pigeons and parakeets. This path ended in the sky, with the speech of the "seven stars" (the Big Dipper):

7.9

I am not the one who speaks	pi̱ su̱ ngo n ngɔ
the seven little speaking stars are the speakers	sɨ̀ nà pi̱ zɔ̀ pi̱ su̱ ngo

Here, language dissolves into howls and cries of animals. The speaking subject dissolves with it, as his voice melts into the sounds of the earth, the air, and finally the sky. The world speaks *through* the ritualist, who denies that he confronts the ghost as a social person, composed of the multiple relations that shared speech, like shared food, helps to create. "This part of the chant says, 'You owe me nothing; it's the tiger, the bear, the wolf who have spoken and offered to you,'" Li Wenyi commented later. As speech unraveled, the ghost was to follow, emptying itself of relations to the living and dispersing finally into communion with the distant, speaking stars. The patient and her family were intended to follow this dissolution toward a disentanglement of the time-confounded social relations that threatened to immobilize them. The clearest indication of how this was to happen is found in the fifth and final section of the chant, which drew the ghost and listeners on a long excursion through the nation's overlapping hierarchies of economic and administrative central places.

Driving

The final and longest section of the exorcism chant was divided into two parts, called "driving over sky and earth" (*mùts'r mits'r kà*) and "driving to market" (*vùji vɐji kà*).[6] These sections sent the ghost on a journey, beginning in the small mountain settlements surrounding Zhizuo. They were composed of lengthy, paragraphlike segments, each beginning with a cluster of place names, usually places in close proximity. To convey a sense of the structure, fragment 7.10 quotes the first such segment of Li Wenyi's chant in its entirety.

7.10

we've heard of Wòní and Wòk'e	Wòní Wòk'e chì mi jo
heard of T'àlɔ and Bòyide	T'àlɔ Bòyide chì mi jo
heard of Mitɐ́dù	Mitɐ́dù chì mi jo
heard of Nɔ̀molè	Nɔ̀molè chì mi jo
some die bearing sons	t'à mo zò ho shr̠
some die bearing daughters	t'à mo nɛ́ ho shr̠
some die swept away by floods	t'à mo yi gɔ̀ yi ngɔ shr̠
some die crushed by trees or rocks	t'à mo cì tí lo lɔ shr̠
some die by hanging	t'à mo chɐ̀ chɐ̀ lè lí shr̠
some die beneath rolling stones	t'à mo lo nga lo tsa shr̠

your ghost friends live over there	ni chè chɔ̀ ko ka jɔ
your ghost companions live over there	chè pe̱ ko ka jɔ
go to where your ghost friends live	ni chè chɔ̀ jɔ dù yi
go to where your ghost companions live	ni chè pe̱ jɔ dù yi
no land for you ghosts to live on here	ni chè jɔ mi n jɔ
no land for ghosts to stand on	chè ha̱ mi n jɔ
I lead you, ghost, back to the sky	ngo ni t'è chè hæ̀ mù lɔ k'ò t'a̱ gà
I lead you in search of your ghost friends	ngo ni t'è che chɔ̀ ju̱ gà bɛ
I lead you in search of your ghost companions	ngo ni t'è che pe ju̱ gà bɛ
we've heard of Lɔ́p'ɔ̀gæ̀ and Mogotsobò	Lɔ́p'ɔ̀gæ̀ Mogotsobò chì mi jo
heard of T'àlobò and Ayejíne	T'àlobò Ayejíne chì mi jo
heard of Bagamo and Chachude	Bagamo Chachude chì mi jo
your ghost friends live over there	ni chè chɔ̀ ko ka jɔ

After each cluster of place names, Li Wenyi repeated the list of deaths that create wild ghosts and beseeched the ghost to return to its companions. The chant advanced from one group of place names to the next by alternating between repetitions of these lists and appeals, in which both structure and semantic content were identical, and passages containing place names, in which the structure was the same but the semantic content—the place names—was not. The route traced was complex and circuitous: this version had a total of seventy-five place names. Nevertheless, participants in exorcism rituals repeatedly insisted to me that the names described a specific path, crucial to the ritual's success. Beginning with villages only a few minutes' walk away, the route made a clockwise spiral through the mountains. This spiral expanded until it reached nearby county towns, intersected more distant prefectural capitals, descended to the provincial capital, and then plunged into the Jinsha River, which, becoming the Yangtze, took it through Sichuan Province and down to the cities of Wuhan, Nanjing, Shanghai, and finally Beijing. I was told repeatedly that any chant that didn't line up place names along such a route would not succeed in returning the ghosts to their place of origin.

This statement fascinated me. I tried to trace one chanted list on a published map, coming up only with a nest of crossed lines. I bought large sheets of white paper and attempted to draw my own map. This failed too, and I discovered I had little sense of the lay of the surrounding mountains and villages, even those to which I had traveled. Finally Li Zhiwu, who was learning about exorcism rituals along with me, volunteered to draw a map. He produced several attempts, two of which are shown here as guides to the geography of exorcism chants.

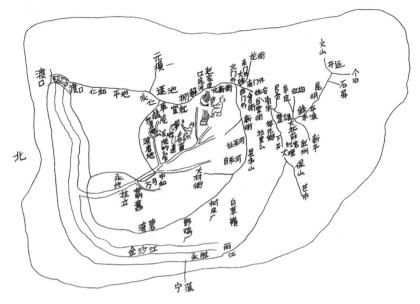

Figure 7.7 Li Zhiwu's first map of a wild ghost's route (with Chinese characters enlarged for clarity). The outside perimeter line is the boundary of Yunnan Province; north is to the left. The human figures represent ritualists performing exorcisms at Zhizuo's two most important exorcism sites. Double lines represent rivers; a truck is crossing the Jinsha River (the upper portion of the Yangtze) at Dukou near the northern border. Single lines represent roads. Place names are written in Chinese characters, some (at the center of the map) transliterated from Lòlongo.

Li Zhiwu began his first map (see Figure 7.7) with the horizon of the wild ghost's activities, drawn as a single line around the edges of the paper. One might think that the encompassing aerial view of modern cartographic practice would be entirely alien to the context of these chants. On the contrary, a domain view was proper to wild ghosts. Even before Beijing, they began in the sky, selecting their victims from the vast, crumpled landscape below. From their playground at the peak of the white clay mountain, the view expanded far beyond the next ridge—the horizon of all ordinary views—taking in range after range of mountains, extending even to the brown, sinuous shape of the Jinsha River in the extreme distance. Still, Li Zhiwu's map was no view from a mountain peak. It was, predictably, the boundary of the nation, familiar from countless official maps and school exercises. As his drawing progressed and this horizon filled in, Li Zhiwu redesignated it the boundary of Yunnan Province (which has a shape roughly similar to that of the nation). In the center of the bounded space, he drew the two streams through the brigade, where exorcisms were performed, and then inscribed Chinese transliterations of the first names from an exorcism chant we had recorded. Although he had designated the left edge of the map as north, after the flow of the streams, the names were oriented neither to the four directions nor to the boundary horizon, but only to the paths and streams; if the path on this side of the creek led to Bojəti and Cidemòjɔ, the path on that side led to Mozòti and Mómɔ̀lɔ. This was a landscape traversed on foot. When traveling between these places, locals walked paths over the ridges rather than making the much longer bus journey down and around through county and township centers.

These wanderings through mountain villages with Lòlongo names ended in the county town of Dayao. Here, the chant slowed to circle the four gates of the city walls, destroyed in the 1950s. Outside each gate, it found men murdering one another: "outside the east gate, outside the west gate, every day they shoot each other, every day they stab each other." The ritualist Li Yong had invoked this passage to describe the 1948 raid on Dayao by Ding Zhiping's army of "Communist bandits" (quoted in chapter 4, fragment 4.2). These words might as easily have evoked subsequent state campaigns in which violent or murderous acts were seen to spread from Dayao into the mountainous hinterland under its jurisdiction. This town marked the limit of experience for most brigade members. A few had ventured into Sichuan or toward Kunming, traveling by bus or truck. But for most, the lowland towns and cities beyond Dayao could only be imagined.

Here, the "driving over sky and earth" portion of the chant ended, and the "driving to market" part began. The first stop of this segment of the tour was Yongding (Wòchò, in Lòlongo), the central market town of Yongren County, where many brigade members traveled once or twice a year (and which had administrated Zhizuo since 1962). It was a macabre scene, a market peopled with dead officials eating piles of meat and drinking the best tea and alcohol:

7.11

Wòchò holds market on the day of the dog	Wòchò chì ji mæ̀
nine days of revelry	ji mæ̀ kɔ́ ni mæ̀
nine days of drinking	ji cɛ kɔ́ ni cɛ
drinking the finest tea	yi mæ̀ lò yi mæ̀
drunk on the day of the snake	ji cɛ cæ ni mæ̀
little ghosts in the street	ji ka chè zò jɔ
ghost officials in the street	ji ka chè tsɤ̀ jɔ

in one day they kill three goats	chì ni sa p'æ sɿ̀
in three days they kill nine goats	sa ni kɔ̰́ p'æ sɿ̀
more meat than they can eat	hò tsò ka n do̱
piled like sand on a beach, it is said	hɔ̀ ji bæ læ go du̱ rò
more grain than they can eat	tso tsò ka n do̱
forked rivers flow past, it is said	nḛ́ yi sɔ̀ lɔ lɔ go du̱ rò
[they] await your coming, ghost	chè lɔ lɔ nì hɔ
[they] will wait until the ghost comes	chè n lɔ lɔ nì hɔ

In another familiar market town, Nijiu (Nɔ́gɔ̀, in Lòlongo), the ghost was asked to gather the offerings of grain and salt in its ragged apron and famished hands, sell them, and buy new clothing to wear:

7.12

Nɔ́gɔ̀ holds market on the day of the mouse	Nɔ́gɔ̀ he ji mæ̀
nine days of revelry	ji mæ̀ kɔ̰́ ni mæ̀
nine days of drinking	ji cɛ kɔ̰́ ni cɛ
water flows and splashes	yi wú bǜ p'è jɔ
water turns up gold	yi tò cæ p'è jɔ
we bring out *dan*s of rice for you	ni t'è̱ lí sɿ́ lɔ̀ gɔ̀ do̱
bring out *dou*s of buckwheat	mò shr də gɔ̀ do̱
bring out *sheng*s of grain	mò tsò shə̰ gɔ̀ do̱
offer bowls of salt	dò kæ cí t'è̱ gɔ̀
stretch out your apron	ni p'a pi̱ cí k'ɔ lɔ
don't lose it through holes in the cloth	mæ me t'à rə̰ mó
stretch out your hands	le ká ci k'ɔ lɔ
don't lose it between your fingers	le shɔ́ t'à rə̰ mó
walk about and sell it	ni vǜ yi kà̰ yi jɔ yi
ghost shirts over there	ni chè p'à ro ka jɔ
ghost hats over there	ni chè k'à ro ka jɔ
go buy ghost shirts to wear	ni chè p'à ho yè yi
go buy ghost hats to wear	chè k'à ho k'o yi
change your clothing	yi lǽ yì ts'ì
change your overcoats	go lǽ go ts'ì

The tour continued, first toward county towns in northern and western Yunnan and then on to prefectural and district capitals (Chuxiong, Dali, Baoshan, and Lijiang). On his map (Figure 7.7), Li Zhiwu attempted to place each name in relation to roads through the province, but here he also took into account the four directions. The initial boundary line, drawn in the conventional manner with the north side on top, contradicted his experiential sense that the rivers through the brigade flowed both north and to the left. To keep the left side of the map north, he had to extend the southern route, leading toward Kunming and other towns to the south and southeast (such as Gejiu and Wenshan), toward the map's upper right corner, which, according to the shape of the initial boundary, should have been the northeast.

At Dukou, on the border with Sichuan Province (marked on Figure 7.7 with a truck crossing a bridge), the chanted journey was given over to a new, fluid mode of transport, as the ghost plunged into the river, joining a cargo of the drowned:

7.13

three bubbling streams merge	p'ɔ̀ lɔ̀ yi sa tsǝ̱
twelve great rivers merge	né yì ts'r̀ nì tsǝ̱
on that side shrimp play in three places	k'ó bò a tsǝ sa mè cà
your ghost friends are over there	ni chè chɔ̀ k'o mo ngɔ
on this side white fish play in three places	hé bò ngó p'ɯ sa mè cà
your ghost companions are over here	ni chè pe̱ hé mo ngɔ
little officials in the river's center	né ka̱ tsɻ̀ zò jɔ
friends of officials in the river's center	né ka̱ tsɻ̀ chɔ̀ jɔ
on that side they wear silk clothing	k'ó bò yi bo yì
on this side they sport stylish clothing	hé bò yi he yì
on that side they hold red flags	k'ó bò chì ni vɛ
on this side they wave green flags	hé bò chì ngǝ vɛ
follow the river, you ghost	ni chè yi né yi jɔ lɔ go
we give you the river as your steed	né yi mò mo pe̱ tsæ̀ gɔ̀
ride the river like a fine horse	né yi mò mo pe̱ tsæ̀ yi

Here, at the juncture of road, river, and provincial boundary, the route ran off Li Zhiwu's map, forcing him to make a new drawing (see Figure 7.8). For this final leg of the ghost's journey, Li Zhiwu began again with the national horizon. But this time he followed all the conventional rules for mapping the nation, making the top north, and orienting the nation with reference to its outside—placing Korea (drawn as an island) to the northeast, Taiwan to the southeast, and Hainan Island to the south. Taking his cue from conventional representations of the national geography, he made the Yangtze River the map's outstanding feature. He then continued marking place names from the recorded chant, which took the ghost through the great river cities of Chongqing, Wuhan, Nanjing, and Shanghai. The chant described daily markets in each city, where ghost officials drink golden wine, wear yellow silk, and eat meat piled like sand on a beach. Markets are the true home of wild ghosts, the chant implied. Their gross displays of riches, with which

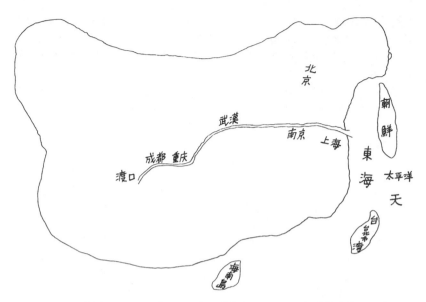

Figure 7.8 Li Zhiwu's second map of a wild ghost's route (with Chinese characters enlarged for clarity). The outside perimeter line is the boundary of China; north is to the top. Korea, like Taiwan and Hainan, is represented as an island. The double line is the Yangtze River, running from Dukou through Chengdu, Chongqing, Wuhan, Nanjing, and Shanghai.

officials conspicuously indulge themselves, are associated with the insatiable envy and greed thought to characterize wild ghosts. At Shanghai, this theme gained another form of expression. Inspired, perhaps, by the glossy pages from fashion magazines with which many youths in Zhizuo adorned their rooms, the chant described Shanghai (with the city's name spoken in Chinese) as a paradise of jewelry and women's clothing:

7.14

go over there to Shanghai	ni Shanghai ko ka yi
your ghost officials are there	ni chè tsɨ̀ ko ka jɔ
embroidery needles and thread	chì po̠ vɔ̀ cɔ̀ jɔ
every kind of earring	nó jo nó kʼo jɔ
bracelets and rings	lè jo lè dɔ́ jɔ
shoes of every style	chí nɔ chí be jɔ
more clothing than you can wear	ni pʼa yì ka n do̠
piles of silk	yi po̠ kʼɔ bà jɔ
looms and spindles	tsà sɔ yì ní jɔ

The ghost's final destination on land was Beijing. Following the conventions of official maps, Li Zhiwu placed Beijing up the coast from the mouth of the Yangtze, to the north. But Li Wenyi's chant implied that the river could take the ghost directly to Beijing: it made the entire nation into a single rivuline flow, or digestive tract, with Beijing at its excretory end. There, ghost officials spent every day in political meetings. It was the home of the most powerful of ghost officials, associated with uncounted violent deaths—the leaders of the Cultural Revolution. Li Wenyi's version named Lin Biao, who died in 1971 when his airplane crashed after an abortive attempt on Mao's life, as the king of wild ghosts and Jiang Qing, Mao's wife and a member of the Cultural Revolution's "Gang of Four," as their queen. This segment required a Chinese vocabulary to speak of political meetings and plane crashes; Chinese words were used for the names "Beijing," "Lin Biao," and "Jiang Qing" and the phrases "hold meetings" (*hui kai*) and "died in a plane crash" (*wang ruo fei*).

7.15

go over there to Beijing	ni Beijing ko ka yi
your ghost kings live there	ni chè tsɨ̀ ko ka jɔ
every day they hold meetings in Beijing	Beijing ni pi ni hui kai lè jɔ rò
Lin Biao died in a plane crash	Lin Biao wang ruo fei
Jiang Qing hanged herself	Jiang Qing chæ̀ chæ̀ lè lí shr̠
your ghost king Lin Biao, go follow Lin Biao	chè tsɨ̀ Lin Biao ni Lin Biao chɔ yi go
your king is over there	ni tsɨ̀ ko ka ngɔ
I shall lead you to Beijing	ngo ni t'æ̀ chè hæ̀ Beijing he gɔ̀ do
go to where your ghost friends live	ni chè chɔ̀ ro ka yi
go to where your ghost companions live	ni chè pe̠ ro ka yi
if the road returns, don't you return	ni jo̠ kò ni t'à kò
if the road strays, don't you stray	ni jo̠ te̠ ni t'à te̠

After Beijing, the ghosts were asked to disperse into the seas and the sky. The chant ended as it had begun (in fragment 7.2), invoking the origins of wild ghosts in the sky among mists and white clouds, nurtured by Mùgòhǽd̠ə, verified by P̠imæ̀menè, and dispatched to earth by Cánìshunì.

Li Wenyi's chant and Li Zhiwu's cartographic experiments juxtaposed two distinct landscapes. The first part of this final section contained a litany of known places, voiced in a language spoken only by their inhabitants, articulated through affinal kinship in ritual exchanges at weddings and funerals and mutual visits to trade labor. This was lived landscape, a network of mountain routes and trails, given form through the rhythms of ascent and descent, ridge and ravine, sunny slope and shady slope that dominated the experience of every ambulatory journey through these mountains. As the journey progressed down the rivers toward Shanghai and Beijing, however, another landscape came into view. This was the abstract landscape of the nation, a vast, imagined surface, organized and circumscribed by a centrally located power. Li Zhiwu marked this landscape on his maps as the boundary line that gave them coherence, orienting them to the four directions and aligning them with the nation's outside. Exorcism chants asked their listeners to perform some version of Li Zhiwu's cartographic exercises as they followed the trail of place names from county towns to prefectural and provincial capitals and down the rivers that linked their mountains to the centers of political and economic power.

Li Zhiwu's difficulty in fully reconciling the paths, streams, and villages of the nearby mountains with the abstract orientations of the national boundary illustrates the troubled relationship between these two landscapes. In the exorcism chant, the ghost's route crossed no threshold dividing the inhabited lands of mountain villages from the wild cities of the nation's center where ghost officials congregated. The ghost's travels folded together the intimately inhabited places of bodies, houses, and paths with the abstract, imagined space of the nation. This difficult interleaving attested to the deeply ambiguous origins of violent death. On the one hand, death from violence had come welling up from the national center, like a river backing up into a flood or like indigestible food backing up from the lower portions of a digestive tract. But on the other hand, violent death had found its way along a long and circuitous route through the intimately known and frequently traveled paths that linked neighbors and kin.

As chapter 8 explores, this ambiguous double origin was a crucial issue for Zhizuo residents as they sought to rebuild a community shattered by the losses of the famine and the Cultural Revolution. In the case of the youthful Li Jie, it reflected the multiple ambiguities of her "madness" as understood by her kin and neighbors. Her affliction drew mystery and fearsome potential from far away in time, in her grandfather's suicide during the Cultural Revolution. Where might the responsibility for that death be traced? To Lin Biao, Jiang Qing, and the Maoist policies of chaos they had fomented? Or to the kin and neighbors who had tormented the former official, avenging famine deaths? Li Jie's possession by her baby brother had drawn on this inheritance of pain, giving her the extraordinary power to demand that her husband's parents burn all their nicest household articles. But her trouble was also clearly bound up with relations and passions close at hand—with memories of "bearing" one baby that another baby evoked and with her difficult transformation from a daughter, shaped by relations with one household, to a daughter-in-law, shaped by relations with another. The voice of a baby speaking through her mouth had made present both a troubled history of violence welling up from national centers and more intimate personal histories of losses and transitions. The ritualist's voice was intended to unwind these histories on a long journey through a double landscape: intimate and distant, lived and imagined.

With the chant's final repetition complete and the offerings cooked, divided, and consumed, the participants exited the site in a single file. Men and boys went first, walking one at a time through the upstream arched willow doorway. As each passed under the arch, Li Wenyi showered him with water from his wand, dipped in the river. "It is the doorway between the world of people and the world of wild ghosts," he told me later. "A wild ghost official guards it, keeping the ghosts back; as you leave, they fall off your shoulders and stay behind. But you must not look back, or they might follow you."

As the men were leaving, Li Jie's mother-in-law opened a chest that had been carried down from her house. She draped the house/arbor/body effigy for the white *gu* with layer upon layer of children's clothing and then set it alight. With the help of two other women, both close neighbors, she began to pile on the fire the things that had been brought from her house: shoes, hats, pails, knives, pots, stools, sieves, baskets, a teapot, more clothing, embroidered aprons, an umbrella, a sewing box full of thread, embroidered strips, a bench, a cabinet. Finally, she tossed in the chest as well. As she placed each possession on the fire, she chanted these words, naming each item:

7.16

I give you this [item]	ngo ni t'è [item] gɔ̀
don't say you don't see	n hɔ ni n bɛ gɔ
don't say you don't understand	n sa ni n bɛ gɔ

When she was finished, the women filed through the arch, Li Jie among them, baby on her back. Her mother-in-law threw a last strip of cloth on the fire, now high and raging, and walked through. Li Wenyi followed without glancing back, sprinkling himself. The rite was over; all the participants dispersed for home, leaving the fire to burn itself out.

Walking

In discussing Li Wenyi's exorcism chant, as with all the *nèpi* I have touched on so far, I have focused exclusively on referential content. In this, I have been influenced by Zhizuo residents' own preoccupations. Like many peoples in East and especially Southeast Asia, Zhizuo residents were extremely articulate about ritual practice. Ritualists and ordinary people alike believed that all rites had meanings that might be dissected and explained. People often spent hours talking over each step of a ritual and arguing about why it was done this way and what effects it should have. It was the same with ritual language. Even when they did not understand a *nèpi* because of its arcane vocabulary, its unfamiliar syntax, or its rapid performance, people believed that each verse and word had a meaning that might be retrieved through exegesis. For this reason, my efforts to transcribe and translate *nèpi* texts were widely viewed as worthwhile. Many people, with varied levels of ritual expertise, were willing to help out, painstakingly disassembling each verse and venturing multiple interpretations for each word or phrase, striving to make clear sense out of language that was often nonsensical at first hearing (and subsequently producing clarity and coherence in my translations that were not always present in the original).

Ritual was viewed primarily as effective communication. Healing rituals such as exorcisms were intended to cut out a particular nonhuman entity from the surrounding world, give it ears and eyes for sensing, present it with a claim that it was a source of trouble or pain, describe in lavish detail the offerings presented to it, and explain in the clearest terms what was expected of it in return. Nevertheless, all this communication followed highly formalized conventions. Lòlopʼò ritual language is *poetic* in the sense that its affective force depends largely on its formal properties. I have attempted to convey a feeling for some of these features in my transcriptions, through spacing and indentations. In the remainder of this chapter, I would like to investigate more explicitly a few of the formal properties of exorcism chants. There is no space here (nor do I possess the expertise) for a thorough analysis of these properties; the discussion focuses only on a few obvious features that will allow me to point out a coincidence of the chant's formal properties with its semantic message—a coincidence that lends affective force to these chants and contributes to the potential for relief they create.

To understand poetic artifice, the great linguist Roman Jakobson once claimed, one need only consider the etymology of the terms "prose" and "verse." The former term derives from the Latin *proversa,* "speech turned straightforward," the latter from *versus,* "return." With this in mind, wrote Jakobson, "we must consistently draw all inferences from the obvious fact that on every level of language the essence of poetic artifice consists in recurrent returns" (1966, 399). The Lòlongo term for poetic language, *mèkòbɛ,* is similarly suggestive: *mè* means "mouth"; *kò,* "to turn" or "to return"; and *bɛ,* "speech." The essence of artifice in Lòlongo ritual language also consists in "recurrent returns," most obviously in rich, layered parallelisms of meter, rhythm, and semantic content. Jakobson was fond of quoting Gerard Manley Hopkins on parallelism: "The artificial part of poetry, perhaps we shall be right to say all artifice, reduces itself to the principle of parallelism" (Hopkins 1959, quoted in Jakobson 1960, 351; 1966, 399). For Jakobson, parallelism was the outstanding feature of what he referred to as the "poetic function" of language. This function draws attention to the performance of language as a source of affective power (1960, 356). Following this suggestion, Greg Urban has argued that, in the case of Shokleng origin myths in South America, the recurrent returns of parallelism gradually draw the listeners into the myths, binding them together in relation to this common object of fascination:

> Each fragment becomes a sign vehicle that draws attention to the fragment that has come before it. Individuals in the presence of the discourse sense these iconicities, and the iconicities in turn draw them into it, acting as a source of attraction, a glue that binds individuals to it. That glue is its source of power, its ability not only to bind given individuals to itself, but simultaneously, because they are bound to a common object, to bind individuals to one another. The poetic function is the source of a true social solidarity in addition to a represented one. (Urban 1991, 102)

In Urban's argument, the gradually accumulating returns of poetic language serve as a source of fascination that absorbs the listeners' attention, drawing them into the poetry, and making it a common ground on which they find themselves moved in unison. Urban contends that the referential content of Shokleng origin myths makes a kind of argument for social solidarity. The language in which they are performed reinforces this argument by creating in its listeners a *feeling* of social solidarity.

Exorcism chants create a similar coincidence of poetic function and referential content. Here too, each fragment of language indexes previous fragments, pulling the listeners into the chant and moving them along with it. But while these returns might draw the listeners into a common experience, it is not an experience of social solidarity. The parallelisms of exorcism chants draw affective force from a particular kind of bodily motion, the motion of walking. As the chant walks the ghost "from the right hand to the left hand and to the river's tail," repetitions of parallel structures on several levels perform the bodily rhythms and reassurances of walking. The chant's poetic function draws the listeners along on the ghost's walking journey. On this journey, I suggest, listeners are moved to unravel the intense entanglements, corporeal and social, in which some find themselves embroiled.

Exorcism chants perform walking rhythms of the kind people use to walk over steep and irregular mountain paths—not the simple, insensible alternation of left and right that suffices to carry one along a flat, paved sidewalk or street. Rather, these are progressive alternations, in which left and right succeed each other, but in which each left step is subtly different from the one before, as the foot feels out the earth's irregularities and conforms to them. The recurrent returns of the chant create such progressive alternations on several levels at once. We have already seen (in fragment 7.10) how, on a macroscopic level, the "driving over sky and earth" portion of the chant performs an alternation between two types of structural units. One type names and describes places; the other lists the species of violent death and asks the ghost to join its friends and companions. As the chant advances over the landscape, it alternates between these two sets, as though between left foot and right foot. With each alternation, however, the form of the chant varies, as though each footstep is feeling out a different configuration of the ground beneath. More microscopic instances of such alternation thickly texture every part of the chant, as we can discover by examining a few illustrations from portions of the chant's final section.

Lòlongo poetic language is largely built of distichs, couplets bound together by semantic and formal similarities. These distichs are often constructed by simply repeating the first line and replacing one of the syllables with a syllable that forms a semantic pair with the first, such as "friend/companion," "son/daughter," or "give/go":

7.17

| go to where your ghost friends live | ni chè *chɔ̀* jɔ dù yi |
| go to where your ghost companions live | ni chè *pe̱* jɔ dù yi |

Other distichs are created by replacing two or more contiguous syllables, again with words that form semantic pairs:

7.18

| some die boiling herbs as vegetables | t'à mo *dò tsò jɛ tsò* shr |
| some die from stabs or slashes | t'à mo *cì lè dɔ lè* shr |

Such distichs form building blocks for larger combinations of related couplets. In one very common form of combination, semantic pairs alternate, like a left foot and a right foot, with each alternation taking place in a slightly changed semantic context. In the "driving over sky and earth" section, the most frequent such combinations employ the semantic pairs *chɔ̀*, "friend," and *pe̱*, "companion":

7.19

your ghost friends live over there	ni chè *chɔ̀* ko ka jɔ
your ghost companions live over there	ni chè *pe̱* ko ka jɔ
go to where your ghost friends live	ni chè *chɔ̀* jɔ dù yi
go to where your ghost companions live	ni chè *pe̱* jɔ dù yi

Another principle by which distichs are produced replaces a pair of alternate syllables that also form a semantic pair with another semantic pair. Here the distich is structured so that the third syllable in the first line becomes the first syllable in the second. This is most often done with numbers or body parts—units that can form sequences larger than pairs:

7.20

| in *one* day they kill *three* goats | *chì* ni *sa* p'æ sɨ̀ |
| in *three* days they kill *nine* goats | *sa* ni *kɔ́* p'æ sɨ̀ |

Sometimes this pattern is extended to four lines, with each new line using the third syllable of the previous line as its first syllable, creating a rolling alternation. Here the chant takes advantage of a double meaning for the syllables *ji* ("to sicken" and "skin") and *mɛ* ("to finish" and "groin") to produce a tightly structured pattern:

7.21

[you] struck his *head* to *sicken* him	*wú* tæ̀ *ji* jæ su̱
struck his *skin* to *finish* him	*ji* tæ̀ *mɛ* jæ su̱
struck his *groin* with an *arrow*	*mɛ* tæ̀ *che* jæ su̱
used an *arrow* to shoot him	*che̱* pa mò jɔ su̱

Often, four-line segments are created by alternating line pairs, much as syllables are alternated in the preceding examples. Some such segments perform a simple alternation, in which alternate lines repeat with one or more syllables replaced. Here the third line is a variation on the first, the fourth a variation on the second:

7.22

stretch out *your apron*	*ni pʼa pi* cí kʼɔ lɔ
don't lose it through *holes in the cloth*	*mɛ me* tʼà r̩ɔ mó
stretch out your *hands*	*le ká* ci kʼɔ lɔ
don't lose it between your *fingers*	*le shá* tʼà r̩ɔ mó

Other segments perform a more complex, rolling alternation. Fragment 7.23 presents a pair of distichs in which contiguous lines and alternate lines both form formal pairs. (In order to make this complex pattern easier to grasp, I have chosen to translate syllable by syllable, preserving the word order and letting the syntax drop out.)

7.23

market revelry nine days revelry	ji mæ̀ kɔ̩ ni mæ̀
market drinking nine days drinking	ji cɛ kɔ̩ ni cɛ
water revelry tea water revelry	yi mæ̀ lò yi mæ̀
market drinking snake day revelry	ji cɛ cæ ni mæ̀

This is a progressive, rolling alternation: the second line replaces alternate syllables in the first; the third line replaces those in the first that the second line repeats and repeats those it replaces; the fourth line repeats syllables from all previous lines but makes a further addition (the syllable *cæ*) contained in none of the previous lines. Given that these passage are also embedded in the larger alternation between segments that name places and segments that list types of death, we can see that the entire chant is closely textured by multiple levels of parallelism, each embedded within others.[7] The dominant form of these parallelisms is a progressive alternation, as between left foot and right foot, with each left or right step feeling out a slightly different configuration from the one before it.

In previous chapters, I have commented on how deictic semantic pairs, such as "over here/over there," "this side/that side," and "this slope/that slope," are frequent participants in ritual language. Often, as they point out spatial alternations, such pairs parallel the formal alternating structure of the chant. This creates a kind of double alternation in which both semantic content and formal properties participate. In fragment 7.24, notice the pairs *k'ó bò/hé bò*, "that side/this side," and *k'ó mo/hé mo*, "there/here":

7.24

on *that side* shrimp play in three places	*k'ó bò* a tsɔ sa mè cà
your ghost friends are *over there*	ni chè chɔ̀ *k'ó mo* ngɔ
on *this side* white fish play in three places	*hé bò* ngó p'ɯ sa mè cà
your ghost companions are *over here*	ni chè pe̱ *hé mo* ngɔ

This is a progressive alternation of lines. The third line echoes the first, replacing "that side" with "this side" and "shrimp" with "white fish." The fourth line echoes the second, replacing "there" with "here" and "friends" with "companions." In terms of the passage's formal properties, the alternations are strictly temporal, one each fragment replacing another along a single temporal line. But with the addition of alternating spatial terms, the "recurrent returns" of the passage are invested with a spatial dimension in which one side replaces the other. This conforms precisely to the configuration of spatio-temporal flow (over the landscape) and spatial alternation (from side to side of the body) produced by walking.

It is as if the bodily rhythms of walking are the principle of production for the chant's language. Bodily motion is transformed into language, as alternation accumulates upon embedded alternation. The chant's semantic content—the ghost's own walk—follows this endlessly generative production, but it cannot keep pace with it. My selections from this chant were initially chosen for their referential content rather than their form, and they do not make clear how ceaselessly repetitive every part of the chant is. Especially in the final "driving" sections, the addition of each bit of semantic content—some place names and sometimes a few descriptive verses—is followed by the repetition (sometimes two or three repetitions) of entire segments that have been chanted many times before. What drives this endlessly repetitive generative flow is, of course, the chant's cadence. It is in the cadence that the rhythms of walking are most directly performed, for, unlike most alternations of lines or passages, the cadence occurs at the pace a body takes as it walks.

Nearly all of the examples of ritual language presented earlier are consistently composed of pentasyllabic and heptasyllabic verses with a trochaic cadence. Of course, nearly every passage quoted also contains exceptions to this rule, but most of these exceptions are embellishments on a pentasyllabic or heptasyllabic core. Most of the six- or eight-syllable lines in exorcism chants are simply five- or seven-syllable lines with personal pronouns (usually the first person *ngo*, the second person *ni*, or the third person *rɔ*) added to the beginning of the verse. This added pronoun is always unstressed.

7.25

ghost companions live over there   chè chɔ̀ no̱ ka jɔ

7.26

your ghost companions live over there   *ni* chè chɔ̀ no̱ ka jɔ

Occasionally ritualists preface a line with two personal pronouns followed by the particle *t'ȅ*, which indicates a subject-object relation between the pronouns. This creates eight- and ten-syllable lines from the chant's pentasyllabic and heptasyllabic trunk:

7.27

I will find *your* ghost companions   *ngo ni t'ȅ* chè chɔ̀ ju gɔ̀ bɛ

7.28

I will lead *you,* ghost, to stand in the sky   *ngo ni t'ȅ* chè hɛ̀ mùɪ lɔ hɔ gɔ̀ do

Other embellishments include adding unstressed particles such as *go, do,* and *lɔ* to the end of the line. My point is that none of these additions breaks up the fundamental trochaic rhythm. One-syllable additions are slipped unstressed into the pause between lines; three-syllable embellishments simply preface a line with one trochaic unit and an initial unstressed syllable that, again, is made part of an interline pause. Were the chant to be performed while walking, one foot would fall on every stressed syllable, and in the majority of cases the left foot and right foot would alternate at the beginning of every line—since most lines have an odd number of stressed syllables.

It is instructive to contrast the obstinately trochaic cadence of Lòlongo ritual language with the language of Ch. *jintishi,* the "modern verse" of the Tang and Song. *Jintishi* poetry is also built of five- and seven-syllable lines, but in contrast to the simple walking rhythms of Lòlongo ritual language, each line of *jintishi* is broken by a caesura that divides it into an iambic phrase before and a trochaic phrase after. Consider, for example, a poem of Li Duan, an eighth-century native of Hebei Province. Like exorcism chants, it leads a social being on a geographical/cosmological journey. And as Francois Cheng (1982, 25) notes, it ultimately identifies bodily movements with cosmological ones. (Here I have used double vertical lines to indicate the caesura that divides each line of the poem.)

summit of Mount Incense-cup	˘ ˊ ˊ ˘ ˊ xiang lu‖zui gao ding
There high hermit dwells	˘ ˊ ˊ ˘ ˊ zhong you‖gao ren zhu
Sun dusky, descends the mount	˘ ˊ ˊ ˘ ˊ ri mu‖xia shan lai
Moon bright, remounts the summit	˘ ˊ ˊ ˘ ˊ you ming‖shang shan

Though these verses are pentasyllabic, their cadence is quite different from that of exorcism chants, as is the cadence of all *jintishi* poetry. In Lòlongo ritual language, we find the following:

pentasyllabic verses	ˊ ˘ ˊ ˘ ˊ
heptasyllabic verses	ˊ ˘ ˊ ˘ ˊ ˘ ˊ

Jintishi poetry, in contrast, employs these cadences:

pentasyllabic verses	˘ ˊ ‖ ˊ ˘ ˊ
heptasyllabic verses	˘ ˊ ˘ ˊ ‖ ˊ ˘ ˊ

Cheng describes the caesura that divides iambic and trochaic hemistichs in *jintishi* as a "seawall against which rhythmic waves strike. After each [iambic] wave there follows a return wave, which engenders a contrary [trochaic] rhythm" (Cheng 1982, 46). He argues that this rhythm is founded on the forward thrust and backward pull of yang and

yin in Chinese cosmology. *Jintishi* poetry does not walk like Lòlongo ritual language: it moves to advancing and receding rhythms of heavenly
bodies or ocean waves.

While Lòlongo ritual language is overwhelmingly dominated by
trochaic cadence, the cadence does occasionally vary. The most striking
of these variations employ caesura superficially similar to those of *jintishi*. The chant for Agàmisimo described in chapter 5 also contained a
"driving over heaven and earth" (*mùts'r mits'r kà*) section, which described the spirit's journey over the geographical landscape as it drove
food, drink, and fertility in a right-hand spiral toward Zhizuo. On the
road, the cadence is identical to that of exorcism chants:

7.29

over there in Yongren	Yongren ju̱ ká ngɔ
let no food sit there	tso mè ju̱ t'à ti̱
no drink rest there	dɔ mè ju̱ t'à ti̱
no earth for sons	zò jɔ mi n ngɔ
no land for daughters	né jɔ mi n ngɔ
no earth for feet to sink into	chì t'o chì hé mi n ngɔ
no soil for fingers to plunge into	lè je̱ lè hé mi n ngɔ

Once the food, drink, and fertile earth come to rest in Zhizuo, however,
three of the heptasyllabic lines are negated and transformed into sexta-
syllabic lines, each divided at the center by a caesura between stressed syllables:

7.30

earth for feet to sink into	chì t'o chì‖hé mi ngɔ
soil for fingers to plunge into	lè je̱ lè‖hé mi ngɔ
earth for plows to turn	lɔ lɔ̀ hé‖do mi ngɔ

The caesura of *jintishi* poetry awaken the dynamic movement of each
line by dividing even and odd numbers of syllables and by separating

trochaic from iambic cadence (Cheng 1982, 46). In this chant, however, the caesura interrupt the dynamic rhythm with a static cadence, in which symmetrical trochaic phrases center on the break produced by two contiguous stressed syllables. As Agàmisimo reaches his destination, the dynamic rhythm of walking is replaced with a static symmetricality.

In the "driving to market" section of exorcism chants, a similar negation, also producing a static and symmetrical cadence, occurs in a single couplet repeated at moments when the ghost arrives in a named market town, where it rests in the company of ghost officials, eats piles of meat, drinks jugs of wine, and buys silk clothing before moving on to the next town or city (see fragment 7.11).

7.31

| [they] await your coming, ghost | chè lɔ lɔ nì hɔ |
| [they] will wait until the ghost comes | chè n lɔ‖lɔ nì hɔ |

As in the chant for Agàmisimo, the cadence walks where the entity it leads walks and rests where it rests.

It is likely that the flow of alternations in exorcism poetry, returning one after the other, embedded one within the other, serves as a "source of fascination for the listeners" (as in Urban 1991, 102), drawing them along on the ghost's journey. The "driving" sections of exorcism chants recapitulate the walk to the summit of the white clay mountain that Zhizuo residents once undertook at every bad death. This journey took ghost and participants out of the inhabited world to regions inhabited only by wild animals and dancing ghosts. This movement is forged again in exorcism chants, a journey in language that also requires the participation of the afflicted. People come to exorcisms not only to help eat, as the ghost eats, but also to help hear, as the ghost hears, and, in hearing, to walk, as the ghost walks. Perhaps it is necessary to take this journey even more in language than on foot because the unity of habitations in which social persons take form is made of language as much as of the materials of body, house, and landscape. The language of exorcism chants is resolutely material, produced through the rhythms of the body as food is produced in the rhythms of labor. As Jean-Jacques Lecercle puts it, "Language is the end-product of a chain of semiotic processes some of which have physical reality in the body" (1985, 53). Here, however, the chain returns to the body and to the other, more expansive habitations through which social persons take form.

Conclusion

How might the poetry of walking give relief from pain? Pain is double from the start. It has two origins—white *gu* and black *gu*, near and far, upstream and downstream, experience and inheritance, mouth and anus. To exorcise pain is to walk it away, to send it on widening circuits: first of what is given in bodily experience, then of what arrives from past times and far places; first of what belongs to social mouths that speak, then of what belongs to solitary anuses that excrete. Pain walks away, following rivers and digestive tracts to their excretory ends. But to walk, pain must be led by language. The origins of this leading language are also double. It issues from a single learned mouth here by the stream, but also from the world, the manifold surrounding mouths of musk deer, pigeons, and stars. One hears it here with half an ear, letting the stream flow by, waiting for the end. But one also walks along, counting footsteps and place names, some to which one has walked, some of which one has only heard. As pain follows language, so do its listeners, finding their walking pace in its layered and alternating rhythms of left and right, ridge and ravine, energy and fatigue. Walking with language, one is absorbed into the current of names, the flow of rivers, the glitter of markets, the strange wealth of imagined cities. Walking, one forgets oneself and the anguished histories that enmesh and entrap one—from the drudgery of life with a new infant under a mother-in-law's thumb to a parent's mysterious grief over a grandfather's suicide. One forgets for a time; those around let go for a bit; things grow better for a while.

It is not an exotic or farfetched scenario. Who has not forgotten himself or herself on a walk? Who has not become absorbed into the world, as rhythms of left and right both heighten the body's presence and give it over to the landscape's flow? Walking creates a delicate interplay of perception and reflection. Surprises emerge from the landscape and are left behind; new thoughts come into being; old ones gradually loosen their hold. "A kind of fluid oscillation between external objects and inward ideas and images may ensue, one whose very rapidity blurs the borderline between physical and mental experience" (Gilbert 1991, 11). In many ways, walking is similar to poetic language: it closely combines a formal rhythmical structure (the body's alternations) with a referential content that arises as temporal succession (this dialectic of perception and reflection). Perhaps this is why poetry describing and performing ambulatory journeys is so common in many languages. As Roger Gilbert notes in his study of the genre, walk poetry gives reflection over to temporal process: "Thought ceases to be wholly cognitive, directed toward some final object of knowledge, and becomes instead a process of wandering as wayward and impulsive as the walk itself" (1991, 11). Walking in language and walking in the body both open one up to the world, giving one over to the rhythm of mind and world modifying each other in turns. The ritualized walk poetry of exorcisms does all this in a particular idiom, the idiom of raveling and unraveling the social and material relations of which persons are composed. The sculptural language of exorcisms models a tangled moment of social personhood: the lived places of body, house, and landscape congested in difficult or quarrelsome social relations; the layered flows of seasons and generations reversed to infect the present with past anguish. Moving with deliberate rhythms through spatial and temporal geographies, the walk poetry of exorcisms unravels these congestions, restoring smooth relations in lived places, allowing difficult memories to recede into past time.

As healing practices, exorcisms were about forgetting. But the diagnoses to which they responded were about remembering. Before every exorcism was a diagnostic search for the multiple and ambiguous origins of pain. Who was responsible for past violence, and how might the communal wounds that its recurrent returns kept open be healed? Chapter 8 shows how Zhizuo residents addressed these questions in talk about the "age of wild ghosts," the prolonged era of social chaos that arrived only a few years after the famine.

CHAPTER EIGHT

The Age of Wild Ghosts

One winter night I attended a funeral for Luo Cheng, a Party member of long standing and the former principal of Zhizuo's elementary school. As Luo Cheng had lain dying of hepatitis complicated by heavy drinking, his fellow schoolteachers had talked over how they might commemorate him as a Party member without giving offense to his family. His sons and daughters were making their own preparations for an elaborate and boisterous nightlong vigil, with dancing, music, much drink, and the slaughter of many goats and chickens. Now that mortuary rituals were tolerated, though not sanctioned, by local government and Party organs, such a night vigil (*kukædo*, "emerging from the courtyard") was de rigueur upon the death of an elderly person in any self-respecting family. On the evening of the vigil, the teachers dressed up in their finest, donned red arm bands, and walked together to Luo Cheng's house. I walked with them as a guest of the school and for the borrowed prestige of my connections to provincial state agencies.

Among the hundreds of guests crowded into the courtyard, the mood was apprehensive. Official Party culture and so-called nationality religion, or even superstition, were to meet, perhaps to clash. After night fell, the principal called out over the hubbub of weeping, singing, and chatting voices for a moment of silence and read a speech about Luo's career in formal standard Chinese. The teachers then dispersed into the crowd, shedding their Party identity with their red arm bands. But in the tense atmosphere generated by their arrival, something else happened, for which this funeral would long be remembered. As was characteristic of this kind of event, few people witnessed it. As was also characteristic, it gained a public, even theatrical, existence in the days that followed, in impromptu gossip sessions. I heard of it from a woman who had not witnessed it but who had heard of it from Luo Cheng's son's wife, who claimed she had seen it herself.

It appears that one of Luo Cheng's sisters, keeping vigil over the corpse inside the house, was possessed briefly by a ghost. She began speaking in a man's voice, soon recognized as the voice of Luo Cheng's wife's brother, Yang Guowen. We have met Yang Guowen before: he was the Party secretary of one of Zhizuo's two management districts during the Great Leap Forward, and he was the official whom Qi Deyi blamed for his brother's death. Yang had harmed many during the Great Leap and famine years; he had played a crucial role in the final destruction of the *ts'ici* system in 1965; and he had died a demeaning and violent death during the Cultural Revolution. Yang's sister, Luo Cheng's wife, had died two years ago. Had he outlived her, Yang would have been the most honored guest at her funeral, with a prominent part to play in the ritual proceedings. "Sister's husband," Yang Guowen's ghost was reported to have said through Luo Cheng's sister's mouth, "I am sorry for not attending my sister's funeral. I have been very busy, running about here and there, attending this death and that. I have many duties now, as king of the wild ghosts."

Two days after the funeral, as this story circulated through the brigade, Luo Cheng's family gave him an exorcism, burning all his possessions beside the river. Luo Cheng had died from common diseases of poverty—hepatitis and alcoholism—not from any species of violence that required exorcism. Nevertheless, with this rite Luo Cheng's family hoped to rid their household of both his ghost and that of the notorious former brigade Party secretary. They hired a ritualist to plead with Yang Guowen and Luo Cheng to ride the Jinsha and Yantgze Rivers like white steeds across the nation's breadth to Beijing, where they would meet with Lin Biao and Jiang Qing, emperor and empress of wild ghosts. Like other efforts to send away the violently dead of recent decades, this one anticipated a difficult moral question. While responsibility for the wounds and deaths of the famine and the Cultural Revolution could clearly be tracked down across the nation's breadth to a distant source, the immediate agents of violence in most rural communities had just as clearly been kin and friends. The question of how to distribute the responsibility for past violence over the troubled gulf between the "distant shore" of the imagined state and the "near shore" of one's intimate, lived community helped give memories of violence their enduring power to afflict (Das 1997, 68).

This chapter explores some of the ways people in Zhizuo confronted this question while telling the story of how Yang Guowen came to be the local boss of wild ghosts in Lin Biao's and Jiang Qing's spectral government. I argue that ghost stories like that of Yang Guowen gradually accumulated in Zhizuo after the famine to form a coherent "strategy of time" (de Certeau 1992). The socialist state in China relied for its power and legitimacy on a specific vision of time in which socialist transformation was to be a series of leaps (Ch. *yue*) or bridges (Ch. *qiao*) along the linear path of national and world history. The state was to be the arbiter of a new social reality, constructed through the deliberate eradication of a painful and shameful past.[1] During the Socialist Education campaign and the Cultural Revolution, time was reworked as activists pulled the past out of the mouths of class enemies through investigation and struggle sessions and as memory was annihilated through public humiliation, torture, and imprisonment. In minority areas such as Zhizuo, official discourse portrayed the state as drawing an impoverished populace out of the obscurity of a primitive past toward a bright socialist future. And crucial targets of this project were the heterodox practices of popular religion, "feudal superstitions" such as the *ts'ici* system, to which minority nationality populations like Lòlop'ò were supposed to be particularly susceptible. In Zhizuo, tales of the violent destruction and spectral return of the *ts'ici* system subverted such campaigns to rework time within an oppositional moral cosmology in which time was neither a road nor a cycle but a spiral through which the effects of past violence returned repeatedly to engage and transform present social relations.

These rival temporal strategies framed different modes of organizing agency to shape local power relations. Marilyn Strathern has deftly defined agency as "the manner in which people allocate causality or responsibility to each other, and thus the sources of influence and directions of power" (1987, 23). In another, related, definition, agency stands for the ways human action is constrained or enabled by enduring social institutions, relationships, and practices (Giddens 1984). Agency in both these senses pivots on understandings and experiences of time. How people allocate the capacity to affect events, outcomes, or behaviors depends on temporal chains of causality. How they imagine lasting institutions, relationships, or practices to constrain or enable action depends on how they find the past to endure, return, disappear, or reproduce itself. This chapter uses ghost stories set between the end of the famine and the present to explore the rival tactics of time and agency that officials, activists, and ordinary peasants employed as they sought to cope with the effects of past violence. In these narratives, multiple modes of producing the past and competing strategies for deciding on the sources of speech and action accumulate to create a specific mode of historical understanding. In this mode, particular violent acts returned continuously to infect the present and—as though by chance—to undermine the efforts of local officials to lead Zhizuo forward along a linear developmental road. Engaging in this subversive temporal strategy by telling and retelling ghost stories was one means by which people in this community continued to search for ways "to inhabit a world made strange through the desolating experience of violence and loss" (Das 1997, 67).

Blood and a Box

As China began to recover from the famine in the early 1960s, it appeared that the system of collective production in the countryside was disintegrating. A number of provinces had begun to allow forms of household cultivation in 1960. Anhui led the way by letting local cadres assign responsibility for agricultural output to individual households, a practice dubbed the "responsibility fields" (Ch. *zeren tian*) system. Similar practices soon emerged in many other parts of the country, including Hunan, Henan, Guangxi, and Guangdong. By the spring of 1962, China's leaders had to contend with the alarming fact that at least 40 percent of peasants were participating in some form of household cultivation. Though cautious about openly voicing support, many of Mao's senior colleagues accepted arguments that agriculture would flourish only if the incentives associated with family farming were again allowed to develop (MacFarquhar 1997, 207–233).

Nevertheless, household cultivation was clearly a threat to Mao's greatest remaining unsullied accomplishment after the Great Leap's failure—the rapid and smooth collectivization of the countryside. In the summer of 1962, after leaning briefly toward permitting household cultivation, Mao changed his mind. The flourishing of responsibility systems, he insisted, was an example of a struggle endemic to communism between the "socialist road" and the "capitalist road" and among the classes that walked each. The struggle would be long and torturous, but the "socialist road" and the system of collectivization must win out (MacFarquhar 1997, 274–283).

The struggle between socialist and capitalist roads would become a core theme of China's next mass movement, the Socialist Education campaign. The documents that laid out the case for this movement in 1963 and 1964 described it as the first widespread class struggle since land reform:[2] it was to pit the broad masses against the exploiting classes of landlords and rich peasants, who were always trying to stage a counterattack. Cadre corruption, incipient capitalist practices such as speculation and profiteering, and "feudal" practices such as gambling, arranging "marriages for sale," engaging in "spiritualism and witchcraft," and "holding religious festivals" were all identified as elements of this reactionary revival (Baum and Tiewes 1968).

The movement began to receive wide publicity by late 1963. By the end of 1964, work teams had been dispatched to thousands of rural locations to investigate and discipline cadres at the county, commune, and brigade levels and to reeducate peasants in the fundamentals of socialist morality. In Yunnan, four counties were selected as test points for the movement in 1964;[3] by 1965, the list had expanded to nineteen, including the northern county of Yongren. (At the end of the Great Leap, Zhizuo and the rest of Zhonghe District had been transferred from Dayao to this much smaller county.) Each county received a work team of thousands of people, who were instructed to ferret out and reeducate those local cadres who had "degenerated into the agents and protectors of class enemies" (CYZZ 1994, 143–144).

One of the cadres investigated was Qi Lin, the chief administrator of the People's Court in Yongren's small county town. The son of poor peasants from Zhizuo, Qi Lin had followed a path unthinkable for poor Lòlop'ò two decades before. He had graduated from Zhizuo's elementary school, attended middle school in the county town, and recently been assigned to the ranks of county cadres. His parents were delighted. Their impeccable credentials as poor peasants and parents of a county official allowed them to realize a dream also once out of reach for members of their class: they had been elected *ts'ici* and *ts'icimo* in Zhizuo.

The rites and festivals of the *ts'ici* system had been revived in 1962 after a hiatus of three years during the famine. When accounting had returned to the level of the production team, the two upstream paddies of the ancestral trust had again begun to rotate from team to team with the title of *ts'ici*. While the harvest from these paddies paid for resumed sacrifices to Agàmisimo and the Lòhə, it was too small to pay for the more public *ts'ici* festivals. In an atmosphere of optimism that followed the famine's end, production team leaders began to sponsor these festivals openly. The *ts'ici*'s production team put on the feast of the *ts'ici* rotation, and the two Chemo teams that farmed the lower ten fields of the ancestral trust joined with youthful volunteers from around Zhizuo to plant the entire ancestral trust on the customary date, the fourth month's second day of the dog. As argued in chapter 5, these festivals were powerful assertions of reproductive metaphor, drawing thick connections between the productive and reproductive practices of growing rice and bearing and nurturing children. As crops and infants both began to survive again after the famine, Zhizuo residents must have felt that the festivals helped to renew the streams of life and death the Great Leap and the famine had so traumatically reversed.

When the reliquary box representing the titles, obligations, and estate of the *ts'ici* was carried in a midnight procession to Qi Lin's parents' house in the first lunar month of 1964, Qi Lin's parents were overjoyed. Three decades later, however, Qi Lin's single surviving brother, Qi Chun, recalled that the box had descended on his father's house like a curse, which would decimate his family and plague its surviving members for the next thirty years. That spring, Qi Lin's youngest brother fell off his harrow while racing his ox over the ancestral trust fields, and a few months later he died suddenly. It was the worst of portents for his parents' tenure as host couple in the *ts'ici* system. This omen was confirmed in the following months. In February 1965, as Qi Lin's parents prepared for the festival that would move the reliquary box on to the next production team, Qi Lin admitted to interrogators from the county's Socialist Education work team that his parents, back in Zhizuo, were "religious frauds" and the ringleaders of a "superstitious sect."

Immediately after Qi Lin's confession, a work team was organized to take the Socialist Education movement to Zhizuo. Yunnan's provincial Party Committee had recently placed new emphasis on bringing the campaign to mountainous minority regions. It had designated the district of Tanhua, bordering Zhizuo and also populated mainly by speakers of the Central dialect of Yi, a "mountainous nationalities district Four Cleanups test site."[4] No fewer than 184 cadres from the army and from county and prefectural Party Committees descended on Tanhua's villages to "carry out socialist education among the cadres and masses, raise class consciousness, promote the socialist road, and develop production" (CYZZ 1994, 144).

Zhizuo fared better: initially, only two cadres were assigned to this brigade's work team. The team leader was a native of Zhizuo, county Party Committee secretary Yang Chaosheng. He had a personal stake in the affair, as his father was Yang Guowen, Party secretary of Zhizuo and the brigade's most powerful official. (In 1962, the two management districts created in Zhizuo during the Great Leap had been reunited into a single brigade [Ch. *dadui*].) Another county-level cadre accompanied Yang Chaosheng on the day-long walk to Zhizuo. There, they met with Yang Guowen and with the brigade's assistant Party secretary and its militia secretary. Aware that his father and his cronies were logical targets for the Socialist Education movement, Yang Chaosheng made them official members of a campaign work team, which would focus not on the sins of local cadres but on the activities of Zhizuo's "superstitious sect."

The morning after arriving in Zhizuo, these five cadres walked in procession down a path from the brigade government building to the village of Chezò, where Qi Lin's parents' house was located. Luo Guotian, the militia leader of the 1940s whose house the government building had once been, had built it to be visible from the entire valley. In the tumultuous decades that followed Luo's execution, locals had learned to watch the path that led to the house's front door as a barometer of official activity. Many remembered viewing the line of five officials from afar as they descended to Qi Lin's parents' house and demanded that the family turn over the reliquary box. Qi Lin's brother, Qi Chun, recalled hiding with his parents and sisters behind the locked and barred door. That night, the entire family fled to a seasonal house higher in the mountains. The next morning, the five officials again descended along the path and ascended again in a defeated, straggling file. The third morning, most of Zhizuo must have been watching as the five descended for a third time, carrying a roof beam. Using the beam as a battering ram, they broke down Qi Lin's parents' gate, climbed the ladder to the loft, seized the reliquary box, and carried it back to the brigade government building.

The next day was the last day of the lunar year. Had things gone otherwise, hundreds of people would have arrived at Qi Lin's parents' house scrubbed and dressed in new clothes for the festive transfer of the reliquary box. Instead, representatives of every household in the brigade were summoned to the courtyard of the government building for a mass meeting. The meeting must have lasted hours, with cadres making long speeches repeating points from the recently issued Twenty-Three Articles that outlined the shape of the Socialist Education movement.[5] Those who described the meeting to me years later, however, would speak of only one event, which could have taken only a few minutes. In mass meetings and struggle sessions, work team members and local cadres were often joined by local activists, who displayed enthusiastic loyalty to new policies in efforts to gain Party membership. Two such activists, both young women, were prominent in this meeting. These two activists emerged from an inner room onto a balcony above the courtyard, carrying the wooden reliquary box. I continue the story in the words of Li Zong, a brigade member who was in his early twenties at the time:

> They came down the stairs and put the box in the middle of the courtyard. Yang Chaosheng [the work team leader] opened it up and dumped out the things inside. There was a little bottle and some bones. The reason no one can tell you whether there were two or six bones, tiger, ox, or human bones, is that no one had ever opened that box until then. And just then everything was very chaotic. Yang Lizhu [one of the activists] said, "See this box! We are here to destroy it! There is nothing to fear from this; it's just an old box. It's just feudal superstition." Then she sat on the box with her buttocks. She was menstruating, and she left some blood on the box's lid. That was not civilized! Then Yang Hua [the other activist and Yang Guowen's wife] also sat on it.

The pollution of menstrual blood was believed to be like infectious disease, a contagion that might be spread by sight and hearing as easily as touch. *Ts'ici* had taken care that pregnant and menstruating women did not look on the reliquary box. Each time the box had been brought out from its attic hiding place, it had been preceded by a crier, who shouted, "All those with recent dead, all pregnant women, all menstruating women, give way!" In retrospect, Yang Lizhu's "uncivilized" act was seen to have driven the ancestral spirits out of the box and transformed them into wild ghosts, bent on revenge against their attackers and descendants.

After this meeting, the work team formed an Art and Literature Propaganda troupe (Ch. *wenyi xuanchuan dui*). The troupe used the public defeat of Zhizuo's "superstitious sect" as inspiration for a prefecturewide campaign against superstition. Its four members worked out a farcical skit centered on the reliquary box. Yang Chaosheng, the work team leader, took the lead role, lecturing on how this dusty old box had been the center of a superstitious cult for hundreds or thousands of years. Another troupe member donned the hempen clothing, sandals, and hat *ts'ici* had worn during their year of service, chanted under his breath, and feigned offerings to the box. Two young women, one of whom was Yang Lizhu, made speeches denouncing this superstition and recounting its heroic annihilation. The skit was never performed in Zhizuo, but many there imagined every show to end with Yang Lizhu again sitting on the box. The troupe toured the prefecture, stopping in at least four county towns. Its final stop was a mass meeting in the prefectural capital of Chuxiong. Stories of this assembly that filtered back to Zhizuo had Yang Chaosheng again spilling the bones and bottle from the box and Yang Lizhu again sitting on it. The troupe eventually returned to Zhizuo and deposited the box in an attic room of the brigade government building. "Even those destroyers of the Four Olds [Ch. *po si jiu fenzi*] didn't dare destroy that box," one Zhizuo resident commented. "It's probably still there, though of course it's empty [*kɔ̩*]."

Ghost Stories

When I attempted to elicit recollections of the Cultural Revolution from people in Zhizuo, many responded with biographical vignettes about those who had participated in demolishing the *ts'ici* system. Brigade members related these tales in a hurry, out of doors, as a brisk litany of deaths and misfortunes.

According to many, the person most directly responsible for bringing the Cultural Revolution to the brigade was Yang Lizhu, the activist who had left her menstrual blood on the reliquary box. It was said that her role in the Art and Literature Propaganda troupe had made her a committed radical. In August of 1966, inspired by Mao's reception of Red Guards at Tiananmen, the Chuxiong Party leadership began creating Red Guard groups in the prefecture's middle schools. In October, Yang Lizhu joined such a group as it formed among middle-school students in Yongren's county town. Wearing on their left arms yellow bands printed with the characters "Red Guard" (Ch. *hong wei bing*), Yang and a band of students walked to Zhizuo and occupied the elementary school there. From this base, the Red Guards launched attacks on the brigade government and the Socialist Education work team. Before the end of the year, the work team dissolved, and its only nonnative member left Zhizuo.

The Red Guards began to hold nightly struggle sessions against brigade cadres and former work team members. By early 1967, the brigade government had been overthrown, and a Revolutionary Leadership Small Group, appointed by the military, had taken over the brigade. Later that year, Zhizuo's Red Guards split into two groups, allied with two Red Guard factions that were engaged in armed battle in other parts of the prefecture and province (CYZZ 1994, 146–147). One of these groups occupied the school, the other the brigade government building, and they spent their energies launching verbal attacks against each other from these bases.

Accounts of this period in Zhizuo focused on struggle sessions, for which much of the brigade's population would gather nightly in the schoolyard. Once the Small Group was established, it led the struggle sessions, employing activists to arrest, beat, and humiliate the victims. A low wooden platform was built in the yard's center. Those to be struggled against huddled directly in front of the platform, guarded by activists with clubs. They faced the crowd, which divided into activists and Red Guards on the far left side of the yard and "ordinary masses" in the center and on the right. In the far right corner to the rear, people labeled as "landlords, rich peasants, counterrevolutionaries, and bad elements" huddled in a wooden enclosure, or "cowshed" (Ch. *niupeng*).

The activists and "ordinary masses" alike took literally Jiang Qing's widely publicized 1967 call to "attack with words, defend with arms" (Jiang 1968, 53; CYZZ 1994, 147). A session leader shouted questions and accusations at the struggle targets about their past activities, thoughts, and loyalties. When words did not wound deeply enough, people made their curses material by hiding bamboo spikes in their fists to beat especially hated victims. At the end of the session, victims were dragged off to be shut into "cowshed" cells in the brigade government building, where they bled and waited for the next night's struggle. The victims eventually included everyone who had been a brigade cadre or production team leader during the Great Leap and afterward. By late 1969, even many former Red Guards had also become targets. Activists investigated ritualists and diviners, labeled them "cow demon snake spirits" (Ch. *niugui sheshen*), and held sessions to beat them. "There were no rules," one man recalled. "One evening, they grabbed the county Party Committee secretary Yang Chaosheng [leader of Zhizuo's Socialist Education work team] and Qi Weidong's old father, who was just a poor peasant and had never done anything but farm. They stood them up side by side and beat them at the same time. Only Mao and his wife were safe."

The first and most notorious victim of struggle sessions was Yang Guowen, the brigade Party secretary. Soon after Yang Lizhu and her

Red Guards occupied the school building in 1966, they arrested Yang Guowen, beat him nightly, and forced him to admit crimes against the people. Some of the enemies he had accumulated during the famine beat him with bamboo spikes, drawing blood. After two weeks, he escaped and hanged himself from a tree. Shortly thereafter, his wife, Yang Hua, the second woman to sit on the reliquary box, died of an unspecified illness.

Yang Guowen's son, Yang Chaosheng, fared little better. In the autumn of 1966, inspired (as Yang Lizhu had been) by his role in the Art and Literature Propaganda troupe, he became the leader of a county-wide drive to destroy the Four Olds (old customs, old habits, old culture, and old thinking). As people in Zhizuo told it, he burst into a neighboring commune's Buddhist temple with a Red Guard retinue and forced a monk to perform a farcical divination ceremony. The monk drew a bamboo lot printed with the words "Destruction to your family, death to your kin" (Ch. *jia po ren wang*). "Yang Chaosheng laughed," one man narrated. "He was full of himself. 'I'm a powerful cadre; my father is a cadre; my wife is young, my children healthy. How could my family be destroyed?' But then his father [Yang Guowen] committed suicide. His stepmother [Yang Hua] died of an illness. Then his wife died, no one really knows of what."

Grieving for his wife, Yang Chaosheng drank heavily. He made drunken fun of another activist's enthusiasm at a mass meeting and was subsequently demoted, arrested, and made the target of struggle sessions for three years. "His father was dead, his wife was dead, and he himself was wearing a counterrevolutionary's hat," the narrator continued. "Then his house was hit by lightning. Terrible! Tiles flew everywhere, and there was a big hole in the roof. 'Destruction to your family, death to your kin' is a terrible thing!"

For others, the revenge of the collective ancestral spirits was more direct. Yang Lizhu survived the beginning of the Cultural Revolution by only months. According to Zhizuo residents, the ghosts she had spawned drove her mad: "She was possessed by ghosts [*nèt'æ*]. She ran around screaming, 'Why did you sit on me? Now do you know my power? Your body was unclean, your buttocks had blood, now do you know my power?' Six months later she died." The militia secretary, who had been second in command to Yang Guowen throughout the Great Leap and the famine and who had been the second local member of the Socialist Education work team, was also hounded to death by the *ts'ici* ghosts:

His illness came and went. His mother said that when he was ill he would see an old Lòlop'ò man wearing a round cap, hempen shoes, and a hempen apron [the costume of *ts'ici*] in the doorway. As soon as he saw this person, he would pass out and shit in his bed. His mother thought that old man was Agàmisimo, and when there was no alternative, she would climb Agàmisimo's hill and slaughter a sheep there. . . . He was ill on and off for ten years; for ten years he lay in his bed covered with his own shit. Before his death, they made a [duplicate] reliquary box in his house and used it to sacrifice to Agàmisimo. That didn't help either. . . . Then one winter up at [the high-mountain hamlet] Henilɔ, he froze to death in a snowstorm. More and more snow fell in the days after his death, and they didn't find his body until two weeks later. The stink was terrible, and no one would help his wife and son carry the corpse down.

The final member of the ruling elite during the Great Leap and the famine and the third local member of the Socialist Education work team was the assistant Party secretary. Like Yang Guowen, he committed suicide after being beaten in struggle sessions. And, like that of the militia secretary, his corpse rotted before it was buried:

He just disappeared. People thought he had run back home to hide, but his family was also looking for him. Years later, after the Cultural Revolution was over, his mother had a dream; it was very clear. In the dream he told her, "Mother, I've been struggled against fiercely, and I have no way to keep on living. I've thrown myself off a cliff, and now my body has rotted, though my bones are still there." He named the place and asked her to get people to pick up his bones and bring them back. He told her not to be sorry, because after his death he looked in the book of fate and found that he would have lived only a year more anyway, even if he had not committed suicide. His mother looked for his bones in that place and found them. She saw from the clothing and a notebook he had carried that this was indeed his own body.

Those who told these stories tallied up the catastrophes on their fingers: the three who had led the brigade through the years of the Great Leap and the famine died horribly. Among the five who participated in the Socialist Education work team, only one escaped: the nonnative, county-level cadre who had left Zhizuo at the beginning of the Cultural Revolution. Of the four who participated in the Art and Literature Propaganda troupe, the only one spared was Li Yishu. "All the others in the troupe cursed the reliquary box, spat on it, or sat on it. But Li Yishu simply dressed up as a *ts'ici* and pretended to make offerings to it. He made fun of the box, but he didn't insult it. Before he left on that tour, his parents told him, 'Whatever you do, don't touch that box.' This is the reason he is still alive. He is fine; he is not even sick."

Eventually a final name would be added to the list of deaths. Shortly after Yang Lizhu brought her band of Red Guards to Zhizuo, the Destroy the Four Olds movement had begun. This movement had been inspired by Lin Biao's speech at the August 1966 rally when Mao received the Red Guards at Tiananmen. "We will energetically eradicate all the old ideas, old culture, old customs, and old habits of the exploiting classes," Lin had declared. "We will sweep out all the vermin and clear away all the obstacles. We will make vigorous efforts to establish proletarian authorities and the new ideas, new culture, new customs, and new habits of the proletariat" (quoted in Bennett and Montaperto 1980, 73). After this rally, bands of students all over China raided the homes of the "backward classes" and destroyed "old things"—including furniture, clothing, art, and imported goods. Soon, the Destroy the Four Olds movement expanded to include public property such as temples, churches, museums, and parks.

In Zhizuo, there was little to destroy. Red Guards made halfhearted raids on the houses of former landlords and rich peasants to look for embroidered clothing and silver jewelry, but the clothing was inconsequential and the jewelry easy to hide. Zhizuo's single, tiny Buddhist shrine, perched above the river's tail, had been destroyed during the Great Leap. Zhizuo residents almost never made lasting representations of spirits, ancestors, or ghosts—no statues, paintings, or carvings of spiritual or mythological figures. The most prominent physical evidence of "old ideas, culture, customs, and habits" was the two giant trees representing Agàmisimo and Shr̀mògù, the spirit of lightning, on the hilltop above Chemo and the matching trees representing the weather spirit Mijù and Shr̀mògù on the opposite hilltop above the village of Méabò. Neighboring tall trees had been cut to feed the fires of the dining halls and foundries during the Great Leap, and these two pairs of trees now dominated every vista of Zhizuo's inner valley. Yet the young Red Guards overlooked them.

Yang Guowen's successor as brigade Party secretary, however, did not. Luo Zicheng had been chosen to fill this post by the Revolutionary Leadership Small Group in late 1967. He was remembered as a relatively harmless leader, more interested in keeping things on an even keel than in producing and attacking "enemies of the people." Still, during the Cultural Revolution, the position of any cadre was precarious. "In order to demonstrate his contribution to the Party," a former brigade cadre told me, "Luo Zicheng did a thing that people would not ordinarily do."

> Even during the Destroy the Four Olds movement, no one had dared cut those two trees. But one morning Luo Zicheng walked up Agàmisimo's hill with an axe and chopped them both down. That was in 1970. In 1978, he froze to death in the snow. He was walking toward the brigade government from Chemo. He was drunk, and he slipped and fell in the gully and hit his head. The snow covered up his body. One morning, the supply and marketing cooperative manager walked down to the gully to get water. One of his buckets fell off his carrying pole and rolled down the gully. When he bent to pick it up, he discovered the head of Luo Zicheng's corpse there. It scared him horribly. During his funeral, Luo Zicheng inhabited his mother's body. She entered his house, saying [in his voice], "I'm cold. Please light me a fire." Then she lit a pine torch, walked to the gully where he had died, and built a fire there. All the people at the funeral watched her do this.

At the root of each misfortune, storytellers emphasized, was the actor's moral responsibility for the transformation of the collective ancestral spirits into wild ghosts. The words of the possessed Yang Lizhu, the old Lòlop'ò man who appeared to the militia secretary, and the manner of each death—by suicide, befouled in excrement, frozen in the snow—were listed as evidence that each catastrophe could be attributed to the vengeful *ts'ici* ghosts. But these tales also implied that the famine dead flocked behind the ancestral spirits like a band of bright parakeets, eager to participate in their revenge. Five of the seven victims of the *ts'ici* ghosts had formed the core of Zhizuo's government during the famine. Brigade Party secretary Yang Guowen, along with his son, Party Committee secretary Yang Chaosheng, and his wife, Yang Hua, the second activist to sit on the reliquary box, were roundly hated for using their high positions to eat well during the famine while others starved. The militia secretary and the brigade's assistant Party secretary were also blamed openly for famine deaths. Only Yang Lizhu and Luo Zicheng were not directly associated with the famine. Those who beat Yang Guowen, Yang Chaosheng, and the brigade's assistant Party secretary during struggle sessions were openly motivated by fury over their role in the famine; the tales of their spectral misfortunes drew their force from the sense that hundreds of ghostly famine dead were also eager for revenge. The moral order to which these stories appealed, an order in which past violence and injustice returned repeatedly to haunt those responsible, participated in a specific strategy of time. This strategy drew on cultural resources familiar to Lòlop'ò, such as practices of possession and exorcism, to defy official rhetoric about time as a linear road or path and the selective freedom from responsibility for past violence that this rhetoric implied.

Roads and Time

Official historiography in post-Liberation China was pre-occupied with metaphors of time as a path, Ch. *daolu,* uniting the idea of an intellectual or moral way, doctrine, or method with that of a road leading forward. One of the attractions of Marxism for Chinese intellectuals during the May Fourth period was that, as a path directed toward a future point the West had not yet reached, the trajectory of world history it outlined did not leave China at a permanent disadvantage (Levinson 1966, 134). Mao devoted considerable scholarly effort to reconceptualizing more than three thousand years of Chinese history as a path through universal stages of development: slave society ending with the fall of the Shang, feudalism rising with the Zhou and Qin, semifeudalism and semicolonialism commencing with the Opium Wars, a transition to bourgeois-democratic revolution beginning with the Revolution of 1911, and a stage he called "New Democracy" that spanned China's civil war and heralded the transition to socialism (Starr 1979, 258–264). Socialist transformation was to be a series of leaps (*yue*) and bridges (*qiao*), abbreviating the path of China's historical development to quickly overtake Europe and the United States.

By the time of the Socialist Education movement, the dominant metaphor for socialist transition was a struggle between those taking the "capitalist road" and those adhering to the "socialist road." Socialist Education work teams dispatched to Chuxiong's mountain regions were explicitly enjoined to "lift the lid on the struggle between the two roads" and "promote the socialist road" (CYZZ 1994, 144). The Socialist Education movement opened a period when promoting the socialist road meant violently obliterating what lay behind. Those who could not turn away from the past were bound to get lost along deviating paths such as the various rightist heresies summed up under the phrase "capitalist road." In 1964–1965 and throughout the Cultural Revolution, young

Party activists and radicals were motivated by repeated and strident demands from the center to demolish the past in order to leap forward along a road never yet traveled.

The metaphor of time as a road or path struck deep resonances in Lòlop'ò culture. We have seen that time was made material in the walked and spoken paths of the *ts'ici* rituals. Traveling a chanted path of place names, the ancestral spirit Agàmisimo swept through the surrounding landscape in a spiral, turning around the central villages toward the right hand, in the direction that grain is milled and dancers step, gathering health and fertility to deposit in the central valley. The reliquary box retraced the inner edge of this spiral, as it proceeded year by year from village to village in a right-hand circuit of the central valley. The festive transfer of the reliquary box at the new year made use of similar paths, danced toward the right hand, turning one year over into the next with multiple allusions to one lifetime turning over into another. Taken together, these rituals treated various domains of time—the yearly agricultural cycle, the time of life and death, and the longer institutional time of the *ts'ici*—as material roads or paths. These were not linear paths unfolding in continuous development toward the future, like the "socialist road." They were nuanced circuits or spirals, each turn covering ground similar to the turn before while encountering new obstacles and deviations.

Implicit in these chanted paths was an understanding of the relation between present action and enduring social practices and relationships. In chapter 7, I argued that such temporal paths are embedded in the structures of poetic ritual speech, or *mèkòbɛ* (*mè*, "mouth"; *kò̠*, "to turn" or "to return"; *bɛ*, "speech")—speech that turns in (or returns to) the mouth. This poetry is composed of formally parallel units that can be compared to paragraphs, encompassing smaller parallel units at the level of lines and yet smaller ones at the level of words and syllables. Each parallel unit, whether longer or shorter, is a "return," *kò̠*, that gathers its meaning from all that come before it while imposing nuanced formal and tropic turns on the returning structure. Skilled practitioners of ritual poetics use the multilevel parallelisms of poetic language to elaborate witty or emotive metaphors that resonate back through each of the parallel cycles of the speech. This poetic speech diagrams assumptions about the place of action in the flow of time,[6] a flow composed of longer circuits or returns, such as a lifetime, encompassing shorter ones, such as an agricultural year. The meaning of speech and deeds takes form through the recurrent returns of past years and generations, but each return requires nuanced innovations that resonate back through the preceding cycles, adding new layers of meaning to past events.

Some of the ritualists I became acquainted with in Zhizuo speculated that the syllable *kò* in the term *mèkòbɛ* might also refer to the return of the same speech to the mouths of successive generations of speakers. Although ritualists modified and elaborated the chants they learned as apprentices, they did not consider themselves the authors of their own speech. Their chanted speech "returned to the mouth" (*mèkò*) from the mouths of the previous generational cycle. As chapter 5 described, this speech was associated with ancestral authority and potency. But it also embodied a dangerous potential associated with the spiral flow of time, the potential of a reversal in which undigested fragments of the past back up along the path of time to infect the present. When speech from the past was controlled through the agency of an ancestor or a powerful spirit medium, it was *nèpi*, authoritative "speaking to ghosts." When it escaped such controls, it became, like any other sudden or chaotic reversal of spatial or temporal flows, *chènè t'æ*, "possession by wild ghosts." Words that descended (*jɛ*) on one's head, entangled themselves (*vî*) in one's body, and voiced themselves (*bɛ*) through one's mouth took their force from the reversed paths of wild ghosts, paths that spiraled backward in time and toward the left hand in space.

Admonitions to stride forward along the socialist road involved a mode of allocating responsibility for actions that Lòlop'ò came to associate with ruptures in time's flow and possession by wild ghosts. The Socialist Education movement and the Cultural Revolution were struggles against a structure of power founded on cadres' control over property—in the countryside, primarily collective land. Marilyn Strathern has argued that where power over the bodies, speech, or actions of others depends primarily on property relations, people are seen as effective agents when they own themselves and their actions. If others control the actions of a person through ownership of property or labor, that person is seen to be acting as an agent for others (1988, 158). The Cultural Revolution promoted another structure of power altogether. To exhibit their influence over the speech and acts of others, activists such as Yang Lizhu disavowed authorship of their own acts. To become effective agents, they convinced others that their every word and deed sprang from a source outside themselves and their networks of kin and friends: the person and thoughts of Chairman Mao. As Mayfair Yang (1994) has shown, activists often spoke as though they were possessed bodily by the Chairman's thought. Yang quotes a middle-school student's diary: "The staple foods of my spirit every day are the majestic thoughts of Chairman Mao. Each time I open up the *Works of Chairman Mao* a red sun emerges in the midst of my heart and warmth spreads over my whole body. Each time I gaze upon the portrait of our Great Leader Chairman Mao it's as if all up and down my body I've gained an inexhaustible strength." The teacher commented in the margin: "Our bodies' every vein is filled with the thoughts of our Great Chairman Mao, and every single one of our accomplishments are flashing with the magnificent brilliance of Chairman Mao" (Yang 1994, 261). Such bodily possession by the Chairman and his thought was a crucial political strategy, especially during the violent stages of the Cultural Revolution. Words and acts that did not originate in Mao Zedong Thought were all too likely to flow from a bad class background or a tendency to walk a deviant historical road. The viciously contested origin of speech and deeds was the basis on which millions were beaten or driven to suicide and on which opposing armies of Red Guards waged bloody factional battles.

Like the metaphor of time as a path, the practice of naming a remote agent as a source of action had precedent in Zhizuo. People possessed by wild ghosts changed their facial expressions abruptly, developed immense strength, tore off their clothes, or ran about erratically. Sometimes, as in the case of Yang Lizhu, they used the voice of the dead to remonstrate with themselves or their families or to demand extravagant offerings. To many in Zhizuo, the abrupt changes in manner of youngsters who became Red Guards or Party activists could be explained only as possession by wild ghosts or similar forces. Their unremitting references to Mao and his thought confirmed that their speech descended on them from outside and above or backed up the rivers from Beijing, where the Chairman resided and wild ghosts were sent. Their unfamiliar slogans, chanted in Mandarin and Yunnan dialect, languages their elders understood imperfectly, seemed like the half-coherent ravings of the possessed, obsessively mouthing demands in alien voices.

Each story of possession and death helped consolidate this understanding. Each participated in a narrative mode codified in exorcism ritual—a "chronotope," in Mikhail Bakhtin's felicitous phrasing (1981). In this chronotope, a traumatic event such as the bad death of a loved one instituted a cycle of repetition and return that reverberated into past and future. Its structure was captured with precision in the distinction between white *gu* and black *gu* upon which ritualists insisted as they exorcised wild ghosts. A bad death transformed the deceased into a white *gu*, a wild ghost, whose most insistent characteristic was its inevitable return to afflict those who mourned it. To delay or prevent this return, one had to seek the origin (*ju*) of the white *gu*: this origin was to be found in a black *gu*, a wild ghost official. The black *gu* itself had an origin in the previous descent of another black *gu*, perhaps the ghost that had killed the mythical Pimæmenè in childbirth, and so on, through the ghosts of animals who devoured one another in the wild and the ghosts of stars that died in their catastrophic falls from the heavens. The ultimate origin of this chain of black *gu* was indeterminate, fading off into the unfathomable reaches of the black sky. Yet as black *gu* descended along this chain on the heads of their victims, they drew in their wake, like flocks of brilliant, chattering parakeets, crowds of white *gu*—the ghosts of kin, neighbors, and friends.

The deaths of those who perished in the Cultural Revolution cycled into the future as memories that plagued their kin and descendants for decades to come. They cycled into the past through previous scenes of violence: their immediate origins could be traced, through the evidence of possession, to the theatrical transformation of the ancestral spirits into wandering ghosts—a bad death for living spirits. This scene itself was a descent of indeterminate black *gu* from the wild reaches of the sky, and these black *gu* drew in their wake the known unsettled dead, who gathered round to help devour the living soul—the dead of the famine, never properly mourned. Each story of the death of a member of the Socialist Education work team or the Art and Literature Propaganda troupe was a claim that violence against the collective ancestral spirits had reversed the temporal spiral of life and death and let loose these known wild ghosts upon their descendants. Each was an insistence that the Cultural Revolution was an effect of the famine's unavenged injustices returning to infect the present. These stories served Zhizuo residents' thirst for justice against those who had gorged during the famine while others starved, while deflecting anger from still-living people who might have been held responsible for the violence of the Cultural Revolution—those who, for instance, beat Yang Guowen with fists of bamboo spikes, or those who refused to help the militia secretary's wife and son carry his frozen corpse home. Naming ghosts as the ultimate cause of deaths in the Cultural Revolution helped people bridge some of the schisms between kin and neighbors these deaths had opened.

The wild ghost chronotope at play in these stories described the socialist state in its full moral complexity: it was both an indeterminate, imagined entity that possessed actors (in both senses of possession), motivating them from afar, *and* a collection of determinate agents who bore moral responsibility for their actions through past and future time. Ghost stories outlined this paradoxical relationship clearly. On the one hand, they traced the wounds and deaths of the famine and the Cultural Revolution to an indeterminate origin—unknown ghost officials who held meetings far away in Beijing or even beyond, in the far reaches of the sky. On the other hand, they assigned responsibility for this violence to specific, named kin and friends, whose guilt was proven by their horrible deaths. These stories confronted the tortured question of how to apportion blame for starvation and violence between the distant, imagined center and one's own kin and neighbors. Yet the wild ghost chronotope also cleared a space for the regeneration of community in the face of past violence. It allowed final judgment on a person's culpability for violence to be reserved until after that individual's death. The manner of a death and the events it precipitated were taken as evidence of guilt; the rites of mourning and exorcism allowed kin, neighbors, and friends to come to terms with their fury, fear, grief, or shared guilt in relation to the deceased. Thus, as they mourned Luo Cheng, his family and friends accepted an agonistic relationship with the memory of Yang Guowen, former brigade Party secretary, now local boss of wild ghosts. Yang's appearance at Luo Cheng's funeral implicated both Luo and the kin whom his ghost would now plague in the violence Yang had precipitated. Luo Cheng's family recognized this implication as they exorcised the ghosts of Luo and Yang together (as white *gu* and black *gu*). In this way, they accepted a degree of shared moral responsibility both for the harm Yang Guowen had done and for his horrible death.

Stories of ghostly deaths thus probed the relationship between the living community and the imagined state, searching for an ethical ground on which to re-member social relations still devastated by the effects of past violence. This search produced a kind of subversive vision: it represented the state as a spectral chain descending from the outside and allying with kin and neighbors to work intimate effects on body and psyche, and it worked toward reconstituting social relations dismembered by this alliance on other terms, independent of state power. As critiques of the "sources of influence and directions of power" of local officials, these ghost stories were inevitably disruptive to the authority of those officials. During the period of decollectivization and market reforms, people in

Zhizuo put these disruptive effects to efficient use. By the time I heard the stories in the early 1990s, the wild ghost chronotope had been fine-tuned to a collective strategy for subverting local authority. This mode of tracing the origin of certain events to the spectral return of past violence worked to deflect the force of new mass campaigns and to undermine the effectiveness of the local cadres who had replaced Yang Guowen, Luo Zicheng, and their cronies.

Household Cultivation

After brigade Party secretary Luo Zicheng was found frozen to death in a gully, the *ts'ici* ghosts remained quiet until 1980, the year Zhizuo adopted household contracting (Ch. *baochan daohu*). In 1978, peasants and basic-level cadres in many locales in China had taken advantage of the political opening created by Mao's death and the struggle over his succession to experiment for a second time with household cultivation. As in 1962, provinces that had suffered most severely during the famine, such as Anhui and Sichuan, led the way. Dali Yang (1996, 149–153) shows how such local initiatives influenced a hard-fought controversy over agricultural policy at the center, with reformers using the economic success of these experiments to win out over their opponents and silence skeptics. As central policies gradually relaxed, peasants and local leaders became bolder in experimenting with reform, and the resulting acceleration in the adoption of household cultivation and other "responsibility" systems was reflected in further policy liberalization. The center went from explicitly prohibiting household contracting during the Third Plenum of the Eleventh Central Committee in 1978 to forcefully promoting it as central to the Deng Xiaoping regime's new agenda for "socialist modernization" by 1982.

Still, central policy lagged behind local initiatives. In Chuxiong Prefecture, a few production teams had adopted responsibility systems of various styles in 1978. Prefectural leaders took note of one team that more than doubled its gross production with a system of contracting production to groups of laborers and encouraged other teams to follow suit. By the end of 1979, some 87 percent of the prefecture's teams had initiated some form of contracting to group or household (CYZZ 1994, 165). In March 1980, the prefectural Party Committee issued an ambiguous directive encouraging contracting to the group but stating that household contracting should remain confined to poor mountainous regions, where residence was scattered and transport difficult (CYZZ 1994, 166). Zhizuo's brigade cadres took this as clear encouragement to adopt household contracting, and over the next few months they met to divide up Zhizuo's collective land. Every production team allocated each of its households a portion of land based on the number of household members. Each team member was assigned an equal portion of desirable irrigated paddy land, dry terraced land, unterraced swidden land, and forest for cutting firewood. This system would remain in place, with few substantial modifications, through the 1990s.

In most of rural China, households were required to turn over a portion of their harvest on contracted land to the state as tax and to sell further quotas to the state at state-set prices. But Chuxiong's mountainous areas were in the midst of a devastating economic transformation that made this impossible. Between 1950 and 1978, the population of these mountains had nearly doubled, while the amount of arable land had expanded only slightly. As land per capita shrank, mountain residents had sustained themselves by producing hempen cloth, aided by high hemp procurement prices. In the late 1970s, however, market reforms had caused hemp prices to plunge (as discussed in chapter 3), and by the time collective land was divided, people in Zhizuo had come to rely almost entirely on grain land for their income.

This land was far from adequate. Each person in Zhizuo received an average of .36 *mu* of rice paddy land, farmed in rice in the summer and wheat or barley in the winter, and .93 *mu* of unirrigated terraces, farmed in maize or potatoes in the summer and wheat or barley in the winter. The poorest production teams had no rice paddy land to divide, and they distributed only about 1.1 *mu* per person of unirrigated land.[7] Few households could produce on this land all the grain they needed to eat. Although some were able to generate substantial extra income by illegally harvesting timber, most depended heavily on supplies of state relief grain, which began flowing in 1981. Despite the introduction in the mid-1980s of high-yield grain varieties, chemical fertilizers, and new agricultural techniques, most households remained dependent on relief grain through the 1990s. Per capita grain production was 196 kilos per year, while the poorest households produced only about 63 kilos per person each year. Households received from 20 to 80 kilos of relief grain per person per year.

Household cultivation produced a decisive shift in the character of state power in China's countryside. During the Mao era, the center's economic and ideological aspirations and struggles focused with intensity on brigade and commune cadres. As the actors who coordinated the minimal units of collective production—commune, brigade, or team—these beleaguered functionaries were crucial mediators between state policies and local realities. They were responsible for extracting the products of peasants' labor, managing the quality of their work, regulating their consumption, and overseeing their ideological improvement. At the same time, however, as Vivienne Shue (1988) has argued, local cadres were the chief obstacle to the penetration of state power into the countryside. They were resourceful defenders of their locales, evading or distorting policies the peasants they lived with would not accept, seeking to soften procurement demands by underreporting production, and attempting to wrest more state allocations for their collectives. Given their importance in facilitating and frustrating the plans and aspirations of higher levels of state authority, it is no wonder that these cadres were the frequent targets of campaigns to rectify their corruption, punish their ideological missteps, and avenge the center's own failures. The Socialist Education movement fixed on them the blame for the Great Leap's waste and stupidity and the famine's agonies; the Cultural Revolution ran them through gauntlets of fear, public blame-taking, and ritualized violence. Throughout, local cadres were both the fulcrums and the resistant objects through which state power manifested itself in the countryside. Their bodies were stage and players for the theater that generated images of the state for local consumption.

With decollectivization, this intense focus shifted from local cadres to households. The productive resources of the agricultural economy were entrusted to household heads; the state's plans to stimulate production and commodify the agricultural economy devolved directly on household operations. In areas where rural industrialization was rapid, local cadres quickly achieved new importance as the managers of corporate village or township enterprises, but households nevertheless remained the chief arena where state agricultural policies took effect and met opposition. In Zhizuo, where rural industrialization never occurred, nearly all households were placed in the problematic category of "hardship households" (Ch. *kunnan hu*), dependent for their livelihood on state allocations of grain and subjected to increasingly intense state efforts to assess their economic circumstances and reform their agricultural practices. Team and brigade leaders calculated the resources and output of each household, pressing those with lower than average production for explanations and rectification. At each step in the involved

process of applying for and collecting relief grain from the state bureaucracy, farmers found their household operations subject to exacting
scrutiny: detailed records were kept on amounts and kinds of all grain
and livestock produced, and food needs were calculated on the basis
of a standard figure of 1 kilo of grain per adult per day. Beginning in
1985, households in Zhizuo were subjected to a sustained campaign to
develop and rationalize their agriculture. Ordinary Zhizuo residents,
whose dealings with officialdom had once been limited almost exclusively to contacts with production team leaders and brigade cadres now
found themselves in frequent interaction with grain officials, tax collectors, agricultural experts, and police—all concerned with how much
land of what types they farmed, how much grain they produced, how
many mouths were eating it, and how much money they spent on entertainment such as drinking, weddings, and mortuary rites rather than
on agricultural improvements such as chemical fertilizer, plastic sheet-
ing, and high-yield seed varieties. The local cadres who had once fudged
figures and distorted policies in defense of their locales had turned
around to become the more direct instruments of state demands on and
surveillance of this new basic unit of production and consumption.

In the Mao era, an image of the state as the hollow core of a productive
unity took shape for people in Zhizuo in the struggle over community
resources—the collective harvest and the ritual sites where people had
gathered to negotiate death, life, and the health of their community with
cosmic forces. This image reflected in microcosm the state's own projec-
tions of a national productive unity: despite the era's chaos and frag-
mentation, the state continued to trumpet a vision of the nation as a
unified body incarnating a single will for production. In Zhizuo, resistance to this image centered on the emblems of a communal productive
unity—the reliquary box and ritual sites of the *ts'ici* system—and chose
as its victims those who brought destructive state forces to the center of
this unity—brigade cadres and activists. Now, daily confrontations of
household members with the plethora of officials who sought to survey
and manage their production and reproduction shaped an altered image
of state and nation. The state was to assert itself as the generative center
of each household's productive unity; the nation was to be the additive
sum of household operations, linked in a web of commerce, each contributing to the common project of economic expansion. In response,

people in Zhizuo assembled a transformed strategy of spectral subversion, with a new canon of stories about the wild ghosts of the *ts'ici* system. In these stories, instead of springing from symbols of communal productive unity, the *ts'ici* ghosts emerged from land farmed by individual households. Instead of wreaking revenge on community leaders, the ghosts killed or possessed household members. In opposition to the intensifying relationship between households and the imagined state, this new strategy efficiently undermined the authority of local cadres to push development projects. In opposition to the new image of community as merely the sum of productive households, it reasserted a vision of a local domestic community drawn together through its agonistic orientation toward an incommensurable past.

Spectral Subversions

Two tiny, triangular rice fields in the valley's center were included in the land parceled out in 1980. These were the uppermost portion of the *ts'ici*'s ancestral trust. Nestled in the overgrowth at one margin lay the smooth, white stone of the Lòhɔ, their guardian. As noted in chapter 6, during the Mao era these two fields had stood in for the entire 10-*mu* ancestral trust, which sprawled down the riverside below them. Carved away from the main body of ancestral trust fields when agricultural producers cooperatives were formed in 1955, they had been rotated yearly among production teams for another decade. Scores of women and schoolchildren had dug out their margins in 1958, disciplining them in preparation for tractors and harvesters that never arrived. The Socialist Education work team had stopped their rotation in 1965 and allocated them to a Chemo production team. In the 1980s and 1990s, they became the focus for a new series of stories of deaths and possessions. As though by chance, but with the collusion of hundreds of families in Zhizuo, these stories delayed rice transplanting over a wide stretch of the region's most productive land year after year, causing local officials immense trouble and frustration. Relating these stories, Zhizuo residents made subtle but gleeful fun of the brigade leadership, caught between deaths that everyone attributed to vengeful ghosts and pressures from higher levels to carry out household contracting in a rational manner, overcome local superstitions, and develop the agriculture of this economically distressed area.

As the valley's land was carved up in 1980, it appeared that no Lòlop'ò member of the Chemo production team was willing to accept a contract to farm these two fields. People could not forget that ever since 1965 the two tiny fields had posed a problem for the production team to which they had been allocated. Li Yong, a team member, explained:

> After those fields were collectivized, who cared about the Lòhɔ? Our team should have performed the rite, but because of the Destroy the Four Olds movement, no one dared. With no ritual, women in the team were afraid to walk into that land to transplant it. But some women were in the Party; they could destroy *anything*. They weren't afraid, and they replaced the women who were. Sometimes outside work teams planted the fields. Sometimes the team leader and the others who were responsible for the team, like the agricultural specialist, helped transplant, even though they were men. Sometimes there was no outside work team and no Party activists, so the team leader would get people who were deaf and mute [Ch. *yaba*], who didn't understand anything, to transplant. The *ts'ici* ghosts understood that these people were not responsible. All the way up until household cultivation, no one else dared transplant those fields.

Now, it was said, any household that dared to cultivate the fields without first sacrificing to the Lòhɔ was bound to anger the *ts'ici* ghosts. The production team leader, a Lòlop'ò man, appealed to the team's handful of Han families. Han team members should take the lead in rejecting the feudal superstitions of the Lòlop'ò majority, he argued. Reluctantly, Zhang Jianyi accepted the contract. Zhang was a nephew of the notorious Han landlord Zhang Wenxin, shot during the campaign against counterrevolutionaries in 1952. During the Mao era, Zhang Jianyi had been labeled a "rich peasant," made to work in punishment work teams, and hauled out periodically for public humiliation in struggle sessions. In 1978, he been rehabilitated along with millions of others in the national reconciliation that followed Mao's death. Still, as one of his neighbors put it, "he was used to doing what he was told." His household farmed the two fields for one year. The next spring his mother died, and he requested that the contract be canceled.

Disturbed by Zhang's mother's death, the production team leader turned the matter over to the brigade leadership. The brigade chief convinced Qi Bao'en, another member of the team, to accept the contract for the two fields. As chapter 4 describes, Qi was an accomplished ritualist, who had once served as *ts'ici*. Before dawn on the customary day for planting the ancestral trust, Qi walked to the two fields, secretly propitiated the

Lòhə, and directed his sons and daughters-in-law to plow and plant the land. "We had no trouble planting those fields," Qi told me.

> I said the Lòhə's *nèpi* correctly. I did everything right, and we had no trouble. When we were finished planting, I walked over to Mijù. I did the sacrifice for Mijù two years in a row. The second year, the rain came right after I was finished. It rained so hard that there was no way to get home, like dumping water from a bucket over your head. In the *nèpi*, you ask it to rain three nights and four days, and it did! [He laughs.] People over there really respect me now! But my wife and son were afraid; they oppose feudal superstition. So after two years I refused to plant those fields again.

After Qi Bao'en rejected the contract in 1983, brigade cadres persuaded another Lòlop'ò team member, Li Mingzhi, to accept the contract. He delayed his transplanting until two weeks past the traditional date, creating a formidable new complication. Until now, this hot-potato land contract had primarily been an entertaining source of scandal and speculation. Li Mingzhi's procrastination vastly expanded the scope of the scandal, drawing in the entire membership of Zhizuo's largest and wealthiest production teams—every household that farmed rice within sight of the former ancestral trust. Before the demise of the *ts'ici* system, the several hundred *mu* farmed by these households had been transplanted in rice only after the ancestral trust land was planted. Even between 1965 and 1980, production team leaders had generally arranged to plant the two representative ancestral trust fields before any of the surrounding land. After 1980, as stories spread about the *ts'ici* ghosts' attacks on households that cultivated the trust fields, those who farmed the surrounding land waited to transplant their rice until the two troubled fields were planted. Now, as Li Mingzhi procrastinated, all his neighbors delayed their own planting, watching their rice seedlings grow long and sickly green. Finally, fearing that his seedlings would expire in their seed beds, a Han named Gu Yin had his household transplant its land, two weeks past the customary date. All those with land nearby, including Li Mingzhi, quickly followed suit.

A member of Gu Yin's household died within the year. Li Mingzhi's brother died too, and Li petitioned the brigade to take back the contract for the troubled fields. The brigade leadership reassigned it to one of their own, Gu Liliang, a brigade cadre from a Han family. Gu Liliang's household transplanted the two fields for six years, each year delaying transplanting for weeks past the customary date and seriously impairing production in hundreds of *mu* of surrounding land. Some claimed that Gu Liliang warded off the *ts'ici* ghosts by secretly hiring Qi Bao'en to propitiate the Lòhə. Qi told me that he had indeed quietly performed this sacrifice for several years. No one was paying him, he said; he was simply making it safe to plant his own fields, next to the contested land. In 1990, Gu Liliang's mother-in-law died, and he asked the brigade government to take the contract elsewhere. His fellow cadres convinced him to plant for another year. After the transplanting season of 1991, however, he retired from the brigade government and refused to cultivate the fields again.

After scouring the brigade for Han families thought to be less committed to Lòlop'ò collective ancestors, the brigade government turned over the contract to Zhang Jianliang, brother to Zhang Jianyi, who had been the first to accept it. "Perhaps Zhang Jianliang has forgotten that the *ts'ici* ghosts killed his own mother," one Chemo resident said to me in the spring of 1992. Perhaps Zhang Jianliang was reminded, for a month before the customary transplanting date, he backed out of the contract. At the last moment, brigade cadres again appealed to Qi Bao'en, implicitly agreeing to look the other way as he propitiated the Lòhə that year.

In 1990, the central government had launched a nationwide Socialist Thought Education movement (Ch. *shehui sixiang jiaoyu yundong*), intended to rationalize aspects of the system of contracting land that had begun to escape the control of local cadres. Yongren County's Party Committee sent a two-member work team to Zhizuo in late 1991. The team immediately began investigating the brigade's finances, adjusting household contracts for the first time since 1980, hiring laborers to repair deteriorating irrigation ditches, and promoting new methods of planting and fertilization. Early in 1993, the work team leader vowed that he would solve the absurd production problems plaguing this superstitious brigade. Every year, the confusion surrounding those two tiny rice paddies delayed cultivation in hundreds of *mu,* team leader Dong complained to me. This was simply unacceptable in an area where most peasants relied on government grain subsidies. "Socialist thought education" meant combating harmful feudal superstitions, he declared, but in this era of reform one could no longer openly punish superstitious peasants.

He had given the problem much thought, he said, and he had decided that the best way to resolve it was to contract the troublesome fields to Zhizuo's elementary school. He was confident that the teachers, being educated cadres, would not share the common people's backward beliefs.

As the transplanting season drew near, team leader Dong proposed this solution to the teachers. After a long and vitriolic meeting, they refused the contract. "Social pressure" was one teacher's laconic explanation. Stung, Dong vowed that the campaign work team and five brigade cadres would personally plant the fields that season. But as the traditional planting date approached, resolve seemed to dissipate. The brigade Party secretary left for a meeting in the township center, two more brigade cadres absented themselves to seasonal houses high in the mountains, and team leader Dong himself found pressing business in the county town.

In 1993, two nights before the customary date for planting the ancestral trust, I was startled awake by a woman's voice outside my window. The voice was screaming in a high, hoarse tone, repeating two or three phrases that I could not understand. In the morning, I sought out Li Zhilin. The voice had also awakened him and his mother, with whom he lived. They had been talking the matter over when I walked into their courtyard.

"That woman has been mad [*t'æ*] off and on for a long time," Li Zhilin told me. Her name was Qi Hai. She was the sister of Qi Lin, whose betrayal of his family in 1965 had initiated the events that destroyed the faltering *ts'ici* system. She had married into a Chemo household, one of several that shared the courtyard at Ts'icizò, where the original ancestors had made their first home. After Luo Zicheng chopped down Agàmisimo's giant pine, Qi Hai and her husband had moved to a remote hamlet. The other families in Ts'icizò had also moved away, and the houses there now stood derelict.

Up in their high-mountain settlement, far from the scrutiny of cadres and work team leaders, Qi Hai and her husband had set up a Misi on the hill behind their house. They sacrificed a goat and a chicken to it twice a year on the days Agàmisimo had once been propitiated. Qi Hai's husband's brother lived with them; he wore the hempen clothing, hempen sandals, and round cap of a *ts'ici*. Still, the *ts'ici* spirits plagued this family incessantly, turning them mad, making them ill. "They are like wild ghosts [*chènè*]; no matter what you offer them, they refuse to leave you," Li Zhilin said. Even Qi Hai's brother, Qi Chun, was now and again seized with fits of madness. He kept the set of hempen clothing his father had worn as *ts'ici* under his bed to wear on nights when he felt ill.

In any case (Li Zhilin continued), Qi Hai had lately begun to talk incessantly about the *ts'ici* system. Were you to sit with her for an afternoon, she would talk through the entire cycle of *ts'ici* rituals, describing when each should be held, how the effigies should be constructed, what should be said, what should be offered. At rice-transplanting season, the *ts'ici* ghosts possessed her, and she ran about shouting. During the night, she had been wandering the path to the brigade government building. She was screaming, "Why do you let Han plant my *yiləmi* [ancestral trust land]? If you keep letting Han plant my *yiləmi*, I will never stop killing you! Restore my *ts'ici*, or I will keep killing you!"

A day before the customary date for transplanting, three of the brigade cadres and team leader Dong were still absent. People watched from the hillsides of Chemo and Chezò as the brigade's single female cadre, responsible for implementing birth control policies, spent the morning turning the fields with a hoe, a task ordinarily performed by men with oxen and plows. After three hours, she abandoned her hoe and went home, leaving two-thirds of the land unturned.

That night, it was said, the brigade chief paid a visit to Qi Bao'en, the ritualist who had transplanted the fields the year before. Later, Qi Bao'en told me that he had explained to the young man that, to plant the land safely, he must personally perform the rite for its guardian Lòhə. But that was impossible since he and his wife both opposed feudal superstition—and besides, he was too old to walk that far. The brigade chief offered to carry him down the hill on his back and buy the two chickens for the sacrifice with brigade funds. Qi accepted the contract and the chickens; he wouldn't need the ride, he said—his nephews would help him. The next morning, Qi Bao'en's two nephews plowed and harrowed the fields, and by noon his female kin had transplanted them. The following day, hundreds of Chemo and Chezò residents flooded the valley floor to complete the season's transplanting.

Team leader Dong walked back to Zhizuo the next day, passing a bamboo stalk and two paper streamers tied to a mimosa tree near the ancestral trust, clear evidence that the rite to the Lòhə had been performed. He vowed a thorough investigation. But two weeks later, he was accused of adultery with a married woman and was forced to resign his position.

Not long afterward, an investigatory team from the township found the brigade chief and two other cadres guilty of encouraging feudal superstition, demoted them, and appointed replacements. Few in Zhizuo seemed to think much of the new leadership. As one man put it to me, "None of those bumblers and fools will solve the problem of the ancestral trust fields until the Party allows the *ts'ici* to be restored."

In the 1980s, political culture in China underwent a series of profound transformations as people rejected the styles of discourse, forms of personal and political relationships, and modes of gathering and granting power that had prevailed in the previous decade. Those who had been tortured and imprisoned for their pasts were rehabilitated; those who had persecuted them were expected to be forgiven. Gradually, people were allowed to possess their pasts rather than being possessed by them. A bad class background or past errors were no longer assumed to define one's entire personal and social identity. Painted with a broad interpretive brush, these transformations amounted to another shift in the manner of allocating the capacity for effective speech or action. Power was achieved and punishment distributed on the assumption that effective action originated in individual subjects with their own initiative and autonomy rather than in remote sources such as Chairman Mao's thought or a landlord grandfather (Lin, Rosemount, and Ames 1995).

Yet, just as legal punishments were meted out on the basis of actions consciously authored by individuals, Zhizuo residents learned to shift the authorship of certain acts back to a more remote source, the spectral resurgence of past violence. By the mid-1980s, people in Zhizuo had found it possible to be temporarily possessed by a ghost without risking permanent identification with it. Just as speaking as though possessed by Mao's thought was no longer politically useful, one could now speak in the voice of a ghost without being labeled a "cow demon snake spirit," incorrigibly under the sway of feudal superstition. Beyond a general disparagement of Lòlop'ò peasants as "backward" and "superstitious," local cadres found it impossible to take effective revenge on those who refused a contract for the ancestral trust fields because a household member had died, refused to plant their own land before these fields were planted, or used the voices of the collective ancestral spirits to demand the *ts'ici*'s restoration. Peasants and brigade cadres alike interpreted these acts and refusals as the inevitable eruptions of past injustices in the present. And since these afflictions could not be assigned to living, conscious, individual authors, they could not easily be punished.

These persistent returns threw the local government into disarray, defied its efforts to rationalize the system of land contracts, and deflected its attempts to develop the brigade's "backward" agriculture. But they also related this recalcitrance toward local authority to a larger moral drama of justice and revenge, in which the unsettled souls of those who had died in the Great Leap famine and the Cultural Revolution continued forcefully to shape the ways locals imagined their relations to the state bureaucracy. Despite a nationwide effort to erase the effects of past injustices and keep the national imagination fixed on present and future economic expansion (Watson 1994), the events of the famine, the Socialist Education movement, and the Cultural Revolution kept returning to infect the present. As subversions, these returns were particularly effective because they disrupted agricultural production, which reform-minded state agencies had identified as the crucial issue for poor mountainous areas. By the time I left the area in 1993, the brigade government was in disarray. Peasants openly ridiculed local cadres, and brigade officials routinely fled to remote mountain settlements to avoid the visits of higher state authorities. Township and county officials reviled Zhizuo's Lòlop'ò as backward, superstitious, and recalcitrant while finding themselves powerless to take effective action.

Conclusion

The practices of time on which Chinese socialism was founded had made copious use of so-called minority nationality people. Until the late 1980s, historians and ethnographers tracked down traces of primitive communism, matriarchy, or slave society in minority nationalities as scientific evidence in support of the doctrine of history as a universal, linear development. When market-oriented economic development began to displace socialism as history's goal, the poor, backward, and marginal areas in which many minority nationality people had their homes served a similar temporal strategy. As control of the economy was gradually transferred to the market, these areas became a focus for a new discourse of development in which the state would draw economically backward minority nationalities toward the future by overcoming outmoded traditional concepts such as egalitarianism and isolationism in favor of the "commodity thinking" necessary to a competitive commodity economy (Tang 1988; Pan 1992).

Leaders and activists in Zhizuo repeatedly adjusted their modes of allocating responsibility or capacity for action in response to such temporal strategies. During the Socialist Education movement, work team leaders and budding activists gathered power through efforts to dismantle backward "feudal superstition." In the Cultural Revolution, activists found influence through direct identification with the person and thought of Chairman Mao, under the banner of overcoming the "old ideas, culture, customs, and habits of the exploiting classes." During the era of market reforms, brigade cadres sought power by creating plans and projects designed to promote the area's economic development and pull it into the market economy, the new target of history. In each period, the ability to act and to direct the deeds of others depended on a sense of history as a road forward. Nevertheless, each such tactic of agency was eventually reinterpreted not as a motor of history but as an obstacle to or reversal of time's flow. Ghost stories turned the defeat of superstition in the Socialist Education movement into a violent inversion of the temporal movement of life and death. The wild ghost chronotope encouraged the reinterpretation of activists' unmediated connections to the person and thought of the Chairman as ghostly possession. More stories and rumors of death and possession in the 1980s and 1990s frustrated efforts to wean households in Zhizuo from dependence on state relief toward fuller participation in the market economy. Each mode of distributing "the sources of influence and directions of power" was eventually deflected through another practice of time, a practice assembled of rumors, stories, and the protean voices of the possessed.

This temporal practice drew its form from ideas about the nature of person, time, and causal chains constructed in exorcism practices, but it drew its *force* from a specific historical event: the Great Leap famine. This overwhelming cataclysm, for which no Chinese leadership ever admitted responsibility, defeated forever the faith of hundreds of millions of Chinese peasants in the promises of socialism and created the political conditions for the reversal of these promises, which began after Mao's death and continues to accelerate today (Yang 1996). Few in Zhizuo spoke about the famine dead openly, except in the context of the physical and mental afflictions they brought their descendants. Nevertheless, it was clear that many people felt the unappeased presence of these dead. In 1978, after open, large-scale mortuary rituals became possible for the first time since the Great Leap, hundreds of Zhizuo families began to hold funeral rituals for people who had died twenty years before. In the 1990s, supplementary funeral rituals for these dead were still common.

After the famine, the cumulative weight of these unappeased dead had fissured the socialist vision of time, turning it repeatedly back on itself to produce critical alternative visions of state and nation. The destruction of the *ts'ici*'s reliquary box emerged as a traumatic event through cycles of repetition and return, first in the Art and Literature Propaganda troupe's tour of Chuxiong, later in tales of the wild *ts'ici* ghosts' depredations. But this event was itself the return in a focused, public form of the private grief, affliction, and rage that were the famine's residue. The living *ts'ici* system had drawn metaphorically on production and reproduction within families to create a vision of a wider domestic community. Now, in ghost stories, the violently dead *ts'ici* spirits created a vision of the bad death of the domestic unity they had once represented. These stories borrowed the tainted ancestral authority of ghosts to voice demands that can only be seen as calls for justice.

What form might such justice take? The structure of the wild ghost chronotope precluded that it might finally be revenge or reparation. As I was reminded often, the *ts'ici* ghosts were like ordinary wild ghosts (*chènè*) in that they were never satisfied—the more often they killed, the more they were appeased with offerings, the greedier they became. Every act of revenge left behind an excess, a demand for further reparation; behind each ghost was another hungry, blameworthy ghost official, all the way back to Beijing and the sea and sky beyond. Nor could justice be finally located in the new productive regime, the new denial of domestic community, in which production and reproduction were to be undertaken by individual households, linked in a web of commerce, but caught up with the state in exclusive relationships of surveillance and control (as those who find redemption for Chinese peasants in accelerating market reforms imply). The voices of the dead in the narratives retold here hint at an emergent understanding of justice in another shape altogether. The ghost of brigade Party secretary Yang Guowen at Luo Cheng's funeral voiced one such hint: "I am sorry for not attending my sister's funeral. I have been very busy, running about here and there, attending this death and that. I have many duties now, as king of the wild ghosts." Yang Guowen's reprehensible leadership and horrible death made him an intimate partner in every new bad death. In exorcising him, those whom he now afflicted implicitly accepted a degree of shared responsibility for his harmful acts and his death. Justice would mean not further revenge but, rather, an agonistic reconciliation among the living, compelled by returns of the dead.

Another hint might be found in the words of the dead *ts'ici* spirits that issued from the mouth of Qi Lin's sister nearly thirty years after her brother had betrayed both his own parents and the faltering *ts'ici* system: "If you keep letting Han plant my *yilɔmi* [ancestral trust], I will never stop killing you! Restore my *ts'ici,* or I will keep killing you!" Individual Han families planting the remnant ancestral trust fields were the most poignant sign of a new regime in which all production and reproduction were negotiated between individual households and the state. Calls for the restoration of the *ts'ici* were expressions of longing for an order that would make room for affirmations of communal reproductive power, such as the festive collective planting of the ancestral trust. Such demands for the restoration of a vision of generative community were not confined to stories about the *ts'ici* ghosts. They were elaborated with yet more force in opposition to a sustained state effort to seize and control the sources of reproductive power—the birth control campaign. Chapter 9 turns to this effort and the resistances it engendered.

CHAPTER NINE

A Shattered Gourd

"My wife and her friends are all mad [*t'æ*]," said Li Wuyi one evening. We sat by the fire eating rice in a thin broth of red beans. The moon in the courtyard was almost full. Li Wuyi's wife and daughter had gone out to dance. His maternal uncle sat at the bed's head with a bowl of grain alcohol, interrupting the conversation now and again to blow a note as he tuned the bamboo tubes of a gourd-pipe.

I already knew the story; I had heard it several times from others. Qi Ping, a grandmother in her early forties and a friend of Li Wuyi's wife, had been arrested and released a few nights before for vandalizing the brigade government building. It had happened on the fifteenth of the first lunar month. Since 1987, the township government had sponsored a Clothing Competition Festival on this date. Líp'ò and Lòlop'ò from the surrounding region came to dance, and delegations of officials visited to take photographs, make speeches, and compile reports. Qi Ping had danced for hours that night to gourd-pipe music, her fingers intertwined with the fingers of women on either side, the glossy hair of her goatskin catching the light of a bonfire in circle's center.

Near dawn, as the dancers drifted home, Qi Ping and a few friends walked the short path to the brigade government building. The gates were locked, but earlier that night youths had broken down the post on which one gate swung, leaving a gap between gate and wall. The building was empty. Most years, visiting officials slept in its guest rooms; this year, beds had been prepared for them in the school instead, and the school principal had quietly locked them into their rooms after dark. Qi Ping slipped inside.

Birth planning regulations had been lettered on a plastered wall of the porch: each couple was to be limited to two children; a third would be allowed if one of the first two could be certified physically or mentally handicapped; an interval of three to five years should follow each birth; marriage should be delayed until the age of twenty-four for women and twenty-six for men. Somewhere in one of the locked offices upstairs was a list of about three hundred names, written in ball-point pen on a stack of paper—the names of women targeted for sterilization in the birth planning campaign that had ended two weeks before. Someone, probably the youths who had broken the gate, had overturned the tables and thrown the pots and pans into the courtyard. Qi Ping danced around the courtyard, shouting and kicking a pot until her husband found her and hustled her home.

"It's the madness of itchy feet [*chǐlæ*]," said Li Wuyi. "Some women, my wife and her brother's wife, for instance, have this strange affliction. On certain days in the spring, if they don't dance, their legs itch fiercely, as if with a rash." Throughout Li Wuyi's lifetime, even during the worst years of the Cultural Revolution, people had gathered to dance in outdoor sites on the first and fifteenth nights of the first lunar month. On those nights, Li Wuyi said, you can hear couples arguing: "He's tired; he wants to go home. She wants to stay and dance until dawn. 'If I don't dance, my feet will itch!' 'Dance on the road! Dance in the courtyard at home!'"

The morning after her dance, a policeman visiting from the township arrested Qi Ping and questioned her before the brigade cadres. What had she been thinking? The policeman was young, puzzled, and impatient. Qi Ping remained silent; the brigade chief explained that sometimes some women just go mad. It had happened before. During the Clothing Competition Festival of 1989, after dancing energetically all night, Qi Ping and Li Wuyi's wife, Li Siping, had stormed the brigade government building. They had overturned the table and benches on the porch, burst into the kitchen, and thrown the pots and pans on the floor. Superstition was to blame, the brigade chief said. The women thought they were possessed by a ghost, and they went mad. The policeman had other things on his mind—identifying those who had done the real damage to the brigade government building, finding the person who had burned down the bridge at the valley's tail, and investigating rumors of threats to the brigade Party secretary's life. Qi Ping was released, and her husband was warned to keep her from dancing for a while.

This book has investigated transactions between intimate practices of the everyday and the imagined state and nation. My questions about these transactions have taken many forms. How did people in this mountainous corner of China draw on the intricacies of ritual to imagine state power and its effects? How did images of the state intersect circuits of debt and nurture between children and their parents, living or dead? How were such images refracted into the courtyards and upstream rooms of houses as guarantors of patriarchal authority, or as bearers of violence and pain? How did people manipulate memory, language, and ritual to deal with memories of past violence, to seek relief from their continued effects, and to apportion responsibility for their origins? How did practices of the everyday become resources with which to explore questions of community and justice? In response to these questions, a narrative of the relations between daily life and the distant image of the state has emerged from my informants' stories about the past. It is a critical narrative, full of irony, productive of subversive tactics and alternative visions. It describes a gradual movement of the imagined state from outside to inside, from alien to intimate. At the same time, it depicts a widening rift between the everyday and the imagined state and nation.

Stripped to a simple plot line, the narrative goes something like this. In the remembered *ts'ici* system of the 1940s, the state was an external Other, defining a houselike community within. A generative union at the core of this community combined the principles of affinity and descent that animated household relations. This union excluded the imagined state from community affairs, drawing its agents in only to send them on their way and managing the social and moral threats their incursions entailed. In the early 1950s, the new socialist state exhumed and reoccupied the intimately lived landscape, installing itself at the center of communal life as the generative origin of production and collective reproduction. By the end of the 1950s, images of the state as a generative force had become associated with the implacable avarice of the ghosts of those who had died during the famine. During the Cultural Revolution, the state, personified as the specter of Chairman Mao, possessed the bodies and speech of youthful activists and hapless cadres, as famine and chaos were traced to a double origin: to the distant, imagined centers of state and nation, on the one hand, and to the actions of kin and friends, on the other. As state power grew increasingly intimate, infusing the very bodies of children and friends, it became ever more elusive, more spectral, more difficult to grasp and comprehend. The advent of household cultivation in the 1980s accelerated this divergence. As households became the central focus of the arts of governance, the redistributive power of the state moved out of the hands of basic-level cadres to both the market and a network of bureaucratic agencies. The state became faceless, unlikely to be found personified in the everyday, in human form.

Stating it thus makes it abundantly clear that this narrative is an artifice. It is the product of a collective effort, of my informants in dialogue with myself, to give past time a clear trajectory in relation to the concerns of the present. As such, however, it illuminates with precision the most pressing of these concerns, the unvoiced background for Li Wuyi's amused tale of Qi Ping's pot-kicking dance: the birth planning campaign that was under way at the time. Birth planning was the end point of this narrative, the culmination of the state's transformation from personified external Other to abstract internal Other.

Birth planning gave the state access to the most intimate of all realms. Surgeons' scalpels made this access material as they cut into female bodies to perform IUD insertions, tubal ligations, and abortions—the predominant contraceptive methods in rural areas. The objects of these surgical incisions, wombs (*dolomo*), were the most intimate places of all, and fundamental to every vision of social unity. In ritual, wombs expanded into a series of rectilinear shapes: granaries, door frames, reliquary boxes, upstream rooms, and square-cornered mountain valleys, where opposite and complementary principles like male and female, descent and affinity merged to form new social relations and beings. And for those who endured contraceptive surgeries, wombs were direct sources of physical strength and spiritual exuberance. As it directed the scalpels of birth planning surgeons, the state penetrated the social to its mythical origins and the corporeal to its material core.

Yet this state was more evasive of attempts to represent and comprehend it than ever before. It no longer possessed its agents; they no longer voiced personal commitment to its policies; they simply repeated them as emanating from higher sources. In justifying these policies, they no longer appealed to class struggle or even to personal enrichment but to the utterly abstract issues of the "quantity and quality of the population" (Ch. *renkou shuliang yu suzhi*). The rift between the effects of the state on the most intimate aspects of the everyday, on the one hand, and the possibilities for imagining it fully and vividly, on the other hand, was at its widest.

The tale of Qi Ping's pot-kicking dance explored this rift, its confusion, and its costs. Like so many other stories retold here, it emerged in dialogue among several men, some of them implicated in its every turn, one whose lack of history or kin made him a convenient repository for stories of this kind. It was a tale about the afflictions of another—and between its words, as though through the weave of a bamboo sieve, the shadow of yet another could be glimpsed. The shape and attitude of this second Other were difficult to discern, yet they determined the meaning of the tale, the motivations of its players, the past it elaborated, the future it projected. As always, place was crucial. My interlocutors mentioned a few particulars: the lettered wall, the locked office above, the courtyard with its overturned tables and scattered pots, the circles of Qi Ping's dance. Through these details of place, one can discern the ambiguous shape of that baffling Other: written authority transmitted from an indeterminate source above.

As always, this Other can be envisioned only in relation to an object. That object, the target of the authoritative writing lettered on the walls and penned on stacks of paper, was no longer mainly production; it was a problematic, reproducing population. The principal material foundation for this authority was no longer productive fields; it was fertile wombs. These wombs were numbered and assessed in records and reports—more than three hundred of the most problematic were named in a list in the locked office above. Qi Ping's name was not on that list, but those of several of her friends waiting outside were, and her daughter lay in bed ill from the surgery. "She is mad," the brigade chief told the township policeman. "My wife and her friends are all mad," Li Wuyi said to me. Yet both dissembled, for both knew that there is no such thing as, simply, "madness": all madness has a specific origin that may be divined and named, and the route back to that origin is everything.

What was this origin? Qi Ping remained silent after her release, and my male informants reached no consensus. Li Wuyi's best guess was a revealing joke—the madness of "itchy feet." He attributed this malady to a group of women in early middle age, including his wife, who had played active parts in the chaos of the Cultural Revolution. *Le,* "to itch," is a euphemism for *t'a,* "to lust"; it denotes the unpredictable, chaotic, and even fearsome nature of feminine sexuality, with a material foundation in the womb. Cutting into wombs harmed individual bodies and penetrated the social institution of community to the quick, but it also released forces of chaos and exuberance associated with feminine reproductive potential.

Qi Ping's dance was among many acts of rebellion against a campaign of compulsory sterilization carried out in Zhizuo in the spring of 1993. Since the beginning of the one-child campaign in China in 1978, central officials and cultural elites had effected a thorough redefinition of "minorities," as troubled populations in need of eugenic reform. The one-child campaign had twin goals: improving the "quality" of the national population was as urgent as controlling its quantity. In the interest of older goals of "nationality unity," most members of minority groups had been allowed more than one child in the past. In the more recent discourses about "population quality," however, many minorities were repeatedly cited as exemplary of the low quality of China's rural population. "Feudal" and "backward," the minorities of the country's western half were seen to be plagued by inbreeding that led to genetic inferiority. They were represented as beset by health problems, including high rates of mental illness and retardation. Their inferior maternal and infant health care was thought to produce children of low quality, with high rates of defects and deficient intelligence. In the early 1990s, these concerns led to efforts to tighten birth planning among minority populations in provinces throughout western China. Yunnan issued more restrictive regulations for its minorities in 1991, and, in the spring of 1993, Yongren County carried out an intensive sterilization campaign in its mountainous minority regions.

This final chapter tells the story of this birth planning campaign as a tale of the widening rift between the everyday and the imagined state. This campaign's goal was to sterilize all women under the age of forty-two who had borne two or more healthy children. Although tubal ligation was accepted as relatively harmless in many parts of rural China, in Zhizuo it conflicted with deep-seated ideas about the flows of sexual energy through the body and the evil capacity of blockages or reversals in such flows to reverberate through the closely inhabited world. Women targeted for sterilization feared that it would obstruct the currents of sexual energy through their bodies. Thus, along with losing their capacity to renew their families in case of death, they would be robbed of the physical energy they needed to sustain their households, and they would lose their enthusiasm for sexual activity and their exuberance for life—all this for the goal of improving the "quality" of an abstract national population in which their own place was increasingly uncertain. The campaign had many victims. Among them were more than eighty young women compelled to undergo tubal ligation, who experienced fear, humiliation, and varying degrees of physical debilitation. Also among the victims was the young brigade Party secretary who brought the campaign to Zhizuo. Generally powerless, invested at this moment with a frightening power over his friends, parents, affines, and enemies, he began the campaign with hopeful visions of personal advancement and ended it in isolation and despair. All of these victims were caught between harsh violations of their most intimate everyday worlds and the oppressive difficulty of imagining the ultimate agent of these violations.

Birth Planning in Zhizuo

Michel Foucault noted that the regulation of population in relation to economy is the "ultimate end" of the modern state (1991, 103). "It is the population itself," Foucault wrote, "on which [modern] government will act directly or indirectly through techniques that will make possible, without the full awareness of the people, the stimulation of birth rates, the direction of the flow of population into certain regions or activities, etc. . . . The population is the subject of needs, of aspirations, but it is also the object in the hands of the government" (1991, 100). Frank Dikötter (1995) has shown that the regulation of the quantity and quality of the population (Ch. *renkou*) in the name of national rejuvenation was a preeminent concern among the cultural and intellectual elites who envisioned modern government for China in the early twentieth century. In its own program for national rejuvenation, the socialist state began to display a concern with the size and rates of growth of the population in the early 1950s, as it developed a comprehensive economic planning process.

The first national birth planning (Ch. *jihua shengyu*) movement, in the 1950s, focused on propaganda and on the production and distribution of contraceptives, especially condoms, diaphragms, and contraceptive foams and jellies. Though most of this activity appears to have been concentrated in large cities, birth planning also reached the top of the agenda in the remote prefectural capital of Chuxiong in 1957. A birth planning guidance committee was created to propagandize cadres, and exhibitions were organized to demonstrate the use of contraceptives and sell them at low prices (CYZZ 1993, 347). As the Great Leap Forward gathered steam in 1958, however, pronatalism became an element of the optimism required of all cadres, and birth planning advocates were attacked as rightist enemies.

After the Great Leap, the center announced new efforts to promote birth control. Party documents echoed Mao's words: birth control would "move the birth problem gradually from a state of anarchy to one of planning" (White 1994, 274). In Chuxiong, birth planning committees were created for each county, and plans were formed to carry out propaganda "first in the cities then in the countryside, first in the plains then in the mountains." Counties printed handbooks explaining the benefits of contraception and once again held photograph exhibitions and slide shows to demonstrate contraceptive technologies (CYZZ 1993, 348). Before plans to train cadres in the countryside in birth planning work could be put into effect, however, the campaign was interrupted by the advent of the Cultural Revolution in 1966. The issue of birth planning was marginalized for several years as radical politics dominated the agenda.

These first two birth planning movements reached into Yunnan's county towns, but they had minimal effect in the rural areas.[1] It was during the third mobilization, in the mid-1970s, that birth planning was first carried out systematically in Yunnan's countryside. Dubbed the "later, longer, fewer" campaign, this was an intensive, well-organized mass mobilization. It encouraged couples to marry later, wait three to five years between births, and have only two children. The campaign was very successful in controlling fertility in the cities, and it created a dramatic decline in birth rates in many rural areas as well (Chen 1976; Greenhalgh 1993). The movement produced an extensive infrastructure for birth planning work throughout the country. Each of Chuxiong's counties developed a Birth Planning Small Group. County hospitals created birth planning departments, opened birth planning leadership offices, and trained clinicians in the "four surgeries": vasectomy, tubal ligation, IUD insertion, and abortion. County towns held mass training sessions for teams that would tour the countryside and perform contraceptive surgery at village clinics (CYZZ 1993, 347). Beginning in 1973, more than sixty thousand sterilizations, abortions, and IUD insertions were performed each year in the prefecture, as compared to about seventy-five hundred total before 1970. Chuxiong's "later, longer, fewer" campaign culminated in 1979 with a mass meeting in which a large group of pregnant women who had already borne two or more children were "energetically required to adopt remedial measures": after the meeting, 2,597 abortions were performed in twenty days (CYZZ 1993, 354).

Such measures were not applied in most minority areas. The campaign aimed to provide birth control for people with minority status only at their request (Zhang Z. 1986; Peng 1991). A surgical team visited Zhizuo periodically, giving residents their first exposure to any but traditional contraceptive methods.[2] The team performed IUD insertions, tubal ligations, and abortions in improvised clinics in the elementary school and the medical clinic. Women with two or more children were encouraged to undergo one of these surgeries, but no structure of inducements and penalties was introduced to force compliance. During the "later, longer, fewer" campaign, Yunnan's crude birth rate declined from 34 births per thousand to 25 (YSTRB 1990). Nevertheless, the large minority population in Yunnan made the campaign less effective there than in most of China. By 1979, a smaller percentage of fertile couples (54.6 percent) used contraceptives in Yunnan than in any other province but one.

Compulsory birth planning was introduced to Zhizuo in late 1982 and early 1983. The center had announced the one-child policy three years earlier. In response, Yunnan created birth planning regulations differentiating border regions from internal regions, mountains from basins, the countryside from the city, and minority populations from Han (DZY 1991, 2:189). These regulations permitted couples who were both members of a minority to raise two children, regardless of the sex of the first. They also allowed two children to couples in rural households who faced practical difficulties. Chuxiong's regulations were slightly more liberal, proceeding on the principle that "one child is best, a planned second child is permitted at most" (CYZZ 1993, 351–352). Each set of regulations mandated that three to five years should separate births and that all couples should marry late: women should be encouraged to marry only after the age of twenty-four, men after the age of twenty-six.

Before the rural reforms, cadres in nonminority rural areas had encouraged birth planning through structures of incentives and disincentives. Incentives included maternity leave; extra grain or work points; priority in health care, education, and employment; and distribution of housing plots. Disincentives included the loss of work points and the loss of entitlements to private vegetable plots and housing plots for over-quota children. The introduction of responsibility systems, however, had transformed the style of birth planning enforcement. By the early 1980s, rural cadres no longer distributed resources such as work points or higher education. Contracting land to households had also increased the labor value of children, and expanded incomes made fines for over-quota births less effective.[3] Birth planning agencies responded with renewed efforts to mobilize cadres to carry out high-intensity birth planning campaigns, modeled on the mass mobilizations of the Mao era (White 1992). In Chuxiong, a national "birth planning propaganda month" in January 1983 began an intensive effort to extend compulsory birth planning to mountainous minority districts. More than seven thousand new birth planning cadres were trained, and more than seventeen thousand birth planning surgeries were performed in this one month (CYZZ 1993, 354). In this new atmosphere, Zhizuo residents were subjected to intense pressure to limit births for the first time.

⌒

Compulsory birth planning quickly became the most important work of Zhizuo's government. The brigade Party secretary was the birth planning leader, answerable to higher-level authorities. One special birth planning cadre, a young woman, was responsible for birth planning education and propaganda. A female "barefoot doctor" performed gynecological exams and IUD insertion and removal in the village medical clinic. The other four brigade cadres also shared duties of dispensing propaganda, writing reports, and making household visits during birth planning campaigns. Little birth planning work was carried out during the ordinary course of governance. Instead, cadres waited for periodic birth planning campaigns to be organized at higher levels. Indeed, many in Zhizuo believed that cadres allowed couples to have over-quota births during ordinary times to make it easier to complete their quotas of fines to be collected, IUDs to be inserted, and sterilizations to be performed during the campaigns.[4]

Campaigns lasted from a few days to several weeks. Some were simply for propaganda and education; others set specific targets for collecting fines and performing medical procedures. Many included mass meetings, often planned to coincide with the visits of township- or county-level cadres. In the post-Mao era, cadres could no longer simply call a meeting and expect the "masses" to attend. Instead, they sent a youth with a mule to the township center to retrieve a popular film, a projector, and a screen, to be set up outdoors at dusk. The price of admission was to sit through an hour or so of birth planning speeches by local and visiting cadres.

Beyond propaganda, the key work of birth planning campaigns involved door-to-door visits to negotiate with fertile couples. On these visits, cadres attempted to coax women with two children to have an IUD insertion, to persuade those with three or more children to undergo sterilization, or to collect fines for over-quota births. Stainless steel ring IUDs and sterilization were the predominant forms of contraception used in China, accounting for 85.4 percent of all birth control in

1982 and 90.69 percent by 1988 (Deng 1992). Other contraceptives were available at the township clinic, but cadres did not promote them, finding them too difficult to monitor and evaluate. Cadres did not bother with the modest and ineffective rewards allowed by birth planning regulations, such as monthly health stipends and nutrition allowances. Instead, they alternated verbal persuasion with threats of heavy fines and compulsory sterilization. Few in Zhizuo could pay cash fines, but cadres could confiscate livestock from couples with over-quota births. Exemptions from fines or confiscation were frequently granted in exchange for sterilization. Most in Zhizuo feared sterilization: rarely would a man agree to a vasectomy, and few women would assent to tubal ligation after bearing only two children. The infant mortality rate in Zhizuo had historically been very high;[5] there was still little medical care for infants and new mothers; and women feared that if they agreed to sterilization they might lose a child and be unable to bear another. Those women sterilized in the 1980s accepted the operation reluctantly, as the alternative to a ruinous fine, only after giving birth to a third child.

Brigade cadres found these negotiations with their kin, friends, and neighbors onerous. In many campaigns, they relied on the help of a birth planning implementation team from the township. Since the cadres of this team were not locals, they could afford to threaten harsh penalties without fearing reprisals and without being swayed by sympathy for any household's particular plight. The chief intent of birth planning in Zhizuo was to limit births to two children per couple. Brigade and township cadres considered late marriage regulations unenforceable. They were well aware that local sexual practices exceeded the official designation of "'sex' as a procreative act to be performed on the legal site of domesticity" (Dikötter 1995, 186). As described in chapter 3, sex was an accepted aspect of the courting process, which began around the age of fourteen. Girls often became pregnant before reaching the age at which they could legally marry (twenty for women and twenty-two for men under the 1981 marriage law). Abortion was a common consequence of premarital pregnancy. Some girls had babies while living in their parents' houses and continuing to seek spouses. Many moved into partners' households while still teenagers and waited to register the marriage until both partners reached the legal age. Marriage registration was necessary to hold a wedding, but weddings were easily timed to coincide with the legal age of marriage, since by custom nearly all wedding ceremonies were delayed until several years after a couple began cohabiting, usually until after the birth of a first child. In the 1980s, brigade cadres did not try to fine couples who cohabited before registering their marriages.[6] In addition, they did not attempt to make newly married couples postpone their first child, did not demand that women with one child accept IUD insertions, and did not collect fines from those who failed to space their births by three to five years.

In carrying out birth planning, local cadres acted as reluctant agents for a masterful state, whose specific demands might be evaded or manipulated, but whose general intent to control the population (Ch. *kongzhi renkou*) infused every aspect of reproductive activity. Brigade cadres made it clear that they did not wish to press for birth planning; this was the state's requirement, not their own. In struggling to mediate between the demands of higher levels and the reluctance of locals, they negotiated compromises to every formal birth planning regulation: some they diluted; others they reshaped; many they made no attempt to implement. Their informal rules for enforcing penalties and exacting birth planning surgeries were fluid, hardening in response to more stringent demands from above, softening in negotiation with specific households. Yet this very fluidity made every reproductive act a matter of official concern, demanding far more exhaustive scrutiny and arbitration than a clear structure of strictly enforced policies would have required. It was brigade and township cadres who surveilled, negotiated, exacted penalties, and operated on bodies. Yet in contrast to the situation in other eras, no cadre could voice wholehearted commitment to state policies; all deferred the responsibility for birth planning policies to higher levels. None claimed to embody the state, as many had in the Mao era. The effect was to represent a state that was impossible to grasp in concrete or human form — everywhere present but nowhere personified, and obsessively concerned with human reproduction.

Zhizuo residents were accustomed to imagining society as instituted in the acts of bearing and nourishing children. Their retrospective dreams of the *ts'ici* system refashioned a former social community as a (re)productive unity, instituted anew each year in the reliquary box's bridal procession, renewed each season in acts of insemination, conception, birthing, and cultivation performed on the muddy womb-fields of the ancestral trust. Now, bearing and nourishing children instituted a relation not with a social community but with an extrasocial state. This relation was no longer founded primarily on productive labor, as it had been in the Mao era. It emerged instead from fertile, sexed bodies: each reproductive act — marrying or not, bearing children or not, undergoing surgery or not—positioned each household member in relation to an all-important fertile womb. And this relation gave each member an age- and gender-specific place in the new social community: the problematic population, project of state power and its raison d'être. Cadres repeatedly proved to fertile couples that their well-being crucially depended on the population, both local and national—its rates of growth, its age structures, and, most important, the area of arable land it allowed to each member. Cadres learned to manipulate demographic statistics expertly to link local poverty with the problem of too many people reproducing too quickly on too little land. But in the early 1990s, this talk began to change. Cadres began to lace their birth planning lectures at evening films with references to "population quality" and to show how the local population was particularly deficient in this regard. Economically and culturally backward, with below average "quality of body" and high incidence of genetic disease, the local minority population was in need of intensive measures of control and reform. This talk associated Zhizuo Lòlop'ò with the Yi population, which had reached 6 million strong and was rapidly growing. And it made the case that this population was responsible for curbing its own growth in the service of national eugenic goals.

A Quality Population

In the early 1990s, demographers and birth planners took note of an "explosion" of unplanned births in the countryside, a growing "floating population" of peasants who had left their villages to seek work elsewhere (among whom birth planning was particularly difficult), and a coming "third baby boom" as those born during a surge in fertility rates following the Great Leap married and bore children. In response, Party leaders sought to extend the reach of the institutional networks that supported birth planning to the village level, where they would routinize and rationalize birth planning work. Increased funds were directed to rural birth planning stations and contraceptive surgery teams; responsibility systems that rewarded cadres who carried out birth planning successfully and punished those who did not were given new teeth; fines for peasants who gave birth to extra children were increased; and households that could not pay those fines were denied land contracts. Some provinces began to construct retirement schemes for peasants so that they would no longer have to rely entirely on their children to support them in their old age (Greenhalgh and Li 1995).

Central leaders articulated a vision of "holistic" birth planning. Material production and population production should no longer be thought of as separate, they declared. As the forces of material production were gradually released to the control of the market, population production should become the focus of every aspect of the state's work. Long-term economic well-being depended on further reducing the rate of population growth, but just as important was the population's quality. A quality population could be achieved only by drawing together every strand of the work of the state into a coordinated network of institutions and practices. Song Ping, then a member of the Party's Political Bureau Standing Committee, set forth this vision in a *People's Daily* article in February 1993:

> It is necessary to associate material production with population production and associate population production with all aspects of our work. We should adopt a holistic concept of population, which is called by some comrades a "macro concept of population." As the work on family planning cannot be divorced from economic development . . . we must integrate the effort to solve the problem of population with such issues as developing the economy, supporting poor areas and helping them tap their potentialities, turning resources to rational use, protecting the environment, universalizing education, improving the conditions of medical care and public health, improving family welfare, and solving the [problems caused by the] aging of the population. . . . In conducting family planning it is imperative to attach importance to eugenics and sound child rearing. The quality of the population has a bearing on the rise or fall of the nation and future generations. (*Renmin ribao,* 9 February 1993, 3)

In the interest of population quality, the rural population was to be managed directly by an integrated network of bureaucratic state institutions, through projects of economic development, socialist education, health care delivery, pension plans, postnatal education programs, and welfare programs.

The notion that population quality was crucial for the nation's future had gained overwhelming support among Chinese intellectuals and planners in the late 1980s and 1990s. This issue had its roots in early twentieth-century discourses about racial rejuvenation and national renewal. Intellectual elites in the Republican era had expressed concern over birth rates that were higher among the masses than in the educated classes. Some had worried that birth control programs might allow mentally and physically deficient lower classes to swamp the professional classes, who practiced birth control (Dikötter 1995, 120). Many intellectuals in the post-Mao era believed that these predictions had been borne out after several decades of comprehensive birth planning. The health of China's population; its physical stature; its levels of intelligence, culture, and education; its mental health; and the quality of its "thought and morality" were of grave concern, particularly among those who had been allowed to reproduce the most—the rural population, especially its least developed and most culturally backward sectors. Without a comprehensive program to improve population quality, the nation would not compete successfully in the marketplace of the next century.

One object of this discourse was mental and physical defects that were thought to be genetic. In 1988, Gansu Province passed the country's first eugenics (Ch. *yousheng*) law, requiring mentally retarded people to be sterilized before they were permitted to marry. The law was directed at people whose condition was thought to be either inherited or the result of marriage between close relatives, but, as Frank Dikötter (1998, 178) points out, genetic factors were frequently named as the causes of mental health problems that were actually rooted in diet deficiencies (especially the lack of iodine). A national eugenics law went into effect in 1995, prohibiting those with "serious hereditary" disorders, venereal diseases, severe psychosis, or inheritable infectious diseases from reproducing. The law required prenatal testing, followed by termination of the pregnancy if the fetus had a serious genetic or somatic disorder. The discourse of eugenics employed a notion of heredity not limited to genetic inheritance (Dikötter 1998). On the one hand, eugenics aimed at creating a superior population through improving childbearing, nutrition, medical care, and education; on the other, it included the imperative to limit the reproduction of those portions of the population deemed incorrigibly backward in economic and cultural terms. "Idiots breed idiots," as Li Peng famously put it—but the poor, uneducated, undernourished, and medically underprivileged also breed the poor, undereducated, and unhealthy. Many demographers noted that birth planning had been more successful in urban areas than in the countryside, more successful among the literate, the affluent, and the healthy than among the illiterate, the impoverished, and the mentally and physically disabled. Echoing the rhetoric of early twentieth-century eugenicists, a pair of birth planning theorists declared in the prominent Party journal *Qiushi* that the result was "a phenomenon of negative selection [Ch. *nitaotai*] within the population":

> The better-educated urban population is being submerged by a surging wave of rural births; the population size in industrialized zones is being left far behind by the population size in agricultural regions; the rural population is growing faster in impoverished areas than in more affluent ones; and we have large numbers of above-quota births in areas with high illiteracy rates, while the areas with better-educated populations practice family planning. With regard to the contrast between the healthy and disabled, healthy couples are satisfied with having one healthy child, while the disabled population's multiple births probably result in children with various types of hereditary diseases. (Yan and Jin 1992, 41)[7]

The urban/rural distinction was one axis on which the qualities of different populations could be compared; another was the divide between Han and minority populations, especially those of the nation's western half. These non-Han populations were overwhelmingly agricultural and often poor in addition to being relatively uneducated with high rates of illiteracy. They were seen as prone to mental and physical disabilities, as a result of "early marriage and marriage between close relatives." They were rife with "goiters," "dementia," "retardation," and other diseases and conditions, most of which were "probably hereditary" (Yan and Jin 1992, 40–41). A new scientific discourse also evaluated and compared the population quality of different minorities. One study (Zhang 1995) devised a Population Quality Index to rank the nation's eighteen minority populations that numbered more than a million.[8] Population quality, the author declared, has three aspects: "quality of body, quality of culture, and quality of thoughts and morals." Only the first two can be measured easily—quality of body by measuring infant mortality and life expectancy at age one, and quality of culture by measuring relative rates of graduation from elementary school, middle school, high school, and college. Weighting these measurements heavily in favor of quality of body, the study compared the qualities of China's minorities to those of the populations of other continents. The Korean and Manchu populations, in the heavily developed northeast, achieved scores as high as those of North Americans, while Tibetans, Yi, and Hani (another Tibeto-Burman–speaking minority in the southwest) had the worst quality, comparable to that of Africans (Zhang 1995, 24). Other studies measured "quality of thought," using standardized cognitive tests to compare spatial and temporal cognition, analytic and synthetic cognition, perception, and reasoning among different minority groups (Zheng 1996). The minorities of "remote" and "economically backward" regions proved to have the least developed cognitive skills."

This discourse drew urgency from observations that the relative leniency of birth planning policies for minorities had allowed their populations to surge relative to the size of the Han majority. The 1990 census revealed that since 1982, the minority nationality population had grown 38.7 percent, compared to the national growth rate of 14.7 percent, increasing from 6.7 to 8.0 percent of the population (Yang 1993). In Yunnan, the growth rate of minority nationality populations was 29.9 percent in the same period, 17.22 percent greater than that of the Han population (Zou and Miao 1989, 528). Many demographers were careful to point out that much of this growth was a result of changes in nationality composition: since the end of the Cultural Revolution, many more Chinese had claimed minority status than before, including most children of mixed minority-Han marriages. Nevertheless, some birth planners raised nightmare scenarios, claiming that unless population growth in minority areas was more strictly controlled, the minority population could reach 567 million by the year 2048—a shocking 28.5 percent of the national population (Yan and Jin 1992, 38). Moreover, it was clear that populations most deficient in quality were growing the fastest: the natural rates of increase among minorities with high rates of illiteracy and infant mortality were the highest (Yang 1993; Song and Cui 1993).

Yongren County, where Zhizuo was located, was a case in point. By standards of the 1970s and 1980s, Yongren's birth planning was a success. The crude birth rate had dropped from 20.9 per thousand in 1981 to 17.8 in 1988, much lower than the 1988 provincial rate of 24.0 per thousand (YSTRB 1990). But for those concerned with population quality, Yongren was a clear example of "negative selection." Birth rates were much higher among the county's fifty thousand Yi than among its Han population. In 1955, 40 percent of the population had been Yi and other minorities; this had grown to 46 percent by 1980 and to 50 percent by 1988 (YSTRB 1990). These minorities lived in the county's mountainous regions, where the arable land per capita was minuscule and most households depended heavily on relief grain. They were the least educated and least healthy segment of the population with the highest infant mortality rates, shortest life expectancy, smallest stature and chest size, and highest rates of heritable disease. Stricter birth planning among this population became an urgent new priority.

☙

In 1991, Yunnan adopted revised birth planning laws, stipulating that one member of every couple of childbearing age with two or more children was to be sterilized. Sterilization, especially of women, had become the contraceptive method of choice for family planners in much of rural China. In most localities, the only IUD available was the single-ring stainless steel IUD, which had a failure and expulsion rate of about 14.3 percent. Nationally, IUD failure had been identified as an important cause of over-quota births (Kaufman et al. 1992, 78; Tu 1995). Planners in Yunnan noted a proliferation of illegal IUD removals by "witches and witch doctors" and other traditional healers. Vasectomy had gradually fallen out of favor among local birth planners in all but a few locations (notably the Sichuan basin) because it encountered too much resistance among men. In contrast, women in many parts of China had come to view tubal ligation operations as relatively innocuous (Greenhalgh and Li 1995). By 1988, sterilization, largely of women, was the birth control method of 49.2 percent of couples of childbearing age nationwide (Deng 1993). In the early 1990s, in the climate of heightened concern over "population quality," Yongren County administrators chose to carry out the new provincial regulations to the letter. Even minority couples who were allowed two children would be sterilized after the second birth. In early 1993, the county planned an intensive campaign to be focused on the minority population, designed to accomplish the sterilization of every eligible woman.

A Gathering, with Wolves

Zhizuo's Party secretary Qi Haiyun told me about the campaign's beginnings one glum October afternoon in Yongren's county town. I ran into him in the street, slogging through the rain with his two-year-old son on his back. We shared tea in a stall while we waited for the rainy-season downpour to let up. Qi was an edgy, intelligent man of twenty-five, and one of my first friends in Zhizuo. He had grown up in one of the poor villages on the valley's shady side, where water for irrigation was scarce and the fields were small and rocky. He graduated from middle school and married without a certificate at eighteen; his bride had been sixteen. They had lived in Qi's parents' house ever since. Their first child was a girl, now seven years old; the boy was their second. On the strength of his middle-school grades, Qi had been selected to attend a four-month literacy course in the provincial capital shortly after his marriage.[9] This made him a natural candidate for quick advancement in the brigade government. He had attained the post of Party secretary only a month previously, after the former secretary was demoted over the planting of the ancestral trust. Before this, Qi had frequently taken me aside to ask my opinion on schemes for escaping a poor peasant's life—attending college in Australia, perhaps, or teaching Yi language in Japan. The post of brigade Party secretary paid a meager salary and required him to continue farming his household's land. It was not much of a life, he told me, but he was stuck with it for now. Still, the sterilization campaign might prove an opportunity to show higher officials that he was capable of greater things.

The campaign had begun with a countywide meeting of basic-level Party secretaries. It was imperative, they were told, that they lead their brigades to sterilize all eligible women quickly and comprehensively. Qi Haiyun was promised the full support of the township birth planning team and the police bureau. He had no means to resist, even had he wanted to do so. He commanded none of the power to accumulate and allocate state resources that brigade leaders had wielded in the Mao era, and he lacked the networks of informal relations (Ch. *guanxi*) among higher-level Party and government officials that many had developed since. His ability to make this campaign a success was key to his further advancement, not to mention that of several officials of Zhonghe township, where Zhizuo was the largest and most "backward" brigade.

At the meeting, Qi pledged that every eligible woman in his brigade would be sterilized before spring planting. On the principle that cadres should lead by example, the women of his own household—his wife and his mother—would be first. That had been two weeks before. The previous day, Qi Haiyun and his wife, Li Yuming, had walked to the Yongren People's Hospital, where she was given a tubal ligation. For the next few days, she stayed in bed in a guest room, unhappy and in pain, while Qi Haiyun wandered the mud-sodden streets with his child. Eventually, bus service having been suspended by the rain, the four of us walked back to Zhizuo together over washed-out mountain paths, a fifty-kilometer journey. Qi Haiyun perched the toddler on the back of a borrowed burro so that Li Yuming would not have to carry baggage. Still, abdominal cramps forced her to rest frequently. On arriving home at dusk, she went directly to bed, where she stayed, intermittently ill, for the next three months.

In Zhizuo, the campaign was delayed for weeks while Qi Haiyun argued with other brigade cadres about tactics. Eventually, Qi walked to the township with a borrowed mule and brought back a movie. He spent a day setting up generator, projector, and screen on a hill between Zhizuo's two largest villages. By dark, hundreds of people had found their way up the hill with flashlights and pine torches. With the generator rumbling in the background and the light from the projector illuminating him like a spotlight, Qi Haiyun stood to announce the campaign. Every woman in the brigade under the age of forty-two who had already borne her quota of two children was to be sterilized before the spring planting season, he said. Each morning, the brigade government would post in each village a list of women to be sterilized. The lists would begin with women under thirty with two or more children who had had an abortion. Next would be all other eligible women under thirty. Women in their thirties and early forties would be last. The day after her name was published, each woman would walk the twenty kilometers to the township birth planning clinic, where the operation would be performed. If she failed to show up, she would be fined 300 yuan, her household's livestock would be confiscated, and she would be handcuffed and led to the clinic, where the operation would be performed without anesthetic.

On finishing his speech, Qi Haiyun signaled to the projectionist. The film, intended simply to entertain, was a spectacularly bad choice, a thriller about a pack of wolves invading a mountain village somewhere in the southwest. It featured gruesome scenes of wolves devouring helpless women and young children. Angered and confused by Qi Haiyun's speech, most adults left early. The children and adolescents who remained sat entranced as shaggy mongrels, playing wolves, coursed over walls and through doorways. The next morning, the names of twenty young women, brushed in black ink on red poster paper, were posted in central locations around Zhizuo.

Spayed Pigs and Fire Tongs

Initially, Qi Haiyun's threats were very effective. In the first two weeks of the campaign, all those whose names were posted walked to the clinic for the operation. During that time, I sometimes sat up at night drinking with men who agonized over whether to encourage their wives, daughters, or daughters-in-law to have the surgery. These men were furious at Qi Haiyun, fearful for their female kin, and terrified of the consequences of resistance. "They want to sterilize them just like pigs," Li Haicheng fumed after a great-niece was listed. "They want to do them one after another, without anesthetic, like animals." Many others also compared tubal ligation to spaying sows.

The uneven efforts of birth planning teams to disseminate information about contraceptive surgeries had never provided a more vivid or accessible model. Spaying was a common operation, performed at home by ordinary men who had learned the skill from other locals. Sows ready for spaying were already large; it took two or three agile men to catch one and pin it to the ground. The surgeon made a two-inch incision in its side with a sharp knife and slipped his fingers into the wound. He felt for the ovaries, pulled them out, tied the tubes on both sides with thread, cut the ovaries free, slipped the cut ends back into the animal, and stitched up the wound. The operation was noisy and violent. The sow screamed murder; the men swore; blood flew. Women and girls refused to participate or watch, retiring to an inner room until the pig was on its feet again. Such sights could affect a girl's chances for giving birth normally, said Li Qunhua when I asked her why, and as for old women like herself (she was thirty-nine), they found it bloody and unpleasant.

At first, I took comparisons between spaying and tubal ligation to be hyperbolic expressions of the indignity of forced mass sterilization. Soon, however, I learned that they were intended in a more precise sense. One morning, a woman of twenty-five from Qi Haiyun's village collapsed after receiving the surgery. Her family and neighbors carried her across the valley to the brigade clinic and waited outside nervously as she was treated. I ran into Li Zhiwu on the path from the clinic. He was incensed. "It's no better than castration!" he declared. That was ludicrous, I said, losing patience. Going about saying tubal ligation was like castration or spaying sows was silly and irresponsible. It was a false parallel, founded in ignorance, and it could only contribute to the misery of those forced to undergo an operation that, for all its indignities, had few side effects when performed correctly. Li Zhiwu argued with me stubbornly:

LZ: The ancient emperors used to make eunuchs to guard their concubines for them. This is the same, the same thing, only now it is being done by force.

EM: That's just not true! It's not the same at all! They don't take the ovaries out as you do with a pig; they just cut and tie the tubes.

LZ: It is the same! The same logic! Exactly the same as a pig! [On the ground he sketched two ovals, with a curved line emerging from both ends of each.] What they do is they cut the tubes here and here, the ones leading from the ovaries to the womb. That cuts off the flow of *và* [sexual fluids] to a woman's vagina. With a pig, it's very simple—you just cut the ovaries out. With people, you can't cut them out, so you cut the tubes so the organs will gradually wither and die.

EM: But this doesn't mean, as with pigs, that the woman can no longer have sex.

LZ: Never again. Her entire life. The best a couple can do is lie on the bed and feel each other; they can play around like that. But she no longer feels any interest because there is no longer any *và*. And she can do no heavy labor, because she has no explosive strength, the kind of strength that allows you to lift a load of firewood. And gradually, as the *và* backs up behind the break in the tube, her entire lower torso [Ch. *yaobu*] begins to ache, so she has difficulty moving quickly or carrying heavy loads.

EM: Yet you say that a tubal ligation is not as bad as a vasectomy!

LZ: Oh, doing it to a man is the most terrible thing. It breaks up the family, destroys the couple's relationship, and makes it almost impossible for the family to continue to exist economically.

EM: But, again, it's not the same as making an eunuch. I mean, it only keeps the semen from coming out. It doesn't affect the other functions . . .

LZ: It does! You know as well as I that for anything to happen, the man first has to get hard. Well, after this operation, he can't get hard, or he can only get slightly, momentarily hard, sort of soft hard. So the couple can no longer do it. And, since after the man is done, there is no need to do the woman, the woman feels interest while the man doesn't. So what happens to this family? The woman can only go wild [Ch. *luan*], go crazy [*t'æ*].

EM: And if it's the woman who is done, the man doesn't go *luan* or *t'æ*?

LZ: No, men can't. Men won't. After all, if it is the man who is sterilized, the couple can't do it at all. If it is the woman, the man can do it—it's just that the woman feels no interest. And if a man is sterilized, he can do no heavy labor. He can't plow or harrow. This is much worse than a woman, who doesn't have to plow anyway. You have a family where the man can't plow and the woman is *luan,* is *t'æ*. It's the same for a man as for a woman: he has no explosive strength, and his lower torso gradually begins to swell and hurt so every movement is painful.

Herbalists such as Li Zhiwu had more exposure to birth planning propaganda than most. Nevertheless, they rarely mentioned sperm and egg when speaking of conception. Instead they described a mingling of male and female sexual fluids—*và* (corresponding in many respects to the Ch. *jing* of classical Chinese medicine). In this view, a fetus developed from the dynamic interaction of semen and vaginal fluids. These were the external eruptions of flows that circulated through the body's interior at various volumes and velocities. Together with *sr̀*, "blood," and *cè*, "breath" (much like the Ch. *xue*, "blood," and Ch. *qi*, "breath," of classical Chinese medicine), they flowed through human bodies, animating them and endowing them with vital energies.

Và was the most volatile of these substances. Its interruption or excess produced abrupt and dangerous transformations in bodily equilibrium. Once for instance, when I was heading to the city for a break, Li Zhiwu told me the story of a young couple who died expending all their *và* in a single night of passion after several months apart (it was an unsubtle warning to control myself). The volatility of sexual fluids was felt in excessive retention as well as expenditure. A woman who had sexual intercourse with more than one man in a single night put herself in danger, for the fluids of the different men could do battle within her, causing sudden illness, painful swelling, and even death. In healthy bodies, the dynamic quality of *và* created surges of energy for quick movement, flashes of inspiration, and explosive strength. Sterilization operations in pigs and humans selected vital nodes in the system of flows, where intervention suspended the circulation of *và* through the entire body. Halting this flow destroyed the body's capacity for sexual interest and surges of strength or inspiration. And, as in similar blockages of sexual fluid that occurred without surgery, the ligature produced a lifelong disability (called *jotsr̀no*, or "kidney region illness"), in which the *và* gradually accumulated behind the blockage, creating chronic, painful swelling in the lower torso.

In my argument with Li Zhiwu, his talk of the flows of sexual fluids made men's and women's bodies rough equivalents. The obstruction of *và* had the same effects in each. Gender was not innate to these bodies; it was emergent in the sexual and agricultural economies of their households. Vasectomy and tubal ligation differed in their effects not on bodies but on these economies. Here, sowing and insemination were more than merely metaphors for each other; they were related materially in the flows of sexual fluids. A man who could not get hard was a man who could not plow. In this respect, vasectomy was a catastrophe: it destroyed the generative nexus of growing rice and raising children that animated household relations. Moreover, compulsory vasectomy would betray the alliance that had been constructed in the post-Mao era between male household heads and the state (discussed in chapter 3). Conflicted though this alliance was, it nevertheless encouraged male household heads to imagine their sexual and economic potency within their households as being sanctioned by the state. Properly governed, their male potency made their productive and reproductive relations social in the widest sense—contributions to the national body. Just how vital this alliance was to male household heads can be seen in the talk about the *ts'ici* system that challenged it (chapters 4 and 5). Dreaming of the past, men evoked a time when the household and community were instituted apart from the state, in the potent male acts of sowing and insemination under the authoritative gaze of the collective ancestor, Agàmisimo. Dreaming of the future, they evoked a time when the Party would sanction a restored *ts'ici* system, bringing household, community, and nation together under a single, potent sign.

In this view, tubal ligation, though unpleasant, was no catastrophe. A sterilized woman continued to contribute to the productive and reproductive economies of her household in a diminished way. She passively accepted the sexual advances of her husband, cared for her children, and performed her agricultural tasks, which required steady endurance and resistance to nagging pain rather than sudden rushes of strength. This intervention was no more than an extreme version of the sexual discipline men had long sought to impose on women (described in chapter 5). It was not the stagnation of sexual fluids that destroyed the integration of a woman's body with the sexual and agricultural dynamics of her household; it was their excess or exuberance. A woman whose sexuality was not domesticated through intercourse with her husband went *luan*, running about chaotically, and she went *t'e*, mad from an excess of sexual energy. Men burdened with unreleased sexual energy might run about to the houses of lovers, might stay up all night and sleep all day, neglecting their work and dissipating their wealth; but they did not tear their clothes, soil their faces, or dance about with no pants on, as women whose men could not perform were known to do.

So went the discussions among husbands and fathers. In the meantime, however, talk in other venues was creating another understanding of tubal ligation. Two weeks into the campaign, women who had undergone the surgery began to gather with those who feared it in central locations: a rock on a canal where women from Chemo washed their clothes, a spring where women from Chezò drew water, a public grain pounder with a clear view of the village government across a gully. They discussed the surgery's effects, denounced Qi Haiyun and the other brigade cadres, and plotted strategies of resistance. Every morning, ten to twenty women gathered to ambush Qi Haiyun as he emerged from his parents' house. All day they followed him around, shouting at him whenever he set foot outside.

One afternoon, he fled to my room in the school and sat on my bed, miserably attempting to converse with me and Gu Yimin, a teacher in his thirties. A crowd of women filled the balcony outside, laughing and chatting. "What a lot of fuss," said Gu Yimin, slightly drunk. "All over an operation that can't really hurt them." "Only you can know when your abdomen hurts!" shot back one of the women outside, who had been listening in. Once Qi Haiyun gathered his courage and plunged outside, women surrounded him, shouting, poking his chest, and pinching his arms. A group of those who had been sterilized had agreed on a list of four demands, which they shouted at him. First, central policies allowed two children, yet if one of their two should die, they could not now replace the child. Therefore, Qi Haiyun must arrange an adoption for any woman whose child passed away. Second, the operation had made it impossible for them to perform hard labor for the rest of their lives. Consequently, Qi must personally work for each of them all their lives, carrying their firewood, hauling their water, and bearing loads of compost and rice seedlings to their fields—all tasks that demanded the quick strength they could no longer muster. Third, before the operation, they had all been healthy; now they were chronically ill, requiring frequent meals of chicken soup and medicinal herbs. They demanded that Qi Haiyun cover all their medical expenses and buy each of them a chicken a day. Fourth, while it was true that Qi Haiyun's wife had been sterilized and lay ill in bed, his mother and his two married sisters had never had their names posted, even though all three were eligible. Qi was protecting his own family, even as he strove to get rich by destroying every other family in Zhizuo. His closest kin should be sterilized like everyone else.

These demands established a perspective on tubal ligation that was clear even to men, like Li Zhiwu and myself, who could not participate in the talk that generated them. In this perspective, tubal ligation was a catastrophic obstruction of the energies that animated bodies and households. Every woman in Zhizuo had close experience with the deaths of infants and children; all could easily imagine losing one or both of their offspring. As it destroyed their ability to renew their households in case of disaster, sterilization also damaged their households' economic capacities. Sterilized women could continue to labor at the stereotypically female-gendered tasks that came most quickly to mind for married men like Li Zhiwu: transplanting, weeding, harvesting, sieving, pounding, and winnowing grain. Yet women's daily labor *did* require the explosive energy believed to be depleted by sterilization: lifting back-baskets full of firewood, hauling heavy loads of rice seedlings, shouldering paired water buckets, and carrying huge baskets of compost. These were all bearing (*bù*) tasks, central to the poetry of grief, with which women in Zhizuo mourned their dead ascendants and siblings. Sterilized women feared that, by depleting their capacity for bearing, the surgery had robbed them of the ability to bear and nourish their living children, as their parents and siblings had borne and nourished them.

Men feared that vasectomy would disrupt the balance of sexual energies in a household, causing its women to go mad (*t'æ*). Women feared that as it swelled their lower torsos with an accumulation of stagnant sexual fluids and depleted their interest in sexual activity, tubal ligation drained them of precisely this capacity for chaotic and destructive exuberance. We saw in chapter 5 how fears of such feminine excess came to light in talk about rice transplanting. They also found frequent expression in talk about dance. Dance took many forms, from the nighttime partying of youth to the ritually prescribed dances of elderly women at weddings and old men at funerals. In many ritual contexts, dance drew on feminine reproductive capacities to establish new ensembles of relations. At weddings, for instance, ritual dances performed by the bride's female kin renewed the reproductive potential of the groom's household by moving the soul of the bride from her home to a seat beneath the fertile gaze of her husband's ancestors.

Yet in dance, women also disrupted the channels into which their kin sought to direct their reproductive potential. Night dances at weddings and in the first lunar month gave women, married and unmarried, myriad opportunities to establish liaisons with interested men, raising the possibility of capricious reproductive choices. Young women who displayed immoderate enthusiasm for dancing, singing, playing the mouth harp (a courting instrument), and dressing up in embroidered clothing were often diagnosed as having been driven mad (*t'æ*) by an entity called *srkanè* and treated with a rite to drive away this ghost of a girl killed by a jealous lover.[10] Watching their female kin dance, men feared a chaotic slide of reproductive power or sexual energy into destructive excess. Yet for women who danced madly, possessed by "itchy feet" or the joy of movement, dance was an expression of both bodily exuberance and a sexual potential that mocked the controlling glances of kin. The surgeon's scalpel, they feared, would rob them of both.

When used as a verb to mean "to go mad" or "to become possessed," *t'a* puns easily with the verb *t'a*, "to lust" with animal lust. Older men in Zhizuo had long dreamed of exercising control over the "lust" of their female kin. The verses once muttered to the Lòhɔ, guardian of the ancestral trust fields, were a ritual means to this end: "daughters of the fourth month, don't bloom! plug their vaginas with mud! stop them up with green seedlings! pinch their wombs with fire tongs! don't lust, don't lust!" (fragment 5.12, in chapter 5). Now male household heads were being asked to collaborate with another entity, more mysterious than the Lòhɔ and far more efficient, to achieve this same end. Most complied, reluctantly escorting their wives or sons' wives twenty kilometers to the birth planning clinic. Some, however, eventually rebelled.

A Bitter Image

Many men regarded the swelling crowds of furious women with mixed amusement and respect. "They are *so* angry!" Gu Yimin exclaimed. "Every day, they go to the brigade government to argue with the cadres. Then they come back and spend the rest of the day talking. It's their way of spending their time, now that they can't work. They demand that the state [Ch. *guojia*] feed them for the rest of their lives. The cadres there can only say, 'We haven't a pinch of rice here, but you can come to our houses to eat.'" "They have guts [Ch. *danzi*]!" said another man. "Some of those women walk right into the houses of Qi Haiyun and the brigade chief. They lie down on their beds and refuse to move. 'Now you can take care of me for the rest of my life!'"

Other men found in these demonstrations inspiration for their own acts of resistance. Unnamed youths made nightly attacks on the brigade government building, breaking down the doors, overturning the tables, and destroying the pots and pans. The brigade cadres, who often lived in this building, secluded themselves in their houses or departed for remote seasonal settlements. One night, a beautiful, tile-roofed footbridge that had graced the tail end of the valley for more than a century burned down to its timbers. It was possibly an accident, a lovers'-tryst campfire gone wild, but the township police took it as further deliberate sabotage. The night after his wife was sterilized, one young man went from house to house drinking and trying to convince people to help him ambush and kill Qi Haiyun. "If this were the north, Qi Haiyun would be dead now," said the man who told me of this. "He is alive because we Lòlop'ò are so passive. But we have other ways of taking revenge." Some previous brigade Party secretaries had died mysteriously at night, others reminded me.

Initially, little discussion was given to apportioning blame for the birth planning campaign. Qi Haiyun and the brigade cadres, rather than any more distant institution or set of policies, were the clear focus of anger and resistance. Fury at Qi Haiyun was magnified by the sense that he had violated an unspoken agreement that brigade cadres should always put the interests of their locale over those of the state or their own, using every resource at their disposal to deflect the most harmful of state policies from their locales. Cadres in the neighboring brigade of Bozhedi had acted differently, I was told:

> The Party secretary there told the people, "We have been informed from above that all women under the age of forty-two should be sterilized. But whether you comply with this policy is your business, not ours." He told the township government, "Look, there are only four of us cadres. There are hundreds of women eligible for sterilization, and every one of them will resist. What are we four to do? If you want to force them, it is up to you to send enough police to make it happen." And then he went back to the people and said, "In our opinion, none of you should volunteer for this surgery." So now Bozhedi has been granted special exemption from the campaign, as a particularly poor mountain village.

It was true that Qi Haiyun was inexperienced, it was said, but if he had had a scintilla of human feeling, he would have devised similar tactics. Instead, possessed by greed and ambition, he sterilized his own wife first and then energetically pursued others.

Meanwhile, Qi Haiyun's life was miserable. He spent much of his time at meetings at the township and county levels, where his superiors took him to task for the deteriorating relations between the Party and the masses in his brigade. When he returned to Zhizuo, he was hounded everywhere by angry women. It was spring plowing season, and he scrambled to plow his fields; he was the only member of his household who could handle a plow. His wife had not recovered from her surgery, and he spent the pittance his official post paid buying chickens to feed her as she lay in bed. His parents, with whom he lived, were angry. His mother, forty-three, had five children, and she had recently undergone an abortion. Her neighbors and former friends were demanding that she be sterilized, but she was afraid. She blamed her son.

The campaign ended abruptly, a week before the lunar new year. Concerned about reports of unrest in Zhizuo, the Yongren County government assembled a team of cadres from the Nationalities Commission, the Birth Planning Association, and the Police Bureau to visit the brigade. The team brought a movie projector and a generator, and they announced a mass meeting outdoors. The meeting, which began at dusk, was very well attended. Angry women surrounded the officials, arguing with them. A member of the Birth Planning Association rose to speak, going over once again the goals and rationale of the birth planning campaign. A few stones flew out of the crowd. They missed the official, but one struck a baby strapped to a woman's back. The speeches ceased, the movie was canceled, and the crowd broke up as the mother rushed her baby to the medical clinic. Before leaving the next day, the team announced that the sterilization campaign would be suspended in Zhizuo.

The end of the campaign did not make Qi Haiyun's life easier. Seeking to deflect anger from their level of government, the county team denied that there had been a policy of compulsory sterilization. All birth planning surgeries were voluntary, they said; policies stipulated that refusal could be punished only by a fine of 300 yuan. The loss of livestock and sterilization without anesthetic for women who resisted were not official policy, but had been terrors invented by the brigade Party secretary. Visiting cadres criticized Qi Haiyun openly in front of other Zhizuo residents for mounting an inhumane campaign. The women who had been sterilized—more than eighty in all—followed Qi Haiyun around in crowds, openly pinching and poking him. Nightly sabotage of the brigade government building continued.

One night, when Qi Haiyun's wife and parents were away helping a neighbor prepare for a wedding, six women pushed their way into his house and shouted at him for more than an hour. When they left, he tied an electrical cord to a ceiling beam and hanged himself. The cord broke as he kicked away the stool under his feet. Returning to find him on the floor, his parents put him to bed with a sore neck. I saw him at the wedding the next day, pale and unhappy, wandering nervously from one pine needle "table" of guests to the next, shoveling down a bowl of rice

at one, then getting up again. I did not know of Qi Haiyun's suicide attempt, but it struck me as sad and serious that he could not even participate in this fundamental act of commensality. He invited me home with
him. "If I had the money," he said, "what I would most like to do is buy
a truck or two." "What would you do with a truck?" "Become a truck
driver. Being an official is too bitter."

Qi Haiyun's suicide attempt seemed to soften his neighbors' attitudes
toward him slightly. "That boy's life will be unbearable now," said Li
Wuyi. "He wanted so badly to become an important official and get rich,
but now he will never be an official. He will never be chosen again, for
brigade Party secretary or any other job. His kin all hate him, and his
household is so poor he has to borrow an ox to plow his fields. What
could have made him do this to himself? He is not stupid; he is a very
bright young man. How could he ruin himself and so many other people? People are now saying that it is *yik'ù amùu wo*; it could only be *yik'ù
amùu wo*."

   We have seen this phrase once before, at the beginning of chapter 6.
Yik'ù, the "bitter herb," was remembered to have spread over the landscape during the Great Leap Forward, an omen of calamity. *Amùu wo*
might be translated as "power from the sky" or even "evil from the sky."
Yik'ù combines the sense of a vast bitterness returning from the past
with a portent of catastrophe to come; *amùu wo* brings together the sense
of evil descending on the head of a particular person or household and
the ubiquitous descent of calamity into every corner of the landscape.
The phrase is used in reference to irrational and widely destructive acts
perpetrated by otherwise thoughtful people, as in the Great Leap, when
the deeds of so many defied everything that was just, moral, or even self-
interested. "It is like some strange thing from the sky came into his head
and disturbed his thoughts," expanded Li Wuyi, "forcing him to bring
disaster on himself and on everyone."

   Li Wuyi did not use this phrase in a trivial sense. He had thought the
matter over carefully, he said, and many others agreed with him. It
seems clear that this consensus was implicit recognition that Qi had not
been driven simply by personal greed and ambition; rather, he had been
in the grip of higher forces that had distracted him from the good of the
community, even from his own good. But if so (I found myself asking),
why could Li Wuyi not simply say so? Why did he resort to this vague,

mystical vocabulary when he could have said something more along the lines of my own analysis of Qi Haiyun's behavior?

My explanation focused on the ways in which decollectivization and market reforms had deeply altered the structure of state power in the countryside, shifting it largely away from basic-level cadres and toward a network of administrative agencies, such as birth planning associations, nationalities commissions, development committees, and the police. Qi Haiyun had been promoted to the post of Party secretary as part of this shift. Those who recruited him knew that he enjoyed none of the contacts or experience that allowed older and craftier brigade cadres (like those in Bozhedi) to subvert the demands of higher administrative levels. This restructuring, combined with his own inexperience, gave Qi Haiyun less power to manipulate such demands in the interest of his locale than any brigade Party secretary in memory. This was particularly clear in the context of the most recent push for more stringent birth planning, which, as central leader Song Ping put it, was to be the foundation for a "holistic concept of population" and a unified structure of governance. Basic-level cadres like Qi Haiyun were seen to be crucial to this push. New structures of rewards and punishments for birth planning successes and failures more effectively pressed these cadres to implement the policies of higher levels. Qi Haiyun's options for resistance or subversion were highly constrained, then, and immense pressure was brought to bear on him to carry out the campaign efficiently.

At the same time, agencies at higher levels of government took advantage of the fact that basic-level cadres were the most visible proponents of birth planning in their villages and the natural targets for popular resentment. They encouraged the local cadres to make threats, although the agencies were not willing to back them up in case of trouble. When resistance became overwhelming, these agencies cut the ground out from under Qi, halting the campaign, denying that it had been meant to press so far, and joining in attacks on him and the other brigade cadres. If Qi was to be blamed for anything personally, it would be inexperience, a degree of thoughtlessness about the consequences of ambition, and ignorance of the current nature of state power. The "strange thing" that "came into his head and disturbed his thoughts" was simply a certain gullibility about the state and its promises.

These are my own words, of course, but Li Wuyi and many others in Zhizuo certainly possessed the conceptual vocabulary to have said something similar. Indeed, some individuals had done so, in a fragmentary way, on other occasions. They had been assiduously taught the Chinese analog of this language of organizations, channels of power, policies, negotiations, and resistances. It was the vocabulary employed by the state and its agencies, and many years of listening to speeches, attending political meetings, and hearing newspapers read to them had drilled them in its intricacies. Why, on this occasion, did Li Wuyi speak instead of the "bitter herb from heaven"? The question supposes that he was simply voicing thoughts about Qi Haiyun's instrumental relation to state agencies in another, metaphorical language. This premise—that the language of Chinese folk religion relates to political language as the extended term of a metaphor to its proper term—has been foundational for the anthropology of China. It underlies nearly all discussions of the "Imperial metaphor" in Chinese popular religion—the tendency of these religions to imagine analogs in the world of ghosts and spirits to the world of official bureaucracies. Put simply, these discussions assert that Chinese peasants speak of gods, ghosts, and ancestors as metaphors for officials, strangers, and kin, perhaps to legitimate state authority, perhaps to learn about it, perhaps to resist or manipulate it.[11]

In Li Wuyi's invocation, the phrase "*yík'ù amù wo*" did not use metaphor to rehearse such an assessment of Qi Haiyun's place in a determinate political order. It did not "mystify" or "misrecognize" the state by refashioning it metaphorically as the realm of the sky, from which power descends. Instead, this phrase participated in a very different language, with different aims. This was the language of the ritualized poetics of materials and words to which much of this book has been devoted. It was a resource for thinking *past the limits* of the vocabulary of political determinations and effects toward that which was most fundamental about state power to the lives infused by it. It was a resource for thinking about coexistence with a state imagined as a forceful unity, not merely as a collection of organizations, policies, or causes and effects. It reflected on the image of this unity as fundamental to the "imaginary institution of society," without which social life would not be possible (Castoriadis 1987). Read in the syntax of this language, the phrase "*yík'ù amù wo*" invoked the state as at once an alien Other, vast and distant as the sky, and an interior Other, a "strange thing" disturbing one's own thoughts. It was at once utterly impersonal, with no human analog, and deftly intimate, penetrating head and womb to disturb what was within. Like the "bitter herb" (as *yík'ù* in Lòlongo), it was general, infusing every corner of the inhabited landscape and, in particular, infecting the generative unity of body and house. And like that herb (as *yiku* in Chinese), it was a reflection of past bitterness and a portent of calamity yet to come.

Conclusion

Two weeks after the end of the sterilization campaign, county and prefectural officials returned to Zhizuo to participate in the Clothing Competition Festival (Ch. *saizhuangjie*). This was the centerpiece of state efforts to celebrate the reform-era revival of "nationality customs" in Yongren County. It had been held since 1987 on the fifteenth day of the first lunar month, when Zhizuo residents had once gathered to celebrate the transfer of the title of *ts'ici* from one household to another with feasting and dance. The prefectural Nationalities Commission had published an official myth of the festival's origins, purged of references to the *ts'ici* (Gao and Yang 1989); and newspaper and magazine articles described it as an exuberant, aesthetically exciting, and politically innocent "traditional Yi festival." Its main event was a three-day-long dance on the outdoor site where movies were shown and mass meetings held. Though skeptical at first, many in Zhizuo had come to look forward to the festival as a chance to dress up in their finest and dance. Delegations of officials usually came to open the festival and watch the dancers; choreographers came to gather material for folk dance troupes; photographers came to capture images of Yi women dressed in bright embroidered clothing for feature magazines about minorities; members of the tourist commission came to investigate the festival's possibilities as a tourist attraction. During the day, hundreds of women and children danced in giant circles, their fingers interlaced; after the visitors went to bed, crowds of men from all over the region joined in, dancing around bonfires until dawn.

This year, however, the visitors were disappointed. Only about a hundred women and children showed up to dance. All wore drab daily clothing rather than the brilliant floral pink-and-red embroidered trousers, blouses, and aprons for which they were famous. In the mid-afternoon, a drunken gourd-pipe player in the center of the circle of dancers slipped and fell, smashing the gourd of his instrument on the ground. Distressed, he held up the fragments for the dancers to see. As news of this event made its way over the dance ground, all the women stopped dancing and scattered. "A bad omen," said Li Qunhua quietly, refusing to elaborate before she headed home. Angry clusters of official visitors sat around on the empty dance ground until dusk, when the school principal fed them and locked them in their rooms to keep them from harm. Only after the visitors had retired did some of the dancers return and dance around the bonfires until dawn.

Gourds (*bɔ*) were, of course, central symbols of generative unity. Society had emerged from a gourd. As recounted in chapter 3, a pair of siblings who had survived the flood had lived in their womblike gourd in self-sufficient union until a leaf of the droop-leafed plant had slipped between them, introducing difference into their intimacy and allowing them to give birth to the social world. Gourd-pipes were models of this generative difference in its most harmonious form: womblike gourd skins, penetrated by airy bamboo rods, cemented with beeswax, emitting chords in perfect thirds, a dream of domestic unity. A special pair of large gourd-pipes with double gourds had once led the wedding procession of the reliquary box from one *ts'ici* household to the next, cementing them together as symbolic affines in a dream of generative community. These were the most fragile of dreams, betrayed continuously in practice as people struggled to cope with the incessant violence of their position on the fringes of the nation, reaffirmed in memory and ritual technique as people repeated tales of past unity or sent the ghosts of past violence off to their origins. The mass sterilization campaign had cut these dreams to their core. Dreams of domestic unity had been betrayed again as surgeons' scalpels sliced to the center of the closely inhabited world, crippling bodies and disabling houses. Dreams of generative community had been destroyed again, as the campaign set neighbors and kin against one another, creating hatreds as fierce as those engendered by the Great Leap Forward or the Cultural Revolution.

What was the agent of this violence? This question had emerged repeatedly as people rehearsed tales of the returning ghosts of previous decades' violence. Now it was as pressing as ever and still more difficult. The county officials watching from the hillsides above had voiced the most convenient answer: it was Qi Haiyun, son of Li Siting and Qi Yun, an intelligent but avaricious youth, briefly this brigade's foremost leader, soon to be the poorest of peasants again. Many in Zhizuo repeated this assertion: some of the women dancing in drab aprons at the Clothing Competition Festival were the same who had demanded that Qi Haiyun personally care for them the rest of their lives. Yet by leaving their embroidered clothing at home, these women signaled that they felt another gaze, personified neither by the miserable Qi Haiyun nor by the chief of the Family Planning Association or the uniformed leader of the Police Bureau. It was a gaze elusive of comprehension, present only fleetingly in imagination, yet nonetheless real. It circumscribed their pasts, summing them up as members of the "Yi nationality," economically backward, with generally inferior qualities of body, culture, thought, and morality. It circumscribed their futures, as it counted and assessed their fertile and infertile wombs, keys to their uncertain place in the vast national population. Their hope of finding a richer past and future lay in collective acts like their aborted dance, which drew the daily arts of living in body, house, and landscape to open up this elusive gaze to the force of imagination.

It was that night that Qi Ping slipped into the brigade government building and did her mad dance. I like to think of her up there, plinking a pot around the courtyard, leaping over the tables and stools. Another prankster grandmother, Luo Lizhu, once told me a tale of the mythical Jimìabamo, who used to wander about these mountains playing tricks on people. Once Jimìabamo slipped into an empty house to steal honey. When the family came home, she found herself trapped in the attic. She emptied a pot of honey up there, took off all her clothes, rolled around, and then dumped a bag of wool over herself. She ran down the ladder, holding her clothes under her arm. The family was terrified: "What kind of animal was that? What kind of spirit?" Jimìabamo ran to the river, washed herself off, and got dressed. One young man, smarter than the rest, followed her. "But this is no spirit, Grandmother, it is you!" "Child," she replied, "you don't know me. I'm not your grandmother; I *am* a spirit!" (And she was.)[12] I like to think of Qi Ping emerging from the brigade's attic, its seat of patriarchal power, from whence the reproductive capacity of all in the villages below was regulated, saying to the young man who thought to find her out: Child, you don't know me! You don't know my powers, my despair, the music of my body, the exuberance of my will. In none of this am I another depleted womb for your count!

Still, I know that as she faced that wall with its neatly chalked commands, Qi Ping faced worse terrors than any Jimìabamo encountered in her adventures. Qi Ping had been very poor her entire life and was growing poorer. She had been assigned to a devalued population, obsolete in the nation's crusade to compete effectively in the next century's global market. Her three children and two grandchildren would be further impoverished by a predatory, state-sponsored capitalism that was depleting these mountains of their remaining natural resources to enrich the cities and coasts. Their access to medical care was deteriorating as the system of state medicine broke down and hospitals and clinics demanded fees for their services. As a result, they were found to be ill-favored of body, intelligence, and mental health. They had gained little education, and they would be unlikely to gain more, as elementary, middle, and high schools rapidly increased fees and tuition. As a result, they possessed almost nothing of "culture," as it was measured by those who led the quest for a "quality" national population. In this quest, all their intricate arts of living, all their subtle practices of community, all their best poetic words counted for nothing at all. Qi Ping and her progeny could look forward only to further campaigns to reform these arts for increasingly alien ends.

Under the circumstances, dancing madly was a pretty good response.

Notes

Chapter 1

1. All names of locals in this book are pseudonyms, with the exception only of prominent personages who died before 1955. Most men and women in this area have Chinese names, given to them by their parents when the children are old enough to begin their studies. Before that, children are called by "milk names," usually in their own Tibeto-Burman language. After the birth of a first child, parents are called by the child's "milk name," with the suffix *p'ò* (for men) or *mo* (for women) added. Throughout this text, I have chosen to use Chinese names, as these are the names found in all official communications and written documents.

2. Although the administrative status of Zhizuo had formally changed from brigade (Ch. *dadui*) to administrative village (Ch. *cungongsuo*) in the early 1980s, many locals continued to refer to the area as a brigade. In order to avoid confusion, I follow this usage and call Zhizuo a brigade when referring to the socialist period.

3. Its inhabitants referred to the brigade as Júzò; the Chinese name Zhizuo was used only in writing and by outsiders. I use the Chinese place name here because it is the name that appears on all maps and in written texts. For individual villages and other places in this immediate area, I have used the local, Lòlongo names. More often than not, in general practice, these are written simply by being transcribed approximately with Chinese characters. For names of places outside the immediate area, I have used Chinese names except where otherwise indicated.

4. I describe Zhizuo as lying "mostly in Yongren" because experiments with dividing these mountains into local administrative regions trimmed several outlying valleys off the area once administered by the Zhizuo *ts'ici*, which Zhizuo residents still consider a unity. The core of this area, with its densest concentration of population, formed a single official administrative region throughout the twentieth century: a subtownship administrative unit called a Ch. *bao* until 1950,

then a township (Ch. *xiang*), a brigade (*dadui*), and an administrative village (*cungongsuo*), successively. This core contains Zhizuo's twelve largest villages. Some twelve additional hamlets were also included in the Zhizuo *ts'ici;* most are now in different townships (Menghu and Nijiu) within Yongren County, although a few lie in Dayao County.

5. Alfred Liétard of the Société des Missions Etrangers de Paris wrote the most comprehensive ethnographic account of Central dialect speakers (1913). Liétard's "Lo-o p'o" lived in Zhukula, along the Yupao River in Binchuan County and spoke a dialect that residents of the nearby Baicaolin range could not comprehend. Liétard referred to the inhabitants of the Baicaolin as the "tribe of the Li" and mentioned their impressive production of hempen cloth.

6. The classic ethnography of Northern dialect speakers in English remains that of Lin Yueh-hua (1961). Of the large body of Chinese literature on Northern dialect speakers, see especially Yang H. 1994, Li 1987, and SSB 1987.

7. Ethnography on Yi in Yunnan from the 1950s was collected in the mid-1980s and published in various volumes of a series titled *Zhongguo shaoshu minzu shehui lishi diaocha ziliao congkan.* The best contemporary ethnographic accounts of culture and society among Yunnan Yi are in the yearly journal of the Chuxiong Yi Culture Research Institute *Yizu wenhua;* see also Li 1999. The only extended ethnographies of Yunnan Yi in Western languages remain those by French missionaries such as Paul Vial (1898), Alfred Liétard (1913), and Aimé-Francois Legendre (1913), along with Fr. Luigi Vannicelli's (1944) systematization and reinterpretation of their accounts.

8. Baijing is in present-day Yanfeng township, in Dayao County, Yunnan. During the era of the Qing and the Republic, this was one of Yunnan's three principal salt-producing sites (YXZ 1922; Liu 1933).

9. Zhizuo residents use Chinese terms of measure. The units of measure appearing in this book are as follows:

A *mu* is about 0.167 acre (or 0.067 hectare).

A *sheng* is about 0.96 quart (or 1.08 liters).

A *dou* is 10 *sheng.*

A *jin* (or catty) is about 1.1 pounds (or 0.5 kilogram).

A *dan* is 100 *jin.*

10. This information on household income is drawn from a survey of Yijichang village in Yongren County (YSB 1986, 102).

11. These figures on farmland per capita are taken from administrative village government statistics, collected in 1987 and 1992.

12. In most field research by foreigners in China in the 1980s and early 1990s, institutional sponsors provided such assistants. For the first six months of my field research, my companions were young male ethnographers from the Yi Culture Research Institute, who had grown up speaking versions of the Central dialect of Yi. After six months, for a complex variety of reasons, the institute decided it need not continue providing companions for my research. When they left, I found that I missed the aid and company of these able and dedicated field

assistants, but I also discovered that their presence had inhibited my informants. Many in Zhizuo had assumed that anything said in front of my companions might be reported, under their names, directly to local state agencies and, in the event of a future political cataclysm similar to the Cultural Revolution, might return to haunt the speakers. My own links to state agencies were accurately perceived as more distant, and many in Zhizuo were more open to me when I worked alone.

13. For explorations of the politics of ethnicity in China's southwest, see Diamond 1988, 1995; Gladney 1994; Harrell 1990, 1995; Swain 1995; White 1997; Litzinger 1995, 1998; and Schein 1997, 2000.

14. See, for example, journals such as *Minzu yanjiu* (Nationalities research), *Minzuxue yanjiu* (Nationalities studies research), *Minzu yuwen* (Nationalities literatures), and a spate of local journals dedicated to specific nationalities, such as, for Yi, *Yizu wenhua* (Yi culture), the journal of the Chuxiong Yi Culture Research Institute; *Yixue yanjiu* (Yi studies research), the journal of the Yunnan Yi Studies Association; *Guizhou Yixue tongxun* (Guizhou Yi studies report), the journal of the Guizhou Yi Studies Research Institute; and *Liangshan minzu yanjiu* (Liangshan nationalities research), the journal of the Liangshan Nationalities Research Institute.

15. See, e.g., Chan, Madsen, and Unger 1984; Siu 1989; Potter and Potter 1990; Judd 1994; Yan 1996; Jing 1996; and Kipnis 1997.

Chapter 2

1. Women in Zhizuo divided their mortuary laments into two genres. The song in fragment 2.1 is in a genre called *chr̀mèkò*, "orphans' poetry." Female kin of the dead sang orphans' poetry in a vigil (*kukædɔ*) kept over the corpse from the moment of death until burial. These laments, usually in the form of antiphonal dialogues, described the orphan's life from birth to the death of the parent, elaborated each step of the funeral process, and detailed the labor required to make each of the gifts. A second genre was called *xchɔŋɔ*, "lamenting songs." Women sang these laments at a second vigil (*nihèpi*) held seven days (for a woman) or nine days (for a man) after burial. These were monologues, which described the processes of making offerings of rice, buckwheat, and hemp and which appealed to the newly dead to take a share of the offerings and pass the rest on to other, named, dead kin.

2. Such framing and marking are frequent functions of ritual language across cultures (Keane 1996).

3. My interpretation of Bachelard's *Poetics of Space* (1964) closely follows that of Casey (1997, 287–296).

4. Some readers familiar with the anthropology of China might assume that the orientations in intimately inhabited space outlined here are locally specific to Yi or Lòlop'ò peoples and that this analysis can have little relevance to rural China as a whole. To the contrary, the most perceptive ethnographies of rural China contain hints that similar orientations may once have been widespread. For instance, Ahern's fieldwork in rural northern Taiwan contains vivid evidence

that pregnant women in this area, far removed from the mountains of the south-west, might also have occupied houses where wombs, rooms, and bodies were not governed by Euclidean geometries of inside and outside. In a pregnant woman's bedroom, the woman and the being growing within her shared a space where every action had potential consequences both inside and outside the womb. Ahern's informants told her about a spirit called Thai Sin:

> Although the name means Placenta god, Thai Sin is also, and more impor-tantly, regarded as the child's soul. One informant said, "You could say that just as adults have a *lieng-hun* [a soul], so infants have a Thai Sin." The Thai Sin comes into existence the moment the child is conceived and stays until four months after birth. During its first nine months the spirit is not confined to the fetus, but moves about inside the pregnant woman's bedroom. This movement causes difficulties: if one should happen to strike, break, or cut something in the woman's room when the Thai Sin is in the way, the child's head may be in-jured. If one cuts cloth at the wrong time, the child may be born with a cleft palate; if one breaks a stick, one of the child's limbs may be damaged; if one drives a nail into the wall or digs a hole in the floor, the child may be aborted or born prematurely. After birth the Thai Sin becomes attached to the child's body with increasing firmness, so that at about four months there is no need to fear striking it inadvertently. (Ahern 1974b, 196–197)

Chapter 3

1. In a skillful genealogy of the term *funu* ("Chinese woman"), Barlow (1994a, 1994b) argues that a "Confucian" discourse, which produced women (*funu*) as wives and mothers, conceived relationally within networks of kin, gave way in the early twentieth century to a May Fourth discourse, which created a cat-egory of woman (*nuxing*) as the female sex, conceived biologically as a binary other to man. The May Fourth discourse gave way in turn to a socialist discourse, which produced the state category of socialist woman (*funu*), conceived politi-cally and economically as a producer in, and reproducer of, the socialist polity. Nevertheless, it is clear that the differential relations of daughter, mother, and wife that Barlow tags as "Confucian" remained central in peasant households throughout the twentieth century as a substrate of, or counterpoint to, newer possible subject positions being generated by the elite discourses of the state and intellectuals. It is this substrate with which this chapter is concerned.

2. People in Zhizuo might find Bray's metaphor of a house as a loom felici-tous. Prior to 1980, women in Zhizuo wove hempen cloth on timber-frame looms in their courtyards. They used a simple tabby weave in which each weft goes alternately over and under one warp end (Cheng 1992). This weave was analogous to the rectilinear patterns of alternating positions (on opposite beds) and successive generations (from beds' heads to their tails) evoked in poetic rep-resentations of household life. Still, Zhizuo residents might also point out that, in contrast to the houses Bray describes, in their houses the cloth of descent and alliance unraveled even as it was woven. The warp threads of descent loosened as ancestors were actively forgotten after three generations. Some weft threads

were woven when daughters-in-law married in, but others unraveled when daughters (and sometimes sons) dispersed to other households, while maintaining an attenuated connection to the house of their birth.

3. In the poor, mountainous areas of rural Yunnan, households were most often the *only* basic units of production. In much of rural China, township and village enterprises became widespread in the 1980s and 1990s. But in these mountains, where transportation was difficult and capital and credit scarce, such enterprises were uncommon. By the early 1990s, despite a few failed attempts, Zhizuo's leadership had proved unable to organize any enterprise at a level larger than a household.

4. In addition to those described in this chapter, many other minor household spirits resided in Zhizuo houses. Most households kept a spirit responsible for the domestic animals' fertility and well-being (*lócimìci*) by the barn entrance. Inside the upstream room were spirits of the fire pit (*kolomo*) and "mother and son ghosts" (*nèmonèzò*) in the water cistern. Spirits of health and long life for children (*menè*) resided on the outside of the back wall; spirits of health and fecundity for pigs (*jits'a*) occupied a corner of the courtyard; a tree behind the house was sometimes designated the residence of a domestic thunderstorm spirit (*mògùmi*). Some households maintained spirits to ward off tuberculosis (*junè*); households with Han ancestors sometimes kept a "Han ghost" (*cenè*); some sheepherders kept a "sheep-rash spirit" (*rɔcik'ɔ*); and a few houses had a spirit to keep thieves away (*àrɔ*). Each of these entities was represented by an effigy specific to its kind with a fixed location in the house or its immediate environs, and each had verbal techniques associated with it to encourage its beneficence or counter the harm it might do to those who offended it.

5. This pattern of roof tiles is illustrated in Knapp 1986, 83, fig. 3.55 (5) and fig. 3.56.

6. For descriptions of rural houses in other parts of China as central halls with wings, see Hsu 1948; Chao 1983; Knapp 1986, 1999; and Sangren 1987.

7. See also Yang H. 1990 and Yang F. 1990 for descriptions of courtship among Yi in this region.

8. The strong prejudice against uxorilocal marriage held by Zhizuo residents was not shared evenly throughout Líp'ò and Lòlop'ò areas. In a 1988 survey of fifty-three Líp'ò households in the neighboring township of Tanhua, Yang Fuwang found that only 44 percent of marriages were virilocal; in the other 56 percent, the couple resided in the woman's household or, when both partners were single children, rotated their residence between households (1990, 54).

9. Such couplets have counterparts in a long tradition of parallels and doubles in Chinese literary and aesthetic expression. As Bray (1997, 394) points out with reference to eighteenth-century wives and concubines, the full meaning of such doublings "emerges through the echoings, complimentarities, and contrasts between the pair," as in the paired scrolls that still hang on either side of doorways to houses, restaurants, and offices throughout China, each scroll bearing one line of a couplet.

10. The second line of fragment 3.5 puns on the word *fu* ("to rot"), as in "the radish rots within" (*và tsì và kɔ fu*): its first word, *fu mo*, "to marry out a daughter," can also mean a rotting, sexually frustrated woman.

11. Pine trees are indispensable to the imagery of descent in Zhizuo. Rooted on the mountain behind the large village of Chezò was the giant pine tree of Agàmisimo, an ancestral spirit from whom all Zhizuo Lòlop'ò claim attenuated descent (as discussed in chapter 4). In villages where houses are not piled one behind the other, many Lòlop'ò designate a pine tree directly behind their house as a *mògùmi,* a domestic version of the Shìmògù (a lightning spirit) that stands beside Agàmisimo. Like Agàmisimo, this spirit is associated with the values of the distant ancestors who were said to have first settled Zhizuo.

12. Upstream rooms in most houses contained one or two smooth stones behind the fire pit, seen as household spirits called *kolomo,* who, Zhizuo residents said, watched houses and kept them from harm, like guard dogs.

13. Massive footprints in these rocks were identified as dinosaur prints in the 1950s.

14. As Boon teaches us, this relation of relations is what Lévi-Strauss (1983) identifies as the "atom of kinship"—not a substantive social relation but a "dialectical field of social differences" (Boon 1990, 104). Taken in itself, an ancestral effigy represents the relational core of the "atom of kinship" in its most "mythic" (that is, neither genealogical nor historical) form: "a sibling link and a spouse link: cross-sex siblings with a spouse parallel-sex to one of them" (Boon 1990, 107). As part of a larger ensemble that includes further generations of ancestral effigies and the fertile bed below, this mythic relation of relations opens up to the temporal realities of descent. Its affective power to confer fertility on its descendants, however, flows from its mythic form: "a model of social totality constricted into a bundle of cross/parallel-sex possibilities" (ibid.).

15. On Guanyin's transformation from Indian *bodhisatva* to Chinese goddess of fertility, see Dore 1965–1967 and Sangren 1983.

16. For examples of flood stories told by other peoples in the southwest, see Rock 1935, Fang 1990, Li Z. 1990, and Tao 1986.

17. For a full text of this story, see Mueggler 1996.

18. This lament is described in Mueggler 1998b.

19. On the belief in multiple souls, which was widespread in rural China, see Wolf 1974 and Harrell 1979.

20. Bed's-head spirits were often blamed for calamities, from fire to murder, that caused a household's collapse. One night in 1992, for instance, a drunken young man broke into a house in Zhizuo and threatened an elderly couple and their son with a long pig-slaughtering knife. The son struggled with the attacker, took the knife away, and killed him with it. Later, gossip had it that the dead man had repeatedly caught his wife and the killer sleeping together. But the gossips nevertheless located the root of the tragedy in an incident that had occurred a few nights before. The killer's parents had had a violent argument, and his father, in rage or madness, had pulled the bed's-head spirit off the wall and tossed it in the gully. This act resulted in the failure of the house's sheltering embrace (when the drunken man burst through the door with his knife) and the collapse of household relations (when the killer was arrested, tried, and imprisoned).

21. In other parts of China as well, ancestral tablets kept in homes were sometimes destroyed after several generations. Indeed, the Confucian philosopher

Zhu Xi advocated this practice for the same reason as my informants in Zhizuo: because memory faded as generations passed (Ebrey 1991). Freedman, citing evidence from Addison (1925, 35) and Doolittle (1868, 170), writes that "the tablets of ancestors beyond the third generation (or sometimes beyond the fifth) were burned in some parts of China and in other parts removed to an ancestral temple representing a group larger than the family" (1958, 82). When individual tablets at home were destroyed, people still kept generic tablets or genealogical scrolls, analogous in many ways to the bed's-head spirits of Zhizuo. In the southeast, tablets at home were often removed to lineage halls, where the limit on generations did not apply. As with all ritual practices in China, however, regional variations were considerable. New Territories homes sheltered paper "tablets" recording the names of ten or more generations of ancestors (Baker 1968, 62); Hakka in south Taiwan kept framed documents and tablets listing more than twenty generations (Cohen 1976, 37–38); and none of the fine ethnographics of ancestor worship in Taiwan (Jordan 1972; Ahern 1973; Gallin 1966; Pasternak 1972) found that families there destroyed domestic ancestral tablets (Harrell 1982, 199).

22. There once were other ritual means of actively forgetting the dead. Before the land reform movement in 1952–1953, wealthier Zhizuo residents had held a final, elaborate, night-long mortuary ritual called "sleeping in the wild" (*likádùhè*) several generations after each death. This rite was intended to erase a dead couple from memory, severing the pair's relations of affect and kinship with the living to free them for a return to life.

23. The dominant school of anthropological literature on kinship in rural China is based on fieldwork in the southeast and is associated with the "lineage paradigm" developed by Maurice Freedman (1958 and 1966 especially). Baker (1968), Potter (1968), Pasternak (1972), Cohen (1976), Potter and Potter (1990), J. Watson (1975), and R. Watson (1981, 1988) applied Freedman's model to South China lineage organizations. Ahern (1973, 1976) pointed out incongruencies in this model when applied to Taiwanese lineages, and Sangren (1987) created a powerful critique of it for emphasizing the legalistic ideologies of lineage at the expense of its practical realities. The ethnographic literature on kinship and lineage in other areas of China is thinner. Cohen (1990) has shown that lineage ideologies in the north differed considerably from those described by Freedman, in that patrilineal ties were organized hierarchically on the basis of the relative seniority of descent lines rather than equally on the basis of common descent from a founding ancestor, as in the southeast. The best descriptions of kinship and lineage in the southwest remain those of Fitzgerald (1941) and Hsu (1948), who wrote about the same village in Dali County, Yunnan, the majority of whose inhabitants are now considered to be of the Bai nationality.

24. On such descent groups in the north, see especially Duara 1988, Cohen 1990, and Jing 1996.

25. Descent ideologies vary widely among the peoples now categorized as Yi. Among Northern dialect groups, for whom large agnatic descent groups have historically been a dominant form of social organization, people maintain written and oral records of long genealogies—in some cases up to thirty generations

(Ma 2000). At the other extreme, some Central dialect speakers, such as Líp'ò in Nijiu township, Yongren County, Yunnan, keep only two generations of ancestral effigies, ritually destroying the elder generations. On ideologies of lineage and descent among Northern dialect groups, see Bamo 1994; for a survey of ancestor worship practices among Yi groups as a whole, see Wang 1995.

26. Such mutual inflections are strangely absent from the classic ethnographic literature on South China. In this literature, the perspectives of men and women are most often viewed as rigidly exclusive of each other (as in Martin 1988).

27. See Mueggler 1998b for more detailed discussion of the social impact of hemp prices.

28. As Judd notes, exceptions sometimes arose when a son was taking on his aging father's role in the household or when the senior able male held a non-agricultural registration and was not therefore officially a household member. In the latter case, a wife was designated official household head (Judd 1994, 249). In large numbers of households in some parts of China, the senior able male was employed away from the home and absent for long periods, creating opportunities for women to head households officially and even to replace men in official village positions (ibid., 226). Judd does not distinguish very clearly between the official household (*hu*), with its officially appointed household head (*huzhu*), and the unofficial coresident family, which might have an actual leader (or *jiazhang*) who was not the *huzhu*. Indeed, some powerful senior men had greater influence both within their families and in local politics precisely because they worked outside; they were recognized as their family's undisputed, if mostly absent, *jiazhang,* while their wives were the registered *huzhu.*

Chapter 4

1. On the nationalities classification project, see Fei 1980; Jiang 1985; Lin Y. 1984, 1990; Lin and Jin 1980; Guldin 1994; and Schein 2000.

2. Ascending to power in the last years of the Qing, the Xia family evaded the Qing state's policy of replacing hereditary officials with ordinary appointed magistrates (*gaitu guiliu*). On the history of the *tusi* system, see Herman 1997; Hu 1981; Huang 1968; Li S. Y. 1990, 465–494; Smith 1970; and Weins 1954, 201–240.

3. The *bao-jia* system had existed in northern Yunnan since at least 1726–1731, when Ortai ruled as governor-general of Yunnan and Guizhou Provinces with a mandate from the reform-minded Yongzheng emperor to curb the power of native *tusi* and bring them under the control of the state (Smith 1970). For descriptions of *bao-jia* systems elsewhere in China during the era of the late Qing and the Republic, see Ch'ü 1962 and Duara 1988.

4. The most prominent participants in this debate were Eric Wolf (1957, 1986), Frank Cancian (1965, 1992), John Haviland (1977), and Manning Nash (1964).

5. This myth was chanted during a funeral rite called "tenth-month sacrifice" (*ts'rhonèpi*). For two prose versions, collected in Dayao in the early 1950s, see YSB 1986, 78–79.

6. Chinese ethnographers record a widespread claim among many groups of both Han and non-Han in Yunnan to have descended from immigrants from Yingtian Fu in Nanjing (YSMWCD 1959, 44).

7. The surnames Su, Yin, and Yang, common among Zhizuo Lòlop'ò, were said to have derived from Han settlers.

8. The places along this line of sight most intimately associated with Agàmisimo had been Ts'icizò, where the original ancestors built their houses, and the house where the spirit Cha was kept. Those who had lived in these places abandoned them shortly after the Cultural Revolution, seeking houses where they would not be plagued by the *ts'ici* ghosts. The houses in both places remained empty through the early 1990s.

9. As Zhizuo's bed's-head spirit, Agàmisimo protected its inhabitants from harm when they sojourned. Men who had traveled to labor on the massive public works projects of the Great Leap Forward told me that Agàmisimo had kept them from being crushed by rolling rocks or blown apart by dynamite, as many of their fellow workers had been. Others insisted that Agàmisimo had always protected all in Zhizuo from attacks by wolves, which had been common in Dayao before the deforestation of the 1950s.

10. On the common analogy between underworld bureaucracies and those of the state, see Feuchtwang 1992, Harrell 1974, Ahern 1981, Wolf 1974, Teiser 1988, Kuhn 1990, Kleeman 1993, and Ebrey and Gregory 1993.

11. This group of villages was Zhenamo, in the present-day township of Liuzuo in Dayao County.

12. Several currencies were circulating in Yunnan in the 1930s and 1940s. The common currency was Old Yunnan currency. A New Yunnan currency of about twice the value, as well as the national currency, standardized under the Yuan Shikai administration, of about ten times the value, also circulated (Osgood 1963, 194). These prices are in the national currency. Liu and Yeh list a "national" price (from scattered local sources) in 1933 of 50 yuan for cattle, 48 for horses, and 70 for mules (1965, 136). Given the steep inflation in the 1940s and escalating values for pack animals during and after the war, the prices remembered by Zhizuo residents are feasible.

13. The conscription statistics are drawn from CYZZ 1994, 299. Similar figures do not exist for Dayao and Yongren Counties.

14. For similar metaphors in Chinese literature on physiology and etiology, see Seaman 1992.

Chapter 5

1. The Chinese term "Han" (the unmarked category of all Chinese who are not of "minority nationalities") may be translated into Lòlongo in two ways. Cep'ò are Han of the lowlands, who possess wealth, refinement, and literacy. Kújup'ò (Kúju in ritual speech) is a more explicitly derogatory term, used for local mountain Han, who lack refinement and education. Despite my American nationality, Irish and Swiss ethnicity, and frequent protests, people in Zhizuo habitually referred to me as Cep'ò, since I was wealthy, literate, and alien.

2. This fragment (5.1) is from a *nèpi* used to exorcise from a body or house the "ghost at the river's tail" (*ləmædónè*), the ghost of Magistrate Li, a former Han magistrate of Dayao County (see the following note).

3. Digestion may seem a strange metaphor, given that one product of digestion is human waste, while the products of digestive memory are words. Among the *nèpi* Li Yong loved most was one he used to send away the ghost of Magistrate Li (Li Daye), who afflicted his victims with repeated vomiting. Near its beginning, it employs a couplet used, with variation, in nearly every healing ritual:

he retches his food	tsò nà p'i lɔ su
he vomits his drink	dɔ nà ló lɔ su

Later, it describes the bodily state its words should have wrought:

as he eats the best food	tsò wú hɔ chì ni
he defecates the best food	tsò wú p'ì ɔ̀ lɔ
as he eats the last drink	dɔ mæ hɔ chì ni
he urinates the last drink	dɔ mæ hə ɔ̀ lɔ
let it be thus	k'o ne chì ni go

The chant then sends defecated and urinated food down the stream toward Dayao town, where Magistrate Li once ruled. Among the products of *nèpi* is the smooth flow of waste from healthy bodies. The point of chants such as this is to return this by-product of digestive memory toward the centers from which the evil intentions and harmful acts of people in power arise.

4. See, for instance, the description of exorcism rituals in chapter 7.

5. Zhizuo residents used the Chinese word *wen* in all of the senses rehearsed by Jacques Gernet: "The word *wen* signifies a conglomeration of marks, the simple symbol in writing. It applies to the veins in stones and wood, to constellations, represented by the strokes connecting the stars, to the tracks of birds and quadrupeds on the ground (Chinese tradition would have it that the observation of these tracks suggested the invention of writing), to tattoo and even, for example, to the designs that decorate the turtle's shell" (quoted in Derrida 1976, 123). In each of these senses, *wen* is an inscribed mark, often undecipherable, but never foreclosing the possibility of being read by one who holds the key to its interpretation.

6. This communication among village, market town, and district center was structurally similar to that which Skinner (1964–1965) described for the Sichuan basin.

7. In death ritual, too, the female labor of weeping was initiated by a man. A skilled male mourner was paid to weep for a few minutes before female kin took over for an exhausting daylong or nightlong weeping vigil. As in rice transplanting, women owned the labor of weeping by virtue of their physical nature: men considered extended weeping physically impossible for male bodies to sustain.

8. The funeral flower (*t'àyèngatsì*) is a construction of bamboo and cloth used to represent the soul of the dead during the tenth-month sacrifice, a mor-

tuary ritual held in the tenth lunar month for people who had died during the previous year.

9. Martin (1988, 165) argues that in China such ideologies, in which "the biological birthing that is the preserve of women [is] contrasted to, and subordinated to, the social birthing that men do when they bring ancestors of various kinds to a new life after death," are at best only part of the story. Women frequently hold alternative views, often fragmented and contradictory, which value the process of birth as the foundation of social life.

10. Typhus indicates a group of infectious diseases "characterized by great prostration, severe headache, generalized maculopapular rash, sustained high fever, and usually progressive neurologic involvement, ending in a crisis in ten to fourteen days" (Vardara 1993, 2,064). Of these diseases, the highest mortality is attributed to epidemic (louse-borne) typhus, present in conditions that encourage lice. Murine (flea-borne) varieties are spread to humans by rat fleas or in food contaminated by rat urine or rat feces. Encephalomyelitis is an acute inflammation of the brain and spinal cord. It is usually caused by a viral infection, but it is also sometimes caused by other organisms. Encephalomyelitis viruses are often transmitted by ticks and mosquitos.

11. Corn-drying racks were horizontal grids of pine poles, elevated 7 to 10 feet above the ground with sturdy pine posts. Bundles of peeled hemp stalks were tied to the grid and corn cobs piled over them to dry. Both because they massively divided earth and sky and because they sometimes threatened to collapse suddenly on those below, such racks were used in miniature in death rituals to represent the boundary between the world of the living (*ts'ɔmi*) and the world of the dead (*mómi*). Shr̀mògù was the Charon of that border.

12. In many healing rituals, such groups of marked sticks were made of *bɑ̀tísí̱*, a flexible, slightly malodorous wood, and represented the most dangerous of nonhuman entities. Here they were of *wulusi̱*, a rare, fragrant wood associated with cleanliness and freedom from contamination. Leaves from *wulusi̱* trees were the main ingredient of a fragrant bath women took sixty days after giving birth, to wash away the lingering pollution of childbirth. These groups of sticks thus indicated both the threat Cha was to protect against and the form that protection was to take. The ritualist signaled the end of his chant to Cha by tossing a pair of pine sticks to divine whether the offerings had been accepted. As he stood up from this toss, children, who had been waiting for this moment, rushed forward and fought for one of the thirty *wulusi̱* sticks and six bamboo branches of the effigy. Those who were successful carried their prize home and stuck it into the wall just inside the doorway, where it was supposed to guard the house from disease.

13. Since typhus is readily transmitted through fecal contamination of food, dividing the meat into separate portions might seem a practical way of avoiding contagion in a season when epidemics were feared, in accord with a germ theory of disease. But it probably made little practical difference. The cooks used their hands to divide the meat into piles and to place it in each person's bowl. Indeed, this meticulous division probably occasioned more direct handling of the meat than the usual procedure of passing out handfuls from a basket.

14. I have written of *zhoushen* elsewhere; see Mueggler 1998a.

Chapter 6

1. On the trope of awakening, see Fitzgerald 1996.

2. These figures are probably approximate, since they are from oral recollections. Liu and Yeh list an approximate national market price in 1952 of 160 yuan per head for mules and 8.0 yuan per head for sheep and goats (1965, 136).

3. Kang Sheng's slogan is quoted in MacFarquhar 1983, 103. At the time of the Great Leap Forward, Kang Sheng was an alternate member of the Politburo. In the late 1960s, he emerged as a major architect of the Cultural Revolution and a close advisor to Mao.

4. MacFarquhar 1983 and Schoenhals 1987 give detailed accounts of the history of the Great Leap Forward. Yang 1996, Bachman 1991, and Lieberthal 1987 discuss the politics of this campaign at central and provincial levels. Domenach 1995 provides a case study of the politics leading to the Great Leap in Henan, one of the provinces most severely affected by the famine.

5. David and Isabelle Crook (1959) found a similar situation in Yangyi Commune in Hebei. The Crooks claim that in 1958 the peasants of the poor brigades in the hills relaxed their pace of work, delighted with the subsidies from their comrades in the lowlands, while peasants in the richer lowland brigades also slacked off out of resentment that the poorer brigades were eating their grain.

6. Quoted in MacFarquhar 1983, 84. Tan's speech was quoted critically during the Cultural Revolution in several radical publications, including *Hong qi* (Red Flag), 21 March 1967; and *Ba ba zhan bao* (Eighth of August Combat News), 29 March 1976.

7. During the Eighth Party Congress, Mao committed himself to an all-out drive to mobilize China's five hundred million peasants to create an economic leap forward. The passage is from Mao's first speech to the congress, on 8 May 1958 (Mao 1969, 92; quoted in MacFarquhar 1983, 54).

8. For debate on Justin Lin's (1990) thesis, see Dong and Dow 1993, Kung 1993, Liu 1993, MacLeod 1993, Putterman and Skillman 1993, and Lin 1993.

9. On the reliability of official vital statistics from this period, see also Banister 1987, Coale 1984, and Kane 1988.

10. "Excess deaths" are defined as deaths that exceeded the range of mortality rates that would have been projected based on the tendencies of the early and mid-1950s (Banister 1987).

11. The "five winds" were styles of leadership identified early in the campaign as contributing to production problems. They were the "communist wind" (*gongchan feng*), the "boastful wind" (*fukua feng*), the "wind of commandism" (*mingling feng*), the "wind of blind direction of production" (*shengchan xiazhi-hui feng*), and the "wind of cadre privilege" (*ganbu teshu feng*) (Mao 1969).

12. In 1958, the four counties in Yunnan with the highest Líp'ò and Lòlop'ò populations (Yongren, Yanfeng, Yaoan, and Dayao) were combined into the single large county of Dayao (CYZZ 1994, 131). All figures for Dayao County for the period between 1958 and 1961 refer to this large county. In 1962, Dayao was again divided into four counties. Zhonghe District, which included nearly all of Zhizuo, had been Dayao's northernmost district before 1958, but in 1962 this dis-

trict was transferred to Yongren County. A few outlying villages formerly included within Zhizuo remained in Dayao (YSB 1986, 109; YSTRB 1990).

13. Pierre Janet, Freud's contemporary, who is credited with developing in detail the concept of traumatic memory, noticed that the repetitions of traumatic memory occur automatically in situations reminiscent of the original traumatic event (Janet 1928). Qi Deyi had faced a similar panel of youthful interrogators, probably even in Zhizuo's elementary school, on at least two occasions: after his arrest during the Great Leap and after subsequent arrests during the Cultural Revolution. During the latter instances, he had defended himself with the story of his first arrest—his thought had already been reconstructed, his memory reformed; he no longer recalled any of the words that had made him into a "purveyor of superstition." The Cultural Revolution forced Qi Deyi to refashion the trauma of his brother's death into a narrative that produced a new and safer social identity; my own interrogation of Qi Deyi perhaps stimulated a traumatic repetition of his responses to Cultural Revolution inquisitors. Many of the ritualists with whom I worked in Zhizuo had participated in similar scenarios in the late 1980s and early 1990s. Called before committees of ethnographers to recite knowledge they had been forced to forget twenty years before, they responded with evasions similar to Qi Deyi's. Trauma is a structuring principle of the Chinese state's current ethnographic projects to recover nationality customs and nationality religion. My own ethnography was also frequently complicit in these efforts to reconfigure memory, yet again, by force.

14. These images are all from the tenth-month sacrifice chant (ts'ihonèpi). Contrary to Qi Deyi's assertion, one or two ritualists who had moved to settlements on Zhizuo's outer periphery did actively remember this chant. Ritualists performed this chant before an effigy of pine trees wrapped in many layers of clothing that substituted for the corpse, which was already in the ground. Real corpses were not elevated into trees in mortuary ritual (with the exception of infant corpses from local Han families). Before about 1935, however, the most lavish funeral rites combined the night vigil (kukædo)—in which the corpse was wrapped in clothes, placed in a coffin, and buried—with the chants and gestures of tenth-month sacrifice. In these rites (called tsʒtə), the coffin was elevated above the ground on timbers, and sacrificial animals were killed beneath it. And up until about three hundred years ago, Lòlop'ò in Zhizuo burned corpses (as some Yunnan Yi groups still do [Li 1999]), elevating them on timbers above a cremation fire. In general, mortuary ritual in Zhizuo combines (older?) images of elevation into the sky with (newer?) images of descent into the underworld.

15. During the years of the Cultural Revolution, many Zhizuo residents would take advantage of this policy, moving temporarily or permanently to remote settlements to escape the labor discipline or political chaos of the larger, more concentrated production teams.

16. For predominantly ethnographic accounts of the "Imperial metaphor" in Chinese folk religion, see Wolf 1974; Feuchtwang 1974, 1992; Weller 1987; Ahern 1981; and Shahar and Weller 1996. For predominantly historical accounts, see Duara 1988; Teiser 1988; Kuhn 1990; Kleeman 1993; and Ebrey and Gregory 1993.

17. Arthur Wolf's (1974) discussion of mortuary ritual among rural Taiwanese, which served as inspiration for many further attempts to define and

understand the "Imperial metaphor," draws parallels between gods and living officials, ancestors and living kin, and ghosts and living strangers.

Chapter 7

1. Two other important mortuary rites were not revived: the tenth-month sacrifice (*ts'rhonèpi*), which was performed until 1958 (see chapter 6); and "sleeping in the wild" (*likádùhè*), which ceased to be performed in 1950.

2. Entities once frequently blamed for serious, chronic, or recurrent symptoms included *srkalanè*, the ghosts of a mythical couple who had died in a murder-suicide after their love was thwarted and who specialized in attacking beautiful young women; *melònè*, the ethnically Han spirit familiars of diviners and ritualists, who sometimes turned on their masters; *línè*, the ghosts of unnamed Líp'ò ancestors from the high mountains; *lɔmædɔ́nè*, the "ghost at the river's tail," the ghost of a former county magistrate, who traveled up the river to harm the poor; *puunè*, the statues in Buddhist temples, who sometimes trapped and tortured the souls of those who happened upon them; Ch. *zhouyan-nè*, the "ghost of curses," who harmed those who became involved in protracted disputes; *micèæcè*, the ghost of a former emperor, to whom all new farmland was offered before it was farmed; *ci-shanshen*, who inhabited springs, sometimes trapping the souls of those who happened upon them; the neglected or insulted tombstones of ancestral spirits; and all the "house ghosts" mentioned in chapter 3, if insulted or neglected, especially the bed's-head spirit (*gɔwúdenè*) and the souls of ancestors, resident in ancestral effigies (*nètsr̀*). Most of these entities were still propitiated in the 1990s, though less often than before the Great Leap.

3. Literature on menstrual pollution in China is extensive, and much of it could support an argument that the men's ideas about menstrual pollution described in these paragraphs differ little from ideas throughout much of rural China. See, for example, Topley 1974, Blake 1978, Seaman 1981, Sangren 1983, Furth 1986, Ebry 1993, Liu 1994, Brownell 1995, Bray 1997, and Mann 1997. Ahern (1974b) makes a particularly suggestive case for the interrelation of birth pollution (of which menstrual pollution is one kind) and death pollution in rural Taiwan.

4. The consistent numerology of exorcisms and mortuary rituals seems to belie Li Wenyi's claim. Twos and threes appear everywhere in exorcisms, but there are no sevens or nines. Sevens and nines are used, however, throughout mortuary rituals.

5. Lengthy examples of mourning songs that detail each step in the labor of producing hempen cloth are given in Mueggler 1998b.

6. These two parts of the exorcism chant belong to an important genre of Lòlop'ò ritual language. All *nèpi* for the five *ts'ici* spirits (three of which are quoted in chapter 5, in fragments 5.2 through 5.7, 5.9 through 5.13, and 5.15) contain "driving over sky and earth" sections, as do most for malevolent entities (including the *mæ* of chapter 2). "Driving to market" is more specific to extremely evil nonhuman entities: the only other ritual I know of in which a ghost is driven to market is one for the "tree ghost," *srkanè* (or *srkalanè*), closely related to *chènè*. Of all these "driving" sections, those contained in exorcism chants are by far the longest and most complex.

7. See Cheng 1982; Fox 1977, 1988; and Urban 1991 for related descriptions of parallelism in ritualized speech.

Chapter 8

1. See M. Yang 1994 and Watson 1994.

2. The documents referred to as the Former Ten Points, adopted by the Central Committee in May 1963, and the Latter Ten Points, adopted by the Central Committee in September 1963, with a revised draft adopted in September 1964, were the basic guidelines for the Socialist Education movement in the rural areas. The Twenty-Three Articles, adopted in 1965, repeated and refined many of the instructions given in these earlier guidelines. All of these documents are translated in Baum and Tiewes 1968.

3. The four counties were Yuxi, Anning, Yiliang, and Dali (CYZZ 1994, 143).

4. The "Four Cleanups" was another name for the Socialist Education movement, given more prominence in the movement's later phases in 1964 and 1965. For consistency, I have chosen to refer to the movement in every phase as the Socialist Education movement.

5. The Twenty-Three Articles, formally titled "Some Problems Currently Arising in the Course of the Rural Socialist Education Movement," had been adopted only recently, at a January 1965 work conference of the Party's Central Committee. This document shifted the focus of the movement from harsh criticism and punishment of basic-level cadres to an emphasis on the more fundamental struggle between the two roads of socialism and capitalism and an expansion in the targets of class struggle to include all those with "capitalist tendencies" (Baum and Tiewes 1968, 118–126).

6. The term "diagram" is used here in the sense given it by Charles Sanders Peirce, for whom a diagram is "a type of icon in which the arrangement of parts of the signifier is isomorphic with the arrangement of parts of its object" (Mannheim 1991, 227; cf. Peirce 1940, 105).

7. These estimates of land allocation come from village government statistics collected in 1984, four years after household cultivation began.

Chapter 9

1. The total fertility rate in rural Yunnan grew from 6.03 per thousand population in the mid-1950s to 6.33 between 1964 and 1966, the height of the second birth control campaign (Peng 1991, 218). Peng estimates that there were .57 birth control operations (IUD insertions, sterilizations, and induced abortions) per thousand people in Yunnan during the 1960s, compared to 16.43 for Shanghai and 15.84 for Beijing; this was the lowest for any province for which figures exist (1991, 33).

2. Like peasants elsewhere in rural China, Zhizuo residents used a variety of other methods to control fertility and avoid raising unwanted children, including rhythm methods, withdrawal, herbal methods to induce abortion, neglect or differential care of less-valued children, and, occasionally, infanticide.

3. See Greenhalgh 1993 and A. Wolf 1986. For a contemporary assessment of these difficulties, see Wu and Duan 1982.

4. Zhang Weiguo (1999, 213) describes a similar practice in a village in northern China.

5. Infant mortality rates for Zhizuo residents are difficult to estimate. People in Zhizuo resisted registering their infants until the babies had teeth—the point at which parents felt that a child could be considered a true person. Official data from the 1990 census showed that Yi populations in general had infant mortality rates of 65 per thousand, significantly higher than the national rate (55 per thousand) (Zhang 1995, 20). In Yongren, with a Yi population of about 50 percent, overall mortality statistics reflected poor nutrition and medical care. From 1971 through 1982, the crude death rate in the county averaged 8.7 per thousand, while the provincial rate averaged 8.1 and the national rate 6.4. By 1989, the provincial rate had fallen to 7.3 and the national rate to 6.0, while Yongren's rate remained high, at 8.4 (YSTRB 1990). Most of this difference resulted from the inclusion of mountainous regions like Zhizuo, where nutrition and medical care were much inferior than in the county town and its surrounding plain.

6. Yunnan, with its large minority population, seems to have experienced similar problems with early marriage. Official statistics for 1988 put the birth rate for women from fifteen to nineteen years of age in Yunnan's countryside at 160 percent of the rate for rural China as a whole; this gap was as high or higher throughout the 1980s (Chen 1993). The difficulties cadres faced in enforcing birth planning policies in general throughout rural China in the mid-1980s are reflected in national statistics: from 1984 to 1986, the rate of late marriages (in which the bride was over twenty-three) declined from 58.8 percent to 54.1 percent; the rate of contraceptive use among fertile couples declined slightly, from 85.8 percent to 85.6 percent in the same years (Peng 1991, 54); and the total fertility rate in the countryside grew from 2.51 to 2.87 from 1984 to 1987 (Chen 1993, 29). In Yunnan Province, the total fertility rate in the countryside dropped from 5.82 in 1975, when the "later, longer, fewer" campaign got under way, to 3.48 in 1987; but it remained 21 percent higher than the national rate (Chen 1993, 101).

7. The authors of this article, Yan Tiansan and Jin Cao, were members of the Party Committee of Nanyang Prefecture, Henan Province.

8. The Population Quality Index was developed by modifying the Physical Quality of Life Index (PQLI), developed in 1979 by M. David Morris. The PQLI is a weighted average of indexes of infant mortality, life expectancy at age one, and basic literacy on a 0 to 100 scale (Morris 1979). Its use by international agencies as a measure of life quality has recently been largely supplanted by other, more detailed indexes (van der Lijn 1995).

9. The course Qi attended was designed to combat illiteracy by teaching basic-level minority cadres how to read and write in their own languages. Qi had learned a standardized script compiled from four separate traditional scripts from other Yi areas in Yunnan—Central dialect speakers like Líp'ò and Lòlop'ò had no traditional script of their own. This literacy campaign later expanded into village-level courses for youths who had no middle-school education.

10. Part of a chant for this spirit is transcribed in chapter 5, fragment 5.14.

11. See chapter 6, note 16, for a sampling of the extensive literature exploring the "Imperial metaphor."

12. For a fuller version of this story, see Mueggler 1996, 101.

References

Addison, James Thayer. 1925. *Chinese Ancestor Worship: A Study of Its Meaning and Relations with Christianity.* Tokyo: Chung hua sheng kung hui.

Ahern, Emily. 1973. *Cult of the Dead in a Chinese Village.* Stanford: Stanford University Press.

——. 1974a. "Affines and the Rituals of Kinship." In *Religion and Ritual in Chinese Society,* edited by Arthur Wolf. Stanford: Stanford University Press.

——. 1974b. "The Power and Pollution of Chinese Women." In *Women in Chinese Society,* edited by Margery Wolf and Roxanne Witke. Stanford: Stanford University Press.

——. 1976. "Segmentation in Chinese Lineages: A View Through Written Genealogies." *American Ethnologist* 3(1): 1–16.

——. 1981. *Chinese Ritual and Politics.* Cambridge: Cambridge University Press.

Aird, John. 1982. "Population Studies and Population Policy in China." *Population and Development Review* 8(2): 267–297.

Anagnost, Ann. 1989. "The Transformation of Gender in Modern China." In *Gender and Anthropology: Critical Reviews for Research and Teaching,* edited by Sandra Morgan. Project on Gender and the Curriculum. Amherst, Mass.: American Anthropological Association.

——. 1997. *National Past-Times: Narrative, Representation, and Power in Modern China.* Durham: Duke University Press.

Bachelard, Gaston. 1964. *The Poetics of Space.* Translated by Maria Jolas. Boston: Beacon Press.

Bachman, David. 1991. *Bureaucracy, Economy, and Leadership in China: The Institutional Origins of the Great Leap Forward.* Cambridge: Cambridge University Press.

Baker, Hugh. 1968. *A Chinese Lineage Village: Sheung Shui.* Stanford: Stanford University Press.

Bakhtin, Mikhail. 1981. *The Dialogic Imagination.* Translated by C. Emerson and M. Holquist. Austin: University of Texas Press.

Bamo Axyi. 1994. *Yizu ling xinyang yanjiu* (An investigation of the Yi belief in souls). Chengdu: Sichuan minzu chubanshe.

Banister, Judith. 1987. *China's Changing Population*. Stanford: Stanford University Press.

Barlow, Tani. 1994a. "The Politics and Protocols of *Funü:* (Un)Making National Woman." In *Engendering China: Women, Culture, and the State,* edited by Christina Gilmartin, Gail Hershatter, Lisa Rofel, and Tyrene White. Cambridge: Harvard University Press.

——. 1994b. "Theorizing Woman: *Funü, Guojia, Jiating* (Chinese Woman, Chinese State, Chinese Family)." In *Body, Subject, and Power in China,* edited by Angela Zito and Tani Barlow. Chicago: University of Chicago Press.

Baum, Richard, and Frederic Teiwes. 1968. *Ssu-Ch'ing: The Socialist Education Movement of 1962–1966.* Berkeley: University of California Press.

Bennett, Gordon A., and Ronald N. Montaperto. 1980. *Red Guard: The Political Biography of Dai Hsiao Ai.* Gloucester, Mass.: Anchor Books.

Bernstein, Thomas P. 1984. "Stalinism, Famine, and Chinese Peasants: Grain Procurements During the Great Leap Forward." *Theory and Society* 13:339–377.

Blake, F. 1978. "Death and Abuse in Marriage Laments: The Curse of the Chinese Bride" *Asian Folklore Studies* 37:13–33.

Boltz, Judith. 1983. "Opening the Gates of Purgatory: A Twelfth Century Taoist Meditation Technique for the Salvation of Lost Souls." *Tantric and Taoist Studies* 2:487–511.

Boon, James A. 1990. *Affinities and Extremes: Crisscrossing the Bittersweet Ethnology of East Indies History, Hindu-Balinese Culture, and Indo-European Allure.* Chicago: University of Chicago Press.

Bourdieu, Pierre. 1990. *The Logic of Practice.* Translated by Richard Nice. Stanford: Stanford University Press.

Bradley, David. 1978. *Proto Loloish.* London: Curzon Press.

Bray, Francesca. 1997. *Technology and Gender: Fabrics of Power in Late Imperial China.* Berkeley: University of California Press.

Brownell, Susan. 1995. *Training the Body for China.* Chicago: University of Chicago Press.

Cancian, Frank. 1965. *Economics and Prestige in a Maya Community: The Religious Cargo System in Zinacantan.* Stanford: Stanford University Press.

——. 1992. *The Decline of Community in Zinacantan: Economy, Public Life, and Social Stratification, 1960–1987.* Stanford: Stanford University Press.

Carsten, Janet, and Stephen Hugh-Jones, eds. 1995. *About the House: Lévi-Strauss and Beyond.* Cambridge: Cambridge University Press.

Casey, Edward. 1997. *The Fate of Place: A Philosophical History.* Berkeley: University of California Press.

Castoriadis, Cornelius. 1987. *The Imaginary Institution of Society.* Cambridge: MIT Press.

Chan, Anita, Richard Madsen, and Jonathan Unger. 1984. *Chen Village: The Recent History of a Peasant Community in Mao's China.* Berkeley: University of California Press.

Chao, Emily. 1996. "Hegemony, Agency, and the Re-presentation of the Past: Dongba Culture Among the Naxi Minority of Southwest China." In *Negoti-*

ating Ethnicities in China and Taiwan, edited by Melissa Brown. Berkeley: University of California Press.

Chao, Paul. 1983. *Chinese Kinship.* London: Kegan Paul.

Chen, Pi-Chao. 1976. *Population and Health Policy in the People's Republic of China.* Washington, D.C.: Smithsonian Institution Press.

Chen Shengli. 1993. *Zhongguo gesheng shengyulu shouce, 1940–1990* (Handbook of provincial birth rates in China, 1940–1990). Beijing: Zhongguo renkou chubanshe.

Chen Shilin, Bian Shiming, and Li Xiuqing, eds. 1984. *Yiyu Jianzhi* (A brief account of the Yi language). Chengdu: Sichuan minzu chubanshe.

Chen Zaihua. 1994. "Zhongguo shaoshu minzu renkou shenghuo zhiliang yü minzu renkou fazhan zhanlue" (The quality of life of China's minority nationality population and the strategy of population development). *Renkou yanjiu* (Population research) 18(1): 31–37.

Cheng, Francois. 1982. *Chinese Poetic Writing, with an Anthology of Tang Poetry.* Bloomington: Indiana University Press.

Cheng, Weiji. 1992. *History of Textile Technology of Ancient China.* New York: Science Press.

Ch'ü, T'ung-tsu. 1962. *Local Government in China Under the Ch'ing.* Cambridge: Harvard University Press.

Coale, Ansle J. 1981. "Population Trends, Population Policy, and Population Studies in China." *Population and Development Review* 7(1): 98–110.

——. 1984. *Rapid Population Change in China, 1952–1982.* Washington, D.C.: National Academy Press.

Cohen, Myron. 1976. *House United, House Divided: The Chinese Family in Taiwan.* New York: Columbia University Press.

——. 1990. "Lineage Organization in North China." *Journal of Asian Studies* 49(3): 509–534.

Cong Jin. 1989. *Quzhe fazhan de suiyue* (The years of torturous development). Zhengzhou: Henan renmin chubanshe.

Coronil, Fernando. 1997. *The Magical State: Nature, Money, and Modernity in Venezuela.* Chicago: University of Chicago Press.

Cowie, Elizabeth. 1978. "Woman as Sign." *m/f* 1:49–63.

Croll, Elizabeth. 1981. *The Politics of Marriage in Contemporary China.* Cambridge: Cambridge University Press.

Crook, David, and Isabelle Crook. 1959. *The First Years of Yangyi Commune.* London: Routledge & Kegan Paul.

CYZZ (*Chuxiong Yizu Zizhizhou zhi* [Chuxiong Yi Autonomous Region gazetteer]). 1993. Vol. 1. Beijing: Renmin chubanshe.

——. 1994. Vol. 2. Beijing: Renmin chubanshe.

Das, Veena. 1997. "Language and Body: Transactions in the Construction of Pain." In *Social Suffering,* edited by Arthur Kleinman, Veena Das, and Margaret Lock. Berkeley: University of California Press.

de Certeau, Michel. 1992. *The Mystic Fable.* Vol. 1, *The Sixteenth and Seventeenth Centuries.* Chicago: University of Chicago Press.

Deleuze, Gilles, and Félix Guattari. 1983. *Anti-Oedipus: Capitalism and Schizophrenia.* Translated by Robert Hurley, Mark Seem, and Helen Lane. Minneapolis: University of Minnesota Press.

——. 1987. *A Thousand Plateaus: Capitalism and Schizophrenia.* Translated by Brian Massumi. Minneapolis: University of Minnesota Press.

Deng Guosheng. 1992. "Jieyu xiaoguo wenti ying yinqi gaodu zhongshi" (Problematic birth control results deserve more attention). *Renkou yu jingji* (Population and economics) 74:43–45.

Derrida, Jacques. 1976. *Of Grammatology.* Translated by Gayatri C. Spivak. Baltimore: Johns Hopkins University Press.

Diamond, Norma. 1975. "Collectivization, Kinship, and the Status of Women in Rural China." In *Toward an Anthropology of Women,* edited by Rayna Reiter. New York: Monthly Review Press.

——. 1988. "The Miao and Poison: Interactions on China's Southwest Frontier." *Ethnology* 27:1–25.

——. 1995. "Defining the Miao: Ming, Qing, and Contemporary Views." In *Cultural Encounters on China's Ethnic Frontiers,* edited by Stevan Harrell. Seattle: University of Washington Press.

Dikötter, Frank. 1992. *The Discourse of Race in Modern China.* London: C. Hurst; Stanford: Stanford University Press; Hong Kong: Hong Kong University Press.

——. 1995. *Sex, Culture, and Modernity in China: Medical Science and the Construction of Sexual Identities in the Early Republican Period.* London: C. Hurst.

——. 1998. *Imperfect Conceptions: Medical Knowledge, Birth Defects, and Eugenics in China.* New York: Columbia University Press.

Dillon, M. C. 1988. *Merleau-Ponty's Ontology.* Evanston: Northwestern University Press.

Dirlik, Arif. 1983. "The Predicament of Marxist Revolutionary Consciousness: Mao Zedong, Antonio Gramsci, and the Reformulation of Marxist Revolutionary Theory." *Modern China* 9(2): 182–211.

Domenach, Jean-Luc. 1995. *The Origins of the Great Leap Forward: The Case of One Chinese Province.* Translated by A. M. Berrett. Boulder: Westview Press.

Dong, Xiaoyuan, and Gregory K. Dow. 1993. "Does Free Exit Reduce Shirking in Production Teams?" *Journal of Comparative Economics* 17(2): 472–484.

Doolittle, Justus. 1868. *Social Life of the Chinese: A Daguerreotype of Daily Life in China.* London: Sampson, Low, and Co.

Doré, Henry. 1965–1967. *Researches into Chinese Superstition.* 11 vols. Translated by M. Kennellyu, D. G. Finn, and L. F. McGreal. Taipei: Ch'êng wen.

Douglas, Mary. 1978. *Purity and Danger: An Analysis of the Concepts of Pollution and Taboo.* London: Routledge & Kegan Paul.

Duara, Presenjit. 1988. *Culture, Power, and the State: Rural North China, 1900–1942.* Stanford: Stanford University Press.

DXZ (*Dayao Xian zhi* [Dayao County gazetteer]). 1825.

DZY (*Dangdai Zhongguo de Yunnan* [Contemporary China's Yunnan]). 1991. Vols. 1 and 2. Beijing: Dangdai Zhongguo chubanshe.

Ebrey, Patricia B. 1991. *Chu Hsi's Family Rituals: A Twelfth-Century Chinese Manual for the Performance of Cappings, Weddings, Funerals, and Ancestral Rites.* Princeton: Princeton University Press.

——. 1993. *The Inner Quarters: Marriage and the Lives of Chinese Women in the Sung Period.* Berkeley: University of California Press.

Ebrey, Patricia B., and Peter N. Gregory. 1993. *Religion and Society in Tang and Sung China*. Honolulu: University of Hawaii Press.

Fang Kaisong, ed. 1990. *Ailao Shan Yizu shenhua chuanshuo* (Mythological tales of the Ailao Mountain Yi). Kunming: Yunnan renmin chubanshe.

Fei, Xiaotong. 1980. "Ethnic Identification in China." *Social Sciences in China* 1(1): 94–107.

Feuchtwang, Stephan. 1974. *An Anthropological Analysis of Chinese Geomancy*. Vientiane, Laos: Vithagna.

——. 1992. *The Imperial Metaphor: Popular Religion in China*. London: Routledge.

Fitzgerald, C. P. 1941. *The Tower of the Five Glories: A Study of the Min Chia of Ta Li, Yunnan*. London: Cresset Press.

Fitzgerald, John. 1996. *Awakening China: Politics, Culture, and Class in the Nationalist Revolution*. Stanford: Stanford University Press.

Foucault, Michel. 1991. "Governmentality." In *The Foucault Effect: Studies in Governmentality, with Two Lectures by and an Interview with Michel Foucault,* edited by Graham Burchell, Colin Gordon, and Peter Miller. London: Harvester Wheatsheaf.

Fox, James J. 1977. "Roman Jakobson and the Comparative Study of Parallelism." In *Roman Jakobson: Echoes of His Scholarship,* edited by Daniel Armstrong and C. H. van Schooneveld. Lisse: Peter de Ridder.

——, ed. 1980. *The Flow of Life: Essays on Eastern Indonesia*. Cambridge: Harvard University Press.

——, ed. 1988. *To Speak in Pairs: Essays on the Ritual Languages of Eastern Indonesia*. New York: Cambridge University Press.

Frazer, Sir James G. 1890. *The Golden Bough: A Study in Comparative Religion*. London: Macmillan.

Freedman, Maurice. 1958. *Lineage Organization in Southeastern China*. London: Athlone Press.

——. 1966. *Chinese Lineage and Society: Fukien and Kwangtong*. LSE Monographs on Social Anthropology, no. 33. London: Athlone Press.

——. 1967. "Ancestor Worship: Two Aspects of the Chinese Case." In *Social Organization: Essays Presented to Raymond Firth,* edited by Maurice Freedman. Chicago: University of Chicago Press.

Furth, Charlotte. 1986. "Blood, Body, and Gender: Medical Images of the Female Condition in China, 1600–1850." *Chinese Science* 7:43–66.

Gallin, Bernard. 1966. *Hsin Hsing, Taiwan: A Chinese Village in Change*. Berkeley: University of California Press.

Gao Dingfeng and Yang Yunzhong. 1989. "Yongren Yiuzu saizhuangjie" (The clothing competition festival of the Yongren Yi). *Yongren lishi ziliao xuanji* (Selected material on Yongren history) 1:121–122.

Giddens, Anthony. 1984. *The Constitution of Society: Outline of the Theory of Structuration*. Berkeley: University of California Press.

Gilbert, Roger. 1991. *Walks in the World: Representation and Experience in Modern American Poetry*. Princeton: Princeton University Press.

Gladney, Dru. 1991. *Muslim Chinese: Ethnic Nationalism in the People's Republic*. Cambridge: Harvard University Press.

——. 1994. "Representing Nationality in China: Refiguring Majority/Minority Identities." *Journal of Asian Studies* 53(1): 92–123.

Greenhalgh, Susan. 1993. "The Peasantization of the One-Child Policy in Shaanxi." In *Chinese Families in the Post-Mao Era,* edited by Deborah Davis and Stevan Harrell. Berkeley: University of California Press.

Greenhalgh, Susan, Ahu Chuzhu, and Li Nan. 1994. "Restraining Population Growth in Three Chinese Villages, 1988–1993." *Population and Development Review* 20(2): 364–392.

Greenhalgh, Susan, and Jiali Li. 1995. "Engendering Reproductive Policy and Practice in Peasant China: For a Feminist Demography of Reproduction." *Signs* 20(3): 601–641.

Guldin, Gregory E. 1994. *The Saga of Anthropology in China: From Malinowski to Moscow to Mao.* Armonk, N.Y.: M. E. Sharpe.

Handwerker, Lisa. 1995. "The Hen That Can't Lay an Egg ('Bu xia dan de mu ji'): Conceptions of Female Infertility in Modern China." In *Deviant Bodies: Critical Perspectives in Science and Popular Culture,* edited by Jennifer Terry and Jacqueline Urla. Bloomington: Indiana University Press.

Hansen, Chad. 1992. *A Daoist Theory of Chinese Thought.* New York: Oxford University Press.

Harrell, Stevan. 1974. "When a Ghost Becomes a God." In *Religion and Ritual in Chinese Society,* edited by Arthur Wolf. Stanford: Stanford University Press.

——. 1979. "The Concept of the Soul in Chinese Folk Religion." *Journal of Asian Studies* 38(3): 519–528.

——. 1982. *Ploughshare Village: Culture and Context in Taiwan.* Seattle: University of Washington Press.

——. 1990. "Ethnicity, Local Interests, and the State: Yi Communities in Southwest China." *Comparative Studies in Society and History* 32(3): 515–548.

——. 1995. "The History of the History of the Yi." In *Cultural Encounters on China's Ethnic Frontiers,* edited by Stevan Harrell. Seattle: University of Washington Press.

Haviland, John. 1977. *Gossip, Reputation, and Knowledge in Zinacantan.* Chicago: University of Chicago Press.

Herman, John A. 1997. "Empire in the Southwest: Early Qing Reforms to the Native Chieftain System." *Journal of Asian Studies* 56(1): 47–74.

Hopkins, Gerard M. 1959. "Poetic Diction." In *The Journals and Papers of Gerard Manley Hopkins,* edited by Humphry House. London: Oxford University Press.

Hsu, Francis. 1948. *Under the Ancestors' Shadow: Chinese Culture and Personality.* New York: Columbia University Press.

Hu Q. 1981. *Ming Qing Yizu shehui shi luncong* (Collected essays on the history of Yi society during the Ming and Qing dynasties). Shanghai: Shanghai renmin chubanshe.

Huang, K. H. 1968. "Mingdai tusi zhidu sheshi yu xinan kaifa" (The opening of the southwest and the establishment of the native chieftain system during the Ming dynasty). In *Mingdai tusi zhidu* (The native chieftain system during the Ming dynasty), edited by She Y. Taipei: Taiwan xuesheng shuju.

Jakobson, Roman. 1960. "Closing Statement: Linguistics and Poetics." In *Style in Language,* edited by Thomas A. Sebeok. Cambridge: MIT Press.

———. 1966. "Grammatical Parallelism and Its Russian Facet." *Language* 42(2): 399–429.

Janet, Pierre. 1928. *L'évolution de la mémoire et la notion du temps.* Paris: Cahine.

Jiang Qing. 1968. *Jiang Qing Tongzhi jianghua xuanbian* (Selected speeches of Comrade Jiang Qing). Beijing: Renmin chubanshe.

Jiang Yongxing. 1985. "Cong Guizhou minzu shibie gongzuo tanqi" (A discussion of Guizhou's nationalities classification work). *Minzu yanjiu jikan* (Nationalities research collection) 2:303–316.

Jing, Jun. 1996. *The Temple of Memories: History, Power, and Morality in a Chinese Village.* Stanford: Stanford University Press.

Jordan, David. 1972. *Gods, Ghosts, and Ancestors: Folk Religion in a Taiwanese Village.* Berkeley: University of California Press.

Judd, Ellen R. 1994. *Gender and Power in Rural North China.* Stanford: Stanford University Press.

Kane, Penny. 1988. *Famine in China, 1959–62: Demographic and Social Implications.* New York: St. Martin's Press.

Kaufman, John, Zhang Zhirong, Qiao Xinjian, and Zhang Yang. 1992. "The Quality of Family Planning Services in China." *Studies in Family Planning* 23(2): 73–84.

Keane, Webb. 1995. "The Spoken House: Text, Act, and Object in Eastern Indonesia." *American Ethnologist* 22(1): 102–124.

———. 1996. "Religious Language." *Annual Review of Anthropology* 26:47–71.

Kipnis, Andrew. 1997. *Producing Guanxi: Sentiment, Self, and Subculture in a North China Village.* Durham: Duke University Press.

Kleeman, Terry F. 1993. "The Expansion of the Wen-Ch'ang Cult." In *Religion and Society in Tang and Sung China,* edited by Patricia B. Ebrey and Peter N. Gregory. Honolulu: University of Hawaii Press.

Klein, Melanie. 1975. "The Importance of Symbol-Formation in the Development of the Ego." In *Love, Guilt, and Reparation, and Other Works, 1921–1945.* London: Hogarth Press.

Knapp, Ronald G. 1986. *China's Traditional Rural Architecture: A Cultural Geography of the Common House.* Honolulu: University of Hawaii Press.

———. 1999. *China's Old Dwellings.* Honolulu: University of Hawaii Press.

Kristeva, Julia. 1982. *Powers of Horror: An Essay on Abjection.* Translated by Leon S. Roudiez. New York: Columbia University Press.

Kuhn, Philip. 1990. *Soulstealers: The Chinese Sorcery Scare of 1786.* Cambridge: Harvard University Press.

Kung, James. 1993. "Transaction Costs and Peasants' Choice of Institutions: Did the Right to Exit Really Solve the Free Rider Problem in Chinese Collective Agriculture?" *Journal of Comparative Economics* 17(2): 485–503.

Lecercle, Jean-Jacques. 1985. *Philosophy Through the Looking Glass: Language, Nonsense, and Desire.* London: Hutchinson.

Lefebvre, Henri. 1991. *The Production of Space.* Translated by Donald Nicholson-Smith. Oxford: Blackwell.

Legendre, Aimé-Francois. 1913. *Au Yunnan, et dans le massif du Kin-ho (Fleuve d'Or)*. Paris: Plon-Nourrit et Cie.

Levinson, Joseph. 1966. *Confucian China and Its Modern Fate*. Berkeley: University of California Press.

Lévi-Strauss, Claude. 1983. *The Way of the Masks*. Translated by Sylvia Modelski. London: Jonathan Cape.

——. 1984. *Paroles Données*. Paris: Plon.

——. 1991. "Maison." In *Dictionnaire de l'Ethnologie et de l'Anthropologie*, edited by P. Bonte and M. Izard. Paris: Presses Universitaires de France.

Li Fengming, ed. 1987. *Xinan minzu yanjiu* (Research on southwestern ethnicities). Chengdu: Sichuan minzu chubanshe.

Li S. Y. 1990. "Luelun tusi zhidu yu gaitu guiliu" (A brief discussion of the native chieftain system and bureaucratic consolidation). In *Zhongguo gudia bianjiang zhengce yanjiu* (Studies on frontier policy in ancient China), edited by Ma D. Beijing: Zhongguo shehui kexue chubanshe.

Li Yongxiang. 1999. *Yizu Nisuren de sangzang yishi yi jingwen fanyi* (Funeral rites and documents of the Nisu branch of the Yi). Kunming: Yunnan daxue chubanshe.

Li Zixian, ed. 1990. *Yunnan shaoshu minzu shenhua xuan* (Selected myths of Yunnan's minority nationalities). Kunming: Yunnan renmin chubanshe.

Lieberthal, Kenneth G. 1987. "The Great Leap Forward and the Split in the Yenan Leadership." In *The People's Republic, Part 1: The Emergence of Revolutionary China, 1949–1965*, edited by Roderick MacFarquhar and John K. Fairbank. Vol. 14 of *The Cambridge History of China*. Cambridge: Cambridge University Press.

Liétard, Alfred. 1913. *Au Yun-nan les Lo-o p'o: Une Tribu des Aborigenes de la Chine Meridionale*. Münster: Aschendorffsche Verlagsbuchhandlung.

Lin, Justin Y. 1990. "Collectivization and China's Agricultural Crisis in 1959–1971." *Journal of Political Economy* 98(6): 1228–1252.

——. 1993. "Exit Rights, Exit Costs, and Shirking in Agricultural Cooperatives: A Reply." *Journal of Comparative Economics* 17(2): 504–520.

Lin, Tongqi, Henry Rosemount Jr., and Roger T. Ames. 1995. "Chinese Philosophy: A Philosophical Essay on the 'State-of-the-Art.'" *Journal of Asian Studies* 54(3): 727–758.

Lin Yueh-hua. 1961. *The Lolo of Liang Shan*. Translated by Ju-shan Pan. New Haven: HRAF Press.

——. 1963. "Guanyu 'minzu' yici de shiyong he yuming de wenti" (On the problem of the uses and synonyms of the term *minzu*). *Lishi yanjiu* (Historical studies) 2:175.

——. 1984. "Zhongguo xinan diqu de minzu shibie" (Ethnic identification in China's southwest). *Minzu yanjiu lunwenji* (Treatises on nationalities research) 3:1–9.

——. 1990. "New China's Ethnology: Research and Prospects." In *Anthropology in China: Defining the Discipline*, edited by Gregory Guldin. Armonk, N.Y.: M. E. Sharpe.

Lin Yueh-hua and Jin Tianming. 1980. "Cong lishi fazhan kandongqian woguo minzuxue de duixiang he renwu" (Looking at the goals and tasks of our country's nationalities studies from the perspective of historical development). *Minzu yanjiu* (Nationalities research) 2:50–57.

Litzinger, Ralph A. 1995. "Making Histories: Contending Conceptions of the Yao Past." In *Cultural Encounters on China's Ethnic Frontiers,* edited by Stevan Harrell. Seattle: University of Washington Press.

———. 1998. "Memory Work: Reconstituting the Ethnic in Post-Mao China." *Cultural Anthropology* 13(2): 224–254.

Liu Chün. 1933. "Qingdai Yunnan de yanwu" (The Yunnan salt administration during the Qing dynasty). *Zhongguo jindai jingjishi yanjiu jikan* (Studies on the economic history of modern China) 2(1): 27–141.

Liu, Lydia H. 1994. "The Female Body and Nationalist Discourse: Manchuria in Xiao Hong's Field of Life and Death." In *Body, Subject, and Power in China,* edited by Angela Zito and Tani Barlow. Chicago: University of Chicago Press.

Liu, Minquan. 1993. "Exit Right, Retaliatory Shirking, and the Agricultural Crisis in China." *Journal of Comparative Economics* 17(2): 540–559.

Liu, Ta-chung, and Kung-chia Yeh. 1965. *The Economy of the Chinese Mainland: National Income and Development, 1933–1959.* Princeton: Princeton University Press.

Ma Erzi. 2000. "Names and Genealogies in Liangshan." In *Perspectives on the Yi of Southwest China,* edited by Stevan Harrell. Berkeley: University of California Press.

MacFarquhar, Roderick. 1974. *Contradictions Among the People, 1956–1957.* Vol. 1 of The Origins of the Cultural Revolution. New York: Columbia University Press.

———. 1983. *The Great Leap Forward, 1958–1960.* Vol. 2 of *The Origins of the Cultural Revolution.* New York: Columbia University Press.

———. 1997. *The Coming of the Cataclysm, 1961–1966.* Vol. 3 of *The Origins of the Cultural Revolution.* Oxford: Oxford University Press; New York: Columbia University Press.

Mackerras, Colin. 1994. *China's Minorities: Integration and Modernization in the Twentieth Century.* New York: Oxford University Press.

Macleod, W. B. 1993. "The Role of Exit Costs in the Theory of Cooperative Teams: A Theoretical Perspective." *Journal of Comparative Economics* 17(2): 521–529.

Mann, Susan. 1997. *Precious Records: Women in China's Long Eighteenth Century.* Stanford: Stanford University Press.

Mannheim, Bruce. 1991. *The Language of the Inka Since the European Invasion.* Austin: University of Texas Press.

Mao Zedong. 1969. *Mao Zedong sixiang wansui* (Ten thousand years for Mao Zedong's thought). Beijing: Renmin chubanshe.

Martin, Emily. 1988. "Gender and Ideological Differences in Representations of Life and Death." In *Death Ritual in Imperial and Modern China,* edited by Evelyn Rawski and James L. Watson. Berkeley: University of California Press.

Mauss, Marcel, and Henri Hubert. 1972. *A General Theory of Magic.* Translated by Robert Brain. New York: W. W. Norton.

McKhann, Charles F. 1995. "The Naxi and the Nationalities Question." In *Cultural Encounters on China's Ethnic Frontiers,* edited by Stevan Harrell. Seattle: University of Washington Press.

Merleau-Ponty, Maurice. 1962. *Phenomenology of Perception.* Translated by Colin Smith. New York: Humanities Press.

———. 1968. *The Visible and the Invisible.* Edited by Claude Lefort. Translated by Alphonso Lingis. Evanston: Northwestern University Press.

Morris, M. David. 1979. *Measuring the Condition of the World's Poor: The Physical Quality of Life Index.* New York: Pergamon Press.

Mueggler, Erik. 1996. "Specters of Power: Ritual and Politics in an Yi Community." Ph.D. dissertation, Johns Hopkins University.

———. 1998a. "A Carceral Regime: Violence and Social Memory in Southwest China." *Cultural Anthropology* 13(2): 167–192.

———. 1998b. "The Poetics of Grief and the Price of Hemp in Southwest China." *Journal of Asian Studies* 57(4): 979–1008.

———. 1998c. "Procreative Metaphor and Productive Unity in an Yi Headmanship." *Journal of the Royal Anthropological Institute* 4(2): 61–78.

———. 1999. "Spectral Subversions: Rival Tactics of Time and Agency in Southwest China." *Comparative Studies in Society and History* 41(3): 458–481.

———. 2000. "Procreation and Spatial Production in a Yi Headmanship." In *Perspectives on the Yi of Southwest China,* edited by Stevan Harrell. Berkeley: University of California Press.

Munn, Nancy. 1970. "The Transformation of Subjects into Objects in Walbiri and Pitjantjatjara Myth." In *Australian Aboriginal Anthropology,* edited by R. M. Berndt. Nedlands: University of Western Australia Press.

Nash, Manning. 1964. "Capital, Saving, and Credit in a Guatemalan and a Mexican Indian Peasant Society." In *Capital, Saving, and Credit in Peasant Societies,* edited by Raymond Firth and B. S. Yamey. Chicago: Aldine.

Osgood, Cornelius. 1963. *Village Life in Old China: A Community Study of Kao Yao, Yünnan.* New York: Ronald Press.

Pan Qi. 1992. "Minzu diqu shehuizhuyi jingshen wenming fazhan yingai sheng xin shuiping" (The spiritual development of minority regions must rise to a new level). *Qiushi* (Seeking truth) 24:25–28.

Pasternak, Burton. 1972. *Kinship and Community in Two Chinese Villages.* Stanford: Stanford University Press.

Peirce, Charles S. 1940. "Logic As Semiotic." In *The Philosophy of Peirce,* edited by Justus Buchler. London: Routledge.

Peng, Xizhe. 1987. "Demographic Consequences of the Great Leap Forward in China's Provinces." *Journal of Asian Studies* 13(4): 639–670.

———. 1991. *Demographic Transition in China: Fertility Trends Since the 1950s.* Oxford: Clarendon Press.

Potter, Jack. 1968. *Capitalism and the Chinese Peasant.* Berkeley: University of California Press.

Potter, Jack, and Sulamith H. Potter. 1990. *China's Peasants: The Anthropology of a Revolution.* Cambridge: Cambridge University Press.

Putterman, Louis, and Gilbert L. Skillman. 1993. "Collectivization and China's Agricultural Crisis." *Journal of Comparative Economics* 17(2): 530–539.

Ramsey, S. Ramsey. 1987. *The Languages of China*. Princeton: Princeton University Press.

Rawski, Evelyn S. 1996. "Presidential Address: Re-envisioning the Qing: The Significance of the Qing Period in Chinese History." *Journal of Asian Studies* 55(4): 829–850.

Rock, Joseph F. 1935. "The Story of the Flood in the Literature of the Moso (Nak-hi) Tribe." *Journal of the West China Border Research Society* 7:64–80.

Rose, Gillian. 1996. *Mourning Becomes the Law*. Cambridge: Cambridge University Press.

Rubin, Gayle. 1975. "The Traffic in Women: Notes on the Political Economy of Sex." In *Toward an Anthropology of Women*, edited by Rayna Reiter. New York: Monthly Review Press.

Sangren, P. Steven. 1983. "Female Gender in Chinese Religious Symbols: Kuan Yin, Ma Tsu, and the Eternal Mother." *Signs* 9(1): 4–25.

———. 1987. *History and Magical Power in a Chinese Community*. Stanford: Stanford University Press.

Schein, Louisa. 1997. "Gender and Internal Orientalism in China." *Modern China* 23(1): 69–98.

———. 2000. *Minority Rules: The Miao and the Feminine in China's Cultural Politics*. Durham: Duke University Press.

Schoenhals, Michael. 1987. *Saltationist Socialism: Mao Zedong and the Great Leap Forward, 1958*. Stockholm: University of Stockholm.

Seaman, Gary. 1981. "The Sexual Politics of Karmic Retribution." In *The Anthropology of Taiwanese Society*, edited by Emily Ahern and Hill Gates. Stanford: Stanford University Press.

———. 1992. "Winds, Waters, Seeds, and Souls: Folk Concepts of Physiology and Etiology in Chinese Geomancy." In *Paths to Asian Medical Knowledge*, edited by Charles Leslie and Allan Young. Berkeley: University of California Press.

Shahar, Meir, and Robert P. Weller, eds. 1996. *Unruly Gods: Divinity and Society in China*. Honolulu: University of Hawaii Press.

Shue, Vivienne. 1980. *Peasant China in Transition: The Dynamics of Development Toward Socialism, 1949–1956*. Berkeley: University of California Press.

———. 1988. *The Reach of the State: Sketches of the Chinese Body Politic*. Stanford: Stanford University Press.

Siu, Helen. 1989. *Agents and Victims in South China: Accomplices in Rural Revolution*. New Haven: Yale University Press.

Skinner, G. William. 1964–1965. "Marketing and Social Structure in Rural China." *Journal of Asian Studies* 24(1): 3–43, 24(2): 195–228, 24(3): 363–399.

———. 1977. "Regional Urbanization in Nineteenth Century China." In *The City in Late Imperial China*, edited by G. William Skinner. Stanford: Stanford University Press.

———. 1985. "Presidential Address: The Structure of Chinese History." *Journal of Asian Studies* 44(2): 17–54.

———. 1997. Introduction to *Migration and Ethnicity in Chinese History*, by Sow-Theng Leung. Stanford: Stanford University Press.

Smith, Kent C. 1970. "Ch'ing Policy and the Development of Southwest China: Aspects of Ortai's Governor-Generalship, 1726–1731." Ph.D. dissertation, Yale University.

Song Boping and Cui Li. 1993. "Yunnan teyou shaoshu minzu renkou xian-zhuang ji dui shengchanli tiaoyue fazhan de yingxiang" (The population situation among Yunnan's special minorities and its influence on the rapid development of productive forces). *Renkou yu jingji* (Population and economics) 81(6): 27–35.

SSB (Sichuan Sheng bianjizu [Sichuan Province editorial committee]). 1987. *Sichuan Sheng Liangshan Yizu shehui diaocha ziliao xuanji* (Selections from investigations into Liangshan Yi society in Sichuan Province). Chengdu: Sichuan Sheng shehui kexueyuan chubanshe.

Stalin, Joseph. 1956. *Sidalin quanji* (The collected works of Stalin). Beijing: Renmin chubanshe.

Starr, John B. 1979. *Continuing the Revolution: The Political Thought of Mao.* Princeton: Princeton University Press.

Stein, R. A. 1957a. "Architecture et pensée religieuse en Extreme-Orient." *Arts Asiatiques* 4:163–186.

——. 1957b. "L'habitat, le monde, et le corps humain en Extreme-Orient et en Haute Asie." *Journal Asiatique* 245:37–74.

Strathern, Marilyn. 1987. Introduction to *Dealing with Inequality: Analysing Gender Relations in Melanesia and Beyond,* edited by Marilyn Strathern. Cambridge: Cambridge University Press.

——. 1998. *The Gender of the Gift: Problems with Women and Problems with Society in Melanesia.* Berkeley: University of California Press.

Swain, Margaret B. 1995. "Père Vial and the Gni-p'a: Orientalist Scholarship and the Christian Project." In *Cultural Encounters on China's Ethnic Frontiers,* edited by Stevan Harrell. Seattle: University of Washington Press.

Tang Wenan. 1988. "Lun Yunnan shaoshu minzu jingji tizhi gaige" (On reforming the economic systems of Yunnan's minority nationalities). *Yixue yanjiu* (Yi studies research) 2:137–140.

Tao Xueliang. 1986. *Yizu wenxue zazu* (Anthology of Yi literature). Kunming: Yunnan minzu chubanshe.

Taussig, Michael. 1993. *Mimesis and Alterity: A Particular History of the Senses.* London: Routledge.

Teiser, Stephen. 1988. *The Ghost Festival in Medieval China.* Princeton: Princeton University Press.

Topley, Marjorie. 1974. "Cosmic Antagonisms: A Mother-Child Syndrome." In *Religion and Ritual in Chinese Society,* edited by Arthur Wolf. Stanford: Stanford University Press.

Tu Ping. 1995. "IUD Discontinuation Patterns and Correlates in Four Counties in North China." *Studies in Family Planning* 26(3): 169–179.

Urban, Greg. 1991. *A Discourse-Centered Approach to Culture: Native South American Myths and Rituals.* Austin: University of Texas Press.

Valeri, Valerio. 1980. "Notes on the Meaning of Marriage Prestations Among the Huaulu of Seram." In *The Flow of Life: Essays on Eastern Indonesia,* edited by James J. Fox. Cambridge: Harvard University Press.

van der Lijn, Nick. 1995. "Measuring Well-Being with Social Indicators, HDIs, PQLI, and BWI for 133 Countries for 1975, 1980, 1985, 1988, and 1992."

Tilburg University Library, The Netherlands; available online at *http:// greywww.kub.nl:2080/greyfiles/few/1995/704.html.*

Vannicelli, Fr. Luigi. 1944. *La Religione dei Lolo, Contributo allo Studio Etnologico delle Religioni dell'Estremo Oriente.* Milan: Società Editrice "Vita e Pensiero."

Vardara, Dena R., ed. 1993. *Taber's Cyclopedic Medical Dictionary.* Philadelphia: F. A. Davis.

Vial, Paul. 1898. *Les Lolos, Histoire, Religion, Moeurs, Langue, Ecriture.* Shanghai: Imprimerie de la Mission Catholique.

Wang, Lizhu. 1995. *Yizu zuxian chongbai yanjiu* (An investigation of Yi ancestor worship). Kunming: Yunnan renmin chubanshe.

Watson, James L. 1975. *Emigration and the Chinese Lineage: The Mans in Hong Kong and London.* Berkeley: University of California Press.

Watson, Rubie. 1981. "Class Differences and Affinal Relations in South China." *Man* 16(4): 593–615.

———. 1988. "The Named and the Nameless: Gender and Person in Chinese Society." *American Ethnologist* 13(4): 619–631.

———. 1994. "Making Secret Histories: Memory and Mourning in Post-Mao China." In *Memory, History, and Opposition Under State Socialism,* edited by Rubie S. Watson. Santa Fe: School of American Research Press.

Weins, H. 1954. *China's March Toward the Tropics.* Hamden, Conn.: Shoestring Press.

Weller, R. 1987. "The Politics of Ritual Disguise: Repression and Response in Taiwanese Popular Religion." *Modern China* 13(1): 17–39.

White, Sydney D. 1997. "Fame and Sacrifice: The Gendered Construction of Naxi Identities." *Modern China* 23(3): 298–327.

White, Tyrene. 1992. "The Population Factor: China's Family Planning Policy in the 1990s." In *China Briefing, 1991,* edited by William A. Joseph. Boulder: Westview Press.

———. 1994. "The Origins of China's Birth Planning Policy." In *Engendering China: Women, Culture, and the State,* edited by Christina Gilmartin, Gail Hershatter, Lisa Rofel, and Tyrene White. Cambridge: Harvard University Press.

Wolf, Arthur. 1974. "Gods, Ghosts, and Ancestors." In *Religion and Ritual in Chinese Society,* edited by Arthur Wolf. Stanford: Stanford University Press.

———. 1986. "The Preeminent Role of Government Intervention in China's Family Revolution." *Population and Development Review* 12(1): 101–116.

———. 1995. *Sexual Attraction and Childhood Association: A Chinese Brief for Edward Westermarck.* Stanford: Stanford University Press.

Wolf, Arthur, and Chieh-shan Huang. 1980. *Marriage and Adoption in China, 1845–1945.* Stanford: Stanford University Press.

Wolf, Eric. 1955. "Types of Latin American Peasantry: A Preliminary Discussion." *American Anthropologist* 57:452–471.

———. 1957. "Closed Corporate Peasant Communities in Mesoamerica and Central Java." *Southwestern Journal of Anthropology* 13:1–18.

———. 1986. "The Vicissitudes of the Closed Corporate Peasant Community." *American Ethnologist* 13(2): 325–329.

Wolf, Margery. 1972. *Women and the Family in Rural Taiwan*. Stanford: Stanford University Press.

Wu Jinyi and Duan Deyuan. 1982. "The System of Agricultural Production Responsibility and Control of Population." *Gansu ribao*, 16 January, 4.

Wyschogrod, Edith. 1998. *An Ethics of Remembering: History, Heterology, and the Nameless Others*. Chicago: University of Chicago Press.

Yan Tiansan and Jin Cao. 1992. "Jinren youlu de renkou nitaotai xianxiang: Jihua shengyu zhong renkou zengzhang de jingji sikao" (The contemporary concern of negative population selection: Economic considerations of the impact of birth planning on population growth). *Renkou yanjiu* (Population research) 77:36–41.

Yan, Yunxiang. 1996. *The Flow of Gifts: Reciprocity and Social Networks in a Chinese Village*. Stanford: Stanford University Press.

Yang, Dali. 1996. *Calamity and Reform in China: State, Rural Society, and Institutional Change Since the Great Leap Forward*. Stanford: Stanford University Press.

Yang Fuwang. 1990. "Dayao Tanhua Yizu muquanzhi canyu tantao" (An inquiry into remnants of matriarchy among Yi in Tanhua, Dayao). *Yizu wenhua* (Yi culture) 52–58.

Yang Hesen. 1990. "Chuxiong Yizu gaikuang" (A survey of Chuxiong's Yi nationality). *Yizu wenhua* (Yi culture) 117–140.

Yang Huaiying. 1994. *Liangshan Yizu nuli shehui falu zhidu yanjiu* (A study of the legal system of Liangshan Yi slave society). Chengdu: Sichuan minzu chubanshe.

Yang Jianbai and Li Xuezeng. 1980. "Lu woguo nongqingzhong guanxi di lishi jingyan (On the historical experience of the relationship between agriculture, light industry, and heavy industry in China). *Zhongguo shehui kexue* (Chinese social science) 3:36.

Yang, Mayfair M. 1994. *Gifts, Favors, and Banquets: The Art of Social Relationships in China*. Ithaca: Cornell University Press.

Yang Shuzhang. 1993. "Zhongguo shaoshu minzu renkou de zengzhang yu jihua shengyu" (The growth of China's minority nationality population and family planning). *Renkou yu jingji* (Population and economics) 78:13–20.

YSB (Yunnan Sheng bianjizu [Yunnan Province editorial committee]). 1986 [1952]. *Yunnan Yizu shehui lishi diaocha* (Research into the society and history of Yunnan Yi). Kunming: Yunnan minzu chubanshe and Yunnan renmin chubanshe.

YSDBW (Yunnan Sheng difangzhi bianzuan weiyuanhui [Yunnan Province local gazetteer compilation committee]). 1992. *Yunnan Sheng zhi, 17 juan, gongxiao hezuoshe zhi* (Gazetteer of Yunnan Province, vol. 17, supply and marketing cooperative gazetteer). Kunming: Yunnan renmin chubanshe.

YSJZZ (*Yunnan Sheng zhi jingji zonghe zhi* [Economic statistical gazetteer of Yunnan Province]). 1989–1995. Kunming: Yunnan renmin chubanshe.

YSMWCD (Yunnan Sheng minzu minjian wenxue Chuxiong diaochadui [Yunnan Province nationalities folk literature Chuxiong investigation team]). 1959. *Mei ge: Yizu minjian shishi* (Mei ge: A Yi folk ballad). Kunming: Yunnan renmin chubanshe.

YSTRB (Yunnan Sheng tongji ju renkou ban [Yunnan Province statistical bureau, population office]). 1990. *Yunnan Sheng renkou tongji ziliao huibian, 1949–1988* (Compiled material on population statistics for Yunnan Province, 1949–1988). Kunming: Yunnan renmin chubanshe.

YXZ (*Yanfeng Xian zhi* [Yanfeng County gazetteer]). 1922.

Zhang Ruhai. 1984. *Nongchan jige wenti yanjiu* (Research on some problems of agricultural prices). Shanghai: Renmin chubanshe.

Zhang Tingxian. 1988. "Tan Yunnan Yizu wenzi guifan gongzuo" (On the work of standardizing Yunnan's Yi writing). *Yixue yanjiu* (Yi studies research) 2:76–81.

Zhang Weiguo. 1999. "Implementation of State Family Planning Programmes in a Northern Chinese Village." *China Quarterly* 157:202–230.

Zhang Yi. 1995. "Zongguo de 18 ge baiwan ren yishang shaoshu minzu renkou suzhi fenxi" (An analysis of population quality among China's eighteen minority nationalities with populations of over one million). *Minzu yanjiu* (Nationalities research) 5:19–24.

Zhang, Zeyu. 1986. "Population Policy for Minorities." *Beijing Review* 29(48): 15–18.

Zheng Xue. 1996. "Han, Li, Hui, Mengu he Ewenkezu chengre renshi fangshi de bijiao" (A comparison of adult cognitive style among Han, Li, Hui, Mongolian, and Ewenke nationalities). *Minzu yanjiu* (Nationalities research) 1:26–32.

Zou Qiyu and Miao Wenhou, eds. 1989. *Zhongguo renkou: Yunnan fence* (China's population: Yunnan volume). Beijing: Zhongguo caizheng jingji chubanshe.

Index

activists: during Cultural Revolution, 96, 252, 258, 259, 260, 265, 266, 267, 282, 287; during Socialist Education campaign, 252, 257

Agàmisimo, 111–13, 329n9; failure of state-run market and, 169, 170; *nèpi̱* for, 130, 132, 133, 134–38; rituals for, 130, 131, 132–38; tree of, 110, 112, 113

agency, 252

agricultural producers cooperatives, 171, 172, 173, 176–77, 274

Ahern, Emily, 324n4

ancestral tablets, 326–27n21

ancestral trust lands: creation of, 109; land reform and, 96, 165, 173, 181, 254–55, 274–78; transplanting of, 139–45, 156, 279. *See also* Lòhɔ, the

androcentry, 91

animals. *See* domestic animals; wild animals; *and under specific name*

Art and Literature Propaganda troupe, 257, 258, 260, 261, 268, 283

assemblages, 221

attics, 53, 89–90, 91

Bachelard, Gaston, 41–42, 43, 44, 54, 72

baozhang, 103, 105, 106

barns, 58, 62–63

bearers (in *ts'ici* system), 123, 124–25

bearing: children, 22, 23, 24, 25, 27, 29, 42, 48, 93; tasks, 310

bed's-head spirits, 80–82, 83–84, 326n20

birds: model in exorcism of, 220, 222, 226; sounds of, 227; as wild ghosts, 220, 226, 268

birth planning, 288, 289; compulsory, 293–96; first two movements, 291–92; holistic, 298; "later, longer, fewer" campaign, 292–93. *See also* sterilization

Boon, James A., 326n14

boundaries, 42, 43, 223–24

Bourdieu, Pierre, 59

Bray, Francesca, 52

brothers: contention between, 61–62, 71, 87. *See also* siblings

buckwheat, 129, 183

cadres: agricultural inspection teams of, 180; ancestral trust fields and, 173, 181, 276; attendance of *ts'ici* festival by, 164, 165; birth planning and, 291, 292, 293, 294, 295, 296, 297, 303, 304, 312, 313, 315, 336n6; criticism of sacrifice by, 192; disciplining of, 254; during famine, 190; household cultivation and, 253, 270, 271, 272, 273, 277–78, 279, 280; markets created by, 169, 170; procurement targets of, 186; prohibition of buckwheat cultivation by, 183; Red Guards and, 258; replacement of old institutions with new by, 167, 282; resistance to, 162, 273, 274, 281, 309, 311, 312, 315; shift of state power away from, 315; Socialist Education movement and, 255–57, 266;

market: attended by the living and the
dead, 5–6; driving to, in exorcism
chant, 228, 231–32, 233, 242, 247,
334n6; economy, 281–82, 298; network,
137; reforms and hemp prices, 16, 271;
state-run, 169–71. *See also* supply and
marketing cooperatives
marriage: adolescent gatherings and,
62–63, 149; cross-cousin, 77–78, 149;
of daughter, 67, 69; delayed-transfer,
64–65; late, 286, 295; registration,
295–96; of son, 61, 67; uxorilocal, 64,
69, 325n8; virilocal, 65, 325n8
Mauss, Marcel, 40, 46
memory/memories, 23, 42, 45; the body
and, 155; childhood, 72; collective, 95; as
commemoration, 137, 156; digestive,
128, 129–30, 133, 134, 193, 330n3; double, 102; forgetting, 84, 112, 130, 133,
134, 135, 208, 248, 249, 327n22; kinship
and, 82–83; of places, 103, 161, 168;
scriptic, 127, 128, 129, 130; as self-
representation, 102; traumatic, 333n13;
of violence and disasters, 131, 161, 200,
252, 268, 287, 318
menstrual blood. *See* pollution
Merleau-Ponty, Maurice, 44–45, 48
metaphor, 97; boundaries in, 112; Imperial, 197, 316; reproductive, 99, 121, 122,
134, 141–42, 143–46, 167, 183, 255, 283,
307; of time as a road or path, 264, 265,
267; "turning speech," 155;
vegetable/plant, 66–67, 160–61
Mijù, 111–12, 173–74
millstones, 76
mimesis, 26, 40–42, 46, 47
Misi, 110. *See also* Agàmisimo
mortuary laments, 22–23, 25, 51–52,
92–94, 107, 160, 222, 323n1
mortuary rituals: animal souls dispatched in,
41; cross-sibling relations in, 76–77;
"dawn to dusk offering," 71; day vigil,
193, 210, 250; during epidemics, 152;
goats at, 225; gourd-pipes in, 74; night
vigil, 193, 210, 250, 333n14; numerology
of, 334n4; revival of, 200, 282–83;
"sleeping in the wild," 171, 327n22, 334n1;
the state in, 5–6, 196–97; tenth-month
sacrifice, 192–93, 330–31n8, 333n14, 334n1
mothers-in-law, 86, 209, 211, 237, 238, 248
mourning, 5–6, 23, 71–72, 157, 195–96. *See
also* mortuary laments; mortuary rituals

mutual aid groups, 172
myth: of founding of Zhizuo, 109–10, 133;
"itchy girl," 68–69; of Jimìabamo, 319;
of origin of exorcism ritual, 204; ox (or
tiger), 111; Shokleng origin, 239–40; of
tigress and granary, 86; Wòlòbo̠, 68,
69. *See also* Agàmisimo; gourd house;
Grandmother Wosomo

Nationalist Party, 163. *See also* Guomindang
nationality/nationalities: customs, 98, 102,
126, 317; Han, 15, 18, 19; land reform
and, 165; Lòlop'ò, 99; minority, 19, 165,
252, 281, 301; religion, 98, 102, 250;
Stalin's four criteria of, 13, 125; unity,
290; Yi, 13–14, 95, 318–19; of Zhizuo
area, 13–15, 97, 98–99
nèpi̠, 128–29; for Agàmisimo, 130, 132, 133,
134–38; for Cha, 119, 123, 152, 153–55,
165; for Lòhɔ, 142–43, 146–47; for
srkanè, 150; origins of, 127–28; at trans-
plantation of ancestral trust fields, 139,
141, 142–47; *ts'ici* system and, 131

officials, 2, 17, 103, 273, 317; birth planning
campaign and, 285, 290, 313; collectivization and local, 172, 180, 190, 191;
effigies of, 41, 42, 48; entertainment of,
60–61; metaphors for, 316; in *nèpi̠* for
Cha, 153–56; paper, writing, and,
128–29, 130; ritual and powers of, 49,
50; speech of, 154–56, 167; suicide of,
202, 209; *ts'ici* system and visitation of,
8, 96, 99, 105, 106, 117–18, 132, 197; underworld, 6, 167, 196; view of Zhizuo
of, 2, 38. *See also* cadres

pain: divination of, 44; lineage of, 202;
ritual to sweep away, 45, 49–50. *See also*
wild ghosts, black *gu*
parallelism, 239, 240–45, 265
People's Communes, 175, 177–79, 186
People's Liberation Army, 14, 103, 115, 117,
162–64
perception, 44–45
persons, social/personhood, 39, 249; as
"assemblage," 221; as effects of family
and kinship, 52, 222; exorcism and, 201,
208, 249; as fields of entanglement, 223;
language and, 247–48; sedimentation
and, 26; spatial practices and, 54, 157

Designer: Nola Burger
Compositor: Impressions Book and Journal Services, Inc.
Text: 10/15 Galliard
Display: Galliard